D1295780

THE AGE OF VIRTUE

The Age of Virtue

British Culture from the Restoration to Romanticism

David Morse
Lecturer in English and American Studies
University of Sussex

First published in Great Britain 2000 by
MACMILLAN PRESS LTD
Houndmills, Basingstoke, Hampshire RG21 6XS and London
Companies and representatives throughout the world

A catalogue record for this book is available from the British Library.

ISBN 0–333–76031–X

 First published in the United States of America 2000 by
ST. MARTIN'S PRESS, INC.,
Scholarly and Reference Division,
175 Fifth Avenue, New York, N.Y. 10010

ISBN 0–312–22353–6

Library of Congress Cataloging-in-Publication Data
Morse, David.
The age of virtue : British culture from the Restoration to
Romanticism / David Morse.
p. cm.
Includes bibliographical references (p.   ) and index.
ISBN 0–312–22353–6
1. English literature — 18th century — History and criticism.
2. Virtue in literature.   3. English literature — Early modern,
1500–1700 — History and criticism.   4. Didactic literature, English–
–History and criticism.   5. Great Britain — Civilization — 18th
century.   6. Ethics, Modern — 18th century.   7. Romanticism — Great
Britain.   I. Title.
PR448.V57M67   1999
820.9'353 — dc21   99–18157
                                                                        CIP

This book is printed on paper suitable for recycling and made from fully managed and
sustained forest sources.

10   9   8   7   6   5   4   3   2   1
09   08   07   06   05   04   03   02   01   00

Printed and bound in Great Britain by
Antony Rowe Ltd, Chippenham, Wiltshire

For Annabelle

Contents

Acknowledgements

I would like to thank my Sussex colleagues Vincent Quinn, Angus Ross and Norman Vance for reading and commenting on sections of the manuscripts. I owe a particular debt to Siobhan Kilfeather for putting me in touch with some Irish materials directly relevant to the topic.

1

Introduction

This is a study of eighteenth-century culture and of the role that the idea of virtue played within it, but it is by no means my intention to suggest that the age itself was particularly virtuous; rather, as is so often the case, the invocation of virtue tended to be associated with the concern that it was more likely to be absent than present. In one of G.K. Chesterton's Father Brown stories, 'The Three Tools of Death' the worthy priest throws out the enigmatic suggestion that it is because the murder weapon is so large that it has not been noticed. The earth was the 'weapon' – since the body had been thrown out of a window. Similarly in the reign of Anne and three subsequent Georges the allusions to virtue are so thickly strewn that they are likely to go both unnoticed and undeciphered. It is as if, in the vicinity of a country house, you take it for granted that there are gravel-walks and would think it distinctly odd if there were not; whereas in another context gravel-walks would stick out like a sore thumb, indeed might even lead one to rub one's eyes in astonishment. Equally, this very familiarity may lead us to believe that all talk of virtue is bound to consist of sanctimonious platitudes – especially since we are rarely prone to speak of virtue ourselves – whereas these were in fact questions which were taken intensely seriously. So the intention of this book likewise is to take virtue seriously; to chart like the sightings of a great whale both its longtime prominence and subsequent disappearance, to try to grasp it in all its diverse manifestations.

Not only is virtue's most congenial habitat the eighteenth century, it is also plausible to suggest that it flourishes most abundantly between 1700 and 1800. In the morally relaxed and generally cynical atmosphere of Charles II's court virtue was scarcely a word to galvanise men into activity. Its special province was the grandiose world of the heroic play; where royal heroes were as magnificently noble and virtuous as they were

1

splendidly unreal. While the emergence of a pervasive discourse of virtue at the end of the seventeenth century is partly attributable to two influential texts, Shaftesbury's *An Enquiry Concerning Virtue or Merit* (1699) and Locke's *Some Thoughts Concerning Education* (1693), the deeper causes were political. After the Glorious Revolution of 1688 the determining role of parliament in national affairs made it seem increasingly appropriate to analyse the political scene in terms of the model of the Roman republic. In both political systems there were vital liberties to be preserved and in both there was a need to ensure a balance between the various elements that composed it. Those who acted not selfishly but in the best interests of the state and the people were virtuous. Under Anne it was believed that faction and party-mindedness posed a threat to the system; under Walpole, a combination of political corruption and financial manipulation; under George III, the existence of rotten boroughs and a reassertion of royal power. Yet it was already becoming evident that the language of virtue was such as to predicate an *aristocratic* solution to all political dilemmas. With the passing of the 1832 Reform Bill the basis for political corruption was removed, but democracy rather than virtue was now the rallying cry.

Although the many things that people understood by virtue in the eighteenth century will emerge in the course of this narrative it may be as well to begin with some definitions of the word, particularly since we may be likely to feel that there is something rather nebulous about it. Yet equally we may need to be on our guard against the temptation to be too precise since the utility of many words and phrases that we use depend on their vagueness, flexibility or both – there is no point in asking *exactly* what somebody means when they say that somebody or something is 'nice' or 'attractive' or that something gives you a 'buzz' or what specifically such words as 'monster', 'spook' or 'computer' designate. Virtue may be generally associated with moral goodness but it cannot be pinned down. It has neither a centre nor distinct boundaries.

An obvious starting-point for any discussion of virtue in Hanoverian England is Johnson's dictionary (1755) but it is a good deal less illuminating than you might expect. Although Johnson offers ten different meanings of 'virtue', six of them are concerned with 'virtue' in the sense of power, efficacy or agency, whether medicinal or divine, which only leaves four. Virtue is either 'moral goodness', 'a particular moral excellence', 'excellence; that which gives excellence' or it is 'bravery; valour'. This last is the most instructive of the definitions that Johnson offers, since it invokes the virtue of Aristotle's *Nicomachean Ethics* where the model of the virtuous man is based on the soldier as citizen and the citizen as soldier, where the most highly valued qualities are courage, self-discipline and prudence. They are also part of the knightly ethos. Spenser's dedicatory sonnet to the Earl of Cumberland spins a characteristically chivalric web in which virtue involves both breeding and valour:

> Redoubted Lord, in whose corageous mind
> The flowre of cheualry now blooming faire,
> Doth promise fruite worthy the noble kind,
> Which of their praises haue left you the haire;
> To you this humble present I prepare,
> For loue of vertue and of Martiall praise . . .

Yet in Johnson's own more pacific age such military prowess was less crucial to the definition of virtue. Johnson might well have offered three further definitions, more typical of his time.

(1) *Promoting and advancing the public good*
On this definition the virtuous man was one who engaged in political activity not to achieve personal goals or for financial gain but in order to act in the best interests of his country. Such a person would correspond to Thomson's eulogy of the Earl of Wilmington in *The Seasons*:

> A firm, unshaken, uncorrupted soul
> Amid a sliding age, and burning strong,
> Not vainly blazing, for thy country's weal,
> A steady spirit, regularly free . . .

(2) *Benevolence*
It was the Earl of Shaftesbury who initiated the identification of virtue with benevolence in his *Enquiry concerning Virtue or Merit* of 1699. In this sense the virtuous man was a philanthropist who placed the welfare of others before his own personal self-interest. The epitome of such a virtuous man was 'The Man of Ross', a Mr John Kyrle, whom Pope praised in his 'Epistle to Bathurst':

Who taught that heav'n directed spire to rise?
The MAN of ROSS, each lisping babe replies.
Behold the Market-place with poor o'erspread!
The MAN of ROSS divides the weekly bread:
Behold yon Alms-house, neat, but void of state,
Him portion'd maids, apprentic'd orphans blest,
The young who labour, and the old who rest.
Is any sick? the MAN of ROSS relieves,
Prescribes, attends, the med'cine makes, and gives.
Is there a variance? enter but his door,
Balk'd are the Courts, the contest is no more.

The idea of virtue as benevolence becomes associated with the attempt by many philosophers and divines to refute Mandeville's insistence that human beings are driven by pride and self-love and to stress the more sociable side of human nature.

(3) *The distinguishing mark of the aristocrat or gentleman; exhibiting the best qualitites of an aristocrat or gentleman*
Locke writes:

> I place *Vertue* as the first and most necessary of those Endowments, that belong to a Man or a Gentleman, as absolutely requisite to make him valued and beloved by others, acceptable or tolerable to himself.[1]

In this usage of the word, virtue is understood not just as moral excellence but as involving social graces, such as politeness, dignity, even elegance of deportment and bearing. Hence virtue becomes bound up with education since there is the conviction not only that virtue can be taught but that this rather than the acquisition of knowledge or familiarity with languages is what the education of a gentleman must be concerned with. Clearly, as with Spenser, these meanings are interlinked. Normally only an aristocrat could expect to play a prominent role on the political stage and only an aristocrat or well-connected person would be in a position to dispense largesse.

The idea of virtue in a political context implied an individual who was wholly intent on public good and the welfare of his country. This concern with virtue is particularly associated with the party struggles over the War of Spanish Succession between 1710 and 1713 when it seemed that the desire for personal advantage had become the preponderant motive in politics. Tories believed that the Duke of Marlborough and the Whigs were bent on continuing the war more or less indefinitely for their own political advantage and financial gain. Whigs were convinced that the Tory administration, led by Harley, an ex-Whig, and which took power in 1710, was equally self-serving and that it had no greater object in mind than to maintain itself in power and perpetuate its own influence. Bolingbroke, co-leader with Harley of the Tories, subsequently confessed as much in *A Letter to Sir William Wyndham* (1717):

> I am afraid that we came to Court in the same dispositions as all parties have done; that the principal spring of our actions was to have the government of the state in our hands; that our principal views were the conservation of this power, great employments to ourselves, and great opportunities of rewarding those who had helped to raise us and hurting those who stood in opposition to us.[2]

Bolingbroke also goes on to say that they also had in mind the public good but even in his own account of it this is very much an afterthought. This party spirit was challenged by Joseph Addison, himself a Whig, both in *The Spectator* and in his play *Cato* (1713). The connotations of virtue for Addison are complex but clear. The virtuous man stands opposed to party and unthinking party-mindedness, which Addison calls faction. Cato describes himself as

> engaged in a corrupted state
> Wrestling with vice and faction.

Bolingbroke also subsequently admitted that the two parties had effectively ceased to represent any more general interest:

> The two parties were in truth become factions, in the strict sense of the word.[3]

The virtuous man is temperate and moderate, opposed, in the Aristotelian tradition, to extremes and to what Addison was wont to call 'zeal', that is fanaticism. Virtue is self-disciplined, rational, disinterested, patriotic.

However, with the coming of the Hanoverians the whole political landscape altered. George I and George II depended exclusively on the Whigs for their administration since they dared not trust the Tories after their flirtation with the Pretender and their tacit support for the Jacobite rebellion of 1715. The prospect now was a single-party state and, after Walpole became Prime Minister, of a government that would perpetuate itself as much through corruption as royal support. So the whole question of virtue had to be reformulated. For a long time Bolingbroke and his circle believed that in a political world where everyone was either corrupted or corruptible the only possible hope was that the country might yet be saved by a handful of 'superior spirits' who were at once virtuous and patriotic. They might yet be able to do for Britain what Cato and Brutus had done for Rome. In his *On the Spirit of Patriotism* Bolingbroke wrote:

> It seems to me, that in order to maintain the moral system of the world at a certain point, far below that of ideal perfection . . . but, however, sufficient upon the whole to constitute a state easy and happy, or at the worst tolerable; I say it seems to me, that the Author of nature has thought fit to mingle, from time to time, among the societies of men, a few, and but a few, of those on whom He is graciously pleased to bestow a larger proportion of the ethereal spirit, than is given in the ordinary course of his Providence to the sons of men. These are they who engross almost the whole reason of the species; who are born to instruct, to guide, and to preserve; who are designed to be the tutors and guardians of human kind. When they prove such they exhibit to us examples of the highest virtue and the truest piety, and they deserve to have their festivals kept.[4]

At the time such a conception flattered Bolingbroke and his followers. They were the chosen few who might yet redeem all and if they kept themselves in pure and decorous seclusion the time might yet come when their talents would be called upon. Yet, only two years later, Bolingbroke had another idea, perhaps his most important, set forth in his work *The Idea of a Patriot King* (1738). The reason for this change of emphasis is not hard to discern. In 1737 Frederick, Prince of Wales, had quarrelled with his father, George II, and become a focus for opposition to the

King and his administration. Bolingbroke's argument was that what the country needed was a 'patriot king', an independent and virtuous ruler who would act in the best interests of a united people and who would choose his ministers on the grounds of their talent and ability rather than along party lines. Such an argument was well calculated to flatter the prince and also to suggest that there was nothing to fear from the Tories, who would not seek to take control, but who would be happy to take their place alongside other able and uncorrupted individuals in the service of the state. But Bolingbroke may not have been a total opportunist – he was perfectly sincere in deploring both division and corruption in the state and he may have genuinely believed that a patriot king was Britain's last best hope.

When he became king in 1760 George III attempted to put this notion of a patriot king into practice. Political parties in any event did not have either the influence or the cohesion that they had under Anne, and George through his appointed Prime Minister, the Earl of Bute, and with the support of a group of MPs whom Burke styled 'the Court Faction', was effectively able to govern in his own right.

Virtue in politics had for a long time implied a politician of independent mind and judgement who refused to act either at the behest or in the interest of a political party. So the King, in proposing to form a body of his own supporters could claim to be acting in the national interest as Bolingbroke had defined it and could be seen as striving to counteract the influence of a narrow party-mindedness. Burke, in his *Thoughts on the Cause of the Present Discontents* (1770) refers to a pamphlet which had issued from the Court:

> In this piece appeared the first dawning of the new system; there first appeared the idea (then only in speculation) of *separating the Court from the Administration*; of carrying everything from national connexion to personal regards; and of forming a regular party for that purpose, under the name of *King's men.*
>
> To recommend this system to the people, a perspective view of the Court gorgeously painted, and freshly illuminated from within, was exhibited to the gaping multitude. Party was to be totally done away with, with all its evil works. Corruption was to be cast from the Court. . . . A scheme of perfection to be realized in a Monarchy far beyond the visionary Republick of Plato.[5]

Under these new circumstances the notion of virtue in politics needed to be rethought since, if each MP simply acted according to what he claimed were the dictates of his conscience, there would never be any hope of concerted action against the King. For Burke, to leave a political party with which you had been associated was an act of desertion which could not be extenuated by talk of virtue or independence. Political parties, far from being evil, were the necessary means by which policies could be formulated and translated into effective political action:

> Party is a body of men united, for promoting by their joint endeavours, upon some particular principle on which they are all agreed.[6]

So for Burke there was more virtue and integrity attached to belonging to a political party with clearly formulated goals than in an unspecified right to private judgement that could all too easily be bought or influenced.

In his *Reflections on the Revolution in France* (1790), written just 20 years later in response to the most momentous event of the contemporary era, Burke was even more severe on the gospel of individualism, especially when it manifested itself in the idea that a modern generation should simply take an axe to the root of institutions that it found displeasing. It was positively dangerous that they

> should act as if they were the entire masters; that they should not think it amongst their rights to cut off the entail, or commit waste on the inheritance, by destroying at their pleasure the whole original fabric of their society; hazarding to leave to those who come after them, a ruin instead of a habitation.[7]

Indeed, characteristically Burke regarded even a ruin as being better than nothing at all. He suggested to the French that since they had inherited the walls and foundations of 'a noble and venerable castle'[8] it would have been better for them to have repaired the walls and built on the old foundations rather than to start afresh. The very fact that a social formation had endured for a period of time was proof positive that it was a repository of wisdom and virtue. Social institutions provided a secure context for human activity. They offered a prospect of stability and permanence that should not be lightly thrown away. In a context of perpetual change and innovation 'the commonwealth itself would, in a few generations, crumble away, be disconnected into the powder of individuality, and at length dispersed to all the winds of heaven'.[9] The past is a sacred trust that must be protected at all costs. It is not through the auto-authorising action of individuals but through the preservation and perpetuation of institutions and traditions that virtue will be maintained.

In the late eighteenth century it would be difficult to find two figures more contrasted than Burke and Edward Gibbon, author of *The Decline and Fall of the Roman Empire*. Whereas Burke was comparatively insular, a traditionalist, and a devout Christian, Gibbon was cosmopolitan, a rationalist and profoundly sceptical of religion. Yet they were surprisingly brought together by the recognition that traditions and structures are more important in human history than the actions of individuals however virtuous or meritorious. In many ways Gibbon's reluctant acknowledgement of this is the more remarkable. Gibbon had a profound respect for the classical Roman tradition and all it represented. The reason why any narrative about the course of the Roman empire must be a melancholy one is that it must tell how a civilisation that was rational, enlightened, well-ordered and tolerant was supplanted and destroyed by religious fanaticism, whether Christian or Muslim. It is a story not just about what happened to Rome in the past but about what happened to the whole world and about the moral and spiritual darkness that still lingers. One of the most poignant moments in the *Decline and Fall* is when Gibbon defends himself against the charge that he may be both ignorant of and unsympathetic to Islamic culture:

> Our education in the Greek and Latin schools may have fixed in our minds a standard of exclusive taste; and I am not forward to condemn the literature and judgment of nations, of whose language I am ignorant. Yet I *know* that the classics have much to teach, and I *believe* that the Orientals have much to learn.[10]

The classics really do matter. A crucial part of that tradition were the Roman historians in whose footsteps Gibbon followed. Like them Gibbon saw it as a central part of his task to pass judgement on the Emperors and other powerful individuals who occupied centre stage in his account, whether to praise them for their virtue or excoriate them for their corruption and vice. Gibbon undoubtedly believed that it was essential for an Emperor to be both active and virtuous and he was generally disposed to explain the overall decline in terms of the moral failings of particular individuals. Septimus Severus, Valens and Gratian are all charged with contributing to Rome's downfall. On the other hand, Gibbon believed that such an admirable and virtuous Emperor as Theodosius had actually been able to arrest the process:

> If the subjects of Rome could be ignorant of their obligations to the great Theodosius, they were too soon convinced, how painfully the spirit and abilities of their deceased emperor had supported the frail and mouldering edifice of the republic.[11]

Yet the sack of Rome in AD 410 at the hands of Alaric occurred only fifteen years after the death of Theodosius. In the end all individuals, no matter how powerful or virtuous, are diminished by the sheer scale of Gibbon's narrative and it becomes hard to see how this or that intervention can acquire particular importance when there is still a millenium to go. In the end the fate of Rome was determined by more fundamental and long-term causes. If the 'firm edifice of Roman power'[12] in the Age of the Antonines was grounded in military organisation, effective political structure, Roman law, religious and racial tolerance, the universal use of the Latin language; its decline was brought about by internal division and external threat, through the insidious moral corrosion of Christianity and luxury.

The philosophical and religious debate over virtue in the eighteenth century is dominated by the idea of virtue as benevolence. As against Hobbes who had stressed the inevitability of conflict stemming, in a state of nature, from the determination of individuals to attain their own private ends, Shaftesbury emphasised the harmoniousness of the universe and the inherent desire of human beings to be sociable and to live in harmony with others. Virtue, which only human beings possessed, is connected with an idea of the public interest. The desire for Candour, Equity, Trust, Sociableness and Friendship is natural and contrariwise the unhappy few who do not desire these things must be regarded as being perverse and unnatural. Shaftesbury's view of human nature effectively excludes any idea of evil. There are theological implications to the definition of virtue as benevolent, whether explicit or not. The implication is that a benevolent God has created man in his own image and that just as it is only natural that God should be well-disposed to man, whom he has created, it is equally natural that we should feel well disposed towards our fellow creatures and seek both to get along with them and be approved by them. While the virtuous man in the political sphere seeks to do good by acting in the interests of his country, the benevolent man is a more private person who, like the Man of Ross, tries to do good in his own immediate sphere. While the image of the virtuous political leader stresses self-discipline and consistency, the benevolent man, especially in Sentimentalist fiction, tends to be more emotional and spontaneous – it is his heart that tells him what to do.

Shaftesbury's arguments about the social nature of man might have seemed little more than a set of benign platitudes had they not been so abusively attacked by Bernard Mandeville, a Dutch-born physician, in the expanded edition of his *Fable of the Bees* (1723), who far from showing respect for Shaftesbury's retirement from the world because 'he hated all Flattery and Slavish Attendance, the Insincerity of Courts and the Bustle of the World' insinuated that he might be 'a Man of Indolent Temper and Unactive Spirit' unlike the truly virtuous man who would 'exert himself to the utmost for the good of his Fellow Subjects'.[13]

Not that Mandeville believed in virtue since the whole point of *The Fable of the Bees* was to demolish it. The moral virtues are nothing more than a device of politicians to provoke men to 'the utmost Pitch of Self-denial'[14] and perform heroic deeds in a way that is quite contrary to their nature. They are 'the Political Off-spring which Flattery begot on Pride'.[15] For Mandeville all human behaviour, however masked and concealed, is essentially based on pride and self-love. But actually such vices are socially pro-ductive. For it is pride,vanity and self-love that leads men to build costly mansions and purchase expensive luxuries, which in modern commercial societies creates both employment and prosperity. Even hospitals are more likely to be built to satisfy the vanity of a wealthy individual than out of an charitable or benevolent inten-tion. Such alleged noble intentions amount to nothing more than hypocrisy.

Mandeville's mocking, satirical style of arguing proved difficult to refute. For Mandeville did not necessarily claim to be a
philosopher, only a shrewd and knowing individual who was
thoroughly familiar with the motives of men in the real world
and who therefore could not be readily duped. So, in his own
eyes, to point to Shaftesbury's unworldliness was effectively to
have refuted him. Yet, paradoxically, far from prematurely closing
the debate, it was Mandeville who gave the whole controversy a
vital shot in the arm. After Mandeville the arguments about not
just the nature of virtue but about the very possibility of virtue
took on a greater urgency. Frances Hutcheson, an Irish philosopher who became professor of moral philosophy at the University
of Glasgow, followed the general lines of Shaftesbury's argument
but developed it in a more systematic fashion. Hutcheson insisted,
against Mandeville, that men were not just motivated by self-
love and self-interest, but also by Benevolence, whose 'very Name
excludes Self-Interest'.[16] Every human being possesses an inbuilt
moral sense which motivates him to act not just out of self-love
but for the greater good of the whole, what Hutcheson, before
Bentham, described as 'the greatest Happiness of the greatest
number'.[17] Hutcheson shrewdly pointed out that rather than
perversely to try to:

> twist Self-Love into a thousand Shapes, than allow any other
> Principle of Approbation than Interest.[18]

it was more natural and honest to recognise that there are a
diversity of human motivations. This emphasis on the variety of
human feelings was also made by Bishop Butler, who, in his
Sermons (1726) argued that, in normal circumstances, there was
no necessary contradiction between virtue and self-love:

> It is manifest that, in the common course of life, there is seldom
> any inconsistency between our duty and what is *called* interest:
> it is much seldomer that there is inconsistency between duty
> and what is really our present interest; meaning by interest,
> happiness and satisfaction. Self-love then, though confined to
> the interest of the present world, does in general perfectly
> coincide with virtue; and leads us to one and the same course
> of life.[19]

Butler has of course defined self-love away from Mandeville's model of the prideful individual intent on achieving own personal gratification since in his view no one who behaves badly can be either happy or satisfied; but his argument also involves the claim that Mandeville is simply deploying a false antithesis.

Hutcheson and Butler attacked Mandeville's celebration of pride and self-love, but in concentrating on the moral arguments they failed to confront what was possibly Mandeville's most telling argument that, like it or not, pride, vanity and the desire for luxury played a crucial role in promoting economic development and providing gainful employment. For if these things were actually functionally necessary then it was plausible to argue that there was some merit in them. So, arguably the most thoroughgoing answer to Mandeville came from Adam Smith, who, in his *The Theory of Moral Sentiments* (1759) and *The Wealth of Nations* (1776) addressed both the philosophical and economic arguments. But in Adam Smith the whole nature of the discussion is shifted and transposed. In the first part of the century it seemed natural for people to start from the individual and to assume that moral behaviour was grounded in what each individual thought and felt, whether in the dictates of conscience or in the impulses of selfish desire. But Adam Smith, like other leading thinkers of the Scottish Enlightenment saw society as the most important category. To say that man was made for society meant not just that man was likely to be well disposed towards his friends and neighbours but that the nature of man was defined by his place in society. Thus, for Adam Smith, sympathy for others is one of the most powerful of all human motivations. Moreover, all human beings desire the approbation of their fellow members of society and therefore the moral sense is essentially a social sense which prompts individuals to act in ways that will command general approval. But this moral sense is not *for* the individual but for *society* and beyond that it serves to contribute to the harmony of the entire universe:

> The happiness of mankind, as well as of all other rational creatures, seems to have been the original purpose intended by the Author of nature, when he brought them into existence. No other end seems worthy of that supreme wisdom and divine benignity which we necessarily ascribe to him; and this opinion, which we are led to by the abstract consideration of his infinite

perfections, is still more confirmed by the examination of the works of nature, which seem all intended to promote happiness, and to guard against misery. But by acting according to the dictates of our moral faculties, we necessarily pursue the most effectual means for promoting the happiness of mankind, and may therefore be said, in some sense, to co-operate with the Deity, and to advance as far as is in our power the plan of Providence.[20]

Adam Smith disagrees with Mandeville in stressing man's powers of self-command, so that

The man of the most perfect virtue . . . is he who joins, to the most perfect command of his own original and selfish feelings, the most exquisite sensibility both to the original and sympathetic feelings of others.[21]

Mandeville's claim that many virtuous actions are only performed to impress others has no force for Adam Smith since he finds nothing unworthy in the desire for such approval. Indeed it is right and natural that others should approve our actions since our moral sense directs us to act in such a way as will promote the good of society. Here the views of Adam Ferguson and Adam Smith run in parallel. Ferguson says that man is

only part of a whole; and the praise we think due to his virtue, is but a branch of that more general commendation we bestow on the member of a body, on the part of a fabric or engine, for being well fitted to occupy its place, and to produce its effect.[22]

Adam Smith writes:

virtue, which is, as it were, the fine polish to the wheels of society; while vice, like the vile rust, which makes them jar and grate upon one another, is as necessarily offensive.[23]

We are no longer speaking of a virtue that in some way involves great and remarkable actions, but of something that greases the wheels and ensures the smooth running of the system.

It has often been thought that there is a contradiction between Adam Smith's emphasis on sympathy and benevolence in *The Theory of Moral Sentiments* and his emphasis on the self-regarding nature of economic man in *The Wealth of Nations*. We might think that such an inconsistency, though potentially serious, is not altogether surprising given that there is a 16 year gap between the two texts and the fact that they address different conceptual fields. Nevertheless, on the face of it, *The Wealth of Nations* involves crucial concessions to Mandeville, the very author whose 'licentious system' was obliquely disparaged in the earlier work on moral philosophy. The very question – what produces 'the wealth of nations' – is itself a Mandevillian question and much of Smith's attempt to answer it seems very reminiscent of *The Fable of the Bees*. Both men stress that increases in trade and general activity are themselves productive and beneficial.

> Vast numbers thronged the fruitful Hive;
> Yet those vast Numbers made 'em thrive;
> Millions endeavouring to supply
> Each other's Lust and Vanity.

writes Mandeville and Adam Smith seems to agree that it is the fact that men are driven by self-interest that makes the whole system work:

> It is not from the benevolence of the butcher, the brewer, or the baker, that we expect our dinner, but from their regard to their own interest. We address ourselves, not to their humanity but their self-love, and never talk to them of our own necessities but of their advantages.[24]

Indeed, Smith seems to have accepted one of the most damaging implications of Mandeville's argument: that even hospitals are more likely to be built out of vanity than philanthropy. But it seems virtually certain that Smith himself would not have accepted that he had gone over to the Mandevillian side. For one thing all, Mandeville's critics were agreed that Mandeville's error was not to speak of self-love, which they freely conceded did exist, but to explain *everything* in terms of vanity and self-love and to deny that any other motives existed. So in this way the deadly bee's sting of the self-love argument was rendered quite harmless. By showing that apparently self-regarding behaviour benefits everyone and enables the community as a whole to prosper Adam Smith has demonstrated, from quite another perspective, that there actually can be no such thing as purely selfish behaviour. As Adam Smith had already pointed out in *The Theory of Moral Sentiments*, on the first occasion when he invoked 'the invisible hand' that guides our dealings, whether we know it or not, the rich are obliged through their expenditure to benefit the poor, distribute their affluence and 'without knowing it, advance the interest of society'.[25]

Moreover, Adam Smith does not accept the argument that it is luxury that produces economic development. The whole tendency of *The Wealth of Nations* – which is precisely what makes it the founding document of the discipline of economics – is to decouple economic activity from obvious moralistic assumptions, whether this is Mandeville's cynicism about self-love or the Physiocrats idealisation of manual labour. A great many differing factors enter into the production of wealth. Frugality may be as productive as extravagant expenditure. Indeed the expansion of commerce is driven not so much by the production of luxurious items for the few as by the more general diffusion of relatively simple items like nails and pins, knives and forks, glass windows, soap, candles and linen shirts. The general tendency of the development of trade is democratic, diminishing though not abolishing the distance between classes, which is why Smith can say:

> the accommodation of an Egyptian prince does not always so much exceed that of an industrious and frugal peasant, as the accommodation of the latter exceeds that of many an African king, the absolute master of the lives and liberties of ten thousand naked savages.[26]

But in any event the whole nature of the argument has significantly shifted. Smith is no longer particularly interested in attitudinising over virtue and vice, or involving himself in questions about the moral behaviour of particular individuals. It is the system that matters and there there is no cause for concern for an invisible hand guides all.

In the eighteenth-century the idea of virtue was closely bound up with education, since it was almost universally agreed that the paramount goal of education must be virtue rather than either learning or the acquisition of social accomplishments, though these were still regarded as important. This emphasis owes much to the influence of John Locke's *Some Thoughts concerning Education* (1693) since Locke emphasises over and over again that it is virtue that is central to education:

'Tis Vertue, then, direct Vertue, which is the hard and valuable part to be aimed at in education.[27]

By virtue Locke means such qualitites as honesty, innocence, sobriety, industry, modesty and generosity, but perhaps the most important quality that Locke aims for under the general rubric of virtue is self-control:

denying ourselves the Satisfaction of our own Desires, where Reason does not authorise them.[28]

Since Locke is well aware that the children of aristocrats are all too frequently indulged either by servants or their parents it is essential that they should not be wilful and always insist on getting their own way. Yet, although Locke puts a premium on self-control, his method is relatively progressive since he disapproves of both beatings and rewards as ways of motivating the student since he believes that they will be injurious to his character. In anticipation of Rousseau – who, from another point of view simply takes Locke's overall approach still further – Locke is not particularly interested in book learning and instruction in the Latin and Greek language. His distinct preference is for practical activities like gardening and carpentry. He acknowledges that it it is customary for Latin and Greek to be taught and since this is so Locke does not specifically rule it out, but he is continually warning that there is a real risk that an education in the classics may well be at the expense of virtue. The, tutor, Locke insists, should be one:

who thinks *Latin* and *Language* the least part of Education; one who knowing how much Vertue, and a well-temper'd Soul is to be preferr'd to any sort of *Learning* or *Language*, makes it his chief Business to form the Mind of his Scholars, and give that a right disposition: which, if once got, though all the rest should be neglected, would, in due time, produce all the rest: and

which if it be not got, and setled, so as to keep out ill and
vicious Habits, *Languages* and *Sciences*, and all the other Accomplishments of Education will be to no purpose, but to make
the worse, or more dangerous Man.[29]

Locke is so concerned with the tutor's role in the formation of
his pupil's character that he does not view the instructor's preoccupation with attaining accuracy in the Latin language as being
merely pedantic and superficial, he is genuinely worried that in
the process moral education will be totally neglected.

Locke's misgivings about the teaching of Latin went further
than the Latin language since he also was concerned about the
use of imaginative literature, with its general lack of regard for
truth. Nevertheless, there were many in the eighteenth century
who believed that both classical literature and a study of history
could be crucial in the formation of a virtuous character in the
overall context of a virtuous education. Even Locke conceded that
Cicero's *Offices* was useful for 'the Principles and Precepts of
Vertue'[30] and Rousseau who followed Locke in trying to steer
the child away from books advocated the study of Plutarch's *Lives*.
But for most eighteenth-century gentlemen the value of the classics was indisputable. Bolingbroke believed that the citizens of
the Roman republic were themselves inspired to virtue by the
narratives of heroic deeds and by the busts they erected to the
memory of the great, in this way.

> The virtue of one generation was transfused by the magic of
> example into several[31]

and even in later and more decadent days history could still serve
to keep such values alive:

> When Tacitus wrote, even the appearance of virtue had been
> long proscribed, and taste was grown corrupt as well as man-
> ners. Yet history preserved her integrity and her lustre.[32]

For Lord Chesterfield Roman history was an indispensible part
of the education of a gentleman. Taking note of the fact that his
son was was now reading Roman history he stresses that he should
study it with care and attention because of its very considerable
moral significance;

History animates and excites us to the love and practice of virtue; by showing us the regard and veneration that was always paid to great and virtuous men in the times in which they lived, and the praise and glory with which their names are perpetuated, and transmitted down to our times. The Roman History furnishes more examples of virtue and magnaminity, or greatness of mind, than any other.[33]

In a similar vein, the Scottish author, James Dunbar, author of *Essays in the History of Mankind in Rude and Uncultivated Ages* (1782) – writing in the wake of MacPherson's fabricated Ossianic poems – (1762–3), at a time when it was widely believed that simplicity of culture was most favourable to virtue, stressed the centrality of classical literature in any project of moral education. Increasingly the classics were seen not just as an end in themselves but as part of a general pattern of moral advancement:

> to stop the career of Vice is the ultimate end of well-directed education. This was felt by the great writers of antiquity. They erected a temple to Virtue and exhausted in the opposite character all the thunder of eloquence.[34]

Still, there always the worry, expressed by James Beattie in his essay 'On the Utility of Classical Learning' that exposure of young minds to the more salacious aspects of classical literature might counteract its more edifying potential, though he concluded that the classics were bound to improve the mind. They 'cannot now corrupt the heart or understanding of a person who is a friend to truth and virtue'.[35]

The heyday of the classical education in the public schools was yet to come, yet already there were attempts to promote virtue through the use of vernacular sources. The Scottish historian, William Robertson, wrote in the dedication of his *History of Ancient Greece* (1786) to the Prince of Wales:

> Your ROYAL HIGHNESS, too, is now at that Age, when the interesting Scenes displayed in this History are apt to make the most lively impression on the mind. When therefore you shall contemplate the immortal Heroes of Greece, sacrificing their Passions to their Reason, pursuing the Suggestions of Honour in opposition to the Allurements of Pleasure, and

courting Danger in the Service of their Country; their Patriotism, their Virtue, their Magnanimity, will awaken their
Kindred-feelings in your ROYAL HIGHNESS'S Breast, and
inspire You with the noblest Emulation.[36]

Unfortunately, despite this impassioned plea, the future Prince
Regent proved to be rather more interested in pursuing pleasure
at Brighthelmstone in the company of Mrs FitzHerbert. Besides
history there was also the possibility of encouraging virtue through
readings selected from the English poets. In 1780 Thomas Tomkins
published *Poems on Various Subjects Selected to Enforce the Practice
of Virtue*, based on selections from such writers, as Milton, Pope,
Thomson, Goldsmith, Cunningham and Gray in the hope that
they would

> allure those who are inattentive to the excellence of virtue, and
> direct their thoughts to the noblest qualifications.[37]

Rousseau, through his publication of *Emile* (1762), became the
most influential educational theorist of the eighteenth century
but the effect of Rousseau's work was to turn the whole project
of raising and nurturing a virtuous individual into a highly problematic, even self-contradictory activity. For although Rousseau
exalts what is natural in man he sees the task of developing this
nature as extremely complex since he believes that all the forces
of the contemporary world are bent on destroying it. At the very
beginning of *Emile* he announces that someone who was left to
themselves from birth would become *more* of a monster than others:

> Prejudice, authority, necessity, example, all the social condi-
> tions into which we are plunged, would stifle nature in him
> and put nothing in her place.[38]

So education in Rousseau is less concerned with actually teaching
the child something, as with ensuring that the child should not
be exposed to influences that are likely to be harmful:

> Education consists not in teaching virtue or truth, but in pre-
> serving the heart from vice and from the spirit of error.[39]

Although Rousseau's emphasis on spontaneity and self-direction
are by no means contrary to the general spirit of the times,

Rousseau often disconcerted his contemporaries by his paradoxical use of language. Thus, in one of the most notorious passages of *Emile* Rousseau writes:

> Let us lay it down as an incontrovertible rule that the first impulses of nature are always right. . . . The only natural passion is self-love or selfishness taken in a wider sense. This selfishness is good in itself.[40]

Rousseau was thought to be encouraging precisely the kind of selfish, wilful behaviour that Locke had made it his mission to combat – not unreasonably since Rousseau, who was well acquainted with Mandeville as his esssay *On the origin of Inequality* shows, seemingly goes out of his way to redefine virtue as its very opposite. Yet clearly Rousseau did not believe that his pupil should simply please himself and he later develops his notions in a way which is much more in accordance with contemporary opinion:

> Extend self-love to others and it is transformed into a virtue, a virtue which has its root in the heart of every one of us.[41]

Yet Rousseau *was* different in that he deeply distrusted the world in general and did not regard the human drive towards sociability with quite the same complacency as Shaftesbury, Hutcheson and their followers:

> Man's weakness makes him sociable. . . . Every affection is a sign of insufficiency; if each of us had no need of others, we should hardly think of associating with them. So our frail happiness has its roots in our weakness. A really happy man is a hermit. . . .[42]

Man's disposition to be sociable make him into a conformist. It sucks him into a world of competition, luxuriousness and self-display, nurturing the vices of vanity, envy and pride. So Emile is to be brought up in the country and educated by the example of Robinson Crusoe. Although Emile himself must be taught to be honest and direct, the tutor is justified in using all manner of subterfuge to keep him that way. 'Precaution' is a crucial word in Rousseau's educational vocabulary. All manner of precautions will be needed to shield the pupil from the world and even when he is grown up he may yet need to be protected, shielded and diverted from all that is potentially corrupting. So, although Rousseau believes passionately in virtue, it is always and everywhere under threat and the possibility of erasure. If Bolingbroke's Romans were the virtuous citizens of a virtuous republic, Rousseau's virtue can scarcely find a place to stand. The individual is important but the world is all encompassing and infinitely more powerful. Under the conditions of modern civilisation the preservation of virtue will require something very like a miracle.

What we find emerging in all three of these discourses, political, philosophical and educational is a much clearer awareness of the limitations of the individual. What, thereby, also becomes clear, is that virtue does not simply designate noble, public-spirited or benevolent behaviour it has, in effect, been a kind of short-hand for a model of the world – the classical world – in which the intervention of a single individual could really count. It was the French Revolution, above all, that destroyed such aspirations because the events that took place were so rapid, so complex and so unpredictable that they made the whole idea of exercising a decisive influence on events seem problematic in the extreme. Yet, this had been the Roman model – a model which many actors on the stage of the French Revolution aspired to follow. Roman virtue was epitomised not just by Cato and Brutus (who, admirable as they were, had nevertheless been ultimately unsuccessful in their efforts to preserve the Roman Republic) but by such legendary figures from Livy's early history of Rome as Horatius, Mucius Scaevola and Quintus Cincinnatus. Horatius had slain all three of the Curiatii after his two brothers had already fallen in the combat. Mucius, though he failed to kill Lars Porsena the leader of the Etruscans, nevertheless convinced him to make peace by holding his hand in a flame as a demonstration of Roman fortitude. Cincinnatus, summoned from his farm to be dictator in the hope that he can save Rome, duly restores morale and defeats the Aequians. Everything in this legendary world can be transformed by the actions of a single man. But in the modern world the very possibility of it is becoming questionable. Napoleon comes closest to reviving the ideal of the classical hero, but while Alexander, Julius Caesar and many subsequent Roman emperors invariably prevailed on the battlefield, Napoleon found the force of circumstance too great for him. His invasion of Russia failed. He was defeated at Leipzig and again at Waterloo.

Yet it has to be admitted that virtue has always been passing, has always been the subject of nostalgia and is invariably invoked only to be lamented. Even Spenser, whose commitment to virtue was second to none could write in the Proem to Book V of *The Faerie Queene* (published 1596):

> Let none then blame me, if in discipline
> Of vertue and of ciuill vses lore,
> I doe not forme them to the common line
> Of present dayes, which are corrupted sore,
> But to the antique vse, which was of yore . . .

The very existence of a classical tradition in which the idea of virtue was foregrounded meant that it was virtually inevitable that later eras would seem morally inadequate by comparison. Indeed there was never any serious possibility that the moderns, whatever else they might boast of, could seriously hope to challenge the ancients on the specific ground of virtue. Virtue was what the ancients were good at.

Nevertheless, the eighteenth century went in search of virtue as if in pursuit of the philosopher's stone. For if virtue was elusive this simply served to confirm the thought that it really ought to exist – *somewhere*! In the reign of Queen Anne and of the first two Georges the prevalence of first faction and then political corruption made it indispensable that men should be found who would not only stand apart from the pressures and inducements of the times but positively resist them. But the virtuous politician proved to be rather a chimerical beast and Swift, at least, was forced to fall back on the idea that horses, at least, could be relied upon to be both honest and virtuous. But, strangely, although virtue was generally perceived as the prerogative of aristocrats and gentlemen, there were few indeed who actually believed that such pampered and indulged individuals were likely to be virtuous. Indeed, the whole history of the novel, from Richardson and Fielding to Jane Austen, is based on the idea that if you want virtue you should look to the lowly, whether without fortune, feminine, illegitimate or actually servants – these are the only people you can hope to rely on. Beyond that, in the reign of

George III, London is increasingly seen as the corrupt metropolis, the seat of an increasingly overbearing and oppressive empire, where trade and the exploitation of the colonies promotes consumerism, luxury and decadence, and where Britain is increasingly perceived not as a reincarnation of the Roman republic, but as a brutal repetition of the Roman Empire. In such a context, only the provincials, only the oppressed, are likely to be virtuous.

Indeed, virtue had been so extensively redefined in terms of the lowly, the feminine, the primitive and the culturally marginal that the aristocratic connotations of the term were virtually obliterated. But once the French revolution was perceived as ushering in a new age of democracy and 'Liberty, Equality, Fraternity' became the rallying cry, it became increasingly obvious that any talk of virtue implied harking back to the spirit of some long lost *status quo* rather than looking forward to a democratic future. The idea that the world might be redeemed from corruption by a saving remnant, which had seemed so appealing in the age of Walpole, now seemed a great deal less compelling. The conservative, even reactionary implications of deploying the word 'virtue' now seemed obvious. Among the British Romantic poets it seems as significant that Blake, the son of a hosier, and Keats, the son of a livery-stable keeper, should have been hostile to virtue as that Shelley and Byron, both aristocrats, should have been most nostalgic for the ideals for which it served as a complex shorthand. But in any event, the very idea of virtue was beginning to seem increasingly rigid and narrow. Either 'virtue' designated an impossible perfection or else it was a denial of human complexity, but whatever it was it suggested a cardboard cut-out more than the hero. The very idea that there was some kind of pattern of virtue into which an individual might fit, suggested something fixed and stereotyped, something cast from a mould, albeit antique. An important step along the way toward rejecting virtue – and thus toward creating the general ethos of Romanticism – was taken by Boswell in writing *The Life of Samuel Johnson*. Boswell could very easily have taken the decision to present Johnson as a model of virtue and piety and could have provided abundant evidence that he was. But instead he chose to present his longtime companion and hero in intimate and revealing detail, showing him as at once admirable and flawed. Boswell's Johnson is forceful, formidably quick-witted and intelligent, undeniably eccentric. Johnson is, as we say, a 'character'. But despite all this, for the

Romantics, Johnson was too much the establishment figure to embody their idea of a hero. The change that they brought about is epitomised by Carlyle's discussion of Cromwell in *Heroes and Hero-Worship*. When Carlyle is discussing the Puritan Revolution he admits that he finds it difficult to regard Hampden, Eliot and Pym as heroes even though in theory there is much to admire:

> They are very noble men, these; step along in their stately way, with their measured euphemisms, philosophies, parliamentary eloquences, Ship-moneys, *Monarchies of Man*; a most constitutional, unblameable, dignified set of men. But the heart remains cold before them; the fancy alone endeavours to get-up some worship of them. What man's heart does, in reality, break-forth into any fire of brotherly love for these men? They are become dreadfully dull men! . . . One leaves all these Nobilities standing in their niches of honour: the rugged outcast Cromwell, he is the man of them all in whom one still finds human stuff.[43]

What Carlyle is really saying is that he cannot warm to Hampden, Eliot and Pym because they are *virtuous* – because they represent an abstract, aristocratic ideal. It is Cromwell who is the hero because despite all temptations he remains the resolute outcast, who is great, like Johnson, partly because of his faults and not in spite of them. If the hero were virtuous he could not be as remarkable as he is!

2
Virtue's Vicissitudes

Since the emergence of 'virtue' as a talismanic word is so intimately bound up with the party rivalries of the age of Anne, it is instructive to examine the status of virtue in the Restoration period, when its mandates were noticeably less compelling, when it was experiencing the darkest hour that precedes the dawn. It might well be thought that in the aftermath of Civil War that there would be a pervasive disillusionment with all forms of idealistically motivated politics – especially where that was inclined to take the form of opposition to the king – and equally that in consequence the desire for personal advancement at court would inexorably take precedence over any high-minded concern for the well-being of the commonwealth. Certainly there was both opportunism and widespread cynicism, and yet the idea of virtue still continued to exert a certain fascination over men's minds. For at this time, the idea of virtue was important for any understanding of the role of the monarch. Although Charles II could scarcely be regarded as especially virtuous in his capacity as a private individual, virtue nevertheless had a particular significance for those who wished to priviledge the power and prerogatives of the king. George Savile, Marquis of Halifax, who was to offer the crown of England to William and Mary, was widely regarded as a moderate and a peacemaker, yet even he could write in his *The Character of a Trimmer*:

> Our Trimmer cannot conceive that the power of any prince can be lasting but where 'tis built upon the foundation of his own unborrowed virtue.[1]

However it is important to note that the notion of virtue here carries very specific connotations: the monarch must act clearly, openly, and in good faith. He needs to be trustworthy. So more generally, a virtuous individual is someone who displays loyalty,

26

fidelity and consistency. Regrettably, neither Charles I nor Charles II acted virtuously in this sense – both concealed much from their Parliaments and behaved erratically in their relations with them. Although folklore has it that peace and tranquillity were restored in good king Charles's golden days, in reality the suspension of the political tension was shortlived; since all the old conflicts and suspicions immediately resurfaced in 1669 with the news that James, Duke of York and heir to the throne, had converted to Catholicism. In turn the political turbulence of seventeenth-century England meant that it was wellnigh impossible to plausibly present on the English stage a character as Corneille's Cid, who is such an unimpeachable servant of the Spanish king. This is in part because such a character in an English context would seem either too good to be true but perhaps more importantly because, despite the Restoration, the political options were too complex to offer either any self-evident solution or any single focus of loyalty. It was only with the accession of Anne, a monarch who was both legitimate and universally acceptable, that clarity was – momentarily – restored to the British state. Yet, in a fallen world virtue had a kind of numinous hovering presence, like a vision of the Holy Grail that will only be vouchsafed to someone who is too perfect for the world.

In the Restoration virtue carries with it the idea that it is either superhuman or hypothetical. With Dryden there is the *beau ideal* of the royal hero, whose exemplary merit lies at the heart of the newfound genre of the heroic play, which seeks simultaneously to celebrate virtue and to link it with the values of a monarchic and hierarchical society. Yet it finds ironic reflection in Restoration comedy where to be either honest or predicatable is to be a fool or a gull. For its part the heroic play in no way attempts to imitate real life or to present probable characters in recognisable circumstances. Instead it revels in the outlandish and exotic and celebrates characters whose capacity for heroic action, magnaminity and self-sacrifices is so great as to be almost unbelievable, but which for that very reason is all the more admirable. The first English heroic play was Sir William D'Avenant's *The Siege of Rhodes*, first produced as an opera in 1656 and revived as a play in 1663. Davenant was influenced by Corneille in offering a drama that hinged on chivalric themes of love and honour but subordinated them to a lavish action-packed spectacle, which, as in *The Cid* focused on a last ditch stand against the Muslim foe. D'Avenant himself was something of a moralist, offering in the preface to his epic poem *Gondibert* a formula which well serves to define the heroic play:

> I may now beleeve I have usefully taken from Courts and Camps the patterns of such as will be fit to be imitated by the most necessary men; and the most necessary men are those who become principall by prerogative of blood, which is seldom unassisted by education. Or by greatnesse of minde, which in exact definition is Vertue.

Such heroic literature is not simply aristocratic it is conceived of as actually producing greatness by offering exemplary models on which aspiring heroes can model themselves. Yet *The Siege of Rhodes* itself did not necessarily lead in this direction. Heavily imitated as it was in such dramatic works as Orrery's *Mustapha* (1668), Dryden's *The Conquest of Granada* (1672), Crowne's *The Destruction of Jerusalem* (1677), Banks's *The Destruction of Troy* (1677), there was no particular necessity for the grandiose representation of sieges and last ditch battles to instruct: since they were just as likely to involve palace intrigue, treachery, confusion and immoderate, sadistic violence. Indeed in such plays as Settle's *Empress of Morocco* and *The Conquest of China* and Nathaniel Lee's *Tragedy of Nero* and *Caesar Borgia* this was precisely the direction in which Restoration 'tragedy' did go, surpassing the excesses of the Jacobean theatre, yet without either its psychological intensity or moral seriousness. It was Dryden above all who in *The Indian Queen*, *The Conquest of Granada*, and *Aureng-Zebe* created a heroic drama, dedicated to the celebration of virtue.

The Indian Queen (1665) is quite explicitly concerned with the education of a ruler. At the opening of the play Montezuma, a general who has been successful in battle, is angered when the Inca of Peru turns down his request for the hand of his daughter in marriage. Acacis, son of the Mexican queen, who has been captured in battle and who represents the play's pattern of virtue advises Montezuma against both anger and disloyalty:

> Your honour is obliged to keep your trust . . .
> Subjects to kings should more obedience pay.

Acacis's concern to protect the Inca and his daughter, despite the fact that they are on opposing sides, and his anxiety about the fate of Amexia, the true queen, who his own mother has supplanted, impresses Montezuma, who observes

Excellent prince!
How great a proof of virtue you have shown,
To be concerned for griefs, though not your own.

Montezuma and Acacis become good friends despite their rivalry for Orazia's hand, and Montezuma tries to model himself on Acacis's altruistic and unselfish example. At the end of the play Acacis, believing that Orazia is to die, commits suicide, and Montezuma is revealed to be the long lost son and heir of Amexia, the legitimate queen. By now Montezuma is worthy to be King, a man in whom, as he himself says, the spirit of Acacis lives.

In 1670 Charles II appointed Dryden as Poet Laureate and Historiographer Royal and from this point onward his role as ideologist of the monarchy and royal apologist becomes more and more conspicuous. The same year saw the first performance of his most ambitious work to date, the two part *Conquest of Granada*; a play dedicated to the king's brother, the Duke of York and the future James II, who had converted to Catholicism in the previous year. The play makes use of tried and tested ingredients. There are internal conflicts and rivalries in a city under siege. The play concludes with a last minute revelation in which Almanzor, the heroic defender of Granada, the last Muslim stronghold in Spain, is identified as the long lost son of the duke of Arcos, the Spanish general. Almanzor is tested through a conflict between his love for Almahide and his duty to Boabdelin, King of Granada, whose queen she is. Yet there are specific local identifications since Dryden compares the Duke of York to his hero. Almanzor's struggles to defend Granada against a background of totally self-interested and selfish behaviour by the Segry and Abencerrago factions resemble the efforts of the duke of York, whose naval victories against the Dutch at Harwich and the Hague took place against a background of internal dissention, as Parliament repeatedly delayed the voting of essential supplies. King Boabdelin's complaints in the play are very much to the point:

Cursed is that king, whose honour's in their hands.
In senates, either they too slowly grant,
Or saucily refuse to aid my want:
And, when their thrift has ruined me in war,
They call their insolence my want of care.

Charles II was particularly sensitive to this want of co-operation because, so soon after an initial honeymoon period for the monarchy, it brought back unfortunate memories of 'ship money' and the conflict between parliament and King that had led to civil war. So Dryden did intend collapse of Granada and the Muslim empire in Spain as a warning to all those backsliders and carping critics in the House of Commons that loyalty and national unity were essential.

Neverthless, in the light of Dryden's dedication of the play to the duke of York it is surprising that Almanzor is not more idealistically presented than he is. For while Almanzor is undoubtedly presented as a noble, valiant and in many respects virtuous character, he is nevertheless clearly flawed since, even at his best, his behaviour is typically impulsive and self-regarding rather than controlled and altruistic. Dryden justifies this in his essay 'Of Heroic Plays' by insisting that he will never subject his characters to 'the French standard, where love and honour are to be weighed by drams and scruples',[2] and by invoking such classic precedents of the headstrong, vainglorious hero as Achilles in *The Iliad* and Rinaldo in Tasso's *Jerusalem Delivered*. However, there is rather more to the story than this. In *The Conquest of Granada* Dryden seems to have taken on board Hobbes' claim that all human behaviour is self-interested, but then seems to have tried to show that it can be both noble and virtuous despite this. Although in the first part Almanzor acts for himself first and foremost switching sides from Boabdelin, the King, to his rebel brother Prince Abdalla and back again; in the second part he acts more honourably, protecting Boabdelin from rebellious crowds and securing his release from imprisonment. Although he does these and other good deeds out of love and respect for Almahide, these motivations are clearly self-interested, yet Dryden implies they have an ennobling effect just the same. But clearly Dryden, in response to the climate of cynicism at the time, is already back-pedalling away from absolute standards of virtue.

At the best of times the Restoration was scarcely a favourable time for moral earnestness. With the impeachment and flight in 1667 of the Earl of Clarendon, who had been briefly revered as chief minister to the King and longsuffering survivor of the Protectorate, it was clear that there was no longer to be much faith in great men either. Indeed the sheer difficulty of striking even a moderately idealistic note is indicated by the fact that Almahide, the most unimpeachable character in the play, was played by Nell Gwynn – who was unable to play the role until she had delivered herself of the King's bastard son, to be styled the Duke of St Albans. Nevertheless Dryden's attempt to make his hero more sympathetic, because less than perfect, backfired. In George Villiers' merciless parody of Dryden as the self-important dramatist, Bayes, in *The Rehearsal*, the moral emptiness of Almanzor (Drawcansir) is clearly exposed in the following conversation:

> *Johnson*: Pray, Mr. Bayes, who is that Drawcansir?
> *Bayes*: Why, sir, a fierce hero that frights his mistress, snubs up kings, baffles armies, and does what he will, without regard to numbers, good manners, or justice.
> *Johnson*: A very pretty character.
> *Smith*: But, Mr. Bayes, I thought your heroes had ever been men of great humanity and justice.
> *Bayes*: Yes, they have been so; but, for my part, I prefer that one quality of singly beating of whole armies above all your moral virtues put together, 'y gad.

The problem that Dryden has created for himself is that in striving to make his super hero somewhat less than totally superhuman is that it does not serve to make him either very credible, or very sympathetic, or, indeed, particularly admirable. The result is a well-intentioned intellectual and dramatic muddle.

By contrast *Aureng-Zebe*, performed four years later in 1676, is Dryden's most successful attempt to present a virtuous hero on the Restoration stage and, in fact, one of the few plays by Dryden which comes close to justifying its pretensions. In part this is due to the fact that Aureng-Zebe's desire to be virtuous makes life more difficult for him rather than easier, but it is also because Dryden's theme, derived from a contemporary rivalry for the Indian throne, had a clear contemporary relevence. Just as Aureng-Zebe and his three brothers, Darah, Sujah and Morat, are led to struggle for the succession when it is believed that the 70-year-old

Emperor is mortally ill so, in Britain the whole question of the succession to Charles II was placed on the political agenda by the Duke of York's decision to convert to Catholicism.

While the Duke's allegiance to Rome as a matter of personal conviction did not necessarily exclude him becoming King, it created an atmosphere of uncertainty, both as to what might happen in the future and also made parliament and the British people more anxious about the possibility of Catholic conspiracies in the present. Such suspicions were not entirely unjustified, given that Charles II had entered into secret agreements with Louis IV to carry on with a fruitless war against Holland, which seemed perverse, given that Holland as a Protestant country, was a much more natural ally. These worries were the blue touch paper that would be lit by the alleged Popish plot of 1678, but Dryden's play shows that, as a supporter of the future James II, he was already concerned at the undermining of the monarchy and the possibility that James's position as legitimate successor could be challenged.

Aureng-Zebe shows Dryden moving towards a definition of virtue which is more private than public, more stoic than republican, in that he is beginning to distrust the very possibility of moral political action. The play is dedicated to the Earl of Mulgrave, a supporter of the Duke of York, in terms that strongly assert this:

> A popular man, is, in truth, no better than a prostitute to common fame, and to the people. He lies down to everyone he meets for the hire of praise; and his humility is only a disguised ambition. . . . How much more great and manly is your lordship, is your contempt of popular applause, and your retired virtue, which shines only to the few.

By 'popular man' Dryden undoubtedly had in mind the Earl of Shaftesbury, whom he was soon to pillory in *Absolom and Achitophel*, who, after the collapse of the governing group known as the Cabal in 1673, had become the chief thorn in the side of Charles II and who was to become the chief proponent of the idea that the Duke of York, as a Catholic, should be excluded from the succession. All this led Dryden to the notion that being virtuous was essentially a thankless task.

In *Aureng-Zebe* the hero, despite his loyalty to his father and his bravery and self-sacrifice in defending him nevertheless finds

himself unpopular, since the Emperor resents being in his debt
and being placed under unspecified moral obligations:

> O Aureng-Zebe! thy virtues shine too bright,
> They flash too fierce: I, like a bird of night,
> Shut my dull eyes, and sicken at the sight.
> Thou hast deserved more love than I can show;
> But 'tis thy fate to give, and mine to owe.

Although Dryden may regard himself as an opponent of Hobbes,
the play nevertheless presents a Hobbesian world of bitter and
unappeasable conflict, where there can never be life without desire
and without fear, where there is:

> a perpetuall and restlesse desire of Power after power, that
> ceaseth onely in death.[3]

The very existence of fathers and sons creates rivalry and the
desire for absolute domination in *Aureng-Zebe*. The four sons and
their father struggle against one another for the throne of India
and when Darah and Sujah have been eliminated the struggle
only intensifies, since the remaining participants, The Emperor,
Aureng-Zebe and Morat, his ruthless brother, are also rivals for
the hand of Indamora, the captive Queen. Indeed the situation
strongly invokes René Girard's notion of mimetic rivalry, since
the Emperor only seems to desire Indamora because he knows
that Aureng-Zebe loves her. 'Love' seems totally saturated with
connotations of power – Nourmahal, frustrated by her rejection
by the Emperor, becomes totally obsessed with Aurenge-Zebe, a
relationship which is technically incestuous, even though he is
not her son. Aureng-Zebe remains virtuous – even though his
jealousy is aroused by Indamora's apparent love for Morat – but
he persists in seeing such virtue as a disadvantage rather than a
self-validating moral code:

> How vain is virtue, which directs our ways
> Through certain danger to uncertain praise!
> Barren and airy name! thee Fortune flies
> With thy lean train, the pious and the wise.
> Heaven takes thee at thy word, without regard,
> And lets thee poorly be thy own reward.

The world is made for the bold impious man,
Who stoops at nothing, seizes all he can.
Justice to merit does weak aid afford;
She trusts her balance, and neglects her sword.

In the end virtue *is* rewarded since the Emperor regrets his self-interested actions and offers both the crown and the hand of Indamora to Aureng-Zebe – but this, far from seeming some inevitable culmination, has very much the air of a close-run thing.

The task of celebrating virtue which Dryden had set himself in his heroic plays was not necessarily a doomed enterprise even in an age where the very possibility of heroism and virtue were doubted: since the very rarity of such qualities could make them the worthy object of memorialisation. The problem was more that the heroic play effectively celebrated the Restoration itself. It took as axiomatic there were rightful and legitimate kings who had under all circumstances to be obeyed. All challenges to their authority constituted usurpation, which though bad enough in itself, must necessarily usher in anarchy and total political collapse. In England, though the usurper, Cromwell, had triumphed for a while, the danger had now been averted and a traditional order restored. What made the heroic play seem not just implausible but anachronistic was the political frenzy that surrounded the Popish Plot and the subsequent Exclusion Crisis. As Shaftesbury rallied Protestant England against the dark machinations of Rome it was suddenly crystal clear that the very same political and ideological forces that had led to the execution of Charles I and which had seemingly been defeated for good were actually still very much in evidence. It was not just James's succession to the throne that was at stake but the very authority of the reigning king. In such a divided and highly politicised world even a loyal supporter of the King and the Duke of York, which Dryden was, could no longer expect to speak of virtue even if he believed in it – which he did – since it would simply be exposed as a coded political discourse rather than as a language of morality. From this point onward the heroic play could only ever be self-evident propaganda.

Although Dryden's *All For Love* (1678) was almost certainly largely complete before Titus Oates's disclosure of a Popish plot, it neverthless shows that Dryden was already moving away from the concept of characters who could offer a pattern for moral action. Dryden's greater pragmatism is obliquely reflected in his dedication of the play to the King's chief minister, the Earl of Danby, whose great merit is not so much to have been virtuous, like the Duke of York or the Earl of Mulgrave, as to have restored the King's finances. His decision to revert to the native tradition of Shakespeare rather than to follow the exalted precedent of Corneille and Racine is presented as a victory for commonsense and decency. The decision of Hyppolyte in Racine's *Phèdre* to say nothing to his father about his stepmother's amorous advances shows not so much a sublime decorum as poor judgement. He should:

> choose rather to live with the reputation of a plain-spoken, honest man, than to die with the infamy of an incestuous villain.

All For Love, is seen as a perverse and superfluous attempt to rewrite one of Shakespeare's supreme dramatic masterpieces – which in a way it is – but it also needs to be read against the background of its day. In calling the play *All For Love*, in writing out the part of Octavius and amplifying the role of Octavia, Dryden was explicitly offering the public a place centred on love rather than virtue and on a hero, Antony, who has been deliberately chosen because the concept of virtue does not fit him, which is 'too narrow/ For his vast soul.' It is conceived of as a battle between rival queens (Nathaniel Lee's *The Rival Queens*, about the struggle between Roxana and Statira for the affection of Alexander, had been performed in the previous year) for Antony's love – a play that no one could really object to. Instead of offering a hero and heroine who strive to be impossibly virtuous Dryden stresses the honesty and straightforwardness of Antony amd Cleopatra. Antony regrets his own transparency:

> Why was I framed with this plain, honest heart
> Which knows not to disguise its griefs and weakness,
> But bears its workings outward to the world?

while Cleopatra condemns Antony for his continuing involvement with Octavia:

> Did you not o'errule,
> And force my plain direct, and open love,
> Into these crooked paths of jealousy?

If French heroes and heroines suffer by bottling up and concealing their emotions in accordance with artifical codes of etiquette,
their British counterparts are tormented by the exposure of their
deepest feelings. But if they suffer it is in the name of love *not*
virtue.

Dryden's avoidance of virtue is still more evident in his remarkable response to the Exclusion crisis, *Absalom and Achitophel*
which appeared in 1681. This poem is usually described as a satire,
but while such a designation is virtually inevitable it is nevertheless very far from the 'snarling muse' of Dr Johnson. Indeed,
precisely what is so remarkable about the poem is that in an
atmosphere of hysteria and polarised political opinion Dryden
contrives to be so serene and so genial, to offer an analysis of
the nation's dilemma that seems relatively sane and dispassion-
ate. Dryden's task, of course, was politically sensitive since he
effectively had to exonerate Monmouth, the King's illegitimate
son and chosen candidate to ensure a Protestant succession, from
any blame or involvement in the furore that had grown up around
him. Moreover, to condemn Shaftesbury unmercifully when he
had such widespread popular support, was likely to be counter-
productive. So Dryden's chosen strategy was to avoid contrasts
in black and white in the presentation of a more colourful and
diversified picture; to see the situation as a comedy of errors rather
than a battle between good and evil. Charles II may not be either
a good or noble king and his sexual indiscretions may have been
manifold, but, like his Biblical predecessor, King David, his sexual
'warmth' points to an essentially affable and well disposed person. He is mild and merciful, which may mean that he is often
perceived as weak, but those who believe this will be undeceived.
Monmouth, the king's natural son, (Absalom) is essentially a naive
innocent, who can be all too easily manipulated by a cunning
political leader like Shaftesbury (Achitophel). Yet even Shaftesbury
is partially exonerated, for although his restless and reckless desire
for power is dangerous to the state, Dryden concedes that he
could have been of service to the state 'had he been content to
serve the crown'. So the dangerous catalyst has been the unruly
spirit of the British people, so reminiscent of the Jews in the Old
Testament:

> The Jews, a headstrong, moody, murmuring race,
> As ever tried the extent and stretch of grace;

God's pampered people, whom, debached with ease,
No king could govern. nor no God could please.

The combination of unstable demagogue with a restless populace
makes for a deadly cocktail:

Achitophel, grown weary to possess
A lawful fame, and lazy happiness,
Disdained the golden fruit to gather free,
And lent the crowd his arm to shake the tree.
Now, manifest of crimes contrived long since,
He stood at bold defiance with his prince;
Held up the buckler of the people's cause
Against the crown, and skulked behind the laws.

So Dryden actually calls for reformation from those he ostensibly
satirises. The King must stand firm against this challenge to his
authority. Monmouth, cruelly misled, must disassociate himself
from Shaftesbury; while even Shaftesbury himself can still reclaim
himself as a legitimate politician by repudiating the mob. Yet the
paradox of the poem is that the man who stands to gain most
from Dryden's intervention and who is a key figure in the exclusion
crisis's cast of characters, James, Duke of York, is effectively absent
from the poem. *Absolom and Achitophel* is *Hamlet* without the prince.
Yet James, the king's brother, is the virtuous man:

His brother, though oppressed with vulgar spite,
Yet dauntless, and secure of native right,
Of every royal virtue stands possessed;
Still dear to all the bravest and the best.

But James, though virtuous is not popular, so his cause is best
served by focusing on the prospect of a triumphantly assertive
Charles:

Once more the godlike David was restored,
And willing nations knew their lawful lord.

Virtue is most virtuous when it is invisible – as in *The Spanish
Friar*, Dryden's play of the same year, where, Sancho the legitimate King of Spain, never actually appears.

Virtue takes a back seat in *The Spanish Friar* since affairs of state are subordinated to an ostensible sub-plot, focused on the immoral activities of an unscrupulous friar – no doubt because Dryden sought to deflect anti-Catholic feeling onto a relatively harmless object. But even the political world is murky. Dryden's plot centres on the love of Torresmond for Leonora, the queen and daughter of a usurper. Leonora contemplates the execution of Sancho and even Torresmond, who at the end is revealed to be Sancho's son, justifies the woman he loves with some remarkably opportunistic reasoning:

> Kings' titles commonly begin by force,
> Which time wears off, and mellows into right;
> So power, which, in one age, is tyranny,
> Is ripened, in the next, to true succession.
> She's in possession.

So Alphonso's comment:

> Virtue must be thrown off; 'tis a coarse garment,
> Too heavy for the sunshine of the court

seems not so much cynicism as a realistic assessment of the state of affairs.

A similar disillusionment marks Otway's *Venice Preserved* (1682). The play has often been seen as an anti-Whig tract since it ridicules Shaftesbury in the characters of Antonio and Renault, but in fact the play is remarkably detached. There is nothing admirable about the state of Venice, for the senators constitute a ruling class that is corrupt, venal, ruthless and oppressive, yet the conspirators who seek to overthrow them are for the most part equally violent and unscrupulous. The only real exception to this is Pierre, who is a genuine idealist, a man outraged at the direction in which Venice is heading:

> We have neither safety, unity, nor peace,
> For the foundation's lost of common good;
> Justice is lame as well as blind amongst us;
> The laws (corrupted to their ends that make 'em)
> Serve but for instruments of some new tyranny,
> That every day starts up t'enslave us deeper.

But Pierre's involvement with a motley rabble of self-serving plotters cast doubts on his judgement – not least on his faith in Jaffeir who betrays them all. The very idea of virtue has become problematic and although the word occurs almost as often as it does in *Aureng-Zebe* (31 as compared with 36) there is no longer much sense that the word designates anything very real. The defining point of view seems to be expressed by Renault:

Yes, clocks will go as they are set. But Man,
Irregular Man's ne'er constant, never certain.

If there is no honour among senators and no loyalty to the state, there is no loyalty among the conspirators either. Instability rules.

Such instability is equally prominent in the world of Restoration comedy, which in its unremitting focus on deception and sexual intrigue certainly precludes virtue and makes even such residual qualitites as honesty and fidelity seem highly problematic. The rake and his correspondent figure the sexually demanding and promiscuous wife take part in a ceaseless dance of infidelities, driven by restlessness and the passion of the moment. In Etherege's *The Man of Mode* (1676) the rakish hero Dorimant erects this into a philosophical principle:

We are not masters of our own affections, our inclinations daily alter; now we love pleasure, and anon we shall dote on business: human frailty will have it so, and who can help it?

Morality therefore appears as a superogatory system of rules that have no real bearing on actual life. Restoration comedy does not claim to satirise or castigate vice in the Jonsonian manner but to project as forcefully, frenetically and grotesquely as possible. At best there is a somewhat hypocritical attack on hypocrisy as in Wycherley's *The Country Wife*, in which Margery Pinchwife is distinguished from her urban equivalents, not by her innocence, but by the shamelessness with which she pursues men other than her husband. But in such a context it is very doubtful whether there is really anything left to veil. Yet despite the obvious cynicism of such comedy there does remain a slightly surprising attempt to salvage something at least of human nature – to insinuate that your hero is in no way to be taken as a paragon of virtue is nevertheless the best of a bad lot. Dorimant is shown discarding

Mrs Loveit in favour of Belinda before finally transferring his affections to Harriet. On the face of it he is now a reformed man, determined to settle down to a peaceful life in the country, but whether we believe in his reformation or not the play still asks us to think well of him. Unlike Sir Fopling Flutter he is not absurdly narcissistic and effeminate. He recommends himself to the ladies because he is manly, witty and straightforward. If he flatters women through good nature and good manners he neverthless claims 'I am honest in my inclinations'.

If Dorimant is not exactly sincere, Etheredge suggests that he come as close to it as you are likely to get. Beneath an engaging and well disposed exterior there beats a comparatively loyal heart. In Wycherley's *The Plain Dealer* (1674) his aptly named Manly, a rough and rugged sea captain, is made of very much sterner stuff. Indeed Wycherley implies that he is, under normal circumstances, too much of an man to stoop to intrigue and subterfuge. His honesty, integrity and fidelity in love make him as close to a virtuous character as you are likely to get, but for his pains he is betrayed by Olivia, the woman he loves, by marrying in his absence Vernish, his only friend. *The Plain Dealer* becomes a revenge play, where the humour such as it is stems from Manly's determination to humiliate Olivia publically. But although Wycherley asks us to admire Manly, his endorsement is hardly unequivocal, since his willingness to trust people only leads to acute unhappiness and seems to represent some kind of questionable error of judgement. The only other admirable character in the play, Fidelia, a woman who loves him and who has followed him to sea in man's clothes seems to have strayed in from the comedy of another epoch. Plainly Manly is too good for the age he finds himself in.

Such virtue is still harder to find in Wycherley's celebrated successor and alleged disciple, William Congreve. On the basis of his claim in the prologue to *Love for Love* to follow in Wycherley's footsteps:

As Asses Thistles, Poets mumble Wit,
And dare not bite, for fear of being bit . . .
Since the *Plain-Dealers* Scenes of Manly Rage,
No one has dar'd to lash this Crying Age.
This time, the Poet owns the bold Essay,
Yet hopes there's no ill-manners in his Play:
And he declares by me, he has design'd
Affront to none, but frankly speaks his mind.

and because of his notorious abandonment of the stage after *The Way of the World* Congreve has often been represented as a writer trying to function in a milieu that was beneath him. On this account Congreve's drama is the fine flower of the age, delicately poking its head above a circumambient morass of coarse grasses and weeds. But all this is really folklore based on a need to think well of a dramatist whose work long continued to hold the stage through its ingenious plotting, grotesque caricatures and some vague sense of poetic justice. It would actually be more pertinent to suggest that Congreve represents the moral nadir of Restoration comedy and that it was not without good reason that Jeremy Collier, sanctimonious though he may have been, chose to focus his attack on the stage upon him. Certainly Congreve's first play, *The Old Batchelor*, is unrepentently squalid – the intrigues of Vainlove and Bellmour with Araminta, Belinda and Laetitia, the spouse of Fondlewife, the banker constitute the ice-cream sundae that is topped with a hot sauce – the marriage of Heartwell, the old batchelor to Vainlove's cast-off and notoriously complaisant mistress, Sylvia. Heartwell only escapes total humiliation through the discovery that Sylvia is married already. Indeed this is the real ethic of Congreve's plays: we are asked to admire those who are adroit and sophisticated as they outwit and get the better of those who, from the perspective of the play are boorish, naive and ridiculous. While it goes without saying that we should laugh at rustics and coxcombs, the most persistent target are the elderly of both sexes (that is over 50) who are ridiculous, not so much because they are ridiculous as because they are old and still have pretensions to love. In this way Congreve's comedy is actually quite cruel.

The one play of Congreve that contradicts much if this is *The Double-Dealer* in which Maskwell, the principal character and arch-intriguer is frankly presented as a downright villain. A further awkwardness of this is that since Mellefont, the ostensible hero, is the victim of Maskwell's machinations he does not necessarily emerge in a very favourable light. Indeed Congreve felt obliged to defend himself from precisely this criticism:

> Another very wrong Objection has been made by some who have not taken leisure to distinguish the characters. The Hero of the play, as they are pleas'd to call him, (meaning Mellefont) is a Gull, and made a Fool and cheated. Is every Man a Gull and a Fool that is deceiv'd? . . . But if an Open-hearted Honest

Man, who has entire confidence in one whom he takes to be his Friend, and whom he has obliged to be so; and who (to confirm him in his Opinion) in all appearance, and upon several tryals has been so: If this Man be deceived by the Treachery of the other; must he of necessity commence Fool immediately, only because the other has proved a Villain?

But Congreve in protesting so much gives the game away. We cannot fail to note that he carefully distances himself from any idea that Mellefont is to be thought of as the hero and indeed he is too passive and too colourless to be this. Mellefont is to be married to Cynthia, daughter of Sir Paul Pliant but has upset Lady Touchwood, his aunt by rejecting his advances. Maskwell plans to discredit Mellefont and marry Cynthia is his place by trapping him into an assignation with Lady Touchwood in her chamber, where Lord Touchwood can discover him. The plot goes astray when Lady Touchwood learns that Maskwell is to marry Cynthia and becomes jealous. The play turns on the contrast between appearance and reality. Maskwell appears to Lord Touchwood as 'Honest Maskwell' and as one possessed of 'Manly Virtue' but in the end it is the innocents Mellefont and Cynthia who benefit as Lord Touchwood:

> ... hastens to do Justice, in rewarding Virtue and Wrong'd Innocence.

But it is hard to respect Mellefont when at an early stage Maskwell unfolds the entire plot to his face:

> I have undertaken to break the Match, I have undertaken to make your Uncle Disinherit you, to get you turn'd out of Doors; and to – ha, ha, ha, I can't tell you for Laughing – oh she has open'd her heart to me. – I am to turn you a Grazing, and to – ha, ha, ha, Marry Cynthia my self; there's a plot for you.

Honest or not Mellefont is duped in the most humiliating fashion and we are more inclined to respect, perhaps even admire, the daring, shameless, ingenious Maskwell who runs rings round him.

Love For Love is perhaps Congreve's most appealing comedy in that it is his one play, despite its pretensions to satire, that aspires to be nothing more than frankly humorous through its presentation of a wide range of ludicrous characters ranging from Miss Prue the foolish, ignorant country girl and Ben, a naval simpleton, to Foresight, an old fogey totally immersed in astrology and Sir Sampson Legend, the pompous, bullying father of the play's hero, Valentine, whom he proposes to disinherit in favour of Ben, because of the vast debts that Valentine has incurred in wooing Angelica. There is nothing particularly admirable about Valentine but he inaugurates a stage tradition of a likeable, well-meaning if rather self-indulgent young men that continues into the eighteenth century with Sheridan's *The School for Scandal* and Goldsmith's *The Good-natur'd Man*. To evade signing over his fortune he feigns madness in the style of Hamlet – a gesture that prompts Angelica to show more evidence of her affection for him than she has hitherto. She then purports to test him still further by agreeing to marry his father. Valentine in despair resigns his inheritance, whereupon Angelica, convinced of his sincerity, agrees to marry him after all.

Congreve's last play *The Way of the World* gestures in the direction of the rake reformed. In the past Mirabell has been something of an unscrulous womaniser. He has a long-standing affair with Mrs Fainall before marrying her off to Fainal and purports to make love to Lady Wishfort in order to advance his relationship with Mrs Millamant her niece. It seems that he and Millamant are genuinely in love. The one obstacle to their happiness is that Lady Wishfort has the power to deprive her niece of half her inheritance. Millamant plans to forestall this by shaming Lady Wishfort, through a marriage to his servant, Waitwell, masquerading as Sir Rowland, a gentleman. Fainall, effectively the villain and successor to Maskwell, seems likely to frustrate this scheme by threatening to expose his wife's past, but this in turn is frustrated by Mirabell's revelation that he has power of attorney over Mrs Fainal's property. We must believe that Mirabell and Millamant are more genuine because they are in love but cold-blooded analysis suggests that it is more appropriate to think of Mirabell and Fainal as two of a kind – indeed Congreve goes out of his way to suggest similarities between them. In Congreve glamour effectively takes the place of virtue or integrity – it is hard to imagine performances of either *Love For Love* or *The Way of the World* in which Valentine and Angelica, Mirabell and Millamant, are not far and away the most attractive people on stage, so an audience wants the beautiful to win and to believe that they deserve to. But we must also note how mercenary the characters are. Even Mellefont and Cynthia, who speak of running away without regard to

Portion, Settlements and Joyntures

do not do so. If Valentine is proved to be a faithful lover he nevertheless marries an heiress with his own fortune intact, while Millamant and Mirabell are certainly not prepared to start life together on half income. At the end even the likeableness of such characters becomes questionable – like elaborate royal icing on a cardboard cake.

When it was performed in 1700, five years after *Love For Love*, *The Way of the World* must have seemed slightly dated since in the interim there had been a distinct shift away from the hard-hearted, cynical mode of earlier Restoration drama. This tendency was initiated by Colley Cibber's first play, *Love's Last Shift* which received its premiere in 1696. In the play, Amanda, whose husband Loveless has abandoned her after only six months marriage to travel abroad, succeeds in winning back his love by masquerading as a promiscuous woman of the town. Cibber acknowledged that the play was unusual in presenting a more moral character:

Nor do the bad alone his colours share;
Neglected virtue is at least shown fair

though he conceded that to do so was to go against the taste of the time:

A honest Rake forego the Joys of Life!
His Whores, and Wine! t'Embrace a dull chaste Wife:
Such out-of-fashion Stuff! But then again,
He's lewd for above four Acts, Gentlemen!

The switch from bawdy humour to elevated sentiment is indeed abrupt and makes the play seem crude and clumsy in its overall conception, but it nevertheless strikes a significantly new note in its willingness to take the part of a woman and to actually talk about an unhappy marriage. Before Cibber, marriage is largely presented as a convenient starting point for having extra-marital affairs, which can be carried on indefinitely to the mutual satisfaction of both husbands and wives. But for Cibber infidelity is actually a moral issue – the question Amanda asks of her husband:

> Conscience! did you ne'er feel the checks of it? Did it never, never tell you of your broken Vows?

is not one that we would expect to be asked in a play of this kind. Cibber suggests that this should not be so and stresses that in marriage it is usually the woman who is the loser. As Lord Foppington says in *The Careless Husband*:

> a fine Woman when she's married makes as ridiculous a Figure, as a beaten General marching out of a Garrison.

Nevertheless Cibber's happy ending was so obviously contrived that by comparison Vanbrugh's two plays, *The Relapse* and *The Provok'd Wife*, which appeared in the following year (the first as a deliberate sequel to *Love's Last Shift*), seem more satisfactory if only because they make no real attempt to resolve the situation. In each case Vanbrugh presents an unhappy marriage in a more or less serious main plot but leaves it dangling as a kind of problem play by foregrounding a comic sub-plot in the final scenes. In fact neither situation lends itself to a resolution, since Loveless has already relapsed once, protestation of fidelity at the end would scarcely be very convincing. In *The Provok'd Wife* he has treated his wife so contemptuously that Lady Brute would utterly lose our respect if she were to seek a reconciliation. In fact Cibber's *The Careless Husband* (1705), a play well respected in its own time but since then unjustly neglected, is the one work that manages both to express the marital tension between Lord and Lady Easy and resolve it in a way that is psychlogically convincing. But of course to look at human relationships in this way is far removed from the themes that the Restoration comedy had habitually addressed.

The sentimental turn in English comedy which Colley Cibber initiated is typified by Farquhar's best-known plays, *The Recruiting Officer* (1706) and *The Beaux's Strategem* (1707), both of which are significantly located not in London, but in the provincial towns of Shrewsbury and Lichfield. While there are intrigues in these plays there are no victims and most of the characters are likeable and good-natured. In *The Recruiting Officer* Sylvia, daughter of Justice Balance, who loves Captain Plume – despite her father's opposition to their marriage – runs away from home dressed as a man and eventually gets her way after she had been arrested for scandalous behaviour and handed over by her own father to Plume as a recruit. In *The Beaux' Strategem* Aimwell and Archer, two gentlemen who have fallen on hard times, travel to Lichfield in the hope of retrieving their fortunes. They are given the opportunity of doing so when they rescue Dorinda and Mrs Sullen, to whom they have become attracted, but characteristically confess. No one will be gulled. Mrs Sullen is freed from an unhappy marriage. Aimwell learns that he has inherited his father's fortune; plotting has become a completely harmless activity. For Farquahar the age of cynicism about human nature was past. In the prologue to *The Beaux Strategem* he writes:

> When strife disturbs, or sloth corrupts an age,
> Keen satire is the business of the stage.
> When the Plain-Dealer writ, he lash'd those crimes,
> Which then infested most the modish times:
> But now, when faction sleeps, and sloth is fled,
> And all our youth in active fields are bred;
> When, through Great Britain's fair extensive round,
> The trumps of fame the notes of UNION sound;
> When Anna's sceptre points the laws their course
> And her example gives her precepts force:
> There scarce is room for satire . . .

Under Anne and the union virtue has been restored.

3

Virtue Excluded

The eighteenth-century obsession with the idea of virtue was above all the product of political infighting between Whigs and Tories that reached its maximum intensity under Queen Anne but which continued with almost equal virulence under the Hanoverians, even though after 1715 the Whigs remained permanently in power. Under Anne the concern was that with the selfish and factional spirit of party prevailing there was a serious danger that there would be no place in the nation's councils for genuinely patriotic and disinterested statesmen who would be prepared to place the interest of the country as a whole before the desire to aggrandise a single sectional interest, whether Whig or Tory. Under George I and George II, and especially after Sir Robert Walpole became the first recognised Prime Minister in 1721, the concern was somewhat different though essentially similar: to ensure that there still would be public spirited citizens and, especially Members of Parliament, who would be prepared to speak out against the government despite Walpole's determination to crush all criticism through co-optation and bribery. A particularly clear example of how this could work was provided by Thomas Gordon, co-author of *Cato's Letters* – which had criticised the Whig hegemony – who in 1723 accepted Walpole's offer of a sinecure as First Commissioner of Wine Licences. But in both cases virtue designated the very reverse of what generally prevailed, whether violent partisanship or political corruption.

The notion of virtue was classical and Roman. Although Britain was not actually a republic the Roman analogy acquired as cogency that it has never possessed before, partly because the consequence of the Glorious Revolution of 1688 was to limit the power of the King and partly because it was strongly believed that this settlement of 1688 needed protecting and preserving from its enemies of whatever persuasion, just like the Roman Republic. But in Britain virtue was invariably defined as a lack. Virtue was needed precisely because it was conspicuous by its absence. The virtuous, almost by definition, were those who lacked power.

In the age of Anne the notion of virtue was largely bound up with the literary and political careers of two men – Jonathan Swift, a Tory and Joseph Addison, a Whig – who in their different ways demonstrate just how crucial the pen could be as a tool of political advancement. For propaganda was crucial to the new politics. Journals and pamphlets could play a vital part in influencing public opinion. Perhaps for the first time the real debates of the nation were fought out not so much on the floor of the House of Commons as beyond its walls and in print.

For Swift the notion of virtue was complexly bound up with a sense of tradition. Though others perceived him – rightly – as anarchic and subversive, Swift viewed himself as a conservative, a defender of familar and well-tried ways, a supporter of the ancient against the moderns and 'virtue' was a complex but lucid shorthand which could designate all of this. In adopting such a position Swift was powerfully influenced by his years at Moor Park as secretary to Sir William Temple, for Temple was not only a denigrator of all things modern but an unrepentent and often uncritical exponent of classical learning. As a scholar, gentleman and archetypal old fogey, Temple occasionally got things badly wrong – especially when Bentley was able to show that the Epistles of Phalaris, which he had extravagantly praised, were a forgery. Yet he was undoubtedly learned in his own way and his trenchantly argued indictments of contemporary culture undoubtedly struck a nerve. Temple argued that not only in classical Greece and Rome but in many other societies from China to Peru besides, it was possible for men to be both virtuous and creative because their existence was simpler and more straightforward and because, in such a world, personal honour had a prominent place. He asserted:

> I think nothing is more evident in the world, than that honour is a much stronger principle both of action and invention than gain can ever be.[1]

Indeed for Temple the very controversy that he initiated, as the so-called Battle of the Books, was itself a symptom of what he deplored. He contrasted the wisdom, learning and patriotism of such a scholar as Confucius which served to stabilise society with the unsettling role of knowledge in the modern era, where it serves.

> ... for little more than to raise doubts and disputes, heats and feuds, animosities and factions in all controversies of religion or government.[2]

Holland, where he had served as ambassador for many years, had served to focus and exemplify his fears: it was divisive, self-centred, pre-occupied with financial gain. To many in the late seventeenth century the United Provinces were both a portent and a warning. Holland was an unnatural country, born out of the sea through technological expertise, whose astonishing commercial rise seemed equally unnatural and precarious. Precisely because the Dutch saw everything in terms of their own selfish short-term advantage they were a people who could not be trusted or depended upon as everyone knew; yet despite this the British were compelled to rely on an alliance with the United Provinces to defeat France in the War of Spanish Succession, in the process becoming, according to Swift 'the dupes and bubbles of Europe'. Against the calculating and opportunist spirit of the moderns Temple was unrepentently old-fashioned. He concluded his essay on 'Ancient and Modern Learning' by quoting Alphonsus, King of Aragon:

> ... among so many thing as are by men possessed or pursued in the course of their lives, all the rest are baubles, besides old wood to burn, old wine to drink, old friends to converse with, and old books to read.[3]

Although Temple believed in the universality of human nature, and delighted in using his wide reading to substantiate his views, he nevertheless believed that there were crucial differences between the modern and ancient world: besides 'avarice and greediness of wealth' there was also the 'vain ostentation'[4] of contemporary scholarship, which he viewed as an essentially parasitic activity. Poetry was important for the moral role that it could perform, since it was essentially concerned with 'the praise of virtue, or virtuous men' because:

> ... under the disguise of fables, or the pleasure of story, to show the beauties and rewards of virtue, the deformities and

misfortunes or punishment of vice; by example of both to encourage one, and deter men from the other.[5]

but in the modern world the ethical dimension of poetry had effectively disappeared. The typical modern author was Rabelais who subjected everything to indiscriminate ridicule. Yet despite his overall sense of pessimism Temple did have a rather surprising solution to the problem of modernity that was to be remarkably influential: if Britain were to be ruled by a virtuous monarch the nation really could be transformed:

> I cannot but observe to the honour of our country that the good qualities amongst us seem to be natural, and the ill ones more accidental, and such would be easily changed by the example of princes and by the precepts of laws; such I mean, as should be designed to form manners, to restrain excesses, to encourage industry, to prevent men's expenses beyond their fortunes, to countenance virtue, and to raise the true esteem due to plain sense and common honesty.[6]

Temple certainly has an extensive programme of legislation in mind but the whole project depends on a virtuous ruler in the first place. This constant and to us somewhat optimistic faith in a model monarch who will initiate the moral rebirth of a nation is a thread that runs through seventeenth- and eighteenth-century politics. If the high hopes held out for Charles II were soon dashed, they were raised again for William of Orange. Swift and Pope believed that the virtues of Anne would be diffused through the kingdom, while Bolingbroke, disillusioned with Hanoverian support for the Whigs, longed for a patriot king. For a brief historical moment it seemed as if George III, particularly as he was British born, might at last be the promised Messiah, but after his descent into madness it became doubtful whether such a massive investment in the personal character of a monarch could ever be repeated.

Swift followed in the footsteps of his mentor, Temple, in his commitment to the faith that in the modern world virtue was always in danger, whether from the opportunism of politicians, the financial manipulations of city merchants or from the manoeuvrings of self-serving generals such as the Duke of Marlborough. Moreover he was to repeat his patron's departure into political exile, a destiny which though it had an excellent classical pedigree, was far more painful for Swift precisely because it was involuntary. Whereas Temple lived out his days in the grandeur and tranquillity of Moor Park still close to the capital, Swift though a Dean and in Dublin from 1713, he was neverthless on the wrong side of the Irish sea and acutely conscious that he could never again enjoy the influence he had had as a confederate of the chief minister, Robert Harley, at the very centre of things. While Temple was often bland, Swift was invariably bitter. While Temple would serenely appeal to the past and invoke the classical tradition as if it were unproblematic, Swift had too acute a mind to ever be uncritical of anything. Swift's conservatism often turned out to be disconcertingly radical in practice. His passionate and coruscating intelligence was always getting him into trouble. From *A Tale of a Tub* (1704) he was feared and distrusted as a loose cannon, which might always be fired in the most unexpected direction.

A Tale of a Tub epitomises many of the paradoxes of Swift as a writer and polemicist – which he unceasingly was. Ostensibly it speaks for tradition, sanity and ancient virtue; for the *via media* of the Anglican church against the contrasted extremes of Roman Catholicism and Dissent. Yet what makes Swift's latterday claim, in 1710, that he had nothing more than this in mind – and anyway why should it matter when it was all so long ago? – is that all this leaves totally out of account the book's violent, anarchic and disruptive tone. To focus very literally on the 'argument' of *A Tale of a Tub* is not only to miss the point, but to wilfully blind oneself to what positively leaps off the page. Rather what Swift positively revelled in was the totally novel freedom and anonymity of print culture which offered him a soapbox to say anything and everything he liked. In the process of 'giving a loose to his soul' – as Robert Frost has it – Swift could send up those who were ostensibly on his own side just as much as the actual enemy. However hard we may try to believe that Swift's praise of Lord Somers is sincere, or that both here and in *The Battle of the Books* (published with *A Tale of a Tub* but written earlier in 1697) he is simply acting out of loyalty to his patron, Sir William Temple, there are bound to be doubts. For Swift, with his lack of deference and critical intellect was actually far closer to the Moderns like Bentley than he would actually care to admit. In his 'apology' for the *Tale* he boasts that:

> ... he has not borrowed one single hint from any writer in
> the world ... He conceived it was never disputed to be an
> original. (p. 6)

Yet this same claim in the body of the text would have been
treated with ridicule. After all, if Bentley was vain, fond of displaying his learning and self-importantly digressive, was not this
also true of his aristocratic opponent Sir William Temple? Moreover,
had Sir William lived to see the publication of *The Battle of the
Books* – and it may be significant that he did not – he could hardly
have approved of a book which reduced what he regarded as
very serious issues to pantomime and farce. Moreover, Swift, by
publishing anonymously evades all responsibility for his actions
and deliberately sends up all the procedures by which texts were
traditionally validated by adorning his tale with a panoply of
prefaces, dedications, digressions and recondite allusions. In his
cloak of invisibility Swift becomes powerful and potentially dangerous. As Swift purports to mock his subversive master of ceremonies
it becomes all the easier to assume that voice, effortlessly blending
into the motley crowd of fools, quacks and mountebanks. All the
high pretensions of contemporary controversy, religious, scientific
or literary, are effortlessly demolished as Swift, anticipating Warhol,
stresses the ephemerality of it all. Addressing Prince Posterity
the author observes:

> It ill befits the distance between your Highness and me to send
> you for ocular conviction to a *jakes*, or an *oven*, to the windows
> of a *bawdy-house*, or to a sordid *lantern*. Books, like men their
> authors, have no more than one way of coming into the world,
> but there are ten thousand to go out of it and return no more.
> (pp. 16–17)

Swift's characteristic linkage of posteriors and posterity, of mind
and body, is not just scatological: it demonstrates both his determination not to take on board the assumptions of high culture
and his own psychological distance from it. Yet it is this observ-
ance of the proprieties and the niceties that maintains the
aristocracy and their cultural pretensions.

Swift may well have been sincere in believing that his *Tale* would
serve to vindicate the Anglican church but by linking the Battle of
the Books with religious controversy he at best muddied the waters,

at worst totally undermined his whole line of argument. Of course his claim that significant parallels could be found between Catholics and Dissenters needed little in the way of intellectual justification at a time when James II had offered freedom of worship to both compratively recently. Ian Higgins has plausibly suggested that Swift was influenced by the writings of Charles Leslie, a severe critic of Catholics and Dissenters alike, who wrote:

> Jesuit and Puritan are convertible Terms, in the Point of Loyalty, only that the Jesuit is the Elder Brother.[7]

and who, perhaps crucially, employed one of the key figures of the *Tale*:

> ... he that will make *Separation* for every *Error*, will fall into much greater *Error* and *Sin* than that which he would seek to Cure. It is like tearing *Christ's* seamless *Coat* because we like not the *colour*, or to mend the fashion of a Sleeve.[8]

However, polemic is one thing, allegory another, and Swift's use of the figure as he develops it gets increasingly out of control. Rectitude involves either maintaining the garment as it was or restoring it to its orginal state – but who is to say where restoration becomes innovation? In *A Tale of a Tub* Swift tells of three sons, Peter (Catholic), Martin (Anglican) and Jack (Dissenter) who are left three plain but serviceable coats by their father, who insists that they must not be altered in any way. All three rebel against paternal authority by adding various adornments to them, but when Jack tries to make amends by ripping off all the accretions he destroys the coat as well. Only Martin does the right thing, by trying to remove as many stylistic innovations as he can, without actually damaging the coat. He begs Jack:

> of all love, not to damage his coat by any means; for he would never get another. (p. 67)

Yet the lack of symmetry between the Reformation controversies and the argument between Ancients and Moderns makes Swift's attempt to align them highly awkward. For it is hard to duck the conclusion that there was a modernising bent to the Reformation, since it involved viewing tradition critically and, equally, that it is the denial of the validity of any such a critical perspective that links the Ancients with Catholicism. In any event Swift should perhaps have realised that those who hurl custard pies may seem as undignified as those who are hit by them and that such carnivalesque proceedings would also bring the Church of England, which sought to be above such controversy, into disrepute.

Again, Swift's strongly held views about truthfulness, clarity and directness of language meant that in practice he was making common cause with such leading figures on the Modern side as Hobbes, Descartes and Locke. Swift was as worried as anyone about how language could be purged of the corruptions that now afflicted it. Although Swift undoubtedly believed that the Moderns were arrogant, opinionated and untrustworthy he would nevertheless have much sympathy with Hobbes's peremptory dismissal of the Catholic theologian, Suarez:

> When men write whole volumes of such stuffe, are they not Mad, or intend to make others so.[9]

and he would have agreed with Hobbes' insistence that clear thinking depended on a precise and careful use of language:

> The Light of human minds is Perspicuous Words, but by exact definitions first snuffed and purged from ambiguity.[10]

But Swift reverses the direction of this argument by claiming that it is the wilfullness and narcissism of the Moderns that unsettles language, and makes both the existence of truth and the very possibility of reaching agreement as to what that truth is, highly problematic. Yet in Swift's discussion of the Aeolists he adopts Hobbes's tactic of characterising social disorders by figures of sickness and disease. The very notion of the Aeolists as blown up with wind invokes Hobbes' carnivalesque definition of 'Spirit' as

> . . . nothing but the blowing into a man some thin and subtile aire, or wind, in such a manner as a man filleth a bladder with his breath.[11]

while, by locating the Aeolists in the Greek 'Land of Darkness', Swift recalls the Kingdom of Darkness that Hobbes speaks of in book IV of *Leviathan*. Perhaps the most significant reminiscence of *Leviathan* may be the fact that Swift's brothers adorn their coats with shoulder-knots: for Hobbes describes how the Christian church introduced what he calls three knots on 'Christian liberty': excommunication, bishops and the papacy.[12] This may well explain why Swift as an Anglican did not believe that the additions could be dispensed with altogether, since to dispense with bishops in the manner of the dissenters would involve all manner of disorders and the destruction of Christian discipline.

It was Swift's strong sense of himself as a Church of England man that enabled him, at least in his own mind, to stand aside from the bitter party conflicts between Whig and Tory that characterised the age of Anne. Originally Swift had been a Whig and he seems to have regarded himself as a supporter of the the the Glorious Revolution of 1688, both insofar as this represented the Anglican church and the rights of the people against the King. However, most aspirants to high office within the church tended to be Tory, largely because the Whigs were widely regarded as being prepared to look favourably on the cause of dissent. Despite Swift's own hostility to dissent this does not seem to have figured prominently in his political calculations and his support for the Tories stemmed almost entirely from the fact that they opposed Britain's continued involvement in the war of Spanish Succession under the leadership of Marlborough. But Swift regarded opposition to the war not as a party matter but as a cause which all good men and true should support because the war was at once disreputable and dishonest and contrary to the national interest. So although Swift wrote in *The Examiner* at the behest of Robert Harley he saw himself not as a hireling but as one candidly speaking out in the cause of virtue and truth.

Undoubtedly Swift viewed the whole matter of the conduct of the war through the spectacles of Sir William Temple, who would certainly have been aghast at the very thought of fighting France on Holland's behalf and financially supporting her at the same time. But there were other strong reasons for opposing the Whigs as well. For one thing they had treated Queen Anne, the ruling monarch, with scarcely concealed contempt. Swift not only reverenced the Queen but believed, like Temple, that a virtuous monarch, as she was, was crucial to any reformation of manners. In his 'Project for the Advancement of Religion, and the Reformation of Manners' (1709) he argued that if a virtuous monarch were to make it in

> ... every man's interest and honour to cultivate religion and
> virtue; by rendering vice a disgrace and certain ruin to prefer-
> ment or pretension: all which they should first attempt in their
> own courts and families.

then

> ... things would soon take on a new face, and religion receive
> a mighty encouragement. (Vol. 2, pp. 47–8)

So Swift was not just objecting to the war on the grounds of
cost, or because the essential question of Britain's national interest had been lost sight of but because he saw it as a canker of
corruption that was damaging the moral health of the whole
country. Furthermore, the war since its continuance was based
on the self-interest of Marlborough and city merchants represented a swerve away from the ideal of virtue, which involved
public-spiritedness and a concern for the common good. As he
wrote in *The Conduct of the Allies*:

> ... we have been fighting for the ruin of the public interest
> and the advancement of the private. We have been fighting to
> raise the wealth and grandeur of a particular family, to enrich
> usurers and stock-jobbers, and to cultivate the vicious designs
> of a faction by destroying the landed interest. (Vol. VI, p. 59)

In an article in *The Examiner* for 23 November 1710 Swift made it
clear how massive was the distance between Marlborough and
the illustrious military heroes of the Roman past by comparing
the cost to a grateful nation of each. Swift estimated the cost of
a Roman triumph, including a statue, trophy, crown of laurel
and triumphal arch at less than a thousand pounds; Marlborough's
emoluments by contrast amounted to some £540 000. Swift's
hyperbolic comparison was designed to register not just the price
of the war, but the gulf between a culture where the central value
was virtue and one where greed and self-interest ruled.

In his *Examiner* articles Swift frequently deplored the spirit of
party. He wrote that 'we are unhappily divided into two parties', (Vol. III, p. 13) referred to 'the cant words of Whig and
Tory' (p. 162) and the 'two fantastic names of Whig and Tory'
(pp. 165–6) and complained that

... instead of inquiring whether he be a man of virtue, honour, piety, wit, good sense, or learning, the modern question is only whether he be a Whig, or a Tory: under which terms all good or ill qualities are included.

From Swift's point of view a man of honour and virtue could not ever strictly be a Whig or Tory, since this would involve his resigning his right of private judgement, which made him a person of integrity in the first place. It would be easy to either regard Swift as a hypocrite for writing this when he well knew that he was writing for Harley and the Tories, or as an artful propagandist who knew that people were more likely to be won over by his arguments if they believed that he himself was independent and detached. The real question is whether Swift really was so naive as to believe that Robert Harley, Anne's chief minister from 1710 to 1714, was honest when the whole world, as it were, knew him to be a wily and self-serving politician of the type that Swift otherwise deplored. Perhaps he was initially prepared to give Harley the benefit of the doubt: partly because he felt that Harley in dislodging Godolphin and changing political sides really was acting as the Queen's loyal servant, in getting rid of ministers she did not want, and partly because no one else was likely to be able to bring the war to an end. While Swift acknowledged Harley's desire for high office he still felt that

he was a person of as much virtue as can possibly consist with a love of power.

Years later he would come to see just how damaging that qualification was but in the interim he viewed Harley as the man of the hour, perhaps even a man of destiny, whom he would faithfully serve. Moreover, to turn the argument the other way round: if the Whigs were above all the party of *faction* – with all the sinister Roman connotations that that word carried – if the Whigs really were determined, as Swift prophetically suggested

to alter and adjust the Constitution to their own pernicious principles (Vol. III, p. 104)

then an effort to thwart their designs must have some pretensions to virtue.

Since Swift himself at this particular moment in time was not actually being rewarded for his services he could still convince himself that in opposing the war he was simply expressing his own convictions even if, at bottom, advancement was as much in his own mind as in that of the despised and detested Whigs. What Swift desperately wanted to believe was that there was a crucial moral distinction between those who simply set out to act virtuously and in the public interest, regardless of whether their virtue was ever acknowledged or rewarded, and those who were prompted by venal self-interest and nothing more. But Swift's idealism blinded him to the complex power struggles that were going on, as is evident from his attempts to 'reconcile' the leading figures in the administration, Bolingbroke and Harley. The effectiveness of Swift's articles for *The Examiner* depended on the clarity with which he outlined his sense of what was going on for country gentlemen of a generally Tory persuasion, based on his own conviction that he was at the centre of things and in the confidence of the great and powerful. But there is a certain pathos to this. For only Harley, the master calculator, who told everyone something different and who was clever enough to remember just what he had said to whom, really knew his way around all the webs of power. Swift was so good at justifying things because he only knew the half of it. In all these complex intrigues no one trusted anyone else – certainly Bolingbroke and Harley did not – and ironically no one felt that they could altogether rely on Swift either. Swift was 'employed, but not trusted' wrote the Earl of Orrery.[13]

Whereas, for Swift, virtue is defined as a determination not just to fight for truth, but to seek out the very heart of battle and give no quarter, Addison is seen as a man of a very different stamp: a man of almost heroic mildness, who not only deplored the violent controversies of his age – even failing to respond when personally attacked – but who still more significantly ushered in a more genial, tolerant and more tranquil age by his own personal example. For Macaulay there is something almost saintly in this:

> His humanity is without a parallel in literary history. The highest proof of virtue is to possess boundless power without abusing it. . . . He was a politician; he was the best writer of his party; he live in times of fierce excitement, in times when persons of

high character and station stooped to scurrility such as is now only practised by the basest of mankind. Yet no provocation and no example could induce him to return railing for railing.[14]

Arguably what Addison and Steele endeavoured to do in the *The Spectator* was to create a cultural space free of antagonism and controversy, a kind of hostelry in print, where under the genial eye of an attentive mine host, visitors could enjoy lively conversation and polite gossip, provided that they left their swords and their instinctive prejudices at the door. Initially, we must think of this space as more imaginative than actual – for the historical moment of the original *Spectator*, from 1 March 1711 to 6 December 1712 is itself absurdly brief – yet in those pages, Addison above all set an example of urbane and civilised communication that the world would ultimately follow. So Macaulay, reviewing his biography in *The Edinburgh Review* in 1843 clearly felt that the periodical for which he was writing could not have existed had it not been for Addison. Indeed Addison's reputation is very largely created in this Victorian retrospect. Edward Young writing in 1759, though eager to praise him nevertheless implied that his reputation had rapidly waned by alluding to 'the long-hidden lustre of our accomplished countryman'.[15] Johnson praised Addison primarily as a stylist. It was Macaulay and his readers in the turbulent 1840s who valued the apostle of moderation and good sense, who

... without inflicting a wound, effected a great social reform, and who reconciled wit and virtue, after a long and disastrous separation, during which wit had been led astray by profligacy, and virtue by fanaticism.[16]

Addison, a Whig himself, is one of the principal beneficiaries of the Whig interpretation of history.

There are real problems with this vision of an Addison who transcends the hurlyburly of party politics and a *Spectator* that floats above a collective hubbub. It is all too easy to gloss over the fact that both Addison and Steele were active and effective propagandists for the Whig cause who carved out a political career for themselves in a way that Swift, for all his gifts, was never able to do. Addison first achieved political office in 1706 as a reward for *The Campaign*, a poem that celebrated Marlborough's victory at the battle of Blenheim. From 1708 until his death in

1719 he was a Member of Parliament. He was Chief Secretary for Ireland under Lord Wharton from 1709 until the fall of the Whigs in 1711, but he was able to resume this office in 1715 when the Whigs triumphantly returned to power under the new Hanoverian dynasty. Steele acquired a gazetteership under the Whigs which he lost in 1710. In 1713 he became an MP and the following year published a pro-Hanoverian tract, *The Crisis*, which caused him to be expelled from the House of Commons. For this he was rewarded by George I, on his accession with a knighthood and various governmental sinecures, including the post of Supervisor of the Drury Lane Theatre. By 1714 Steele had certainly become the violent partisan and even Addison was not quite the chaste and decorous figure of Macaulay's imagination. In a publication of 1713, *The Late Tryal and Conviction of Count Tariff*, which criticised the terms of the Tory-negotiated commercial treaty with France, Addison inserts into an admittedly fictional context, a highly damaging picture of Swift as an unscrupulous hireling, the 'Examiner':

> It was allowed by everybody, that so foul-mouthed a witness never appeared in any cause. Seeing several persons of great eminence, who had maintained the cause of Goodman Fact, he called them ideots, blockheads, villains, knaves, infidels, atheists, apostates, fiends, and devils: never did man show so much eloquence in ribaldry.[17]

Addison may not have relished the fray quite as much as Swift, but here at least he did not shrink from it – and the target was a former friend!

To view *The Spectator* as the self-conscious dawning of a new and more tolerant era certainly misrepresents the situation. In 1711 Addison and Steele were 'resting' between roles. There is no evidence to suggest that they took a long term view of the situation anymore than did anybody else. Harold Wilson's view that 'a week is a long time in politics' would certainly have commanded widespread assent. While *The Spectator* certainly gave the two collaborators the opportunity to express themselves in a way that was not directly political, their project can be more fully understood if we recognise that their goal was *not* to be impartial and non-partisan as to help to create a more relaxed and low-key political climate, which, they believed, would be more

helpful to the Whigs. We have to remember that the political
events of 1710 were not just damaging to the Whigs but psychologically demoralising as well. They had held office throughout
Anne's reign. They were prosecuting what they regarded as a
tremendously successful war against Louis XIV under the leadership of the Duke of Marlborough, whose wife was also the
queen's principal confidant and adviser. They believed themselves
be the the authentic guardians of the revolution settlement of
1788 and the one party that enjoyed widespread popular support.
But in 1710 all this was shattered. The Duchess of Marlborough
was dismissed by the Queen and replaced by a new favourite,
Abigail Masham. Godolphin was dismissed as Prime Minister and
replaced by Harley. The Tories won a crushing victory in the
General Election. Perhaps most ominously of all the Whig attempt
to control the High Church wing of the Church of England by
impeaching Henry Sacheverell, who had attempted to whip up
hostility towards Dissenters by preaching against 'false brethren
in Church and State', backfired. Not only did the church hierarchy rally round him there was actually rioting in the streets of
London when his trial began in 1710. Suddenly, and most unexpectedly, the Whigs were outcasts.

In this somewhat hysterical atmosphere Addison sought to
promote moderation not just because he believed in it – which
he undoubtedly did – but because he believed that a cooler and
more rational climate of opinion would be helpful to the Whigs.
If the Tory gentry, like Sir Roger de Coverley, were gently
reminded that they had rather more in common with gentleman
merchants from the City, like Sir Andrew Freeport, than with a
Protestant rabble out of control; if, instead of reacting out of an
instinctive paranoia they recognised how necessary it was that
all persons of quality should work together for the national good;
if they were disposed to recognise that a wide range of issues
that had been artificially manipulated into matters of ideological
contention could be resolved pragmatically, then all the political
fever stirred up by the War of Spanish Succession could subside.
The sub-text of the 'de Coverley' papers is that Sir Roger is indeed
a lovable if somewhat eccentric and anachronistic Tory patriarch,
but it would really be much more sensible if he carried on with
his fox-hunting and left things in the capable hands of men of
the world like Sir Andrew Freeport, who is knowledgeable, sensible and worldliwise. Regrettably, the rustic squiarchy have started

barking furiously like dogs unexpectedly awakened from their slumbers and now it is really just a matter of pacifying them and settling them down to sleep again. Merchants like Sir Andrew are as indispensible as they are unacknowledged, they are the very salt of the earth, transcending all pettiness:

> They knot mankind together in a mutual intercourse of good offices, distribute the gifts of nature, find work for the poor, add wealth to the rich, and magnificence to the great. (68)

One of the ways in which we can recognise that Addison is very much of his age is that, when he deplores faction, he is by no means being even-handed but, like everyone else, sees it as epitomised above all in the attitude of his opponents. While Whigs are working tirelessly in the national interest to promote British influence and trade by prosecuting the war against France, the Tories are recklessly and selfishly sowing the seeds of discord at a time when the nation should be as one. (Contrariwise, of course, from the Tory point of view, the Tories are striving to preserve Church and State and protect British interests in the face of a Whig administration that places the profits of Whig financiers and Marlborough above human life itself.) No it is not altogether surprising that Addison should note that

> ... the spirit of party reigns more in the country than in the town ... (126)

since this is, preeminently the habitat of Tory country squires, or that, far from the sophisticated coffee houses of the City he should encounter

> ... a kind of brutality and rustic fierceness, to which men of politer conversation are wholly strangers. (126)

While Sir Roger de Coverley and Sir Andrew Freeport may themselves converse amicably enough, you would be much more likely to encounter such boorish behaviour amongst the Sir Rogers of this world than the Sir Andrews. Although the countryside may present a tranquil appearance it is here that senseless grudges, feuds and vendettas are carefully cultivated – as is the case with the squire and parson in Sir Roger's neighbouring village, who are permanently at each others' throats. From the Whig point of view the dangerous thing about party politics – which undoubtedly carries with it the implication that it is the Tories who have made the spirit of faction an evil in the state – is that it produces an essentially tribal and irrational sense of partisanship where nothing can be sensibly discussed. The all-pervasiveness of party politics was, of course, quite unprecedented. Geoffrey Holmes points out:

> It was not only the public lives of Augustan Englishmen, however, that were encroached upon and tormented by their political animosities. They spilled over into such unlikely areas as the administration of poor relief, as well as deeply colouring the religious life, the professional and business life and even the social and recreational life of the age. There were party coffee-houses and taverns; party clubs; and an abundance of party newspapers and periodicals. . . . There was party patronage of the stage and party rivalry on the race-track. London even had its Whig and Tory hospitals – St. Thomas's and St. Bart's – as well as its recognised Whig and Tory doctors, its Garths and its Friends, to attend the party men in their illnesses or deliver the babies of their often equally partisan wives.[18]

Addison is disturbed by such a politics of prejudice and mindless polarisation of every aspect of life but he is confident that if only reason can prevail reason will be on the side of the Whigs. When Addison objects to ladies who wear patches on their faces that proclaim their political allegiance he seems to be suggesting that it is the ladies above all, the chosen addressees of *The Spectator*, who should lead Britain away from an ideological politics since their doing so 'only serves to aggravate the hatreds and animosities that reign among men.' (81) Yet his purpose is actually much more convoluted than this apparently simple request. For the wearing of patches is one of the clearest instances of a tribalism that lies beyond reason and the prevalence of this custom at a time when the Whigs are out of favour can only serve to intensify the sense of isolation they already feel. For Addison and Steele a de-ideologised politics is both sensible and desirable, since a rational political sphere is bound to favour the Whigs! Nevertheless, if we are obliged to expose Addison's habitual bias this does not necessarily mean that we should question his sincerity. Addison genuinely believed that the intensity of party conflict was not just undesirable but morally harmful and he believed this for a multiplicity of reasons. For one thing such violence always contained within it the threat of civil war. For another the indiscriminate and intemperate language of political pamphlets created an atmosphere of confusion in which even the most honourable and dedicated of statesmen could be presented as a charlatan who had no other goal than to line his own pockets. Merit was nothing, reputation everything, yet no one's reputation could be expected to survive for long. For Addison the whole business of contemporary satire was fraught with danger:

> Our satire is nothing but ribaldry, and billingsgate. Scurrility passes for wit; and he who can call names in the greatest variety of phrases, is looked upon to have the shrewdest pen. By this means the honour of families is ruined, the highest posts and greatest titles are rendered cheap and vile in the sight of the people, the noblest virtues and most exalted parts exposed to the contempt of the vicious and ignorant. In the light of this foreigners would regard us a 'a nation of monsters'. (450)

Yet the situation could not wholly be attributed to the scurrility of popular journalism. More seriously still, under the corrosive influence of a party spirit, even the judgement of the leading politicians themselves could become seriously warped through their very belief that they had the well-being of their country at heart:

> Zeal for a public cause is apt to breed passions in the heart of virtuous persons, to which the regard of their own private interest would never have betrayed them. . . . How many honest minds are filled with uncharitable and barbarous notions, out of their zeal for the public good. (125)

So part of the cause for which Addison is arguing involves a turning away from such public concerns to a more private sense of virtue and morality. He suggests that it is more advantageous to mankind

> . . . to be instructed in wisdom and virtue than in politics; and to be made good fathers, husbands, and sons, than counsellors and statesman. (124)

From this point of view Addison, with Shaftesbury, is one of the prime movers in a redefinition of virtue that reorientates its focus towards personal morality, to the conscience of the individual in his face to face relationships rather than in his sense of public duty. On an obvious level this manifests itself in narratives of how individuals are moved by the sufferings of prisoners, slaves or madmen rather than in general arguments about what society should do about them. Nevertheless, almost paradoxically, Addison still believes in the public-spiritedness that is a direct manifestation of the love of one's country. So the sub-text is that this must not be driven by zeal, that is, the spirit of fanaticism as displayed by the likes of Dr Sacheverell, nor should it be infected by the narrow partisanship of party. Addison's second important move in the redefinition of virtue is to align it with the spirit of moderation and goodwill. Addison proposed 'to inspire my countrymen with mutual good-will and benevolence'. (556) In his essay on 'The Beauty and Loveliness of Virtue' he wrote:

> The two great ornaments of virtue, which shows her in the most advantageous light, and make her altogether lovely, are cheerfulness and good-nature. (243)

The virtuous man is essentially non-combative is his relationship with others and therefore one of the most important consequences of this is that there is no cause, however seemingly right or just, that can validate intemperate behaviour. For Addison there is a very big difference between virtuousness and righteousness:

> I must own, I never yet knew any party so just and reasonable, that a man could follow it in its height and violence, and at the same time be innocent. (399)

The most virtuous man of all may well be – the spectator!

In 1713, the interminably prolonged War of Spanish Succession was finally brought to an end with the signing of the Treaty of Utrecht. In 'Windsor-Forest' the young Tory poet, Alexander Pope hailed the coming of a 'Sacred Peace' which he saw as ushering a new golden age. Augusta, the tutelary spirit of London announces

Safe on my shore each unmolested Swain
Shall tend the Flocks, or reap the bearded Grain.

At a stroke Britain is transformed into Arcadia:

> See Pan with Flocks, with Fruits Pomona crown'd,
> Here blushing Flora paints th'enamel'd Ground,
> Here Ceres' Gifts in waving Prospect stand,
> And nodding tempt the joyful Reaper's Hand,
> Rich Industry sits smiling on the Plains,
> And Peace and Plenty tell, A STUART reigns.

As it turned out Anne was to die in the following year, to be replaced by a Hanoverian monarchy which would deliver power to the Whigs for several decades, so Pope's complacency was to be short-lived. Addison, on the other hand, was deeply concerned at the lack of stability and rectitude in British politics and feared the worst. These anxieties were expressed in his play *Cato*, which was performed in the same year. It enjoyed a remarkable success, running for 20 days and selling over 10 000 copies. In writing a tragedy about a completely virtuous hero Addison had, of course, defied the rules laid down in Aristotle's *Poetics* but in the political climate of the time, when all parties were concerned about maintaining both the constitution of 1688 and the Protestant succession given the lack of an obvious heir to the childless Queen Anne, Cato's concern for preserving the Roman republic had obvious implications. Indeed it was *Cato* more than any other single work that dramatised this parallel between Britain and Rome. The idea of virtue, which had had little importance after the Restoration, was suddenly and dramatically elevated to an unchallengeable centrality in eighteenth-century culture even as the definitions of it shifted and changed. *Cato* put virtue on the map. However, Addison's representation of virtue in the play diverged from the general analysis he had offered in *The Spectator*. True, Cato warns against an 'impetuous zeal' and is depicted as a man at once moderate and steadfast in his defence of Roman liberties. However when Cato laments:

> Rome is no more,
> Oh, liberty! Oh, virtue! Oh, my country!
> [Juba's aside]
> Behold that upright man! Rome fills his eyes
> With tears that flowed not o'er his own dead son!

he endorses the privileging of public concerns over private, which was what Addison, in *The Spectator* had so frequently queried. But Cato is also shown as a caring father with concerns for his sons, Marcus and Portius and for his daughter, Marcia, who says of him:

> Though stern and awful to the foes of Rome,
> He is all goodness, Lucia, always mild;
> Compassionate and gentle to his friends:
> Filled with domestic tenderness, the best,
> The kindest father.

It is in his private life that Cato reveals himself to be an essentially kindly person. Moreover, the moment of his death when he is discovered reading Plato on the immortality of the soul strongly suggests that his virtuousness is as much religious as political. In *Cato* Addison tries to produce a synthesis in all the diverse aspects of virtue become facets of a single gem. Nevertheless the public acclamation for *Cato* was overwhelmingly driven by political considerations. Cato, the unwavering patriot and guardian of liberty, could be a role model for Whig and Tory alike. Although Whigs might regard themselves as the true establishers and defenders of 1688 and although they might detect in the play worries about treachery (Sempronius and Syphax), an allusion to Robert Harley's defection from the Whigs and also to the possibility of some sell-out to the Catholics with Charles, as monarch in waiting, there was something in *Cato* for everybody. Tories could, and did, discern a parallel between the ambitious and seditious Caesar and the conduct of the Duke of Marlborough. It seemed that Cato was a hero for the contemporary moment, no longer a marble effigy but a figure who could step down from his pedestal and return to life. But within the space of two years Cato was to become quite unmistakably a Tory. With a Hanoverian king on the throne and a Whig administration firmly in the saddle the Tories were to feel as virtuous in defeat as their great precursor.

From 1719 to 1720 there was frenzied speculation in shares issued by the South Sea Company. Stocks issued at £100 rose as high as £520 before the price collapsed and fell back to £290. At the time the sheer recklessness with which people gambled in the stocks and the scale of the losses caused aroused considerable public concern not just at the role of the directors who had personally profited by driving up the price of the stocks but the suspected involvement of members of the government. Yet from a certain point of view all this was just a blip. A package of financial measures proposed by Walpole under which the shares were effectively underwritten by the Bank of England and the East India Company saved the day and financial stability was quickly restored. Indeed this was the moment when Walpole made his reputation and created a situation whereby he and his party would rule Britain virtually unchallenged for two decades. But, while modern historians, like J.H. Plumb may be justified in the view that a new stability was created in English politics, it is import-ant to recognise that such a perspective is very much the creation of hindsight; for the psychologically destablising effects of the Bubble bursting continued to be felt. The Bubble seemed to epito-mise a contemporary world of finance and trade where nothing was quite what it seemed, where deception ruled, and where innocents could expect to be cheated and gulled as much by the great and powerful as by the moral dregs of society – the world in fact of *The Beggar's Opera* and Fielding's *Jonathan Wild the Great*.

Perhaps the most forceful critics of the directors of the South Sea Company and of the whole state of British politics which the affair seemed to epitomise were John Trenchard and Thomas Gordon, who, under the name of 'Cato', published a series of letters in an opposition paper, the *London Journal*, from 5 November 1720 until the end of 1723. Since the appearance of J.G.A. Pocock's *The Machiavellian Moment*, *Cato's Letters* have been seen as con-stituting a crucial link between the republican tradition of civic virtue associated with Machiavelli and Harrington and the Ameri-can Revolution, where their example was widely invoked. Pocock suggested strong connections between these apparently diverse and widely separated circumstances:

The 'Machiavellian moment' of the eighteenth century, like that of the sixteenth, confronted civic virtue with corruption, and saw the latter in terms of a chaos of appetites, productive of dependence and loss of personal autonomy, flourishing in a word of rapid and irrational change.[19]

However, the parallelism is by no means as straightforward as this confident formulation might suggest. The plotting of *Cato's Letters* as a point on the curve of a graph linking A to B has the effect of deflecting attention away from the specific circumstances, under which Trenchard and Gordon wrote and of bestowing a spurious clarity and homogeneity on letters which were not only written by two different authors but which, hardly surprisingly, shifted their tone and emphasis in response to a rapidly changing political situation. In a subsequent preface to the collected edition Thomas Gordon complained that the letters had been 'ill understood',[20] which was in fact hardly surprising given both the need to refer obliquely to such powerful individuals as Walpole, deploying classical parallels to illuminate contemporary events, and that their analysis differed as they saw the South Sea Company or Jacobitism as the threat. I would argue that what is significant about *Cato's Letters* is rather the degree to which the authors, though justifiably indignant and outraged, were nevertheless disorientated by the whole South Sea Bubble affair and clearly found it difficult to articulate a coherent response to what they undoubtedly felt was a wholly new state of affairs. Significantly Thomas Gordon wrote of his collaborator, John Trenchard, who died soon after the letters ceased publication:

No man ever dreaded publick evils more, or took them more to heart: At one time they had almost broke it. The national confusions, distresses and despair, which we laboured under a few years ago (i.e. The South Sea Bubble) gave him much anxiety and sorrow, which preyed upon him, and endangered his life so much, that had he staid in town a few days longer, it was more than probable he would never have gone out of it alive.[21]

John Trenchard certainly took the South Sea Bubble to heart but part of the reason why he did take it so much to heart was that he could see no easy solution to the political and moral dilemmas which it presented. Neither Algernon Sidney's *Discourses concerning Government* nor Tacitus's analysis of the decline of Rome in the *Historiae* and the *Annales* – Cato's canonical texts and guides – seemed to have the answers to the current situation. The paradox of *Cato's Letters* can only be fully grasped if we acknowledge that they are simultaneously a call to action and developing and unfolding meditation on why such action is unlikely to take place.

In his second letter, dated 12 November 1720 Cato called for speedy punishment of the directors on the grounds that failure to take action threatened the integrity of the entire state:

> For if any crimes against the publick may be committed with impunity, men will be tempted to commit the greatest of all; I mean, that of making themselves master of the state.[22]

Subsequently, in a letter of 13 May 1721 Cato was to call for the execution of the directors:

> Let us hang up publick rogues.[23]

Yet Cato's call for action that would be simultaneously an act of justice and a vindication of the general honesty and wellbeing of the political was not to be answered. Not only was any response long delayed but it was also so calculatedly mild and ineffectual as to represent a positive avoidance of punishment. Almost two years after the original demand for hanging, in April 1723, Cato lamented:

> The tender and slow prosecution of the execrable managers, the gentle punishment inflicted on them, and the obvious difficulties thrown in the way of punishment at all, were fresh provocations to a plundered and abused nation, and fresh stimulations to the conspirators.[24]

The response that Cato had looked for had not been forthcoming.

At first sight it might have seemed that the South Sea Bubble was a natural fuse to ignite popular discontent. After all only a decade previously the attempt to arraign the High Church Dr Sacheverell, who had preached a sermon questioning the Glorious Revolution and opposing toleration for Dissenters, had led to rioting in the streets of London and the destruction of several meeting houses. Yet this was a sectarian issue. By contrast the South Sea affair was a scandal that all could acknowledge and from which many had suffered financially. And yet much had changed – in large part due to the failed Jacobite rebellion of 1715. Quite apart from anything else the passing of the Septennial Act meant that the administration was no longer subject to the kind of rapid popular response that Cato had hoped for. By 1722 the problem had been sorted out and the Whigs were returned with a greatly increased majority. The involvement of much of the Tory party, led by Bolingbroke, in that event meant that George I, who might otherwise have contemplated a change of administration – especially since he himself had lost £56 000 by speculating in South Sea company stocks – had no realistic alternative. Cato appealed to the King to do something but he, not surprisingly chose to stick with the Whigs and hope that they would be able to sort something out. Indeed the situation was such that it was really in nobody's interest to look for purges. Cato's approach – one that the Whigs had successfully used in the past – was to appeal to the people over the heads of their legislators – but this foundered on the same inconvenient rock. Those who had lost money and who still held shares had a greater interest in having the problem sorted out than in hunting for scapegoats, however nefarious. Moreover, the speculative fever had spread so widely the hypothetical integrity of the nation as a court of appeal was gravely compromised. Even as he protested Cato feared that the nation might 'grow mad again' –

This seems evident, not only from the folly and feebleness of human nature, ever the prey of craft, and ever caught up with shadows; but from our endless gaping after new projects, and our eagerness to run into them. We have been bruised in a mortar, but we are not wiser; while one ruin is upon us, we are panting after another . . .[25]

On classical precedent the only other source of redress for Cato, the only hope of cleansing and rectifying a corrupt polity, would come from a virtuous and public-spirited hero, a Cincinnatus, a Brutus or indeed a Cato but in practise Cato put little faith in great men. This was partly because he acknowledged that such an ideal of public-spiritedness was 'too heroic' for the times but also because his study of classical culture led him to the belief that 'great men' had all too often betrayed the trust that was placed in them.[26] Slowly, but relentlessly, Cato was driven into a logical and practical impasse where both the outcome of events and his own reasoning suggested that there was little or nothing that could be done.

Cato's predicament was the greater because he had very little faith in human nature. Already in his sixth paper he was lamenting:

O the weakness and folly of man! . . . Whoever would catch mankind, had nothing to do but to throw out a bait to their passions, and infallibly they are his property. . . . Once more, O wretched man! Thou willing instrument of thy own bondage and delusion. . . . When a people are undone, it is some consolation to reflect, that they had no hand in their own ruin. . . . But alas, poor England! thou hast not that consolation.[27]

Virtually without exception writers in the British democratic tradition have found it necessary to have some faith in human capacities, but Cato's determination to be realistic allows him no such recourse. Rather, in the spirit of Hobbes, whose language he echoes, Cato views men as desiring machines:

We are never satisfied with being just what we are; and therefore, though you give us all that we desire, or can conceive, yet we shall not have done desiring . . . new acquisitions bring new wants; and imaginary wants are as pungent as real ones. So that there is the same end of wishing as of living, and death only can still the appetites.[28]

But whereas Hobbes stresses the conflict and violence that this leads to, Cato places more emphasis on man's consequent capacity to be deluded and therefore cheated and exploited. Cato is therefore led to the conclusion that the very notion of virtue, anxious as he is to believe in it, is desperately elusive to the point of being chimerical:

O liberty! stop they flight. Oh virtue! be something more than an empty name and sound: Return, oh return! inspire and assist our illustrious legislators in the great work which they have so generously undertaken! Assist, assist, if it be but to save those who have devoutly worshipped thee, and have paid constant incense at thy altars.[29]

There is a distinct pathos in this – not just because Cato's expectation that his plea will bear fruit is minimal but because even his reference to illustrious legislators totally lacks credibility, because if they were what he says they are he would have no cause for concern. In desperation Cato is compelled to fall back on the argument that the only form of virtue that can be looked for is based on self-interest. Some American commentators have plausibly see this as foreshadowing the arguments of Jefferson and Madison; but while such a position may be sustainable in a generally more hopeful American milieu and where public virtue, in the wake of Montesquieu, is clearly differentiated from private virtue in Cato this looks uncomfortably like casuistry. If, in one context, self-interest is 'so wicked and merciless a thing'[30] how can it be miraculously be transformed into an unmitigated good when projected into the public arena, which, as distinct from 'philosophical virtue'?

> . . . is the only virtue that the world wants, and the only virtue that it can trust to.[31]

This virtue is certainly not the virtue that Cato wants – but he knows it is the only virtue, if virtue it is, that he is likely to get. In a way Cato's perspective begins to seem even more cynical than Mandeville's since the whole notion of virtue seems to have more substance in Mandeville's text, even though he persistently mocks it. At all events Pocock's suggestion that Cato believes in 'the moral example of the virtuous hero' and in the people as *'guardia della liberta'* is at best a superficial analysis of Cato's desperate wrigglings on the painful hook of political corruption, at worst a wilful misreading.[32]

Although Defoe was not an opponent of the government, but one of it's journalistic supporters and a man who conspicuously failed to echo Cato's call for the heads of the South Sea Company's directors, he nevertheless found the whole affair of the South Sea Bubble disturbing. As a sometime tradesman and a man who had been bankrupt himself, Defoe recognised that the widespread disposition of the affluent classes to gamble in South Sea stocks had made the whole question of entering into financial relationships with others considerably more difficult, since under more normal circumstances there would always be markers, reports and rumours that would alert the prudent individual that the person he was planning to have dealings with was not quite what he seemed. But in the aftermath of the Bubble there was no one who could be taken absolutely at face value. In the chapter 'Rumour and Clamour, Scandal and Reproach' of his *The Complete English Tradesman* (1726), Defoe describes how the reputation of a tradesman, who was actually a man of substance, was seriously undermined by the idle and malicious gossip of three ladies, part of whose conversation went as follows:

> 2. *Lady.* – Well, I could never have thought Mr— was in such circumstances.
> 3. *Lady.* – Nor I; we always took him for a ten thousand pound man.
> 1. *Lady.* – They say he was deep in the bubbles, Madam.
> 2. *Lady.* – Nay, if he was gotten into the South Sea, that might hurt him indeed, as it has done many a gentleman of better estates than he.
> 1. *Lady.* – I don't know whether it was the South Sea, or some other bubbles, but he was very near to making a bubble of her, and £3,000 into the bargain.
> 2. *Lady.* – I am glad she has escaped him, if it be so; it is a sign her friends took a great deal of care of her.
> 1. *Lady.* – He won't hold it long; he will have his desert, I hope; I don't doubt but we shall see him in the Gazette quickly for a bankrupt.[33]

Defoe is, of course, addresssing the much wider problem of how a tradesman can maintain his reputation for financial dependability and credit worthiness, which is absolutely crucial to his success, but his illustration shows that the Bubble had made everyone much more aware of potential dangers and risks. This greater uncertainty of the modern world is also reflected in Defoe's *Moll Flanders* (1722), especially when it is contrasted with *Robinson Crusoe* (1719), which preceded the collapse in South Sea stocks. Admittedly *Robinson Crusoe* itself displays many misgivings about the Britain of Defoe's day, which are well worth exploring, but if nothing else we must note that when Robinson Crusoe returns to civilisation he finds that, thanks to the honesty of the old sea captain, with whom he first shipped to Africa, and the integrity of the trustees of the plantation he had established in Brazil, he has the considerable sum of £5000 coming to him. In *Robinson Crusoe* there is still a certain dependability in human nature that is sadly lacking in the duplicitous world of *Moll Flanders*.

Defoe himself, as tradesman, soldier, journalist and secret agent, was a worldly man, yet in *Robinson Crusoe* he nevertheless allowed himself to articulate a fairly comprehensive disenchantment with the political and commercial world through whose treacherous

waters he was obliged to steer. *Robinson Crusoe* is a hymn to solitude and it is the image of Crusoe as solitary that has captured
the world's imagination. At a time when most would have conceived such an isolated existence as physically and psychologically
intolerable, and when Shaftesbury in particular had insisted on
man's overpowering need for the society of others, Defoe presented Crusoe's existence as most idyllic when most alone. The
island on which Defoe's hero is cast away, far from being a place
where he might regress to a Caliban-like brutishness, is presented
as a theatre in which Crusoe's moral development can take place.
It is a strangely edifying environment because of its very clarity
and transparency. Crusoe, on his own, is brought to reflect on
God and on the inscrutable workings of divine providence in a
way that he never would in the busy and cluttered context of
British society. Moreover, on the island, he sees as never before
that his destiny is in his own hands and that he must necessarily come to terms with the overall limitations of his situation.
The 'if onlys' and 'what ifs' that ordinarily complicate the human
situation can gain little purchase here. Crusoe becomes virtuous
almost in spite of himself. Since he urgently needs shelter, security and sustainence he has no alternative but to engage in incessant
labour. He not only is compelled to focus his attention on what
is genuinely requisite to his existence but he now sees clearly
that the luxuries, that in the civilised world seem so important,
are not simply unobtainable but totally dispensable. Where Crusoe,
like everyone else, once saw money as the one indispensable thing
he is now able to grasp its hollowness – unlike tools which serve
a genuine purpose money is simply a symbol of value, which,
outside society, means nothing. On the island he is freed from
desire, precisely because there is nothing to desire and no reason
to desire it. His lot is better than he had realised and he is led to
express his thanks, that through the intervention of divine providence, he has discovered that he is happier in this solitude than
he could ever have been amid the temptations and pleasures of
the world. Crusoe's grotesque clothing – his suit and shapeless
cap of goatskin – is also fraught with moral significance; for in
society he would be a figure of ridicule, but here, where no one
can see him, it simply does not matter. On the island as a solitary
individual he simply has no reason to indulge in the sins of vanity
and pride. Moreover he is happiest when most alone. The foot-
print is an ominous token of the dangers of communal existence,

initially inspiring him with intense fear and anxiety and ultimately summoning him back to the world of rivalry and violence from which, for so long, he has been mercifully spared. But if man is inexorably led to virtue and godliness only under circumstances of extreme privation and in the intense clarity of solitude, what purchase can they gain elsewhere?

Certainly virtue is a much more distant prospect in *Moll Flanders* and this has more to do with the nature of the world than with the character of Moll herself. Despite Moll's somewhat hyperbolic insistence on her own wickedness, which is doubtless bound up with the pretence that her confessions have a didactic function:

> Let the experience of one creature completely wicked and completely miserable, be a storehouse of useful warning to those that read. (p. 214)

We cannot but conclude that she is something of an innocent and an ingenue. Certainly she is far from the calculated and ruthless villainy of her successor, Roxana. On the contrary Moll is impulsive and reckless. A woman who genuinely cares about people and who shows an often surprisingly capacity for loyalty. Moll is progressively initiated into deceit and thereafter crime by a variety of mentors, ranging from the two brothers Robert and Robin, who seduce her, the sea-captain's widow and the gentleman from Bath to her 'governess' the midwife, who teaches her to steal gold watches and to dress like a man. She is of course responsible for what she does but we are always concious that she is moving in a world where imposture, misrepresentation and deceit are the norm rather than the exception. If Moll finds it all too easy to blend into the background Defoe suggests there is a kind of inevitability about it, given her general thoughtlessness and lack of moral education. A constantly repeated motif in the novel is that of deceiving the deceiver especially where marriage is concerned. Moll's attempts to pass herself off as a woman more highly born and more affluent than she is are justified by the captain's wife:

> . . . at last she made this unhappy proposal to me, viz., that as we had observed, as above, how the men made no scruple to set themselves out as persons meriting a woman of fortune of

their own, it was but just to deal with them in their own way, and if it was possible to deceive the deceiver.

The captain's lady, in short, put this project into my head, and told me that if I would be ruled by her I should certainly get a husband of fortune, without leaving him room to reproach me with want of my own. I told her I would give up myself wholly to her directions. (p. 61)

As the result of all this scheming the Virgina tobacco planter, whom she bigamously marries, turns out be to her own brother and she is forced to return to England. But some years later the perils of such deception are repeated. She persuades a man whom she believes to be a wealthy Irishman that she is a woman of substance but soon after their marriage he confesses that he has no estate, she that she has no money – a disconcerting prospect for both:

'Why', says I to him, 'this has been a hellish jiggle, for we are married here upon the foot of a double fraud: you are undone by the disappointment it seems; and if I had had a fortune I had been cheated too, for you say you have nothing.' (p. 117)

What makes this even more convoluted is that Moll and Jemmy, who turns out to be a highwayman, subsequently meet again in Newgate and are able to start the new life together in the New World that Moll had hoped for some two hundred pages earlier.

The miraculous twists and turns of Defoe's novel may exemplify the inscrutable working of divine providence but they also demonstrate what a risky place the world seemed to be in the aftermath of the South Sea Bubble. There is an especially curious episode in *Moll Flanders* that seems to epitomise this sense of life as perplexing, uncertain and kaleidoscopically shifting. Moll, now fully embarked on her career as pickpocket and thief, decides for no particular reason to dress up as a widow, though, as a widow, twice over, she has a stronger claim to do so than most:

I had taken up the disguise of a widow's dress; it was without any real design in view, but only waiting for anything that might offer, as I often did. It happened that while I was going along a street in Covent Garden there was a great cry of 'Stop thief, stop thief.' Some artists had it seems, put a trick upon a shopkeeper, and being pursued, some of them fled one way and some another; and one of them was, they said, dressed up in widow's weeds, upon which the mob gathered about me, and some said I was the person, others said no. (pp. 191–2)

Moll is only able to extricate herself from this very awkward situation with considerable difficulty while the actual con artist makes good her escape. Defoe suggests that this remarkable coincidence represents a kind of poetic justice, it can even be regarded as some kind of providential warning. Yet there is also a mirror image effect. If Moll has been engaged in a dangerous imposture, hoping in some ill-defined way to find something to her advantage, she encounters, in the other widow, a malignant double, who threatens to bring her down just when she least expects it. While Robinson Crusoe was able to see his situation with remarkable clarity in the civilised world such moments are rare. By contrast, when Roxana looks back on her own career

> . . . with Eyes unpossess'd by Crime, when the wicked part has appear'd in a clearer Light, and I have seen it in its own natural Colours, when no more blinded with the glittering Appearances, which at that time deluded me. (p. 79)

For Defoe it is only natural that we should lose our way in the confusions and corruptions of society and that the voice of conscience should grow faint. In narrating her story Roxana stands amazed at her own moral lethargy:

> So is it possible for us to roll ourselves up in Wickedness, till we grow invulnerable by Conscience; and the Centinel once doz'd, sleeps fast, not to be awaken'd while the Tide of Pleasure continues to flow, or till something dark and dreadful brings us to ourselves again.
>   I have, I confess, wonder'd at the Stupidity that my intellectual Part was under all that while; what Lethargic Fumes doz'd the Soul. (p. 69)

In the worldly world it is more common to see through a glass darkly: to fail to see the good, precisely because double dealing is so omnipresent that any moral perspective disappears. Moll might just as well have been the culprit even though she was not. But, equally, she is simply typical of what goes on. Moll's story may certainly lead to censorious judgements on the heroine herself – and Defoe positively invites them – but he also makes it stand as a powerful indictment of the general treacherousness and uncertainty of contemporary life:

> ... every branch of my story, if duly considered, may be useful to honest people, and afford a due caution to people of some sort or other to guard against the like surprises, and to have their eyes about them when they have to do with strangers of any kind, for 'tis very seldom that some snare or other is not in their way. (pp. 213–14)

The story of Moll Flanders offers, on a multiplicity of levels, warning about the deceptiveness of appearances.

For Defoe an integral part of this duplicitous parade was the City of London itself. Although Defoe believed in commerce and trade, in practice he drew a careful distinction between these necessary and, in his view, solidly grounded activities, and the activities of speculators and stock-jobbers, 'whose trade once bewitched the nation to its ruin' as he writes in *A Tour Through the Whole Island of England and Wales*. In this work it is somewhat startling to find him suggesting, that since the City has rapidly expanded through a 'prodigious conflux of the nobility and gentry from all parts of England to London' landlords and builders should recognise that

> ... when the publics debts being reduced and paid off, the funds or taxes on which they are established, may cease, and so fifty or sixty millions of the stocks, which are now the solid bottom of the South-Sea Company, East-India Company, Bank, &c, will cease and be no more; by which reason of this conflux of people being removed, they will of course, and by the nature of the thing, return again to their country seats, to avoid the expensive living at London, as they did come up hither to share the extravagant gain of their former business here. What will be the fate then of all the fine buildings in the out parts, in such a case, let anyone judge.[34]

As Defoe sees it all these grand residences left vacant will progressively decay and fall down.

Such an apocalyptic scenario is even more conspicuous in the work of William Hogarth. Hogarth's career was significantly shaped by the South Sea Bubble. In 1720 he was a young apprentice of 23, left by the recent death of his father with the responsibility for supporting his mother, and it was with cartoons satirising the frenzy of speculation in 'The South Sea Bubble' and the craze for gambling in the lottery. Hogarth suggested that in this atmosphere Honesty and Virtue were the first casualities. But what was to become even more significant in his critique of British society was his sense of the ephemerality and transitoriness of the fashionable world, which the whole notion of 'bubble' epitomised. In his three powerful series, 'A Harlot's Progress', 'The Rake's Progress' and 'Marriage a la Mode' Hogarth made vivid both the notion of moral downfall and the sheer speed with which, in the corrupt and fervid atmosphere of contemporary society such a collapse could take place. As Hogarth's art became increasingly sophisticated he used new techniques to suggest this. In the first two images of 'A Harlot's Progress' Hogarth uses collapsing pots and pans to allegorically suggest the loss of a young girl's virtue, a 'fall'. But progressively his use of such fallen and overturned items convey more powerful connotations since the suggestion of movement makes the images into snapshots of a particular moment which we know will soon pass and give way to something worse. The overturned table in the fifth scene of 'A Harlot's Progress' already serves as a figure of her death in the final scene – especially when strewn on the floor are remedies for venereal disease. But it would be very misleading to imply that Hogarth's focus is on the sins of his protagonists, rather, like Defoe, he draws attention to the predators to contrive to bring about their downfall and on the pervasive moral decadence through which they move. Yet this world though powerful and all-enveloping is also unstable and on the verge of collapse itself. In 'Southwark Fair' the collapsing stage implies the triviality and brevity of all human shows. In the sixth scene of 'The Rake's Progress', which displays the moral degradation of the gambling den, the overturned chair becomes a marker of the Rake's incipient madness but equally significantly, the gamblers in the intensity of their own obsession fail to notice that the fabric of the building is on fire. In much later and even more apocalyptic images as 'Beer Street' and 'Gin Lane' the very buildings are collapsing. We find, as in the South Sea Bubble itself, the representation of a frenzed and reckless humanity indifferent to past, present and future.

This sense of a world that was desperately spiralling out of control and which in the process was leaving all familiar landmarks and reference behind was intensified by the publication in 1723 of an expanded edition of Bernard Mandeville's *The Fable of the Bees*. An earlier edition of 1714 had made very little noise in the world, so it seems highly likely that Mandeville's mocking exposition of a cynical and worldly philosophy now attracted so very much more attention because it seemed to express the mood of the times. Mandeville, a Dutchman and native of Rotterdam who had qualified as a doctor of medicine before coming to England, seemed to epitomise Sir William Temple's sense that Holland was the representative modern society, where individuals pursued commercial advantage and their own individual self-interest to the exclusion of all else. Mandeville put forward two separate but linked theses, both of which were equally disconcerting. Mandeville opens his argument with the words

All untaught Animals are only Sollicitious of pleasing themselves.[35]

and it rapidly becomes clear that as far as he is concerned this analysis applies to man also for as he subsequently insists:

This is the Law of Nature, by which no creature is endued with any Appetite or Passion but what directly or indirectly tends to the Preservation either of himself or his Species.[36]

It follows that Mandeville refuses to believe either that there can be genuine virtue or even self-denial. In Greek and Roman culture especially, the notion of virtue was used by political leaders to control and manipulate the population into performing altruistic actions, hence

. . . the Moral Virtues are the Political Offspring which Flattery begot on Pride.[37]

In the real world there are only passions, usually base, which individuals hypocritically try to cover up in order to present a better face to the world. It is pretty clear that for Mandeville all talk of virtue is at best self-deluded, at worst dishonest even though, in his characteristically teasing style, he often pretended that he himself really did believe in virtue even though he saw such little evidence of it around him:

> If I have shewn the way to worldly Greatness I have always without hesitation preferr'd the Road that leads to Virtue.[38]

This reductive analysis of human behaviour so shocked Mandeville's religious critics, such as William Law and Richard Fiddes, that they concentrated their fire almost entirely on his denial of moral virtue and largely ignored his arguments about modern commercial societies with which they were bound up. Mandeville's opponents denied that it was possible to speak of an 'origin' of virtue in such political and expedient terms and refused to accept that human passions were necessarily as crude and self-centred as he had implied. But Mandeville had yet more uncomfortable sayings in his locker. Modern commercial societies were based on trade and on the production of goods for the market: the greater the demand for goods and services the greater the prosperity and the higher the likelihood that most members of society would be gainfully employed. It followed that Luxury and Vice were not simply socially beneficial but positively essential to the social fabric:

> Vices are inseparable from great and potent Societies.[39]

Thus the thieves and burglars fulfill a useful function by keeping locksmiths employed. But behind Mandeville's provocative formulations there does lie a genuine insight, which is that modern societies are characterised by increasing specialisation and the division of labour which is an irreversable process. We may fantasise about living in a simpler society but it is actually no longer possible for us to go back:

> Frugality is like Honesty, a mean starving Virtue, that is only fit for small Societies of good peaceable Men, who are contented to be poor so they may be easy; but in a large stirring Nation you may soon have enough of it. 'Tis an idle dreaming Virtue that employs no Hands, and therefore very useless in a trading Country, where there are vast numbers that one way or other

must be all set to Work. Prodigality has a thousand Inventions to keep People from sitting still, that Frugality would never think of . . .[40]

The modern world is dynamic, driven, constantly in motion and luxury is the engine that drives the wheels.

Mandeville saw himself as a realist who, through his candour and spirit of mockery, could compel men to recognise that the virtues they purported to revere were neither revered in actuality nor were they particularly worthy of such reverence. But for Mandeville's opponents Mandeville was something very much worse than this. He above all typified just how far the nation had fallen. Not only was it a corrupt and immoral age but through Mandeville, the shameless and wholly unapologetic advocate of vice, it was revealed to be utterly without conscience. So Mandeville epitomised a new and highly dangerous cultural moment. William Law wrote:

The Infidelity of the present Age is very great, and shews such a Contempt of sacred Things, as was hardly ever heard of before.[41]

According to John Dennis:

. . . a Champion for Vice and Luxury a serious, a cool, a deliberate Champion, that is a Creature intirely new, and has never been heard of before in any Nation, or any Age of the World.[42]

Dennis deplored the fact that, in 'so degenerate an Age' people could be so imposed upon by such 'wretched Stuff' that he was actually obliged to answer it.[43] For George Bluet the state of England provided all too direct a confirmation of Mandeville's thesis:

. . . if Vice in General, and Luxury in particular, be the Road to Wealth, we bid fair for growing Prodigiously rich.[44]

For the philosopher George Berkeley, in his dialogue *Alciphron* (1732) the arguments of Mandeville are symptomatic of a free-thinking spirit that challenges and unsettles all traditions and institutions and which portends anarchy and nihilism. Although

Mandeville himself made no remarks subversive of the state, Berkeley has his Mandevillian spokesman, Lysicles say:

> Men who think deeply cannot see why power should not change hands as well as property; or why the fashion of a government should not be changed as easily as that of a garment.[45]

Again, Berkeley stresses the dangerous novelty of this direct challenge to virtue and stresses the seditious nature of such arguments. Crito says:

> But it is the design of our minute philosophers, by making men wicked on principle, a thing unknown to the ancients, so as to weaken and destroy the force of virtue that its effects shall not be felt in the public.[46]

In the short term Mandeville created a deeply pessimistic, apocalyptic mood, a sense of the dissolution of all significant moral values that is reflected not only in Berkeley but in *Gulliver's Travels* and in the image of 'universal Darkness' that closes Pope's *Dunciad*. In the slightly longer term *The Fable of the Bees* shifted the focus of attention away from party strife and political corruption as sources of moral anxiety and paradoxically served to highlight the dangers of precisely the luxuriousness and conspicuous consumption that he had so provocatively defended.

What is particularly significant about *Gulliver's Travels* as a response to the South Sea Bubble, the multi-faceted corruption of Walpole's Whig administration and the pervasive cynicism of the day, is how little it is concerned with political solutions to what was, in the first instance, a political problem. In part this was due to Swift's own sense of powerlessness as he contemplated matters from the other side of the Irish Sea. So long as he had been involved in politics at the highest level he was compelled to believe that a Tory administration would produce a more virtuous politics but by the mid-1720s it had become clear that there was very little likelihood that Walpole's regime would be replaced still less that Swift himself would be involved in any alternative. While Swift's pessimism in *Gulliver* is inescapable what is significant is that Swift utterly refused to give up on the idea of virtue itself as he very easily could have done – so in some perverse way the book does retain an affirmative character.

Certainly Swift's growing preoccupation with Irish affairs, culminating in the celebrated attack on Wood's debased coinage in *Drapier's Letters* (1724) which turned him into a national hero, made him realise that, whatever the importance of politics, there were certainly aspects of human existence more urgent than this. His awareness of the sufferings of the Irish peasantry – the fact that they were compelled to subsist at the lowest possible level, in a state of near animality, scarcely possessed of even the basic necessities of clothing, food and shelter – made him more sceptical of man's pretensions to be something more than this. Indeed, how could human pretensions to virtue, dignity and justice be sustained when such conditions existed. Swift shared Lear's perception of man as a 'bare, forked animal' and his distrust of the imposture of fine garments: 'Off, off, you lendings'. Wigs, robes, shoes, shirts and waistcoats, the whole panoply of human finery, were there simply so that man can conceal his own nature from himself. Clothes symbolise man's eternal pretension be to something grander than he is. It is therefore entirely characteristic that, in his journey to the Houyhnhnms, Gulliver should be desperately anxious to retain his clothes, even though the Houyhnhnms themselves do not wear any, 'in order to distinguish myself as much as possible from that cursed race of Yahoos.' Yet such marks of 'distinction' do not, in themselves, prove anything! (p. 238)

Because Swift depicted man in such a degrading way and seemed to lay so much emphasis on bodily functions his response has often been regarded as pathological and it has become commonplace to proffer psychological explanations for his preoccupation with cleanliness and his corresponding revulsion from the physical. However, while Swift's aversion can scarcely be doubted such a mode of analysis itself offers a reductive explanation of Swifts's complex attitude to the human species. For *Gulliver's Travels*, despite the vividness and circumstantial detail of its writing is a novel of ideas, perhaps the very first. Swift was only able to write it at all by distancing himself from beliefs that he had held dear and, contrariwise, identifying himself with ideas which, in the past, had been an anathema to him. One of the great paradoxes of the philosophical and scientific revolution of the seventeenth century was that while it exalted the power of human reason to arrive at important intellectual conclusions independently, it simultaneously offered an analysis of the human situation that in many ways was far from uplifting when compared with the Christian humanist tradition. The earth was no longer the centre of the universe but simply a planet revolving around the sun. Man was more closely and directly linked with the world of nature. Man's powers of reason, speech and language were certainly remarkable, perhaps unique, but they could be viewed simply as the characteristics that distinguished him from other mammals, just as mammals are distinguished from reptiles by being warm-blooded. Moreover, reason itself is not an altogether unproblematic concept since it may express itself in perverse ways. In *Essay concerning Human Understanding* Locke writes: (IV, XVIII):

> So that in effect religion, which should most distinguish us from beasts and ought most peculiarly to elevate us as rational creatures above brutes, is that wherein men often appear most irrational and more senseless than beasts themselves.[47]

So reason is not an unmitigated blessing – it may also have a disturbing and unforeseeable downside. Hobbes linked man with animals in a more explicit way. For Hobbes the life of men was originally 'nasty, brutish and Short' because there was perpetual violence and conflict between them as in the animal kingdom. Man is distinguished from brutes not just by language but by his capacity to create political institutions that will enable him to carry on his life in a relatively peaceful and orderly fashion. Hobbes begins his discussion of the passions by saying, in a manner that would have disconcerted Plato and the medieval schoolmen,

> There be in animals two sorts of motion peculiar to them.[48]

as if he can simply take it for granted that he can reason from animals to human beings. In this way the uniqueness of man is imperilled. For if reason can build castles it can also demolish them.

Swift detested the arrogance and intellectual presumptiousness of such reasoning but paradoxically he was also willing to press such assumptions to the very limit – to the point where they became both unpalatable and disconcerting. *Gulliver's Travels* is written by a churchman yet the concepts that it deals in are uncompromisingly secular. Swift writes as if the Christian church had never said that man, unlike the animals, has a soul and in

Book IV at least, he describes a human world that is so unappealing that we would scarcely credit that it could have been created by a wise, benificent and loving God. Indeed it is particularly noteworthy that by comparison with Defoe's *Robinson Crusoe* that had so recently preceded it, it conspicuously lacks the plethora of pious acknowledgements of the goodness of God and of the miraculous workings of divine providence. It can, of course, be argued that since *Gulliver* is conceived of as a fantasy it does not necessarily claim to offer statements about the real world, that the circumstances there described are hypothetical and argumentative, and that Swift himself may have access to religious sources of consolation which the book deliberately does not provide. So the book might exhibit the perils of living in a rational universe without God. Indeed, it may well be that Swift's precise intention is to attack man in order to try to save God and that in the writing of *Gulliver* he steps into a parallel Godless universe, while leaving the present one intact.

Just as a judo master tries to turn his opponent's strength against him, so Swift attempts to redirect the power of modern rationalism against itself by working within its own definitions and operative assumptions. The project of abandoning theology, to be guided in all practical matters by human reason and the spirit of scientific enquiry faced, in the early eighteenth century, more significant difficulties than we might be conscious of today. Contemporaneously there was comparatively little that could be put forward in the confidence that it did not raise further yet unsolved and possibly unsolvable problems, yet it was by no means certain that science would ultimately be able to deliver the real knowledge it promised. In the meantime mankind would have to have faith that the promised and foreshadowed dawning would actually take place. This is the world of *Gulliver's Travels* indeed, for Swift, the evidence for a grotesque modern over-confidence coupled with undisguisable intellectual failure was already in. Yet this pride of science ultimately depended on the religious conviction that man did indeed occupy a unique and privileged place in the universe. Descartes had attempted to maintain the absolute nature of the distinction between man and beast by insisting that animals were mere automata, although his successors had to admit that such a hard and fast distinction could not legitimately be made. Beasts clearly did possess a certain amount of intelligence and with it the ability to make 'rational' decisions so the distinction had to be relative rather than absolute. Indeed, Leibnitz, in his *New Essays on Human Understanding* was even prepared to hypothesise that animals more intelligent than man might exist – elsewhere:

> Although in all likelihood there are rational animals, somewhere, which surpass us, nature has seen fit to keep these at a distance from us so that there will be no challenge to our superiority on our own globe.[49]

However, Locke was not prepared to go this far. Locke really wanted to insist on the absolute divide between man and nature even though he reluctantly acknowledged that the power of thinking could not be ruled out altogether in other creatures. For Locke, the solution to the problem lay in the fact that man alone, through his capacity for language, had the power to frame general ideas:

> It may be doubted whether beasts compound and enlarge their ideas that way to any degree: this, I think, I may be positive in, that the power of abstracting is not at all in them; and that the having of general ideas is that which puts a perfect distinction between man and brutes, and it is an excellency which the faculties of brutes do by no means attain to. For it is evident we observe no footsteps in them of making use of general signs for universal ideas; from which we have reason to imagine that they have not the faculty of abstracting, or of making general ideas, since they have no use of words or any other general signs.[50]

Locke's general claim, in the form in which he makes it, is actually not very plausible since dogs obviously recognise other dogs as being similar to themselves, despite the fact that they come in a very wide variety of breeds, and never at all confuse them with cats, which can also vary considerably; so it must be the case that they have some notion of cat and dog even though they may neither possess or use words. What is really at stake is the uniqueness of man which cannot be troubled by such trifling questions as these. But Swift, though a clergyman, was prepared to violate such taboos. Whether or not he knew of Leibnitz's suggestion that there might be animals more intelligent than man and actualised it in the Houyhnhnms, he certainly took on board the worrying prospect of human animality from which others like Locke flinched, as a strategy for undermining the pretensions of modern thought.

In a very specific sense Locke's theory of abstract ideas epitomises the pretensions of eighteenth-century rational man. For what characterises reason is the ability to derive general, universal rules and unproblematisable concepts from the flux and apparent disorder of experience. The characteristic eighteenth-century genre of the enquiry is an intellectual project that surveys a wide range of evidence drawn from cultures widely separated in space and time in order to formulate some authoritative conclusions. Montesquieu's *L'Esprit des Lois,* for example, considers the nature of government not only in ancient Greece and Rome and in contemporary European societies like France, England, Italy and Germany but also in asiatic countries like India and China, which gives his work greater universality and therefore provides a much stronger basis for generalisation. He concludes that there are three main types of government: Republican, Monarchical and Despotic, each of which has its own distinctive principle, respectively: Virtue, Honour and Fear. So these principles are valid for mankind as a whole even if despotism does tend to be oriental. Samuel Johnson's injunction at the beginning of 'The Vanity of Human Wishes'

Let mankind with extensive view
Survey Mankind from China to Peru

typifies this logic of universality, because it implies that intellectual enquiry can only arrive at valid conclusions if non-Western sources are consulted. Yet the enquiry itself is inevitably Western. Relativising dimensions are to be acknowledged only to be cancelled, expanding the foundations of occidental knowledge without actually putting it in question. So there are already some complex argumentative loops. Western man's claim to an authoritative, unproblematisable standpoint is based on his ownership of reason and the protocols that can validate it so reason itself is defined as that standpoint rather than as an ongoing activity that can interrogate its own conclusions. The universal is a Western construct that endeavours to flatten out in the name of reason anything that it cannot readily accommodate. Already rational man is twisting and writhing in his self-created bonds. Yet in contradiction to this a whole series of eighteenth-century writers, themselves deeply engaged in the project of the inquiry, try to question and undermine the power of the Western gaze in which, as in perspective painting, the distinctive vantage point of the observer is subtly erased in the interests of objectivity. In theory the empire has a chance to fight back. Voltaire in *Candide*, Montesquieu in *Lettres Persanes*, Goldsmith in his *Citizen of the World*, Rousseau in his *Discourses* all attempted to hypothesise a position from which Western man could be criticised. Yet the result is strangely unconvincing. For although Europeans might well be concerned about the direction in which civilisation was headed or even about the very nature of civilisation itself they could not question reason or the notion of a humanity defined by this rationality.

By contrast Swift had no such inhibitions. Since Swift was not committed to the universalising claims of reason he was able to take an imaginative leap into a wholly relativistic universe where Gulliver would not only be deprived of the Western pretension to be judge and jury in all things, but – still more disconcertingly – he would encounter others who would simply take him as they found him without necessarily assuming that he was either rational or human – whatever that might be! So what looms largest in *Gulliver's Travels* is the fact that to these alien others Gulliver manifests himself simply a corporeal being rather than intelligence, soul or spirit. Gulliver in Lilliput figures as a huge beast who must be speared and trapped. The Lilliputians must be every mindful that this is a vast and always potentially dangerous creature, which demands to be fed with vast quantities of food and whose ordure is immensely difficult to dispose of. He makes his mark in their world solely through his massive size, which enables him equally to steal the enemy's ships and to extinguish the fire in the royal palace with colossal drenchings of urine. His 'superiority' is wholly adventitious and comparative. But the edge that he accidentally acquires among the tiny Lilliputians is denied him in Brobdingnag where he figures as nothing better than a tiny and rather contemptible animal. The implications of monstrosity and freakishness, already apparent in Lilliput, are more strongly asserted in Brobdingnag. The overall assessment of Gulliver by three of the King's greatest scholars is pretty damning:

They all agreed that I could not be produced according to the regular Laws of Nature; because I was not framed with a Capacity of preserving my Life, either by Swiftness, or of climbing of Trees, or of digging Holes in the Earth. They observed by my Teeth, which they viewed with great Exactness, that I was a carniverous Animal; yet most Quadrupeds being an Overmatch for me; and Field-Mice, with some others, too nimble, they could not imagine how I should be able to support my self, unless I fed upon Snails and other Insects; which they offered by many learned Arguments to evince that I could not possibly do so. (p. 95)

Doubtless this shows the fallacy of reasoning from first principles but it also shows that such a radically divergent perspective is enough to shatter human delusions of grandeur; already the suggestion that man is both a useless and worthless animal – to be developed and intensified in the land of the Houyhnhnms – powerfully adumbrated.

In a very real sense modern rationality, for Swift, was actually not rational at all. This was in part because modern scientific enquiry totally rejected the knowledge and experience of the past and presented itself as a wholly self-sufficient and self-validating enterprise. There is no way in which its conclusions can be externally modified or reviewed. There is no sense of humility, harmony or self-restraint that can restrain it from the most preposterous conclusions: for the fact that other great minds in the past may have judged differently counts for nothing. All are tarred with the brush of scholasticism and obscurantism. Swift believed that modern learning, far from being empirical as it claimed, was essentially theoretical and unworldly. He represented this in *Gulliver* by the island of Laputa which floats high above the real world and is populated by an absurd gallimaufry of theoreticians, inventors and projectors. But Laputa is also the narrow, self-defining world of the British government, which is wholly given up to corruption and which has so lost touch with the people it supposedly represents that it has simply become a power of domination, persecuting those subjects who will not pay tribute, either by denying them sunshine or rain, or by pelting them with stones and rocks. Here, Swift clearly had the fate of Ireland in mind – taxed, constricted and oppressed by a remote and indifferent administration. That the contemporary world defined itself through violence and technology was at the heart of Swift's disillusionment with it. The people of Lilliput, for example, must be regarded as backward since they only possess bows and arrows. They are impressed by Gulliver's scimitar, pistols, powder and bullets. In Brobdingnag the King is shocked to hear Gulliver's matter-of-fact descriptions of the destructive power of the cannon and still more at the indifference of those who employ them:

> He was amazed how so impotent and grovelling an insect as I (these were his expressions) could entertain such inhuman Ideas, and in so familiar a Manner as to appear wholly unmoved at all the scenes of Blood and Desolation. (p. 129)

Technology serves to negate any kind of ethical perspective. Its destructive power, far from being deplored, is actually worshipped and celebrated. But when Gulliver tries to impress the Houyhnhnms with descriptions of

> Cannons, Culverins, Muskets, Carabines, Pistols, Bullets, Powder, Swords, Bayonets (p. 250)

his Master can only regard it as some kind of deformed and perverted substitute for Reason itself:

> He seemed therefore confident, that, instead of Reason, we were only possessed of some Quality fitted to increase our natural Vices; as the Reflection from a troubled Stream only returns the Image of an ill-shapen Body, not only *larger*, but more *distorted*. (p. 251)

Here Swift anticipates the critique of technological reason offered by Horkheimer and Adorno in *Dialectic of Enlightenment*.

However, Swift's most damaging objection to the modern world is that it neither possesses nor believes it needs any concept of virtue. It was therefore inevitable that Swift should engage with Mandeville's denial that the concept of virtue had any real substance and his contrary claim that luxury, selfishness and vanity were essential to the functioning of modern society. In the voyage to the Houhnhnms Swift confronted Mandeville's demoralising arguments by the extraordinary tactic of conceding them completely.

Was Man really just an extraordinarily selfish and head strong as well as cunning Animal.[51]

driven by the most basic instinctual drives? Very well Swift would depict him as the debased, disgusting and violent Yahoo. Was it the case that for man virtue was simply an imposture and a pretence? – very well, Swift would abandon the very notion that man could be a virtuous creature and depict instead a society of virtuous horses, the Houyhnhnms. Mandeville argued that man was not intended to be a predator because of the tender nature of the human skin, and because of the ineffectiveness of his jaws, teeth and nails. Swift once more agrees. Yes, man is useless – Gulliver's Houyhnhnm Master notes that his body lacks 'a Fence against Heat and Cold' (p. 245) and that his nails are 'of no use to my fore or hinder feet' (p. 244). Swift is not impressed with either Mandeville's claim that modern societies are superior because they are more complex and because they can supply more diverse and luxurious requirements. The Houyhnhnms are morally superior precisely because they do have fewer wants and because they live in a world that does not need to be maintained by vice. It is the very lack of parasitical occupations, praised by Mandeville for their contribution to employment and economic growth, that is appealing. Whereas in England

> ... it follows of Necessity, that vast Numbers of our People are compelled to seek their Livelihood by Begging, Robbing, Stealing, Cheating, Pimping, Forswearing, Flattering, Suborning, Forging, Gaming, Lying, Fawning, Hectoring, Voting, Scribling, Stargazing, Poysoning, Whoring, Canting, Libelling, Free-thinking, and the like Occupations. (p. 256)

By contrast with this sublime diversity of the Moderns the Houyhnhnms are a simple, benevolent and virtuous people, who live in the light of their ancient traditions. Until now they have scarcely glimpsed the full horror of an anarchic world, driven by utility and lack of moral principle. In some sense they correspond to the classical tradition in its strongest and most optimistic version, in that they are exemplary and worth copying, and that they instantiate and perpetuate a positive set of values from which mankind might yet learn. The faint hope for humanity that Swift holds out at the end of *Gulliver* is that it might yet be possible (through an embassy to the Houyhnhnms) to revive the virtues and re-civilise Europe – since we still possess the words, if not the qualities they designate.

For Pope, more optimistic than Swift, the problem posed by the political and economic events of the 1720s, was how to reconcile a general conception of benevolent deism with a more immediate and powerful sense of a world in which virtue how denied? How could the seemingly impregnable and undoubtedly corrupt administration of the Whigs, the prevalence of opportunism and knavery, be reconciled with the idea of a harmonious and well ordered universe, presided over by a good, wise and compassionate God? It had become as essential for Pope to justify the seemingly perverse and irrational ways of God as it had been for Milton to explain the seemingly inexplicable occurrence of the Restoration.

This was what Pope essayed in *The Essay on Man* (completed 1734) – but whether the universe was as favourable to man as he there proposed or rather more discouraging as he implied in *The Dunciad* , in either case the significance of virtue is diminished. In *The Dunciad*, in a world of ignorance, self aggrandisement and venality, where morality itself is doomed, the very idea of virtue seems an anachronism. But equally, if, as he asserts in *The Essay on Man*, God is great and man is only a puny being, puffed up with a false self-esteem and prone to overrate his own importance, then man's first and most urgent moral duty is to come to terms with his own imperfection. If self-love is the starting point for Pope's analysis of human nature then he must urgently guard against the tendencies within himself towards narcissism, vanity and pride. Humility is urgently called for. Indeed if man is nothing but a 'vile worm' then Pope becomes strangely reminiscent of his American Calvinist contemporary, Jonathan Edwards, who compared man with a insignificant spider, whom God could at any moment cast into the flames of a terrible fire. On Pope's own analysis God would, of course, never even contemplate such a horrifying course of action, but the curious and convoluted loop in his argument is that if Pope is right to say:

All Nature is but Art, unknown to thee;
All chance, Direction, which thou canst not see;
All Discord, Harmony, not understood;
All partial evil, universal Good.

we are bound to ask how a benevolent God could have made his universe so inscrutable to man that he is required to predicate a *universal* good beyond the actual local evil he undoubtedly perceives and equally how is it that Pope can perceive such sense of an overriding purpose, when the comprehension of it is beyond man's grasp?

It is not hard to perceive contradictions in Pope's general account of the human situation. Moreover, the sheer familiarity of many lines from the poem tend to reinforce our sense that Pope is being at once complacent and simplistic, disposed to smooth away problems rather than seriously to address them. Nevertheless, the *Essay on Man* is a more serious and more intellectually sophisticated attempt to present an harmonious vision of the cosmos than James Thomson's *The Seasons*, which just predates it since the first complete edition appeared in 1730, even though it is normally read in the final revised and expanded edition of 1746. Thomson's vision of Nature is post-Newtonian in that he views it as a complex self-regulating system, where every single aspect of it contributes to and perpetuates its regular overall functioning. Nature typically manifests itself as abundance and plenitude. The universe is dynamic and incessantly in motion. Drawing on much contemporary scientific knowledge Thomson depicts a world that is constantly changing and transforming itself, where everything circulates, deploying a characteristic vocabulary that makes extensive use of such terms as 'pours', 'swells', 'rolls', 'spreads', 'pervades', 'diffuses', 'rises', 'bursts', 'whirls', 'rushes' and 'flows'. This overall perspective is transferred to the social world. As a Whig Thomson views commerce beneficial, not just because it creates prosperity, but because it is likewise stabilising and energising: Britain was for long in a state of confusion and turmoil, but it has now developed into

> this deep-laid indissoluble state
> Where wealth and commerce lifts the golden head.

Thomson's rhetoric denies the very possibility of negativity, which can only figure as some kind of blockage or impediment to circulation. The only blot on his generally smiling landscape is the corruption of Walpole's administration, but needless to say Thomson has no objection to a Whig supremacy, which indeed is precisely what has made Britain a progressive country, only to a government that through its machinations is putting that tradition at risk. For Thomson – as he dramatises through his hero, the Knight of Industry, in his poem *The Castle of Indolence* (1748) – virtue is activity which must struggle against its perpetual adversary, the temptation to slide into lassitude, idleness and corruption. So politics must be redeemed from the stagnation into which it has fallen. Here, Thomson's exemplary figure is Peter the Great of Russia, a nation that symbolically parallels Thomson's native Scotland, who has tamed a continent, civilised a people and subdued her enemies, a pregnant instance of all that 'active government' can do. It seems that what England really needs is a good kick up the backside!

By contrast, *The Essay on Man* is more measured and less ready to reach for easy answers. It is a work of consolation and reassurance and to understand it we need to bring more clearly into focus the specific questions that it was designed to address. The most significant of these was the fact that the belief in divine Providence, the faith that God, from the Crucifixion to the Last Judgement, was deeply concerned in the working out of man's destiny on earth, was being seriously undermined. This was a consequence of discoveries being made with the telescope, producing not only a new astronomy but a new cosmology. It now seemed that the universe was infinitely greater than had hitherto been imagined and that the sun was itself only one of a multiplicity of suns and therefore in itself of very little importance. Addison wrote in *The Spectator*:

> Were the sun, which enlightens this part of the creation, with all the host of planetary worlds that move about him, utterly extinguished and annihilated, they would not be missed more than a grain of sand upon the seashore. (565)

Equally, but implicitly, the dire prospect had to be faced that the disappearance of man would not greatly trouble God either. Moreover, since other galaxies might also contain living creature comparable, or even superior, to ourselves it could not necessarily be taken for granted that God was as intently focused on human affairs as had hitherto been assumed. Such anxieties acquired greater credence as as result of the ongoing religious struggles of the Reformation and Counter-Reformation. For all the participants, whether Protestant or Catholic, it frequently seemed that events turned out in a puzzling and unexpected way given that the future of religion and the whole course of the world was actually at stake. How could people know where they stood? Man's perplexity and awe at the mysteriousness of God's intentions might only lead to a baffled resentment at the unsearchable obscurity of events. And the deeper worry behind this might be that, when you got right down to it, the belief in Providence might just be man whistling in the dark, that God might not much care what happened to man, one way or the other. Contemplating the sheer immensity of the universe Addison wrote:

> I could not but look upon myself with secret horror, as a being that was not worth the smallest regard of one who had so great a work under his care and superintendency. I was afraid of being overlooked amidst that infinite variety of creatures which, in all probability, swarm through all those immeasurable regions of matter. (565)

The particular threat implicit in the idea of an indifferent God is that it opens up the further possibility that God, so far from actually being opposed to the existence of evil in the universe may have already permitted it and tolerated it, and that, in consequence, he may actually have no very urgent intention of doing anything about it. Moreover, any doubts that we may have that God is not fully concerned in the destiny of our human world lead to further worrying questions about whether such a remote and apparently indifferent God can command our whole-hearted love and reverence. So, while in the philosophical and scientific community of the seventeenth century such doubts were heretical and could not be openly and unambiguously voiced, there was an urgent need to overcome the real anxieties raised by scientific discovery through an appeal to more general scientific principles. Effectively such scientific principles constituted a new set of theological axioms, since they could not be fully demonstrated. Rather, like the arguments of the medieval scholastic philosophers, they stemmed from general arguments and assumptions about the nature of God and the nature of the Universe. Since God must be good it followed that the universe must also have been good since he could not have created it otherwise. Equally, although the universe is undoubtedly complex it must be characterised by order, regularity and predictability.

Despite the bewildering profusion and multiplicity it exhibits it must necessarily be governed by a relatively small body of principles. Leibnitz writes:

> Thus, one can say, in whatever manner God created the world, it would always have been regular and in accordance with a certain general order. But God has chosen the most perfect world, that is, the one which is at the same time the simplest in hypotheses and the richest in phenomena, as might be a line in geometry whose construction is easy and whose properties and effects are extremely remarkable and widespread.[52]

Part of God's goodness lies in the fact that he has the mind of a scientist and that – as Einstein was later to insist – he would not wish to baffle or play malicious tricks on man as he endeavoured to understand creation. There could be no cosmic rolling of dice. Kepler must have been very relieved to discover, after 19 failed attempts, that the trajectory of Mars was an ellipse, not just because of his own heroic achievement, but because it showed both that the orbit *was* calculable and that God, in his wisdom, had chosen a comparatively simple and readily identifiable geometrical figure. The universe was orderly and with that notion firmly in mind the scientist or mathematician could proceed knowing that if he could only command sufficient patience he would eventually attain his goal. The problem of evil, which might well be seen as a force for unpredictability and disorder in the universe, could also be approached in a scientific way. If the universe was *necessarily* complex and diverse then it would inexorably follow that some of the creatures within the divine order would be more perfect than others and that many would excel in partial and specific ways. So what is called evil is simply attributable to the fact that not everything in the universe can be perfect. Evil is the product of privation, limitation and lack. In his *Theodicy* Leibnitz compares evil with cold and darkness:

> Evil itself comes only from privation; the positive enters therein only by concomitance, as the active enters by concomitance into cold. We see that water in freezing is capable of breaking a gun-barrel wherein it is confined; and yet cold is a certain privation of force, it only comes from diminution of a movement which separates the particles of fluids.[53]

So good and evil are like hot and cold; they exist together and can be registered on the same thermometer, but evil in reality has no power of its own just as cold is nothing more than the absence of heat.

The universe is a carefully contrived and intricately interwoven structure in which everything has its own specific place, including and especially man. If man after Galileo can seem displaced in relation to the cosmos he nevertheless regains his place in the general order of nature. According to Leibnitz there are no gaps or holes in the system of nature:

> ... the animal and vegetable kingdoms are so nearly joined, that if you will take the lowest of one, and the highest of the other, there will scarcely be perceived any great distance between them.[54]

The magnificent harmony of the divine scheme of things manifests itself in the fact that the amazingly diverse *combinatoire* of plants, insects, birds and animals neverthless ascends by carefully graduated steps towards the supreme perfection of God himself. This is reassuring for a variety of reasons. It demonstrates that the world itself has been carefully planned and that God only decided upon it after carefully considering a very wide number of options. It is therefore, in Leibnitz's often quoted and often misunderstood phrase 'the best of all possible worlds'. It shows that man, if inevitably not perfect, nevertheless still retains a very significant place in the general scheme of things because although he may be, say, less powerful than the lion and less agile than a squirrel, he is nevertheless clearly superior in many other respects. Leibnitz likes to think of man as part of a vast and subtly articulated scale of actualized possibilities where we can always see him progressing several steps beyond the creatures that seem to come closest to him:

> Birds, which are otherwise so different from man, approach him by virtue of their speech, but if monkeys could speak as parrots can they would approach him even more closely.[55]

This way of thinking about the interconnectedness of nature is not necessarily as hierarchical as it might seem. For man is not presented as unique but is shown as being close to the parrot and the monkey and although Leibnitz does not draw attention to the fact, many a reader might reflect that, as part of this diversity man is unable to fly like a parrot or climb trees as well as a monkey. But what gives this sense of an elaborately constructed cosmos is that man is not apart from nature and that God *must* be concerned about man just because he represents some of the most advanced aspects of a universe over which God has obviously taken a great deal of trouble. This is what Pope means in *The Essay on Man*, when, clearly taking his cue from Leibnitz, he writes:

> Of Systems possible, if 'tis confest
> That wisdom infinite must form the best,
> Where all must full, or not coherent be,
> And all that rises, rise in due degree;
> Then, in the scale of reas'ning, 'tis plain
> There must be, somewhere, such a rank as Man.

If we once accept that man is a necessary being then it follows that God must have plans for him and must assume some general duty of care towards him.

Although Pope's intention in the poem was to develop a positive account of God and the human situation, he chose, somewhat surprisingly to base his analysis on the worldly philosophers Hobbes, Locke and Mandeville, who, in their different ways stressed the inescapability of conflict as men egotistically pursue their own goals – at least when there is no state to govern, control or otherwise interpose. This willingness to combine an *a priori* understanding of the universe in general with a more hard-headed and empirical analysis of human nature may have been the reason why Pope saw the chief merit of his poem as that of 'steering a course between doctrines seemingly opposite'. For Pope had the sense to recognise that an affirmative discussion of the human situation could have little value if it were not prepared to confront awkward and potentially discouraging evidence about it. Indeed, both in the factional struggles between Whig and Tory in the age of Anne, and perhaps still more in the struggle over the yet richer pickings that were to be had in the heyday of Walpole, the notion than human beings were motivated by self-love must have seemed pretty inevitable, and in the process quite a few – like Thomas Gordon – changed sides. As a writer who was obliged to support himself by his pen Pope knew all too well that the struggle for honour and reputation in the literary world was just as desperate as in the political. It was just as imperative for him to assassinate the character of his opponents, in *The Dunciad* and elsewhere, as it was for others to denigrate him, either in their own interest or at the behest of others. Literature was very definitely a zero sum game and more prestige for one person meant less for another. So Pope would have understood very well the force of Hobbes's remark:

> The value, or WORTH of a man, is as of all other things, his Price; that is to say as much as would be given for the use of his Power . . . and, as in other things, so in men, not the seller, but the buyer determines the Price. For let a man (as most men do), rate themselves at the highest Value they can; yet their true Value is no more than is esteemed by others.[56]

There are no absolutes in Hobbes's world and none in the world that Pope moved in either. Although Pope did deny that the original state of Nature had been one of lawless anarchy:

The state of Nature was the reign of God.

He nevertheless argued that stasis and harmony could not be regarded as the normal state of affairs:

But All subsists by elemental strife.

In the spirit of Hobbes he saw tyranny and religion as being linked; the domination of one man as the outcome of self-love. Pope's acknowledgement of the significance of self-love was not based purely and simply on a Hobbesian analysis of human society but also on man's place in a cosmological scheme. Here, Pope was certainly influenced by Bolingbroke's insistence on man's place in nature and on his intimate connection with the animal world. This line of argument so shocked Burke when Bolingbroke's reflections on the subject were posthumously published in 1754 that he vigorously condemned them in his *A Vindication of Natural Society* of 1757. Against those who insisted on man's unique nature Bolingbroke argued:

> Man is connected by his nature, and therefore, by the design of the author of all Nature, with the whole tribe of animals,

and so closely with some of them, that the distance between his intellectual faculties and theirs, which constitutes as really, though not so sensibly as figure, the difference of species, appears, in many instances, small and would probably appear still less, if we had the means of knowing their motives, as we have of observing their actions.[57]

What follows from this is the argument that man, like the animals, is driven by certain basic imperatives such a the need for self-preservation, food and shelter, for sex and the obligation to perpetuate the species. In Pope's own words:

> Not man alone, but all that roam the wood,
> Or wing the sky, or roll along the flood,
> Each loves itself, but not itself alone,
> Each sex desires alike, 'till two are one.
> Nor ends the pleasure with the fierce embrace;
> They love themselves a third time, in their race.

This emphasis on self-preservation and self-love, however seemingly modified by Pope's formulations, clearly shows the influence of Mandeville's *Fable of the Bees*. But Pope does not regard himself as making concessions but rather as performing a balancing act that will give all shades of opinion their due. But his desire to be hospitable to all shades of opinion leads to his associating with some rather uncouth companions and to his admitting company that might be better excluded – rather like a minister who finds that some ne'erdowells, whom had he invited to the vicarage, have decamped with items of value while he was making them a cup of tea. Indeed, with hindsight it is puzzling that Pope should have been prepared to make such significant concessions to a point of view that denigrated virtue when he was so anxious to defend it – especially when such views were regarded as cynical and immoral, even atheistical. In general, as we have already seen, the prevailing view of Mandeville was to see his views as potentially dangerous insofar as they threatened to undermine religion and morality, but to see his actual arguments about self-love and pride as being scarcely worth bothering with, since they amounted to little more than a *pot pourri* of superficial paradoxes and half truths. If they needed to be answered it was only because they were in danger of achieving credence through their very notoriety. In the preface to his *Sermons* Bishop Butler denied categorically that human behaviour was analogous to that of animals. Men were not

> ... wholly governed by self-love, the love of power and sensual appetites ...

since they were also influenced by such feeling as friendship, compassion and gratitude and, very significantly

> ... a general abhorrence of what is base, and a liking of what is fair and just.[58]

Moreover, human beings had a conscience, which must inevitably bring their actions and intentions before the bar of the very highest moral standards. Hume's approach to the problem of 'self-love' and the cynical philosophy that insists on it is representative of the dismissive Augustan way with Mandeville. In his *An Enquiry concerning the Principles of Morals* he did discuss the issue but felt it would be sufficient to dispose of the matter in a brief appendix. On the one hand, as with Butler, there *were* many incontrovertable instances of kindness and benevolence to point to; on the other the attempt to

> ... explain every affection to be self-love, twisted and moulded, by a particular turn of imagination, into a variety of appearances[59]

was at once reductive and perverse. So why did Pope make so many damaging concessions to Mandeville when others ruled this completely out of court. In part it was due to the fact that *The Essay on Man* was written in the wake of Mandeville's greatest period of notoriety. At such an historical conjuncture, which was also the moment when Walpole's administration seemed an almost unchallengeable force and when the patronage system that Walpole presided over seemed all pervasive, it seemed that Mandeville's analysis explained so much and cut so deeply that at least some of his arguments from egoism would have to be taken on board. It would not have been realistic to toss them aside. But equally Pope theodicy in *The Essay on Man* itself became influential and after the fall of Walpole in 1742 the need to address the agenda of Mandeville's worldly philosophy now seemed less urgent.

At the same time it has to be admitted that part of Mandeville's fascination for Pope was that he believed that his style of arguing could simply be turned on its head. If Mandeville could show how Private Vices could become Public Benefits and demonstrate how pride and vanity could lead men into performing actions deemed virtuous then Pope would take this seriously and show a whole series of dialectical processes whereby public order is actually generated by lawlessness and anarchy and where self-love can actually lead to a concern for public good. The difference is simply the difference between contraction and expansion. Mandeville shrinks all human behaviour down to a core of self-love; Pope sees that self-love developing and expanding into virtue:

> God loves from Whole to Parts: but human soul
> Must rise from Individual to the Whole.
> Self-love but serves the virtuous mind to wake,
> As the small pebble stirs the peaceful lake;
> The centre mov'd, a circle strait succeeds,
> Another still, and still another spreads . . .

However, what Pope never quite grasps is that his initial admission that self-love is the driving force in human behaviour has devastating consequences for his whole argument. Pope tends to speak of a conflict between virtue and vice as if this were simply a battle between opposing forces, like good and evil, whereas for Mandeville only self-love is real and 'virtue' is epiphenomenal. There is talk about 'virtue' in a hypocritical style of discourse and a pretence that it exists but that is all. So although Pope purports to attach greater weight to virtue it is an etiolated virtue defeated before it has begun and scarcely the irresistable force that he invokes in the above quotation. Indeed so preoccupied is Pope with the macro level, that the micro level in which individual people face important choices about whether to act well or badly virtually disappears. If each person is bound to be a mixture of virtue and vice and if there is bound to be conflict on the local level anyway, then it seems we might just as well leave it up to God to sort things out and harmonise everything at the level of the Whole. It is all rather reminiscent of those nineteenth-century Marxists who were prepared to wait for capitalism to collapse out of its own contradictions without any action on their part. If God is good, the overall working of the universe benign, virtue as such seems more or less superogatory.

Still, Pope was eventually troubled by the rather too emollient implications of his own message. Especially when he reflected on the general ineffectualness of any attempt to shake the massively planted oak of Whig corruption in political affairs, he was made acutely aware that, self-love or no, there was still a massive qualitative distinction to be made between the virtuous man's desire to be well regarded through public service and the selfish man's ruthless determination to achieve his own ends regardless of the social cost. The evidence of Pope's later correspondence is that he and many of those with whom he corresponded most regularly, such as Bolingbroke, Lyttleton, Bathurst, Marchmont, Orrery and Swift, regarded themselves as a small sect of outcast but virtuous individuals who refused to compromise with the customs of a debased and corrupted age. Symptomatic of their mood is the despairing letter written by Lyttleton to Pope in 1738 imploring him to bring all his powers of eloquence and influence to bear on the Prince of Wales, since it was the Prince who seemed to offer the only conceivable way out of the one way street of Whig supremacy:

> Be therefore as much with him as you can, Animate him to Virtue, to the Love of the Publick; and think that the Morals, the Liberty, the whole Happiness of this country depends on your success. If that Sacred Fire, by which You and other Honest Men has kindled in his Mind, can be Preserv'd, we may yet be safe; But if it go out, it is a Presage of Ruin, and we must be Lost. For the Age is far too corrupted to Reform itself; it must be done by Those upon, or near the Throne, or not at all: They must Restore what we ourselves have Given up. They must save us from our own Vices, and Follies, they must bring back the taste of Honesty, and the Sense of Honour, which the *Fashion of Knavery* has almost destroyed.[60]

The conjuction of the terms 'fashion' and 'knavery' is significant since it recalls the general analysis of the literary world that Pope had presented in the *Dunciad Variorum* of 1729, which consisted of 'pomps without guilt' and mediocrity without shame. Yet to make this connection is also to be acutely conscious that there is

a very real question as to whether Pope *should* be taken seriously as a moralist and especially in *The Dunciad* – even in the
final and more ambitious version in four books. Even many of
those who admire the verve, incisiveness and fantastic humour
of the poem may be disposed to concede that it is simply a
personalised attack by Pope on his enemies, which lacks the
underlying seriousness of Swift's *The Battle of the Books* even though
it purports to participate the the same controversy between ancients
and moderns and to expose the inflated pretensions of the latter.
Moreover, to the modern reader, the spectacle of Pope, both well-
connected and extremely rich as the result of his translation of
The Odyssey, sneering at his humble and impoverished rivals, is
not particularly edifying. What makes it worse is that all too many
have taken it on trust that those whom Pope ridiculed were Dunces
– yet Theobald was a more scrupulous editor of Shakespeare than
Pope himself, Dennis a far more perceptive and original critic,
while both Susanna Centlivre and Colley Cibber have their merits as dramatists. Moreover, to disparage Elkanah Settle, who had
only recently died (in 1724) was in very poor taste, whether he
was a Dunce or not. This is history written by the victors with a
vengeance. In one of the more telling passages of Book IV of *The
Dunciad*, which he added in 1742, Pope criticised

> The critic Eye, that microscope of Wit,
> Sees hairs and pores, examines bit by bit

and which therefore fails to perceive the larger picture – but the
same fault is manifestly present in the earlier *Dunciad*. There Pope
becomes so obsessed with gossip and trivia that his claim that
all this somehow amounts to a critique of the age begins to seem
all too reminiscent of the posturing self-importance that he is
only too eager to ridicule in others.

By contrast the revised *Dunciad of 1743* is a considerably more
impressive, despite the fact that much of the text is carried over
from the earlier version, partly because Book IV offers a more
serious and more searching analysis of the age and because Pope's
decision to focus more on narcissism than pedantry finds a perfect target in Colley Cibber. Significantly Samuel Richardson –
who was no more impressed with the later version than the earlier
– saw the substitution of Cibber for Theobald as a confession on
Pope's part

that his Abuse of his first hero was for Abuse-sake.⁶¹

Pope's original focus on Theobald simply revealed his own animus against the man, whereas Cibber as a prominent actor manager, Poet Laureate and a supporter of the Whigs was a much more legitimate and representative target. Moreover, Cibber perfectly embodied that mixture of complacency and self-love that for Pope epitomised the contemporary Dunce as this passage from his autobiography, *An Apology for the Life of Colley Cibber* (1740) abundantly attests:

> It often makes me smile, to think how contentedly I have sate myself down, to write my own Life; nay, and with less Concern for what may be said of it, than I should feel, were I to do the same for a deceas'd Acquaintance. This you will easily account for, when you consider, that nothing gives a Coxcomb more Delight, than when you suffer him to talk of himself; which sweet Liberty I here enjoy for a whole Volume together!⁶²

Cibber purports to mock himself and yet by that gesture implies that someone who is famous for his vanity has nothing to lose by acknowledging it. He typified a culture in which a talent for self-promotion was the only real talent that was either necessary or useful. In focusing on Cibber it became possible for Pope to regain the high moral ground both because he had less of a personal axe to grind and because he could take up the argument that Swift had made in *The Battle of the Books*, whereas the classical writers pursued objectivity and true judgement; like the bee producing honey and wax, thus:

> furnishing mankind with the two noblest of things, which are sweetness and light (p. 113)

the moderns, like the spider, were filled with

> . . . an overweening pride, which feeding and engendering on itself, turns all into excrement and venom. (p. 112)

Hitherto, as we have seen Pope had made significant concessions to Mandeville – indeed in his 'Epistle to Burlington' he seemed to acknowledge that the arguments of *The Fable of the Bees* were wellnigh irresistible. For there, though Pope describes himself as being sick of Timon's 'civil Pride' and ostentatious display, he nevertheless acknowledged:

> Yet hence the Poor are cloath'd, the Hungry fed;
> Health to himself, and to his Infants bread
> The Lab'rer bears: what his hard Heart denies,
> His charitable Vanity supplies.

Here Pope not only conceded that luxury created employment, but more crucially, allowed Mandeville's yet more cynical claim in his 'Essay on Charity and Charity-Schools' that vanity was more likely to lead to good works than benevolent intentions:

> Pride and Vanity have built more Hospitals than all the Virtues together.[63]

But in the later *Dunciad*, perhaps partly under the influence of Warburton, Pope seems to have stiffened his resistance to him – Mandeville is mentioned in the revised Book III and a footnote by Warburton identifies him as the author of a book which

> . . . may seem written to prove, that Moral Virtue is the invention of knaves, and Christian Virtue the imposition of fools.

Again, although *The Fable of the Bees* is not specifically mentioned, Pope and Warburton in another note almost certainly have both Hobbes and Mandeville in their sights when they stress the dangers of 'modern Free-thinking' which establishes '*Self-love* for the sole Principle of action'. The key formulation in Book IV is Pope's suggestion that the new philosophy:

> Finds Virtue local, all Relation scorn,
> See all in *Self*, and but for self be born.

This recalls the suggestion by Lysicles in Berkeley's *Alciphron*

> . . . that moral virtue is only a name, a notion, a chimera, an enthusiasm, or at best a fashion, uncertain and changeable, like other fashions.[64]

Indeed it was Berkeley who brought into focus the destablising implication of Mandeville's thinking and thereby gave a greater urgency to Pope's invocation of a universal darkness: for now it implies not just dullness and stupidity but a profound ethical vacuum in which the absence of values is not even noticed:

and unawares *Morality* expires.

4

Virtue from Below

In the age of Walpole the idea of virtue had come to seem elusive indeed. The net of patronage, corruption and intimidation was flung so wide that it seemed that scarcely anyone could escape its influence. It was certainly possible to speak of virtue in the abstract and even possible, as with Bolingbroke, to dream that under a new monarch, a patriot king, it would be possible for Astraea to return to earth and for virtue to flourish again. Yet the unreality of such speculation was conspicuous to most. The idea of the court as a potential theatre of virtue as hypothesised in Chapman's *Bussy D'Ambois* has always seemed rather optimistic; now the notion of the court as the originary centre of corruption seemed all but inescapable.

Nevertheless and perhaps for that very reason the idea of virtue continued to cast a spell over the minds of contemporaries. Virtue must exist and if it does not – and perhaps cannot – prosper among the great then perhaps it may continue to quietly flourish lower down in society, where moral behaviour might seem more instinctive and where the temptations and opportunities for debasement might seem less glittering. Certainly Samuel Richardson believed that sober people of the middle classes, like himself, were more moral than their presumed aristocratic betters. *Pamela*, which sets the newly developed genre of the novel in motion, is a radical work precisely because it argues that Mr B, a gentleman, is in all respects the moral inferior of Pamela, a servant. After *Pamela* the tendency was increasingly to look for virtue amongst the lowly and unsophisticated yet so familiar are we with this shift in sensibility and values that it is easy to miss the paradoxical nature of Richardson's enterprise. For virtue was quintessentially the mark of a gentleman – even for Richardson's fellow tradesman Daniel Defoe, who wrote:

110

Here began nobillity in Venice, and a just beginning it was;
nobillity, as it ought to be, was made an appendix to, or an
attendant on virtue: True merit, fidellity to, and services done
for, their country, exalted the first patriots of the State, and
establish'd themselves as the rule for those noble persons to
act by in taking subsequent nobility afterwards as the reward
of virtue.[1]

In this myth of origins nobility flows from virtue; but equally, if
ideally, the reverse is true: virtue flows from the possession of
aristocratic status. For this linkage of birth, status and virtue there
are a diversity of reasons. In the first place Aristotle's emphasis
on the way in which a virtuous character can be formed in his
Ethics may then imply that those exposed to more favourable
influences, whether social or educational are more likely to be
virtuous. Having a philosophical tutor like Aristotle would certainly help. Unlike the religious conception of the good, which
may be most fully realised by those who shun the world, the
classical notion of virtue is public, social and civic; its greatest
exemplars those like Socrates and Cato, who though often at odds
with the dominant values of society nevertheless realised their
destiny within it. Virtue tends to imply social position since if it
is virtuous to be just, then power is necessary if that justice is to
be actualised. Virtue may also imply wealth since Aristotle's
magnanimous man who is munificent and generous with his
money can only be virtuous in this way if he has the funds in
the first place. Contrariwise frugality and abstemiousness can
hardly be virtues in the poor whereas with the man of fortune
they necessarily become noteworthy. Addison has Juba say of
his hero:

> To strike thee dumb: turn up thy eyes to Cato!
> There may'st thou see to what a godlike height
> The Roman virtues lift up mortal man,
> While good, and just, and anxious for his friends,
> He's still severely bent against himself;
> Renouncing sleep, and rest, and food, and ease,
> He strives with thirst and hunger, toil and heat;
> And when his fortune sets before him all
> The pomps and pleasures that his soul can wish,
> His rigid virtue will accept of none.

On a humbler level even the eighteenth-century benevolent man, the man of feeling also requires a certain amount of funds in order for him to aid those more fortunate than himself. Mackenzie's Harley must himself have the guinea in order to give it to the beggar and Werther the coin which he presses into the hand of the mother of a mentally deranged man. Virtue in this general analysis is a top-down affair.

Nevertheless there was a widespread belief in the eighteenth century that virtue could be taught and if it was the case that it could be taught then it followed that in principle it could be taught to anybody. Through the influence of such figures as Defoe and Richardson who sought to improve and better their readers by placing such exemplary figures as Robinson Crusoe and Pamela before them the whole notion of moral education became secularised. It was no longer specifically anchored to the sermon or to the moral authority of the church. Increasingly virtue comes to be viewed through the spectacles of tradesmen and the middle class. Defoe, for instance in *The Complete English Tradesman* insists that it is dangerous for the tradesman to be concerned with pleasure which is 'a thief to business', yet he concedes that by contrast:

> To gentlemen of fortune and estates, who being born to large possessions, and have no avocations of this kind, it is certainly lawful to spend ther spare hours on horseback, with their hounds or hawks, pursuing their game.[2]

It is slightly awkward for Defoe to have to acknowledge that there is one law for the aristocrat and another for the tradesmen, particularly since he stresses elsewhere that tradesmen have risen into the aristocracy, but as Defoe says it is after all tradesmen whom he is addressing. Richardson however is not prepared to make such concessions. On the contrary he demands that the aristocracy meet middle-class standards. He is not prepared to make special concessions. The aristocrat and gentleman of leisure is not only no more likely to be virtuous he is distinctly less likely.

The starting point for many of Richardson's reflections on the relationship between education and virtue is Locke's *Some Thoughts Concerning Education*. Locke's influence on Richardson is everywhere apparent but it is particularly evident in the second part of *Pamela* when Mr B gives Pamela a copy of Locke and asks for her comments. Mr B in doing this may have been concerned that Pamela might be too doting a mother but he is also interested in hearing her views on the subject to which she then devotes a series of seven letters. Since Locke's reflections were specifically intended for members of the aristocracy (or at the very least for those able to provide their children with a tutor) and since Locke warned against the dangers of exposing children to the corrupting company of servants:

> They are wholly, if possible to be kept from such conversation: For the contagion of these ill precedents, both in Civility and Vertue, horribly infects Children, as often as they come within reach of it. They frequently learn from unbred or debauched Servants such Language, untowardly Tricks and Vices.[3]

There is a certain irony in a situation, where Pamela, herself once a servant, must offer her comments on Locke. Nevertheless Locke is a good starting point for articulating a moral discourse, since Locke stresses that education is moral or it is nothing. A knowledge of Greek and Latin in itself amounts to very little, for what underpins the ideal of a classical education is the moral example of the great Greeks and Romans:

> But till you can find a School, wherein it is possible for the Master to look after the Manners of his Scholars, and can shew as great Effects of his Care of forming their Minds to Virtue, and their Carriage to good Breeding, as of forming their Tongues to the learned Languages; you must confess, that you have a strange value for words, when preferring the Languages of the Ancient Greeks and Romans, to that which made them such brave Men, you think it worth while, to hazard your Son's Innocence and Vertue, for a little Greek and Latin.[4]

Character-building was just as important for Locke as it was for the Headmasters of the Victorian public schools but we should recognise, as did Richardson, that much of the thrust of such education was necessary in order to militate against the indulgence and pampering which the children of the aristocracy habitually received.

If Pamela, the child of humble yet virtuous parents is naturally

virtuous herself Mr B himself – improved as he is by the lowly
Pamela – freely admits that his privileged background is the reason
for his own irresponsible behaviour:

> We people of fortune, or such as are born to large expecta-
> tions, of both sexes, are generally educated wrong. You have
> occasionally touched upon this, Pamela, several times in your
> journal, so justly, that I need say the less to you. We are usu-
> ally so headstrong, so violent in our wills, that we very little
> bear control.
>
> Humoured by our nurses, through the faults of our parents,
> we practise first upon them; and shew the *gratitude* of our dis-
> position, in an insolence that ought to be checked and restrained,
> than encouraged.
>
> Next, we are to be indulged in everything at school; and
> our *masters* and *mistresses* are rewarded with further grateful
> instances of our boisterous behaviour.
>
> But in our *wise* parents eyes, all looks well; all is forgiven
> and excused: and for no other reason, but because we are *theirs*.
>
> Our next progression is, we exercise our spirits, when brought
> home, to the torment and regret of our *parents themselves*, and
> torture their hearts by our undutiful and perverse behaviour,
> which, however ungrateful in us, is but the natural consequence
> of their culpable indulgence from our infancy onwards. (Vol.
> I, pp. 401–2)

Mr B himself takes it for granted that if he desires Pamela and
wishes to take her for his mistress then his will must be law and
there can be no thought of any obstacle being placed in his way.
What to both Pamela and the reader seems like cynical, calculated and ruthless behaviour is simply the consequence of a
habitual narcissism that has never been challenged, questioned
or crossed.

In her own thoughts on education Pamela sees another factor
at work; the fact that the children of the wealthy and powerful
can be expected to copy the example of their parents:

> Excessive fondness this hour; violent passions and perhaps
> execrations, the next; unguarded jests, and admiration of fashion-
> able vanitites, rash censures, are perhaps the best, that the child

sees in, or hears from those who are most concerned to inculcate good precepts into his mind. (Vol. II, p. 398)

While virtue may be theoretically the birthright, mark and goal
of the gentleman, in practise self-control is all too often perceived
as utterly alien to the aristocratic code. So if the well born child
is to be well brought up Pamela recommends that the young
aristocrat should be led to emulate the virtues of a companion
from a lower social background. If he studies alongside 'the child
of some honest neighbour of but middling circumstances' who
has given indications of his 'natural promptitude, ingenuous temper, obliging behaviour and good manners', then emulation and
rivalry in the pursuit of virtue should result. (Vol. II, p. 398) But
the pattern of virtue needs to be looked for among the lower
orders of society, in circumstances which are less likely to provide a breeding ground for indiscipline and vice.

At this point some readers of Richardson will certainly expos-
tulate, saying: 'Such a lumbering discussion of virtue is all very
well but all it really succeeds in doing is rather stubbornly miss-
ing the point. Pamela's views on the upbringing of children in
the second part of *Pamela*, which, for good reason, few have read,
really have nothing at all to do with the story that gripped Europe:
the prolonged, tortuous and ultimately unsuccessful bid on the
part of a gentleman of fortune, Mr B, to seduce a beautiful servant girl. Here there can be little point in beating about the bush.
Virtue simply means chastity amd Pamela is rewarded because
in successfully repelling the advances of Mr B she puts him in a
position where he feels compelled to make her his wife. Although
there is a good deal of talk of morality in *Pamela* much of it is
actually quite hypocritical, since what is really going on is a battle
of wills and Pamela is quite as determined to get what she wants
as Mr B. Since Pamela as a servant was in no way a suitable
match for Mr B his proposal to make her his mistress was not
unreasonable. His error was simply his attempt to get his way
by force and fraud, which enabled Pamela, morally speaking to
gain the upper hand. Richardson's tale is more complex and more
compelling if we recognise it as a naked struggle for power, making
it perhaps analogous to Laclos's *Les Liasons Dangereuses*, rather
than reduce it to some banal disquisition on virtue, of which the
eighteenth century has all too many.'

I would not deny the pertinence of such an attempt to demystify

Pamela – but I nevertheless feel that in Richardson's time it was actually quite impossible for virtue to mean simply chastity. Even where this seems the literal meaning the word 'virtue' always carries with too many connotations, complications and rhetorical insinuations for it to be understood simply. Virtue is a loaded term in the struggle between the classes and the sexes. Here we should recognise that not only is Richardson using the term to privilege a middle-class system of values over an aristocratic behavioural code, but he is also opposing a Christian and feminine conception of virtue to a classical and masculine one. The virtues which were esteemed in a woman were significantly different from those that dignified a man. A woman was valued for her chastity, but also for her obedience, her patience, her devotion to duty and to her family, her spirit of self-sacrifice. In the classical tradition a virtuous man is courageous, honourable and self-disciplined – the model of the good soldier is never far away. So we do need to stress that although Christ was certainly courageous in his pacific spirit and willingness to turn the other cheek he was very far from such a martial role model. In many respects he was quite effeminate. In *Pamela* Richardson creates a heroine who is suffering yet stubborn, seemingly passive yet bold and resourceful under pressure, patient yet determined – a complex synthesis of traits which Richardson certainly intends as a representation of virtue in some fuller sense. Yet this virtue is feminine. Pamela's struggles – continued by Clarissa and Evelina – initiate a campaign to create a society in which men and women can live side by side more equally and in which the moral advantage will always be held by the woman.

Yet there remains the slightly perplexing question as to why Pamela's struggles are actually necessary. For Pamela after all is not just a transitory object of desire as far as Mr B is concerned nor is she just another attractive servant wench. Pamela, as Richardson is at pains to stress, is highly accomplished. Pamela can dance, sing and play upon the harpsichord. She can sketch and draw and is an expert needlewoman. She can not only read and write but she is an unusually sophisticated and subtle letter-writer. In a very real sense it is her skill with the pen that saves her. Since Pamela has been educated well beyond her own social sphere we must wonder why Mr B, who seemingly both loves and respects her should be prepared to go to such outrageous lengths to insist that he values nothing about her but her chastity.

So Mr B's reductive perception of the whole question of feminine
virtue obliges the reader to acknowledge Pamela as an authentic
moral force, as a genuine exponent of virtue in a wider and more
complex sense. Nevertheless the struggle is important because
Pamela is victorious and Mr B is defeated. This is a surprising
and perhaps even a slightly improbable outcome, but it is important for Richardson because Mr B is compelled to accept Pamela
at her own valuation – as she writes to Mr Williams:

> But, O sir,! my *soul* is of equal importance with the soul of a
> princess, though my quality is inferior to that of the meanest
> slave. (Vol. I, p. 137)

Indeed, even Pamela's own qualification the novel implicitly denies;
since it suggests that birth itself without merit or virtue is nothing. So the stakes surrounding virtue are actually very high. It is
Pamela's belief in her own worth and virtue that gives her the
strength and determination to struggle on; whereas Mr B despite
his various minions ranging from Colbrand and Mrs Jewkes to
John Arnold the coachman and even Mr Williams the clergyman
is effectively weak. In the contest between them Mr B is always
at a psychological disadvantage. As in Hegel the servant prevails
over the master because the master has become ineffectual through
his dependence on others. But Richardson also suggests he lacks
the clarity, determination and strength of will which he needs to
carry out his purpose. He is shamefaced, vacillating and indeci-
sive. Pamela's bold resistance takes him by surprise and has the
effect of making her even more desirable. Mr B's attempts to seduce
her by assuming a disguise only make him look ridiculous and
ineffectual, whereas Pamela on her knees can still remain dominant, proudly proclaiming:

> I cannot be patient, I cannot be passive, when my virtue is in
> danger. (Vol. I, p. 186)

Mr B's struggle to obtain, control and dominate Pamela is inferi-
ority confessed. As an aristocrat it virtually goes without saying
that he is hollow, morally empty and corrupt.

What disconcerted *Pamela*'s first readers was not so much the
overtly sexual nature of the action or even the marriage of a
gentleman to a servant, dubious as that might have been, as the

frankness with which a servant could condemn her social betters. Pamela rejoices in the poverty, honesty and integrity of her humble parents and insists that virtue, not birth, is the only nobility. In verse she insists:

> For, Oh! we *pity* should the great
> Instead of envying their state;
> Temptations always on them wait,
> Exempt from which are such as we.
> Their riches, gay deceitful snares!
> Enlarge their fears, increase their cares;
> Their servants' joys surpasses theirs;
> At least, so judges Pamela.

As long as Pamela is pursued and oppressed by Mr B's advances her claims about the advantages of the servants estate may not seem entirely convincing, but we nevertheless do see that Mr B is a petty, jealous, possessive, insecure man and that Lady Davers is arrogant, bullying and paranoid. Pamela's most radical thoughts on the question of class occur in her comments on a letter from Lady Davers, a copy of which she sends to her parents:

> This is a sad letter, my dear father and mother! One may see how poor people are despised by the proud and the rich! Yet we were all on a foot originally: and many of these gentry who brag of their ancient blood, would be glad to have it as wholesome and as *really* untainted as ours! – Surely these proud people never think what a short stage life is; and that, with all their vanity, a time is coming, when they must submit to be on a level with us.... Poor souls! how do I pity their pride! – O keep me Heaven, from *their* high condition, if my mind shall ever be tainted with *their* vice.... (Vol. I, p. 229)

In this letter, written on Tuesday, we might well feel that Pamela is so sincerely convinced of the moral dangers of a high estate that she genuinely hopes that Providence will spare her from the necessity of ever entering into any connection with the aristocracy, yet in the next letter, marked Wednesday morning she cannot contain her joy at receiving Mr B's proposal of marriage. Doubtless we may say that Pamela will be an ornament to her new position precisely because she will not be blown up with arrogance and pride but the compelling logic of Richardson's position is that Pamela's virtue cannot be rewarded by marriage to Mr B when such an environment endangers it on a multiplicity of levels. If Pamela is just a pretty girl who has got lucky then the story cannot have the moral significance that Richardson clearly intends.

However, if Pamela and Mr B seem mutually unworthy the difficulty can be overcome by theological argument. The blessed interposition of divine Providence which saves Pamela from harm symmetrically saves Mr B from irreparably falling into evil. Mr B as a man touched by God's grace is now a man worthy of Pamela just as Pamela is made worthy of him. As Mr Williams notes with gratification:

> 'How happily, sir,' said Mr Williams, tears of joy in his eyes, 'have you been touched by the divine Grace, before you were hurried into the commission of sins, that the deepest penitence could hardly have atoned for! God has enabled you to stop short of the evil; and you have nothing to do, but to rejoice in the good, which will now be doubly so, because you can receive it without the least inward reproach.' (Vol. I, p. 276)

But if Pamela is virtuous in her struggles and in her resistance to Mr B then the erasure of Mr B's moral turpitude can only serve to imply that Pamela's virtuousness was at best an illusion, at worst a cultivated pretence to promote her social advancement. We do not necesarily need to believe that Pamela is either a hypocrite or 'a subtle, artful little gypsey' (Vol. I, p. 19) the real problem is that with the disappearance of moral danger and Richardson's dramatic struggle between innocence and all encompassing, deeply menacing forces of evil, the novel itself begins to ring hollow. It is as if Little Red Riding Hood found she had made a mistake in thinking her granny was a wolf and found that it really was her dear old granny all along. The contradictions in *Pamela* are not just produced by Richardson's desire to reward virtue – they also are influenced by the contemporary conviction that a benevolent and kindly God would not wish to do his faithful servants harm. Yet for Richardson, as for many of his readers, such a moral vision was ultimately unsatisfying. For virtue to be truly virtue it would have to suffer without even the prospect of relief.

Clarissa, Pamela's successor was to be just such a novel. Virtue, far from being rewarded was effectively punished; a scenario which might seem to call in to question the justice of a Christian God. Yet Richardson, a determinedly didactic writer, realised that despite *Pamela's* great success it had not really been on the right wavelength as far as his readers were concerned. The suggestion that Pamela was more likely to be virtuous because of her humble origins had not gone down well, but perhaps more significantly it encountered a pervasive scepticism, perhaps not very surprising in the wake of Walpole, about the very possibility of virtue in general. It was all too easy to see Pamela as an ambitious, designing minx who achieved her objective of rising in society, thus not so much contradicting the spirit of the age as reinforcing it. So with *Clarissa* Richardson was even more determined to create a character who would gain absolutely nothing from being virtuous and whose motives could not be impugned or called into question. This meant that *Clarissa*, had to be a tragedy in some sense – even if Aristotle had precluded the notion of a totally faultless protagonist, and it also meant that Clarissa had to enjoy a high social status since this would make her subsequent fall all the more conspicuous. Indeed Clarissa's status and reputation provoke the resentment both of her relatives and of Lovelace. Her family find the independence and wealth, which derives from her grandfather's legacy intolerable. Lovelace as an overweening male and a rake is ultimately driven by the desire to humble Clarissa before he can possibly contemplate marriage. Whereas *Pamela* was, in many ways a new fictional departure, the shadow of the classical tradition always looms over *Clarissa*. This is particularly evident when Clarissa herself cites some lines from Dryden and Lee's *Oedipus* as having a special pertinence to her own predicament:

> It were an impiety to adopt the following lines, because it would be throwing upon the decrees of Providence a fault too much my own. But often do I revolve them, for the sake of the general similitude which they bear to my unhappy yet undesigned error.

> To you, great god! I make my last appeal:
> Or clear my virtues, or my crimes reveal.
> If wand'ring in the maze of life I run,
> And backward tread the steps I sought to shun.

Impute my errors to your own decree;
My FEET are guilty, but my HEART is free. (p. 568)

Although Richardson is conscious of the dangers of invoking such
a parallel, which, at a later point in the narrative, might imply
that God had in some sense willingly connived at her downfall
at the hands of Lovelace, it is nevertheless highly significant since
it helps to explain how it is possible for Clarissa to be entirely
virtuous despite having made what might well be regarded as a
series of serious errors of judgement. How, for example, could
she regard Solmes – certainly a physically unattractive and mercenary individual – as a 'monster' and go to such lengths to avoid
marriage to him when the word certainly fits Rochester, the man
who callously and deliberately rapes her much better. Richardson
shuts his eyes to the Sophoclean implication that Oedipus is
brought down by overweening pride and chooses rather to focus
on the obscurity of the circumstances among which he makes
his fatal and fated decisions. Through the example of Clarissa
Richardson wanted to represent virtue not as an immobile, moral
effigy but as a living principle in action, but he could only do
this on the assumption that it was possible for Clarissa to remain
virtuous despite making mistakes. She is virtue unalloyed throughout and the fact that she is caught in a web of worldly
circumstances and deceptive appearances for Richardson only
highlights her extraordinary fidelity and purity. *Clarissa* is a kind
of elaborated and impassioned metacommentary both on *Pamela*,
the reception of Pamela and on what her fate symbolises: the
fact that the vast majority of people are extraordinarily reluctant
to acknowledge that virtue is real and to recognise it when they
see it. Lovelace cannot be allowed to marry Clarissa precisely
because he is the epitomy of all this – it would be the wedding
of scepticism and faith.

Richardson created considerable problems for himself through
his use of the Restoration icon of the rake as the adversary and
antagonist for Clarissa. If the moral seriousness of Mr B's challenge to Pamela was damaged by his general ineffectualness and
lack of high seriousness this would not be so in the case of
Lovelace. It is important to recognise that Richardson intends
Lovelace not just to be a seducer of women but a principled
seducer, a man so dedicated to his self-appointed task of putting
women in their social and sexual place – underneath – that he

can never be deflected from his aim. In this implacable contest his honour and reputation is just as much at stake – perhaps even more at stake – as that of the woman he pursues. In some general sense of Lovelace is the literary descendent of such dramatic precursors as Dorimant in Etheredge's *The Man of Mode* yet Richardson, in the new genre that he has created, finds it hard to evade the connotations and morality of Restoration comedy. If Dorimant, the rake, is cynical and ruthless in his exploitation of women, he is nevertheless presented as an attractive figure: handsome, witty, disarmingly honest in a world where vanity and self-deception are the norm. The perversity of the rake is indicated by Mrs Loveit's charge that he takes 'more pleasure in the ruin of a woman's reputation than in the endearments of her love' yet the portrait is softened by Dorimant's aside in the presence of Harriet:

> I love her, and dare not let her know it: I fear she has an ascendant o'er me, and may revenge the wrongs I have done her sex.

Although arguably Dorimant never really reforms the implication that in the game of love women have the advantage, it is still there. The implication is that men need to harden their hearts in order not to be victimised by a woman's charms and that sooner or later even the most cynical of rakes will be transfixed by the arrow of Eros and finally mend his ways for good. Richardson in his representation of Lovelace was also ready to confirm, that the key to an understanding of the rake was that, deep down, he found women threatening. Even the haughty Lovelace can say of Clarissa: 'I fear her as much as I love her' (p. 734) and lament the passion that has produced his weakness: 'How does this damned love unman me.' (p. 742) For Lovelace sexual relations always involve questions of power. Referring to Anna Howe's relationship with Hickman he says: 'Power makes such a one wanton – she despises the man she can govern.' (p. 866) Nevertheless, Richardson had little sympathy with the male neurosis that the rake represented. He recognised that such boorish and aggressive forms of behaviour were unjust, precisely because they priviledged the male and marginalised women. Richardson was at the sharp end of a movement in the eighteenth century to feminise the upper echelons of society by creating codes of conduct that would place women on a more equitable footing. Yet, although significant progress was made we must also recognise the extent to which inequalities persisted under the guise of promoting civilised behaviour. For example, the notion that gentlemen should be allowed to indulge in bawdy conversation after dinner over brandy and cigars from which women would be excluded was in theory a concession to gentility, but in practise it was a way of symbolically consigning women to an inferior social status. So the rake is not simply a stereotype or type but becomes the epitome of a social world in which the male is dominant. Richardson challenged this. But his general anxiety about the reception of *Clarissa* indicates he was uncertain as to how this would be received and anxious that his novel would be misread. Before publication he sent out sections to a variety of correspondents of both sexes, ranging from such literary lights as Edward Young and Aaron Hill to a number of women friends. Undoubtedly Lovelace was the central problem since the reader's view of Lovelace would also affect their view of Clarissa. In fact the problem of the rake was also that, perhaps predictably, it involved a privileging of the male character. There was the temptation, perhaps even the necesssity of using Lovelace as a window through which to view Clarissa rather than the other way round. For Richardson Lovelace, behind his glamorous and ingratiating exterior was unquestionably a heartless, calculating and ultimately evil man who would certainly be damned even if Clarissa could find it in her heart to forgive him. Mark Kinkead Weekes's suggestion that Lovelace implies 'loveless' is convincing.[5] Yet for most of Richardson's readers a quite contrary analysis prevailed. Certainly, on the surface Lovelace was the cool and cynical seducer, but they believed that deep down here was a man who passionately and sincerely loved Clarissa in spite of himself and his philosophy. If only Clarissa had been able to give him some sign that she cared for him, if only she could have briefly humbled herself to give him some small shred of encouragement, a catastrophe so disastrous for both could certainly have been averted. So *Clarissa* became a tale of star-crossed lovers, who could and should have become united.

In *Clarissa* Richardson continued to stress how deep were the obstacles to the attainment of virtue either among the aristocracy or among the commercial and upwardly mobile middle class, although his argument was less likely to cause offence when his heroine was a lady of independent fortune and no virtuous servant girls were in the offing. As far as the aristocracy was concerned, as represented by Lovelace and his cronies, Richardson was concerned to show that their lack of any well founded code of conduct could be traced back to their defective education. If they were out of control now, this was simply because they had always been out of control. Mr Hickman confides to Lovelace:

> I see more and more that there are not in the world, with all our conceited pride, narrower-souled wretches than we rakes and libertines are. And I'll tell thee how it comes about.
>
> Our early love of roguery makes us generally run away from instruction; and so we become mere smatterers in the sciences we are put to learn; and because we *will* know no more, think there is no more to be *known*.
>
> With an infinite deal of vanity, unreined imaginations, and no judgements at all we next commence *half-wits*; and then think we have the whole field of knowledge in possession, and despise everyone who takes more pains and is more serious than ourselves, as phlegmatic stupid fellows, who have no taste for the most poignant pleasures of life. (pp. 1130–1)

The rake is an arrogant, thoughtless hedonist whose most striking characteristic is a total blindness to his own considerable defects and limitations. The whimsical, tyrannical and uncontrollable nature of such a man as Lovelace is well brought out by Ann Howe, who traces it back to his childhood:

> From his cradle, as I may say, as an *only child*, and a *boy*, humoursome, spoiled, mischievous; the governor of his governors.
>
> A libertine in his riper years, hardly regardful of appearances; and despising the sex in general for the faults of particulars of it who made themselves too cheap to him. (p. 498)

Yet the commercial middle classes are no more inclined to virtue than the aristocracy since although they are prudent and disciplined their preoccupation with enriching themselves blinds them to the existence of genuinely virtuous and moral behaviour. The entire Harlowe family is prepared to collude in enforcing Clarissa's marriage to Mr Solmes, against her will and her express intentions, simply because they regard the match as commercially advantageous. Significantly Clarissa herself is indifferent. She believes that it is goodness rather than status or wealth that makes for greatness. She is

> '. . . fully persuaded that happiness and riches are two things, and very seldom met together.' (p. 106)

She finds Lovelace 'a base low-hearted wretch' despite 'all his pride of ancestry.' (p. 990) For Clarissa you are what you are and in ascertaining what a person is only virtue or merit can count. As she says to Lovelace quite early on: 'You are boasting of your merits, sir, let merit be your boast: nothing else can attract me.' (p. 393)

Yet, what was virtue? Writing *Clarissa* in the aftermath of *Pamela* Richardson was certainly aware that the task of advocating virtue was more complex than he had originally recognised, since in addition to promoting it he had to justify it as well. It was not just that under Walpole the practice of virtue had come to seem rather preposterous, when even the ostensibly corrupted could plausibly argue that there was nothing wrong in taking money for doing what they sincerely believed was the right thing anyway. The acceptance of bribes could seem positively patriotic. What was perhaps more telling than such philosophical opportunism was Bernard Mandeville's pointed demolition of virtue. Mandeville claimed that in any prosperous commercial society virtue was simply a nuisance and an impediment, but this pragmatic reasoning left virtue itself intact.

Mandeville went further in that he suggested that virtue was the product of political ideology:

> . . . the Moral Virtues are the Political Offspring which Flattery begot on Pride.

So virtue far from being the one thing that remained unsullied by the system could be placed in inverted commas and regarded as the most characteristic product of it. In a rather different argumentative move – since Mandeville loved to pile arguments high, supermarket style – Mandeville pretended to believe in virtue but simply asked to see practical exemplifications of it – a challenge which he was confident his opponents would be unable to meet:

> I am willing to pay Adoration to Virtue wherever I can meet
> with it, with a Proviso, that I shall not be oblig'd to admit as
> such where I can see no Self-denial, or to judge of Mens Sen-
> timents from their Words, where I have their Lives before me.[6]

Doubtless even Jesus Christ, a man who had prodigally distributed
wine at a wedding and made conspicuous use of expensive oint-
ments, would have failed to pass Mandeville's test for virtue.
The general spirit of Mandeville's cynicism is echoed by Lovelace.
Lovelace, like Mandeville, sees Clarissa's virtue as stemming from
pride:

> Don't tell me that virtue and principle are her guides on this
> occasion; 'tis pride, a greater pride than my own, that governs
> her. (p. 868)

Lovelace also argues that since the possibility of virtue is so remote
as to be virtually unthinkable he has been peculiarly unfortunate as to be the one man who should happen to cross the path
of the one woman who actually exemplifies it:

> Why then were there not more examples of a virtue so immovable?
> Or, why was this singular one to fall to my lot. (p. 972)

In Lovelace's perverse reasoning the rake simply acts on what
he regards as the general principles of human nature and of
woman's disposition so implicitly the fact that Clarissa is an exception does not actually put the rake's credo in question. But in
mocking and criticising Lovelace's complacency Richardson himself strangely confirms Lovelace's view, since they both believe
that Clarissa's virtue is exceptional and that it stands in stark
contrast to the general spirit of the age. Clarissa was made to be
an icon of virtue in an age of corruption and so what characterises her above all is the spirit of resistance. If as Belford says:

> She was born to adorn the age she was given to ... (p. 555)

she can only adorn it by not being of it. Mandeville of course
would remain unimpressed seeing Clarissa as yet another instance
of a virtue constructed in language rather than exemplified in
action. But we should remember that Lovelace says:

Such irresistable proof of the love of virtue for its own sake – did I never hear of, nor meet with in all my reading. (p. 902)

So Richardson has remedied the moral deficiencies of his age by offering a paragon who can serve as the starting point for moral renewal.

As a heroine Clarissa was even more irresistable than Pamela. Clarissa was pure, oppressed, unambiguous, unmanipulative. In *Clarissa* questions of chastity and rape become allegorically significant in a way that would have been impossible in the earlier novel. Clarissa seems genuinely to stand for something, because she is absolutely determined not to allow others to dictate to her or to allow them to set her agenda, no matter what price she must pay for standing out against them. The issue is not just the position of women in society, important as that is, but the very existence of freedom itself. In the nightmarish, claustrophobic and all encompassing world of the novel, in which nothing is ever quite what it seems, and where the metropolis of London seems to have become a place where the unspeakable has become perfectly normal, Richardson seems to go beyond the case of Clarissa herself to underline the dangers of uncontested governmental power. Clarissa, imprisoned in a brothel protests:

> I have no patience . . . to find myself a slave, a prisoner in a vile house – Tell me, sir, in so many words, tell me, whether it be, or be not your intention to permit me to quit it? To permit me the freedom which is my birthright as an English subject? (p. 934)

Faced with the ruthless and uncontrolled exercise of power Clarissa is determined, courageous, unflinching, uncompromising.

Yet there remains a nagging doubt, as to whether despite all this, Clarissa is really virtuous enough. There are quite a number of question marks hanging over her. Could she be virtuous if she was not prudent? Could she legitimately be regarded as a paragon when she had made so many mistakes and errors of judgement. Again, even contemporary readers were disposed to find Clarissa cold and unsympathetic. Lovelace's assessment of her as proud, self-righteous and self-deluded might evoke a reluctant echo, even where his self-justifying rhetoric was all too apparent. Clarissa, because of the intensity of her predicament, inevitably appears negative and narcissistic but her case also shows how difficult it had become to imagine a boundless, outgoing generosity of spirit. Virtue, Richardson concluded, far from being rewarded, would be hounded from the realm.

What made Richardson's coupling of a woman's virtue with virtue itself so provocative was that it seemed to reverse the priority of the sexes. In the classical tradition where the concept originated, virtue had traditionally been ascribed not just to men but to men of high rank and status. By contrast, to speak of the virtue of Pamela, a servant girl, in any larger sense than that of feminine chastity, must seem distinctly anti-climactic. Moreover, what was at stake was not just what Pamela represented but her very claims on the reader's attention. Many an aristocratic reader may well have wondered what all the fuss was about. Of these, Henry Fielding was certainly one. His initial indignant response to what he saw as Richardson's celebration of the hypocritical wiles of a determined husband hunter was to jeer and mock. In his parody *Shamela* (1741) he has Pamela pulling down her Stays to expose as much as possible of her bosom and practising her airs in front of the mirror before sitting down to read a chapter from *The Whole Duty of Man.* For Fielding Pamela's (and Richardson's) canting, self-righteous morality stems from the puritan insistence that the route to salvation is exclusively through faith and not through good works – thus Parson Williams' sermon on the text 'Be not righteous overmuch' and Pamela's gloss 'tis not what we do, but what we believe, that must save us.' Pamela typifies what Fielding sees as the low church heresy, where the belief that you belong to a virtuous community takes the place of any need to actually be virtuous.

Fielding may have hoped and believed that the boos, jeers, hisses and catcalls of *Shamela* would drive Richardson from the boards, but it was not to be. Richardson, humble and unworthy as he seemed, had become the benchmark for a new type of writing. Fielding was to devote the greater part of his literary career responding to the challenge that Richardson had set, in the process transforming himself from a writer of squibs, parodies, jests and anarchic satires into something resembling a moralist and certainly a writer with a deeply thought out and firmly held point of view.

Yet in his first novel, *Joseph Andrews* (1742) the anarchic humorist is certainly more prominent. *Pamela* can be debunked by a simple reversal of the sexes – for what could be more ludicrous than for Joseph Andrews, Pamela's alleged brother, to respond to Lady Booby's amorous solicitations with the ponderous rebuttal.

I can't see why her having no Virtue should be a Reason against my having any; or why, because I am a Man, or because I am poor, my Virtue must be subservient to her Pleasures. (p. 41)

A response that makes the lady so indignant she insists on his dismissal. However, Fielding himself recognises that the jest of the chaste man cannot, with propriety be milked any more, and for the rest of the novel the ostensible hero plays second fiddle; Sancho Panza to the Don Quixote of Parson Adams. It would seem that, despite the slapstick and the custard pies, the theological debate, initiated in *Shamela*, is continued in *Joseph Andrews*. Martin Battestin has suggested that the novel reflects the latitudinarian emphasis on good works, as epitomised by such preachers as Tillotson, Barrow, Hoadly and Samuel Price.[7] Thus, we may see Parson Adams, who is virtuous, trusting, benevolent, indeed 'generous, friendly, and brave to an excess' as displaying a conspicuous dedication to good works and altruistic actions in a age that is little disposed to acknowledge them. Adams, symptomatically, acts out of an instinctive feeling as to what is right. It is this that makes him appear naive, simplistic and unworldly,

. . . as entirely ignorant of the Ways of this World as an Infant just entered into it could possibly be. (p. 23)

So it is perhaps entirely appropriate that the good parson should be unable to find a publisher for his sermons. Fielding seems to have taken on board some of the arguments then current about the benefits of trade on the one hand and the dangers of luxury on the other. For Adams finds himself called upon to denounce the

. . . Palaces, Equipages, Dress, Furniture, rich Dainties, and vast Fortunes (p. 82)

of some minsters of the Church and to challenge the publican who affirms that trade is the supreme good:

Of what use would Learning be in a Country without Trade? What would all you Parsons do to clothe your Backs and feed your Bellies

by saying

Who clothes you with Piety, Meekness, Humility, Charity, Patience, and all the other Christian virtues. (p. 183)

He also has to urge the supreme importance of charity on the heartless lawyer, Peter Pounce, who pretends to believe that

. . . the Distresses of Mankind are mostly imaginary and it would be rather Folly than Goodness to relieve them. (p. 274)

So in theory Adams's unsophisticated goodness of heart stands as an indictment of the heartlessness of the age. Certainly the good parson is only too ready to wade into action with his stout crabstick on behalf of any good cause that presents itself, but it would be a reader with a heart of stone who would claim that more edification than humour was produced by these encounters. For although Adams ultimately comes off best at the dinner where he is made fun of and cruelly mocked he, nevertheless, appears pretty ridiculous on quite a number of other occasions. At the inn Adams gets into a fight which leads to the hostess pouring a pan of hog's blood over his head. When a hare pursued by hounds is tracked down to within a few yards of the parson, the hounds remove his wig as well as a large part of his cassock. In another altercation, Adams, without his breeches is saturated in urine and has a mop pushed into his face so that Fielding later comments:

It is not perhaps easy to describe the Figure of Adams; he had risen in such a violent Hurry, that he had on neither Breeches nor Stockings; nor had he taken from his Head a red spotted Hankerchief, which by Night bound his Wig, that was turned inside out, around his Head. He had on his torn Cassock and his Greatcoat; but, as the remainder of his Cassock hung down below his Greatcoat, so did a small Stripe of white, or rather whitish, Linnen appear below that; to which we may add the several Colours which appeared on his Face, where a long Pissburnt Beard served to retain the Liquor of the Stone Pot, and that of a blacker hue which distilled from the Mop. (p. 270)

Finally, Adams, hearing Beau Didapper in Mrs Slipslop's bedroom and believing her virtue to be in danger, rushes in to the chamber completely naked only to be confronted by an aghast Lady Booby. Parson Adams is unmistakably a figure of fun and his moral significance is correspondingly reduced. At this point Fielding's fiction is still as anarchic and undisciplined as his drama.

The problem with attributing latitudinarian views to Fielding is not just that it may involve taking Fielding rather more earnestly than he deserves, but that it may involve assumptions about the general laxity of latitudinarian views which are quite unjustified. Fielding was himself often regarded by his contemporaries as one who professed a rather easy and accommodating morality, but we should not therefore assume that the latitudiarian divines were characterised by their desire to offer their followers a great deal of latitude. The stress of good works did not imply that a few benevolent actions here and there could serve to validate and atone for a life punctuated by dissolute and irresponsible episodes. On the contrary good works meant precisely godly living and virtuous conduct. The idea of an easy and convenient morality is the very thing that Tillotson severely criticises in his sermon 'Of the necessity of good works' when he says:

> The plain truth of the matter is, men had rather religion should be anything, than what indeed it is, the thwarting and crossing of our vicious inclinations, the curing of our evil and corrupt affections; the due care and government of our unruly appetites and passions, the sincere endeavour and constant practice of all holiness and virtue in our lives; and therefore they had much rather have something that might handsomely palliate and excuse their evil inclinations, than to extirpate them and cut them up.[8]

Moreover the latitudinarians could be just as hostile to the scurrilities and immoralities of the stage, of which Fielding was a major exponent, as puritans like Jeremy Collier and William Law. In his sermon on the text 'Evil communications corrupt good manners' Tillotson made a point of condemning the plays of the day:

But as the stage now is, they are intolerable, and not fit to be permitted in a civilized, much less Christian country. They do most notoriously minister both to infidelity and vice.[9]

Just because Fielding approved of the latitudinarians it does not necessarily mean that they would have approved of him.

The real quarrel between Richardson and Fielding was not over points of theology but over the correct relationship between men and women. Moreover their common point of departure was the representation of the sexes in Restoration comedy, which in the early eighteenth century was still the dominant literary genre. For both writers the common point of departure was the figure of the rake, as epitomised in real life by the figure of the Earl of Rochester, and as refined and glamorised on the stage by Etherege as Dorimant in *The Man of Mode*. Richardson made it quite explicit that the rake he condemned as Lovelace was based on Rochester. Fielding's own more empathic relation with the libertine tradition becomes overt at the end of *Tom Jones* when Tom insists that he could never be unfaithful to Sophia and asserts his undying fidelity. But he claims he can offer her a still greater pledge of his constancy than his word and by way of proof shows her her own image in the mirror:

> There, behold it there, in that lovely Figure, in that Face, that Shape, those Eyes, that Mind which shines through those Eyes; can the Man who shall be in Possession of these be inconstant? Impossible! my Sophia; they would fix a Dorimant, a Lord Rochester. (p. 973)

At such a moment Tom Jones, though doubtless more innocent and more vulnerable than such rakish precursors, nevertheless becomes a latterday approximation to the rake reformed. What the rake epitomises is the imbalance in the relations between men and women. The rake epitomises an ideal of masculine assertion and dominance. Proud, self-centred, controlled and somewhat heartless he regards women as pleasures that are to be sampled and tossed aside. The rake despises women and although he may behave towards them with affected chivalry he speaks cuttingly about them behind their back. For Richardson and later for Fanny Burney such behaviour is boorish, inconsiderate and always potentially vicious. It is unfair to women who, denied both dignity and personal freedom, are always at risk of being compromised and degraded whatever their social status. So there is a need not only for women to be granted greater respect but for men to develop qualities often perceived as feminine – to become more sensitive, more considerate, more responsive to the feelings of others.

At his glittering best – as Dorimant in *The Man of Mode* – the rake epitomises an ideal of manliness. His merits are thrown into sharp relief by the contrasting figure of the fop, Sir Fopling Flutter. The fop, because he is so preoccupied with the latest Paris fashions, with particular affectations and forms of speech, is a mere shell of a human being. Characteristically Sir Fopling, at Dorimant's, complains that there is no mirror: 'In a glass a man may entertain himself.' to which Dorimant responds: 'The shadow of himself indeed.' The fop, by contrast with the rake, is not interested in women. He is effeminate, narcissistic, self-centred. Dorimant, in pursuing a number of women simultaneously, Loveit, Belinda, Harriet, may seem both thoughtless and heartless also, but in his defence Etherege would argue that they are also pursuing him. The rake is manly, witty, attractive and socially adroit and if he seeks to preserve his independence women can only respect him for it. If he is inconstant this can be attributed to human nature. Dorimant justifies himself by saying:

> We are not masters of our own affections, our inclinations daily alter; now we love pleasure, and so anon we shall dote on business: human frailty will have it so, and who can help it.

But if the rake seems like a butterfly flitting casually from flower to flower this is only an illusion in which he shares. For ultimately even the cynical rake is susceptible to Cupid's darts and the the irresistible passion of love. When he finally meets the right woman the mask of irresponsibility will be laid aside and he will become a reformed man.

What was disturbing about *Pamela* was that the effortless superiority of the male was overturned. Whether ludicrously disguised or coldly plotting Mr B seemed fairly contemptible, yet having him recalled to the path of virtue by a servant girl and lectured on his conduct seemed scarcely better. For Fielding, certainly, masculine honour and dignity were at stake. Even Nicholas Rowe, perhaps Richardson's most significant precursor, in presenting the sufferings that women were exposed to at the hands of unscrupulous men, had never questioned masculine preeminence or that virtue was essentially a male prerogative. Calista, the heroine of *The Fair Penitent*, who is sexually assaulted by Lothario, the rival to Altamont her intended husband, is one of the first characters in literature to explicitly deplore the condition of women, claiming

How hard is the Condition of our Sex,
Thro' ev'ry State of Life the Slaves of Man?
In all the dear delightful Days of Youth,
A rigid Father dictates to our Wills,
And deals our Pleasure with a scanty Hand;
To his, the Tyrant Husband's Reign succeeds
Proud with opinion of superior Reason,
He holds Domestick Bus'ness and Devotion
All we are capable to know, and shuts us,
Like Cloyster'd Ideots, from the World's Acquaintance,
And all the Joys of Freedom; wherefore are we
Born with high Souls, but to assert our selves,
Shake off this vile Obedience they exact,
And claim an equal Empire o'er the World?

yet, the very same Calista can subsequently concede that she is not the moral equal of her father Sciolto. When Sciolto asks her why she turned to folly she replies:

Because my Soul was rudely drawn from yours;
A poor imperfect Copy of my Father,
Where Goodness, and the strength of manly Virtue,
Was thinly planted, and the idle Void
Filled up with light Belief, and easie Fondness;
It was, because I lov'd, and was a Woman.

The virtuous man, on the Roman model, is strong, unwavering, constant. He suppresses personal inclination and rejects the life of ease in order to follow a difficult path of duty, self-sacrifice and public spiritedness. Implicitly it will be very diffficult if not impossible for a woman to be virtuous in this sense. So, from a certain point of view, Richardson in recasting virtue in woman's image and by making chastity such a significant part of the definition, has not just devalued virtue but positively trivialised it. Moreover, the transposition was doubly unfair, for manly men were naturally interested in pursuing the fair sex, yet it seemed that they could only be regarded as virtuous if they were also chaste. Interestingly enough Fielding was not alone in feeling that virtue was a matter that really had nothing to do with the relations between the sexes. Addison had already raised the question in his play, *Cato*. Cato himself is seen as austere, rigid and puritanical but Marcus his son is concerned that his love for Lucia may undermine his capacity for virtue. He says to his brother:

> Portius, thou know'st my soul in all its weakness,
> Then pr'ythee spare me on the tender side,
> Indulge me but in love, my other passions
> Shall rise and fall by virtue's nicest rules.

But Portius is quick to reassure him:

> When love's well-timed, 'tis not a fault to love,
> The strong, the brave, the virtuous and the wise.
> Sink in the soft captivity together.

So the virtuous man may be hard and soft at the same time. Such a conclusion was one that would certainly have recommended itself to Fielding, who very much wanted to believe that Tom Jones in being amorous could nevertheless be virtuous.

Nevertheless, Fielding recognised that in attempting to answer Richardson's virtuous heroine with a virtuous male hero he was embarking on a project that was riddled with paradoxes. It would not be enough to have a hero who was finally converted to the path of righteousness after sinning all the way through, since a person would have no intrinsic merit and would lack the steadfastness generally attributed to the virtuous heroes of antiquity. He conceded that the writers of recent theatrical comedy were inherently implausible in finally transforming 'Notorious Rogues' into 'very worthy Gentlemen' without any attempt to explain or justify such 'monstrous Change and Incongruity'. (p. 406)

Yet a paradigm of virtue in the classical mould would lack credibility or interest while a virtuous prig, for those raised on Wycherley, Etherege and Congreve, would seem, dull, unsympathetic, too untouched by the complexity of the modern urban world. So Fielding's hero, though in some very general sense virtuous, would certainly have to be fallible, while Fielding himself would have to play a complex double game; on the one hand insisting that his novel was a moral discourse or it was nothing, yet nudging the reader to excuse his hero's various peccadilloes and indiscretions. Doubtless, Tom Jones should be prudent but the fact is – he isn't! In a way the fact that he lacks prudence may be an advantage in that it may serve to dramatise his more positive qualities – for virtue without prudence must surely be better than the contrary, exemplified by Blifil: prudence without virtue. Moreover the handsome, dashing and impulsive hero has the advantage over the paragon of virtue in that it is in the power of the heroine, and the heroine alone, to forgive his transgressions. So Fielding is thus able to insist in his prefatory dedication that the book is intended to display 'the Beauty of Virtue' (p. 7), while at the same time remarking that Tom Jones 'bad as he is, must serve for the Heroe of this History'. (p. 119) Insofar as Fielding was influenced by such latitudinarian divines as Tillotson and Isaac Barrow this was not simply because they spoke of the natural goodness of man but even more because they also acknowledged the inevitability – and naturalness – of human fallibility. So Isaac Barrow in his sermon 'Of Self-Conceit' observes:

> In fine, every man is in some kind and degree bad, sinful, vile; it is as natural for us to be so, as to be frail, to be sickly, to be mortal: there are some bad dispositions common to all, and which no man can put off without his flesh; there are some, to which every man (from his temper, inclination, and constitution of body or soul) is peculiarly subject, which by no care and pain can be quite extirpated, but will afford during life perpetual matter of conflict and exercise to curb them: conceit therefore of our virtue is very foolish. And it breedeth many great mischiefs.[10]

Consequently, Tom Jones, as Fielding perceives it, represents the possibility of virtue even if that possibility has yet to be realised, whereas Blifil who appears virtuous already is fatally flawed by his selfishness and self-centredness. This vital difference is early on grasped by Sophia, who justifies her name through a perception that Blifil was 'strongly attached to the Interest only of one single Person' (p. 165), which is also the mark of her own remarkable maturity and discernment. In the course of the novel Tom performs a remarkable number of altruistic actions: he sells his little horse and Bible to aid Black George the poacher turned gamekeeper and his family; he saves Sophia from falling from his horse in the course of which he breaks his arm; he rescues both the Man of the Hill and Mrs Waters; he forgives a man who tries to rob him and subsequently gives him money which he badly needs himself. So Jones is certainly the benevolent hero but, strangely for so impulsive and spontaneous a character, Fielding also proposed him as a stoical one. Tom knowing his own inferior social position, tries to suppress his love for Sophia. He

> ... endeavoured to smother a Flame in his own Bosom, which like the famous Spartan Theft, was preying upon and consuming his very Vitals.

He is demoralised and humiliated by his rejection by Mr Allworthy, who expels him from his house and banishes him from his sight. We are meant to feel that the sentence is harsh especially for one who believes himself an orphan. Jones is subsequently exposed to the trials and temptations of London and to the torment of imprisonment for attempted murder. If Fielding asks us to respect his hero it is not simply for his honesty and good nature, but for his courage, steadfastness and determination. The implication is that if he has been forged in the fire of adversity this is finally proof, regardless of his actual legitimacy, not just that he is a worthy husband for Sophia but that his pretensions to virtue have been validated.

Tom's virtue, if virtue it is, is the more conspicuous because it figures in a world where expediency is the norm. Fielding's own career, as both supporter and opponent of the Walpole government, as irreverent satirist and sober justice, indicates that he was not unaffected by the temper of the times, but it also unexpectedly suggests that his respect for a character like Tom, who does not allow himself to be deflected by such considerations, however overwhelming they may appear, was certainly genuine. Although Sir John Hawkins forcefully objected to what he perceived as the laxity of Fielding's morality, claiming

> He was the inventor of that cant-phrase, goodness of heart, which is every day used as a substitute for probity, and means

little more than the virtue of a horse or dog; in short, he has done more towards corrupting the rising generation than any writer we know of.[11]

and although Fielding was undoubtedly the inventor of a moral system in which every transgression figures as a mere peccadillo, we need also to consider that at the time Fielding was writing Tom Jones might well have been in danger of being perceived as improbably punctilious and altruistic. Fielding certainly saw Tom as a spontaneous and simple figure, bearing with him something of the spirit of a bygone age. Tom Jones is never quixotic, yet the spirit of Cervantes that hovered over many pages of *Joseph Andrews* is also evident at certain moments in the later novel, as when Tom rewards the highwayman who has robbed him, or when he consoles Blifil after Alworthy's rejection of him, despite all the harm that Blifil has done him. Fielding does not simply follow Shaftesbury in recommending benevolence he writes in an age of self-centred behaviour, where such conduct does not seems natural as Shaftesbury had supposed but positively perverse. Fielding's somewhat surprising concern with virtue must been seen in the context of Mandeville's celebration of private vices as public benefits in his *Fable of the Bees* and of the distinction that he there made between virtue and honour:

The Reason why there are so few Men of real Virtue, and so many of real Honour, is, because all the Recompense a Man has of a Virtuous Action, is the Pleasure of doing it, which most People reckon but poor Pay; but the Self denial a Man of Honour submits to in one Appetite, is immediately rewarded by the Satisfaction he receives from another, and when he abates of his Avarice, or any other Passion is doubly repaid to his Pride: Besides, Honour gives large Grains of Allowance, and Virtue none.[12]

A major theme in *Tom Jones* is the hollowness of the honour code and the fact that a whole gallery of characters from Lady Bellaston and Lord Fellamar to Fitzpatrick and Dowling to Blifil, Thwackum and Square, ask for a respect and approbation to which they are simply not entitled. The honour system corrupts even the servants and underlings, like the proprietors of inns and the aptly named Mrs Honour, whose exaggerated sense of their own dignity is intimately linked to those they wait on. The absurdity is aptly reflected in the case of Nell Gwynn's footman who got into a fight when someone called his mistress a whore:

'You Blockhead', replied Mrs. Gwynn 'at this Rate you must fight every Day of your Life; why, you Fool, all the World knows it.' 'Do they?', cries the Fellow, in a muttering Voice, after he had shut the Coach Door, 'they shan't call me a Whore's Footman for all that.' (p. 605)

Virtue in some fairly flexible sense is nevertheless important because it implies a model of personal integrity that is in danger of being lost altogether. *Tom Jones* is often read as a kind of pastoral in which Tom and Sophia, the innocent lovers in some rural idyll find themselves crossed and parted by hostile circumstance only to be reunited. Yet the world of the novel is actually quite insecure. The Jacobite rebellion is in full swing. There are many different causes and focuses for loyalty as Patridge leans to Jacobitism while seeking to restore Tom as Allworthy's true heir, while Squire Weston expostulates:

I had rather be any Thing than a Courtier, and a Presbyterian, and a Hannoverian too, as some People, I believe, are. (p. 276)

What the world of *Tom Jones* lacks is any genuine principle of legitimacy, both on a political and on a personal level. Squire Western claims to a kindly father when he is actually a boorish tyrant, and even the benevolent Allworthy dispenses as much injustice as justice. What we see in *Tom Jones* is a society destabilised by political corruption and by complex internal divisions, where there is no longer any genuine principle of authority. Significantly one group that Fielding is disposed to praise is that of the gypsies where vice is shamed and discredited and where there is still a genuine sense of community. If Blifil is a pretender to Allworthy's throne, Tom Jones, as the bastard son is his sister, is scarcely more legitimate. The world of *Tom Jones* is a world where nothing can be trusted or relied upon and where even a slightly tarnished or sullied virtue can still communicate the integrity of genuine metal. Tom Jones, we feel, is a man for all seasons, an individual who can carry forward the banner of virtue, not in the realms of chivalric legends but in face of the bemusements and blandishments of an actual world.

But Tom Jones's ability to embody such a virtue is undoubtedly bound up with his apparently lowly origins. The fact that Tom is a foundling makes it possible for him to represent qualities that are natural, spontaneous and free in a way that he could not possibly do if he were simply the son of a country squire. This is not to say that Tom Jones is necessarily to be perceived as of lowly birth, even before the secret of his actual origins are finally revealed. The appeal and fascination of Tom even for readers of his own day lies rather in the way in which he is set free from the constraints of convention: that he can be both more wayward and impulsive than the typical gentleman – who is after all not just defined by birth but by his gentlemanly education – and at the same time more – refined and courteous in his manners in a way that we would not expect from one of humble birth. The real significance of Tom Jones is that he exemplifies Fielding's distrust of education and his belief that morality cannot be taught. For Fielding to educate is to spoil. Ironically there is much in Fielding's emphasis that even Locke, the determined advocate of education, might seem to agree with, as when he says:

Everyone's natural genius should be carried as far as it could.[13]

The difference is that Locke is convinced that education really can improve. For Fielding education is always an education in externals and the tutor is one who promotes an improvement in external appearances, then either does not affect the core of personal identity, or if it indeed does so, does so only for the worse. Since Thwackum and Square, the educators of Blifil and Tom, preach one thing and practice another, and since they are severe where they should be understanding and tolerant, all they can do is to produce hypocrites. Moreover, Fielding claims that the crucial defect of their several systems is that they fail to allow for 'natural Goodness of Heart'. (p. 129) Worse still, what natural inclination to virtue has not been extinguished in the passage from childhood to manhood will be finally suffocated by the pretensions and prevarications of polite society. So it follows that to be virtuous it is necessary for Tom to be something of an anarchist and to mingle with society's misfits, scapegoats and outcasts – with Black George, poacher turned gamekeeper, Partridge, the teacher cum barber, his putative and surrogate father, with gypsies and highwaymen. It is not so much that such people are them-selves necessarily virtuous or admirable – Partridge is superstitious and cowardly; Black George is unscrupulous – it is more that in such company Tom is freed from the posing and the postures of the gentleman. He is able to act not in obedience to protocol, but in response to the promptings of his heart. Strangely, for Fielding, as for Richardson, virtue is often in distress; but civi-lised society is at the heart of its dilemmas, yet there is a conundrum at the heart of *Tom Jones* that Fielding cannot satis-factorily resolve. In his dedication he argues that he has strongly endeavoured to 'recommend Goodness and Innocence' and to inculcate the maxim that

> Virtue and Innocence can scarcely ever be injured but by Indiscretion. (p. 7)

Yet, Fielding's real claim would seem to be rather that virtue and innocence cannot be injured even by indiscretion. Tom's virtue, like Patridge's naivety, is somehow untouchable, yet if this is so, why should he be greatly concerned about the supposed corrup-tions of the great world? Fielding asks us to believe in a virtue which is constantly being frayed about the edges, but which both remains virtuous and is never once in danger of lapsing into vice.

Clarissa and *Tom Jones* appeared within a year of one another and it is clear that both Richardson and Fielding carefully read one another's work. Fielding openly expressed his admiration for *Clarissa* but Richardson continued to distrust Fielding, seeing in *Tom Jones* an attempt to

> ... whiten a vicious character, and to make Morality bend to his practices ...

though he conceded that Fielding's

> Vein of Humour, and ridicule, which he is master of, might if properly turned, do great service to ye Cause of Virtue.[14]

But despite their differences both writers evidently took on board some of the opinions of the other. In his last novel, *Sir Charles Grandison* (1754) Richardson tacitly acknowledged that his novels had implicitly excluded men from the possibility of achieving virtue by creating a male hero who was a paragon of virtue. In turn, in *Amelia* (1751), Fielding felt compelled to acknowledge that virtue was a rather more arduous matter than it might have seemed to be in *Tom Jones*. In both writers there is a distinct shift in emphasis in attitude and tone. *Grandison*, in which Richardson presented a more optimistic view of human nature, is a sunnier and more optimistic work than its predecessors; whereas *Amelia*, though it still affirms Fielding's faith in the basic goodness of human nature, nevertheless locates it in a world that is distinctly more sombre and demoralising. Both *Amelia* and *Sir Charles Grandison* are thoughtful and deeply considered works, yet neither is a complete success – perhaps because their authors, in their concern to achieve objectivity and balance and in their desire to bring moral issues into the clearest possible focus, in the process lost spontaneity and became stilted. But what both novels unmistakably show is how deeply committed Fielding and Richardson were to the cause of virtue.

In 1748 Fielding became a Justice of the Peace for Westminster and in 1749 Chairman of the Quarter Sessions. *Amelia* reflected this experience. In the courts where he sat Fielding saw many people who were by no means downright villains, who had been brought down and brought there through a combination of their own lack of judgement and misfortune. This confirmed him in his view that it was not human nature itself but social circumstances and social conditioning that were to blame. When even Amelia succumbs to pessimism and suggests

all Mankind almost are Villains in their Hearts.

Dr Harrison expostulates:

Do not make a Conclusion so much to the Dishonour of the great Creator. The Nature of Man is far from being in itself Evil: it abounds with Benevolence, Charity and Pity, coveting Praise and Honour, and shunning Shame and Disgrace. Bad Education, bad Habits, and bad Customs, debauch our Nature, and drive it Headlong as it were into Vice. The Governors of the World, and I am afraid the Priesthood, are answerable for the Badness of it. Instead of discouraging Wickedness to the utmost of their Power, both are apt to connive at it. (pp. 374–5)

What is generally known as evil is the effect of power and ideology. Nevertheless Fielding recognised that to make this argument stick would not be easy. Tom Jones might exemplify a kind of natural innocence but he could not epitomise genuine virtue, so long as he frollicked around in a world as hospitable and accommodating as a feather bed. Equally, while for many readers the many accidents and contrivances that both advance the plot of *Tom Jones* and get the hero out of many an awkward situation, such opportune deliverances are hardly a regular part of everyday life. So Fielding had to place his innocent hero, Booth, who in many respects is Tom Jones without the luck, and his virtuous wife, Amelia, in a context in which they would have to struggle against misfortune and thereby demonstrate their worth. To err is human but it is nevertheless possible to redeem the consequences of error through a combination of fortitude and determination. As Fielding insists, by way of introduction:

> To retrieve the ill Consequences of a foolish Conduct, and by struggling manfully with Distress to subdue it, is one of the noblest Efforts of Wisdom and Virtue. (p. 16)

So, whereas Tom Jones often seemed like a feather blown hither and thither on a gentle breeze, Booth is a sailor lashed to the mast on a boat whose decks are awash and who has no alternative but to stay the course.

Perhaps rather surprisingly, considering the extent of Fielding's exposure to lower class criminality, in *Amelia* Fielding reaffirmed his commitment to the idea that it was the poor who were more likely to be virtuous. On the face of it Booth, a humble ensign on half pay, who has accumulated considerable gambling debts, and, who through his naivety, remains unaware of the threat to his wife's virtue from the sinister machinations of a certain noble lord and from Colonel James, who he believes to be his faithful friend, is an even more implausible exemplification of virtue than Tom Jones. Yet in reality Fielding's conception is complex. On the one hand he insists that only the lowly have a real potential to be virtuous because they are not exposed to the temptations, corruption and miseducation of the rich. As Booth himself says:

> To confess the Truth, I am afraid, we often compliment what we call upper Life, with too much Injustice, at the Expence of

the lower. As it is no rare thing to see Instances which degrade human Nature, in Persons of high Birth and Education; so I apprehend, that Examples of whatever is really great and good, have been sometimes found amongst those who have wanted all such Advantages. In Reality, Palaces, I make no doubt, do sometimes contain nothing but Dreariness and Darkness, and the Sun of Righteousness hath shone forth with all its Glory in a Cottage. (p. 124)

While the modern critic might be tempted to see this just as Booth's rationalisation of his own situation it is hard to believe that this is not a statement with which Fielding himself would have agreed. So, although the path of virtue lies clear and open before the poor, on the other hand it is doubly difficult for them to advance because of the material adversities they face. Yet these same adversities can be turned to advantage like a sword forged in the flames. Such a moral intention on Fielding's part in turn demands a far greater realism and in the first few chapters, at least, his purpose is impressively realised. He depicts in Kafkaesque detail the absurd and shameful rituals that Booth is forced to undergo when he is falsely accused of beating a nightwatchman. But after this the novel rapidly loses its way partly because it is devoted to convoluted, factitious and essentially hypothetical attempts on Amelia's virtue that lack the real sense of danger and psychological insight that we find in Richardson. Even allowing for the fact that Fielding intends Booth to be both fallible and vulnerable, he never figures as a purposeful moral agent in the face of manifold difficulties in the way that he had initially proposed. He seems rather to be a drifter, a disconsolate and regular loser at the roulette tables, who is happy to find that his number has actually come up.

For his part, Richardson in *Sir Charles Grandison* endeavoured to repudiate the bogus virtue of Tom Jones by offering in his aristocratic hero, a male paragon who could be universally respected and admired. Richardson realised in focusing on the feminine point of view and in representing the wrongs of woman's situation he had in some way made the very idea of masculine virtue seem untenable. Indeed, judging by Mr B and Lovelace, aristocratic men behaving badly seemed to be part of the very nature of things. So Richardson was now anxious to create a near faultless hero who could serve as a model for others. But more than just virtuousness is involved. Grandison must exhibit what are often perceived as feminine characteristics in that he must be sensitive, caring, considerate, a person who invariably gives priority to the needs of others. He must also be able to express his emotions, as when, complimented by Mr Orme on his marriage to Harriet Byron, he bursts into a flood of tears. So virtue is also a kind of code for correcting the imbalance and disharmony between the sexes. But at the same time Sir Charles must be unmistakably manly. He must make virtue sexy. When first introduced, with his perfect flashing teeth, 'his easy yet manly politeness, as well in his dress, as in his address' (Vol. I, p. 181) and his magnificent manly suntan, he is more than a little reminiscent of the swashbuckling Hollywood hero, particularly since he is an expert swordsman, even though he does not believe in it. He is certainly distinctly glamorous. Sir Charles would make the ladies' hearts beat faster even if he did not possess considerable estates and if he were not descended from the best families in England. We learn that

> ... the man who would commend himself to the general favour of us young women, should be a Rake in his address, and a Saint in his heart. (Vol. III, pp. 92–3)

Undoubtedly Grandison represents this *beau idéal*. The ghost of Dorimant has still not been exorcised and Richardson having tried to discredit the rakish image of manliness now feels obliged to let it in by the back door lest his hero seem dull and priggish. If Fielding was in danger of devaluing virtue by reducing it to mere good nature, Richardson is often dangerously close to making it something even more hollow, since what recommends Grandison is that he is charming, amiable, socially skilled and adept at extricating himself from awkward situations. With the very best moral intentions Richardson betrayed his own values, since he had always been adamant that the practice of real virtue could not simply be conflated with the code of the gentleman. Towards the end of *Sir Charles Grandison*, Harriet now his wife, discovers a copy of his religious reflections which Richardson clearly intended to be as surprising as any denouement engineered by Hercule Poirot aboard the Orient Express. For Grandison is even more humble and deeply religious than we have realised:

Let thy Law, ALMIGHTY! be the rule, and thy glory the constant end, of all I do! Let me not build virtue on any notions
of honour, but of honour to thy Name . . . *Fear* of thee is the
beginning of wisdom. (Vol. III, pp. 292–3)

Needless to say the age applauded Richardson's complex synthesis but perhaps predictably Sir Charles's ideality only served
to emphasise the general unreality and implausibility of what he
was supposed to represent. Was it really that easy for the
Grandisons of this world to pass through the eye of a needle?
The suspicion continued to linger that virtue might be more
probably encountered elsewhere – even among servant girls like
Pamela!

The intuition that those placed in a privileged position in society
– and especially those who inherited great titles and estates by
right of primogeniture – found it particularly difficult to be virtuous
reaches a curious culmination with the accession to the throne
of George III in 1760. It is hard to grasp the exalted and optimistic
expectations which so many Britons had of the new king, since
all this was so quickly snuffed out in the general furore created
by Wilkes's over the peace treaty of 1763, which was generally
taken to be an attack on the monarch. In part this was because
George was the first native born Hanoverian king, but it was
also because he was a thoughtful and serious-minded young man
who seemed ideally fitted to fulfil the role of patriot king that
Bolingbroke had called for: a decent, unbiased and fair-minded
man who would rule in the interests of all the people and suppress the spirit of party and faction. Smollett in the 17th issue of
the *Briton* which appeared in 1762 described George III as a

Patriot-king, whose chief aim is the happiness of his people.[15]

In his poem *Gotham* (1764) Churchill insisted:

Weak is that throne, and in itself unsound,
Which takes not solid virtue for its ground.

Churchill, adopting the role of putative monarch of Gotham speculated – quite seriously – on the qualities needed for the task. In particular it was crucial to be a patriot king:

> A patriot king – Why, 'tis a name which bears
> The more immediate stamp of Heav'n; which wears
> The nearest, best resemblance we can show
> Of God above, through all his works below . . .
> To be a common father, to secure
> The weak from violence, from pride the poor;
> Vice and her sons to banish in disgrace,
> To make corruption dread to show her face;
> To bid afflicted Virtue take new state,
> And be at last acquainted with the great.

Although Churchill's comments were general and speculative, there can be little doubt that even at this comparatively late date they were aimed directly at the new king, calling on him to establish a just and truly virtuous administration. In the same vein Goldsmith's *Vicar of Wakefield*, which was written (though not published) in 1761–2, celebrates kingly power as a bastion against the tyranny of wealth, that is, the Whig supremacy, a note which he also strikes in 'The Traveller' (1764):

> Till half a patriot, half a coward grown,
> I fly from petty tyrants to the throne.
> Yes, brothers curse with me that baleful hour,
> When first ambition struck at kingly power;
> And thus polluting honour in its source,
> Gave wealth to sway the mind with doubled force.

Although, again, Goldsmith's remarks are very generalised he is almost certainly invoking Bolingbroke's general discussion of the rise of faction and party that was eventually to lead, under Walpole to the complete political domination of the Whigs. So a heavy responsibility lay on the new monarch's shoulders. He had to put right virtually everything that had gone wrong in the political world since the beginning of the century. One of the most fascinating admonitions to be directed at George III is John Hawkesworth's oriental tale *Almoran and Hamet* (included in *Oriental Tales*, ed. R.L. Mack) particularly since it is obsequiously dedicated to the King himself:

... as the whole is intended, to recommend the practice of virtue, as the means of happiness; to whom could I address it with so much propriety, as to a Prince, who illustrates and enforces the precepts of the moralist by his life.

Again, the timing of the work, at the very beginning of George's reign is highly significant, since it shows just how high the expectations – and anxieties – surrounding the new king had become. Almoran and Hamet, the twin sons of Solyman, represent the alternate faces of royal authority. Almoran, the first born and presumed heir to the throne, exhibits at a very early date the moral corruption that is characteristic of those who know that they are destined to be powerful and who are therefore appropriately flattered and indulged. Almoran is 'haughty, vain, and voluptuous' and, since he expects his moods to be indulged, he is naturally 'volatile, impatient and irascible'. On the other hand Hamet, the younger brother, accepts that he is to occupy a subordinate situation in life. Since he is not fawned over and cossetted, he adopts a more temperate and philosophical attitude to life and one that is not based on the immediate gratification of desire. Unlike his arrogant and overbearing elder brother, Hamet is 'gentle, courteous, and temperate'. The comparative insecurity of his position – since he knows that in the future his life will depend on the unpredictable whims of his brother – leads him to be thoughtful, patient and forebearing. But events take an unexpected turn, for Solyman, on his deathbed, decides that his power will be inherited by both brothers jointly. Clearly, *Almoran and Hamet* represent alternative paths of conduct for George III. Almoran is tyrannical, arbitrary and self-centred – indeed always potentially evil – while Hamet is virtuous, fair-minded and sensitive to the needs of the people. What is interesting is that Hawkesworth's fable implies that it is actually much more likely that George III will be like Almoran, although it also implies that he must strive to be like Hamet, a king from *below*, who can still be virtuous despite the dangers of his privileged upbringing. To take the position of Hamet is also to take the position of a constitutional monarch: to be prepared to have an administration that is based on law, to employ wise counsellors and always to consider the best interests of the people. Hamet is, in effect, a patriot king, but he is also a virtuous man who refuses to act wrongly, even when there are great incentives for him to do so.

For much of the fable Almoran dominates the action since a genie comes to his aid and grants him miraculous powers. But Hawkesworth story is an allegorical representation of the self-destructive nature of tyranny and all Almoran's attempts to control and dominate prove self-destructive. As Hawkesworth concludes

increase of power is increase of wretchedness.

Finally, against all the odds, Hamet's courageous and self-disciplined stoicism finally wins him the hand of the beautiful Almeida and undivided rule over the kingdom of Persia. Hamet may have been the underdog, but it is that very fact that has made him morally superior.

A similar ability to cope with the difficulties and dangers of inferior status is displayed by Fanny Burney's heroine Evelina, who, though of honourable birth, lacks status because her father denies her, her mother is dead and their marriage certificate has been destroyed. Yet this disability is also an advantage. Evelina, who has been brought up under the guardianship of a clergy-man, Arthur Villars, is innocent, virtuous and unsophisticated. Since she has been led to expect comparatively little and to accept a relatively humble position in life she is free from pride of social position and is untroubled by considerations of worldly advance-ment. It has been her guardian's task to curb ambition

. . . as the first step to contentment, since to diminish expecta-tion is to increase enjoyment. (p. 18)

Yet this also means that she seems destined to be a Cinderella; slighted, despised and ignored by all around her. 'Insignificant as I was' is how she parenthetically refers to herself. (p. 34) She is 'nothing' and a 'nobody' (p. 389) – even Lord Orville, whom she is eventually to marry after many setbacks and discourage-ments, initially describes her rather patronisingly as 'a poor, weak, ignorant girl'. (p. 35) The contradiction involved in her social progress and in the whole trajectory of the novel, is that she must gain both knowledge and experience of the fashionable world in order to preserve and protect the virtue that she has, yet at the same time she has to stay as unspoiled as she was at the outset. A certain social adroitness is called for if she is to be both a

. . . stranger to ostentation, and superior to insolence. (p. 338)

She has to be respected as well. What Arthur Villar's calls

. . . her guileless and innocent soul (p. 126)

must face the challenge of the corrupt and corrupting city, passing through it and yet somehow remaining altogether untouched
and untainted by it. So true virtue means facing humiliation and
suffering with courage and determination – something the powerful never have to do – yet it is also an inestimable prize which
they can never hope to attain. In a strange way the confirmation
that Evelina *is* the daughter of Sir John Belmont – a culmination
almost snatched from her before Dame Green confesses that she
exchanged the legitimate baby for her own – almost serves a
validation of her impeccable behaviour, a final stamp of approval.

Evelina's struggle to maintain her dignity and self-respect is
made the more difficult because she is compelled to move in a
society that is almost entirely dominated by men. There are virtually no women to whom she can appeal for support or advice.
Her grandmother, Madame Duval, is ignorant and uncultivated
and, although Mrs Mirvan does her best to asist Evelina, she is
always overshadowed by her violent, overbearing and sexist
husband Captain Mirvan. Only Mrs Selwyn, who makes an
appearance in the latter part of the novel and who is a wealthy
neighbour of Arthur Villars is able to stand up to the menfolk
and hold her own with them. Significantly, the good angels who
watch over Evelina and try to ensure that she comes to no harm
– Villars and Lord Orville – are both men. By comparison with
the world of Jane Austen, where women are more than able to
hold their own, *Evelina* is, for the women, a nightmare of masculine insensitivity, intimidation and aggression. On numerous
occasions Evelina is placed in a position – in part due to her lack
of social standing – where she has little alternative but to submit
to the offensive behaviour of a variety of vain and patronising
men. Even in the early scene when she first encounters Lord
Orville, who is to be the great love of her life, she is shamelessly
pursued by Mr Lovel, who makes no secret of his general contempt for women and who subsequently describes her as a
'toad-eater', that is, a humble dependent. (p. 294) Scarcely has
she escaped the clutches of this dissolute rake than she is pestered

by Sir Clement Willoughby, in what is only the first of a whole
series of debasing and degrading encounters with a man, who
seems to have no memory and who takes it for granted that his
moral slate is being perpetually wiped clean. Evelina is also offended
by the importunate attentions of a Mr Smith and of Lord Merton,

> ... a professed admirer of beauty, but a man of most licen-
> tious character. (p. 276)

While Evelina's objections to the amorous advances of a variety
of men might seem slightly priggish to us, they are validated by
the sheer imbalance of power in society, the fact that a woman
is placed in a position where she cannot maintain her dignity
and self-respect, and where she can have no redress against even
the most insulting types of behaviour. This reaches its apogee in
Captain Mirvan's attack on Madame Duval when, under the pretence of a highway robbery, she is trussed up and left in a ditch,
and in the scene where Lord Merton and Mr Coverly bet for
high stakes on a race between two extremely elderly women.
The lack of respect for women in the society of the time could
not be more clearly demonstrated. For Fanny Burney decorum
and good manners are necessary, indeed indispensible, if there
is to be a society in which men and women can mingle as equals.

Evelina appeared in 1778, just four years after the publication
of Lord Chesterfield's *Letters to his Son*, and it is the first novel to
respond directly to the maxims of good conduct which he advanced
in a correspondence that was never intended for general publication. Chesterfield was of course no innovator. He simple reflected
the values of the aristocratic world in which he moved. Nevertheless, the letters as published do give a coherence and a visibility
to a particular code of behaviour. Fanny Burney undoubtedly
valued Chesterfield's insistence that good breeding involved treating everybody with a proper respect. Chesterfield writes:

> The characteristic of a well-bred man is, to converse with his
> inferiors without insolence, and with his superiors with respect
> and with ease.[16]

In *Evelina* Lord Orville enjoys high social status but he is careful
to treat everyone he encounters with unfailing courtesy and respect.
He possesses

... a politeness which knows no intermission, and makes no distinction, is as unassuming and modest, as if he had never mixed with the great, and was totally ignorant of every qualification he possesses. (p. 113)

He is extremely tactful. His strategic interventions manage to defuse a whole series of disastrous situations. His whole being manifests not selfishness and self-importance but attentiveness towards others. Evelina is embarrassed to be seen by Lord Orville in the company of two prostitutes, with whom she takes refuge when she is accosted by a young army officer in Marybone Gardens. The following day he tactfully expresses concern at the company she is keeping and Evelina, far from being insulted is grateful:

Generous, noble Lord Orville! how disinterested his conduct! how delicate his whole behaviour! willing to advise, yet afraid to wound me! – Can I ever, in future, regret the adventure I met with at Marybone, since it has been productive of a visit so flattering. (p. 241)

Moreover, Chesterfield's stress on the combativeness and insecurity of the socially inferior:

A vulgar man is captious and jealous, eager and impetuous about trifles.[17]

is reflected in Burney's depiction of Captain Mirvan and his circle.

Nevertheless, in other respects Chesterfield was felt to be a treacherous guide – most conspicuously in Johnson's famous declaration that the *Letters* taught

... the morals of a whore and the manners of a dancing master[18]

because he seemed to privilege good manners over actual morals. For many contemporary readers Chesterfield's preference for the lesser virtues of

... gentleness, affability, complaisance, and good-humour,[19]

which he attributed to Caesar, over the stern and intransigent virtue of Cato, would have been decisive evidence of his triviality and evasiveness where serious moral questions were concerned. For Chesterfield it was more important to be well-liked than to be right. The fickleness and unreliability of the Chesterfieldian hero is apparent in a later letter in which he advises his son to be

> ... a Proteus, assuming with ease, and wearing with cheerfulness, any shape. Heat, cold, luxury, abstinence, gravity, gaiety, ceremony, easiness, learning, trifling business, and pleasure, are modes which he should be able to take, lay aside, or change occasionally, with as much ease as he would take or lay aside his hat.[20]

Chesterfield believes that a man of good breeding should be versatile enough to adapt to any social situation, yet such a person runs the risk of being accused of insincerity and lack of integrity. The possibilities for dissimulation in polite society are considerable. For Villars what makes Sir Clement Willoughby especially threatening is that he is skilled at concealing his real motives:

> But Sir. Clement, though he seeks occasions to give real offence, contrives to avoid all appearances of intentional evil. He is far more dangerous, because more artful . . . (p. 115)

But there is worse to come. It is a cause of great concern for Evelina that even Lord Orville's courtesy may simply serve as a mask for darker motives. At a mid-point in the novel Evelina is so embarrassed at the fact that Madame Duval requisitions his coach in her name, that she writes a letter of apology to him. But she is dismayed to receive in return what she regards as a forward and impertinent profession of love. It subsequently emerges that this letter has actually been sent by Sir Clement Willoughby; but for the moment and long after Evelina is deeply shocked. All men are the same it seems. Real motives can be masked by accomplished social skills. Evelina has seemingly been betrayed;

> Never, never again will I trust to appearances, – never confide in my own weak judgement, – never believe that person to be

good, who seems to be amiable! What cruel maxims are we taught by a knowledge of the world! (p. 256)

It is only a short while before she is tormented by the dangers of misconstruction, the risk that Lord Orville may have leapt to a false conclusion, now she finds the task of interpretation equally daunting. Polite society is enigmatic. The world is a dangerous place.

Evelina must navigate her way in society as best she can when the two virtuous men that would wish to help her find that in practice their hands are tied – Arthur Villars because he is remote from the scene of the Action in his country retreat of Berry Hill, Lord Orville because he is constrained by considerations of decorum and good manners. *Evelina* can be regarded as an enquiry into the possibility of virtue in the modern world, as the heroine is gradually led from the moral security of her old mentor, a reclusive clergyman, into the world of fashionable society, where only Lord Orville seems able to be at once virtuous and a gentleman. Villars doubts whether virtue and polished behaviour can mix. In response to an early letter from Evelina he comments;

> I am sure I need not say, how much more I was pleased with the mistakes of your inexperience at the private ball, than with the attempted adoption of more fashionable manners at the ridotto. (p. 55)

His concern reaches a fever pitch in the aftermath of Orville's improper letter when he writes:

> Awake, then, my dear, my deluded child, awake to the sense of your danger, and exert yourself to avoid the evils with which it threatens you. . . . You must quit him! – his sight is baneful to your repose, his society is death to your future tranquillity! (p. 309)

But her guardian, though well-meaning, is too simple to decipher the intricacies of social behaviour and Evelina is thrown back on her own resources. After first receiving Orville's letter she believes that Villars is the only virtuous man but she changes her mind and trusts her own judgement:

O Sir! was there ever another man such as Lord Orville? –
Yes, *one* other now resides at Berry Hill! (p. 320)

Orville's faith in her is matched by her faith in him. Their marriage constitutes a double reinforcement of virtue, for each has
proved their worth to the other – but such an authentic relationship has only been made possible by trial and error and by the
heroine's lowly status at the beginning.

In his educational work, *Sandford and Merton* (1783–9), Thomas
Day was particularly concerned to play down the significance of
manners in the education of a gentleman. At an early point in
the novel Mr Merton insists that the source of all real merit must
lie in the mind rather than in external traits of behaviour:

> . . . dignified sentiments, superior courage, accompanied with
> genuine and universal courtesy, are always necessary to con-
> stitute the real gentleman; and where these are wanting, it is
> the greatest absurdity to think they can be supplied by affected
> tones of voice, particular grimaces, or extravagant and unnatural
> modes of dress; which so far from being the real test of gentil-
> ity, have in general no other origin than the caprice of barbers,
> taylors, actors, opera-dancers, milliners, fiddlers, and French
> servants of both sexes. (Vol. I, pp. 15–16)

Unfortunately Mr Merton's own son is a particularly clear instance
of the damage that can be done to the children of the rich by over-
indulgence and a concern with fashionable appearance because:

> His mother was so excessive fond of him, that she gave him
> everything that he cried for, and would never let him learn to
> read because he complained that it made his head ache. (Vol.
> I, p. 2)

In Jamaica, where the family fortune was made, he was always
dressed in silk or laced clothes, was carried around in a gilt car-
riage and was waited on hand and foot by black servants. But
when he came to England he was virtually an invalid and also
illiterate:

> He was also so delicately brought up, that he was perpetually
> ill; the least wind or rain gave him a cold, and the least sun

was sure to throw him into a fever. Instead of playing about, and jumping, and running like other children, he was taught to sit still for fear of spoiling his cloaths, and to stay in the house for fear of injuring his complexion. By this kind of education, when Master Merton came over to England he could neither write nor read nor cypher; he could use none of his limbs with ease, nor bear any degree of fatigue; but he was very proud, fretful, and impatient. (Vol. I, p. 3)

Like many of his contemporaries, Thomas Day was influenced by John Brown's warnings in his *Estimate*, of the dangers of effeminacy in the modern age. Day saw it as the task of a modern education to combat such tendencies and to revive the classical ideal of virtue based on simplicity of manners and strength of character, to cultivate what he called

. . . the severe and rugged virtues of the Romans. (Vol. III, p. 275)

James Keir, his early biographer, describes how Day would make long journeys on foot through England and Wales in order to come in contact with the common people, who he believed offered a clearer insight into the real tendencies and potentialities of human nature. Such a bias in favour of the lower orders of society emerges most clearly in *Sandford and Merton*, where the pampered Tommy is compelled to take instruction alongside the virtuous Harry Sandford, the son of a farmer, in the hope that this will lead him to emulate his social inferior and moral superior. At the outset of the book Harry saves Tommy from a dangerous snake and later rescues him from being gored by a bull. In virtually every respect Harry is better than Tommy. He is brave and practical. He is industrious and is able to practice many useful skills. He is honest and clear-sighted – objecting to the lesson in fraud and insincerity offered in Beaumarchais's *The Marriage of Figaro*, detecting in the genteel manners of Harry and his peers the desire to inflict pain. Tommy's wealthy and privileged background is clearly shown as a major obstacle in the way of his becoming a worthwhile and moral human being. As Keir puts it:

. . . the hero of this excellent novel is not, as in most of these compositions, a person of noble or princely birth in disguise, but a *young peasant*, whose body is hardened by toil. . . . These many virtues in young Sandford are contrasted by the feebler character of Merton, a boy bred up in opulence, effeminate indulgence, and the pride of wealth and station.[21]

Indeed so sharply is Day's contrast drawn that it seems to put in question his whole educational project. We begin to wonder whether the whole struggle to redeem Tommy is either possible or worthwhile, particularly when Day lays so much emphasis on early impressions in the formation of character. While more recent ages have seen poverty as a major cause of the damaged personality for many in the later eighteenth century riches were likely to be an infinitely more destructive and degenerative force.

Like *Sandford and Merton*, Charlotte Smith's *Emmeline* (1788) reflects the increasingly confident conviction of middle-class writers that those who occupied the highest positions in society were rarely likely to be notable for their moral excellence and that the inescapable explanation for this state of affairs was the pampered and over-indulgent upbringing which they were likely to receive. Although Emmeline, 'the orphan of the castle' as the subtitle has it, is the heroine of the novel she is for much of the time obliged to play second fiddle to the romantic and passionate figure of Lord Delamere, who desperately craves her love and her hand in marriage quite as much as his parents oppose it. For a long time Emmeline's situation as a relatively humble person who is rendered wholly powerless by her dependence on the will of an aristocrat, Lord Montreville is utterly galling, but again adversity brings out a strength of character that might not necessarily show itself under more favourable circumstances. It makes her

> . . . calm in the possession of conscious innocence, and rich in native integrity and nobleness of nature. (p. 335)

By contrast although Delamere's passionate pursuit of her love is initially flattering, the violent and uncontrollable nature of his emotions, his suspicions and fits of jealousy eventually become distinctly alarming. A characteristic product of an aristocratic miseducation he is possessed by an

> . . . ungovernable and violent spirit, hitherto unused to controul and accustomed from his infancy to exert over his own family the most boundless despotism. (p. 117)

Emmeline, though flattered by his attentions, increasingly recognises that he is too unstable to be a suitable partner and is led to
break off her engagement with him. She is gratified to learn that
she herself is the owner of an extensive estate and that, therefore, she need no longer be dependent on anyone or be subject
to external constraint. The impulsive and excitable Delamere is
killed in a duel over Emmeline and Emmeline is left to marry
Captain Godolphin, whom she has long recognised to be the more
sensible and responsible person. Nevertheless many contemporary readers, including Sir Walter Scott, were disappointed in this
rather prosaic conclusion and would have preferred a scenario
by which Emmeline could somehow have been reunited with
her emotional suitor, no doubt suitably chastened by his experiences. *Emmeline* had the pride and the prejudice without the
right result. But Charlotte Smith was anxious to enforce the
moral that an over-indulged young aristocrat, 'the victim of
his mother's fatal fondness and his father's ambition' was by
no means the ideal match for a respectable and sensitive girl.
(p. 527)

In her first novel, *Northanger Abbey* (posthumously published
in 1818) Jane Austen cites a number of literary quotations that
might prove soothing and servicable to her aspirant heroine,
Catherine Morland. Among them, one in particular from Shakespeare, seems particularly relevant to the children of clergymen
and downwardly mobile gentry whom she chose to focus her
attentions on:

> The poor beetle, whom we tread upon,
> In corporal sufferance feels a pang as great
> As when a giant dies.

Their pretensions to being a heroine at all are doubtful, since
there is no likelihood whatsoever that they have been marked
out for a singular destiny or great success. They would scarcely
be in a position to break off an engagement with a great Lord
like Frederick Delamere. There is no possibility that they will
unexpectedly discover themselves to be an heiress after all, like
Evelina and Emmeline. The sole comfort and consolation in their
situation is to show that they can bear their lot with fortitude,
that they can be virtuous whether anyone notices or not!

The novels of Jane Austen are very specifically anti-romantic in the sense that they start out by envisaging as a possible and even likely outcome an event which is actually quite unlikely. If her fiction involves puncturing illusions then these are also illusions in which Jane Austen herself colludes. In *Northanger Abbey* it was never very likely that General Tilney, the owner of such a vast and splendidly maintained residence would look with particular favour on the child of a clergyman with ten children, yet such is the case. The 'surprise' of his disapproval is generated rather by the fact that in the genre, as in the fairy-tale, there is a convention that the lowly shall be raised. Realism enters Jane Austen's novels through the gradually dawning perception that, while the lowly may propose, it is the rich who will finally dispose. There is always a moment when wistful dreaming is brought to an abrupt halt. It is generally assumed that *Northanger Abbey* mocked Catherine Morland's inability to distinguish real life from a Gothic fiction and in particular through her lurid identification of General Tilney with the tyrant of Mrs Radcliffe's *The Mysteries of Udolpho* and the suspicion that he has in some mysterious way engineered the death of his wife:

> Could Henry's father? – And yet how many were the examples to justify even the blackest suspicions! – and, when she saw him in the evening, while she worked with her friend, slowly pacing the drawing-room for an hour together in silent thoughtfulness, with downcast eyes and contracted brow, she felt secure from all possibility of wronging him. It was the air and attitude of a Montoni! (pp. 149–50)

Catherine's speculations are of course very wide of the mark – and are, in fact, quite absurd, yet there nevertheless is a grain of truth in them in that the likes of General Tilney are able to wield an absolute power and authority quite as formidable as the master of Udolpho. What, in fact, makes Jane Austen's gentrified world remarkably reminiscent of Gothic is the sharp and unblinkable disparity between those who are powerful and those who are powerless. It is particularly evident in *Sense and Sensibility* where we are very aware that Mrs Dashwood and her daughters, Elinor, Marianne and Margaret, who have been reduced to living at Barton Cottage, as clients of Sir John Middleton, after the death of Henry Dashwood, have slipped about as far down the social scale as it is possible to go. The rich and established in *Sense and Sensibility* use their power in a ruthless, arbitrary way, as Almoran says in John Hawkesworth's story:

> It is the glory of a prince, to punish for what and whom he will; to be the sovereign, not only of property, but of life; and to govern alike without prescription or appeal.

The unfettered exercise of power can only be relished to the full when there are no pretensions to fairness or justice. John Dashwood was originally going to give each of the three daughters a thousand pounds each in response to his own father's dying request but in the end, largely as a result of his wife's promptings, he decides to give them nothing. Mrs Ferrars decides to disinherit her eldest son Edward and to transfer the income to his younger brother Robert because of her displeasure at his refusal to give up his engagement to Lucy Steele. Yet Robert suffers no comparable penalty when he goes ahead and marries the same girl. Similarly, Mrs Smith, holds absolute power over Willoughby because he is wholly dependent in the income that she alone can supply. Such figures dictate what is to happen; there can be no appeal.

Another Gothic theme which is significant in Jane Austen's writing is that of secrecy. In the writing of William Godwin in particular, secrecy was seen as a source of illegitimate power, an obvious device for controlling and manipulating others. Of course, Godwin, as a radical and an anarchist, was politically poles apart from Jane Austen but she nevertheless seems to have regarded the practice of secrecy and non-disclosure as morally dubious. In *Sense and Sensibility* there is a great deal that is not revealed. Many of Colonel Brandon's actions appear mysterious because he does not reveal that he is the father of Eliza, a child born out of wedlock. Willoughby is the secret seducer of this child. He also does not reveal the importance that Mrs Smith has for him. Elinor is placed at a severe disadvantage in her relationship with Edward because she is not aware that he contracted a secret engagement with Lucy several years previously. Jane Austen is certainly aware that people necessarily live in a world where they do not have access to all the information they might like and where they must play each hand out in the dark, but a sense of bad faith and unfairness still lingers. Elinor is placed in a position where Edward's motives are completely indecipherable as far as she is concerned.

Willoughby's sudden and inexplicable departure from Marianne at a moment when their relationship had seemed so clear and unclouded is a blow so shattering that she can scarcely recover from it. Even his rejection of her alone would have been hard to bear but it seems particularly brutal when she is left so utterly in the dark. Initially Marianne is anxious to make allowances for him but as Elinor points out his lack of candour is definitely damaging. When Marianne asks her sister what she suspects Willoughby of, Elinor replies:

> I can hardly tell you myself. – But suspicion of something unpleasant is the inevitable consequence of such an alteration as we have just witnessed in him. . . . Willougby may undoubtedly have very sufficient reasons for his conduct, and I will hope that he has. But it would have been more like Willoughby to acknowledge them at once. Secrecy may be advisable; but still I cannot help wondering at its being practised by him. (p. 68)

Again, Willougby's letter to Marianne, which causes her to faint, is especially hurtful, not just because of his rejection of her but because of its lack of transparency. Marianne cannot connect this with her own experience. Willougby even contrives to suggest that the lock of her hair which he insisted on taking from her was something which she actually foisted on him. Marianne finds herself in a emotional maze, all so daunting and baffling that it is well-nigh impossible for her to find her way out.

There is a distinct continuity in the tradition of fiction that runs from Fanny Burney and Charlotte Smith to Ann Radcliffe and Jane Austen in that virtue, though certainly bound up with innocence and unimpeachable conduct, comes to be associated above all with the ability to maintain an undaunted and unshakeable spirit in the face of discouragement and adversity. Typically, the heroine is isolated. Indeed this isolation marks the beginnings of the turn towards Gothic. Whereas Evelina can discuss her experiences with her guardian Arthur Villars, both Emmeline and Emily, in *The Mysteries of Udolpho*, find that there is no one they can really turn to for advice or encouragement. Perhaps surprisingly Jane Austen's heroines find themselves in a similar position – starting of course with Catherine in the mock-Gothic *Northanger Abbey*. But Elinor in *Sense and Sensibility*, Fanny Price in *Mansfield Park*, Ann Elliot in *Persuasion*, all find themselves similarly isolated. The idea of virtue returns to its Stoic roots and for obvious reasons. For the Stoics it was imperative to remain impassive and unmoved before the twists and turns of fate, treating misfortune and good fortune alike. As Hegel long ago pointed out Stoicism is a philosophy of powerlessness: it appeals to those and speaks for those who believe that they have no power to influence their own destiny. Such a view seemed very pertinent to many women at this time and perhaps especially to Jane Austen, who was certainly a good deal less privileged than, say, Fanny Burney. If a woman cannot hope to triumph in the game of life like the heroine of romance she can, by acting steadfastly, survive its disappointments and retain her dignity and self-respect. If Elinor is more virtuous in *Sense and Sensibility* this is because – as her mother recognises – she has never forced her own claims on her attention, leading her to forget

> ... that in Elinor she might have a daughter suffering almost as much, certainly with less self-provocation, and greater fortitude. (p. 312)

Although Jane Austen's title certainly asks us to reflect on the contrast between Elinor's sense and Marianne's sensibility, the comparison if pressed too far can be deeply misleading. For the evidence of Jane Austen's novels taken as a whole shows that she herself valued that combination of intelligence and sensitivity which the age designated 'sensibility' – if only because she is critical of those characters who do not possess it. It was not so much that sensibility was a moral fault as that those who possessed it placed themselves in danger through a tendency to judge by comparatively superficial impressions, to be swayed by the emotion of the moment. There is always a element of arrogance in those who have 'sensibility' – typified by Marianne's patronising dismissal of Edward Ferrars, of Colonel Brandon and Mrs Smith – and the novel insists that such snap judgements are invariably wrong. Again Marianne romantically exclaims:

> What have wealth or grandeur to do with happiness? (p. 78)

but her own sentiment must be contrasted with Mrs Jennings's more prosaic but more realistic assessment of her chances with Willoughby:

Well, it is the oddest thing to me, that a man should use a pretty girl so ill! But where there is plenty of money on one side, and next to none on the other, Lord bless you! they care no more about such things! (p. 168)

Yet the appeal of spontaneity cannot be denied. Marianne rejoices in her sense of affinity with Willoughby:

They speedily discovered that their enjoyment of dancing and music was mutual, and that it arose from a general conformity of judgement in all that related to either. . . . Their taste was strikingly alike. The same books, the same passages were idolised by each – or if any difference appeared, any objection arose, it lasted no longer than till the force of her arguments and the brightness of her eyes could be displayed. He acquiesced in all her decisions, caught all her enthusiasm; and long before his visit concluded, they conversed with the familiarity of a long-established acquaintance. (p. 40)

Elinor's objection to the sheer speed of all this seems pedantic and most readers will sympathise with Marianne when she responds:

But I see what you mean. I have been too much at my ease, too happy, too frank. I have erred against every commonplace notion of decorum; I have been open and sincere where I ought to have been reserved, spiritless, dull, deceitful: – had I talked only of the weather and the roads, and had I spoken only once in ten minutes, this reproach would have been spared. (pp. 40–1)

Bu while Jane Austen values sincerity and spontaneity she also distrusts the moment. If there is a sense of affinity between two people it is something, she believes, that can only truly emerge after a long period of trial and testing. Jane Austen's art of fiction is essentially an art of postponement and delay in which gradually, almost imperceptably, the contours of the emotional landscape alter and new perspectives are opened up. Indeed, the problem with her posthumously published novel *Persuasion* is that, in showing how Anne Elliot and Captain Wentworth are gradually enabled to love again after eight years and the breaking of their engagement, she resolves the issue in a mere two hundred pages. We need to *experience* this hesitation and suspension of time and not merely be told about it. The vivid encounter of Willoughby with Marianne when he lifts the injured girl onto his shoulder cannot be the basis for a lasting relationship anymore than Frank Churchill's providential rescue of Harriet from the gypsies. Immediacy is always a lure. Things are not always quite what they seem. The morally equivocal nature of sensibility emerges most clearly in the case of Willoughby. His sudden departure and effective jilting of Marianne seems cruel, yet his subsequent confession to Elinor, that seems partially to redeem him because it suggests that he really did love Marianne, nevertheless reveals the depths of his narcissism. As Elinor points out:

> The whole of his behaviour . . . from the beginning to the end of the affair, has been grounded on selfishness. It was selfishness which first made him sport with your affections; which afterwards, when his own were engaged, made him delay the confession of it, and which finally carried him from Barton. His own enjoyment, or his own ease, was, in every particular, his ruling principle. . . . At present . . . he regrets what he has done. And why does he regret it? – Because he finds it has not answered towards himself. It has not made him happy. (p. 308)

Willoughby has sensibility without integrity, impulsiveness without virtue. But in the final analysis Marianne is very different from the man she has idolised. If she has been inclined to over-indulge her emotions, she is open, honest and genuine in a way that he is not. Marianne has to learn to acquire through painful experience the virtues of patience and fortitude that her sister possessed from the start; to acquire the 'composure of mind' that as the result of 'serious reflection'

> . . . must eventually lead her to contentment and cheerfulness. (p. 299)

Nevertheless, Elinor and Marianne are not quite as different as they might seem. Elinor has been over-shadowed and neglected, forced to play second fiddle to her more emotional sister, but even she, self-abnegating and emotionally repressed as she is, cannot live without hoping and dreaming. She takes an interminable age to reveal her apparently futile love for Edward Ferrars to her sister and to her mother. But she is, if anything, even more irrational in her attitude to the object of her desire than even her sister was. In Jane Austen's writing there is a familiar temptation: first to envisage a pleasing situation with a clear recognition of its ideal and hypothetical nature and then, gradually, almost unnoticeably, to take that wish for a settled fact. Marianne is guilty of this. So is Elinor. Indeed Elinor is peculiarly stubborn. When, in the rambling and complacent account of Mrs Palmer, she hears that her own mother has been driven frantic by the news that Edward is to marry Lucy Steele, even she finds it difficult to take a balanced view of the matter:

> She could hardly determine what her own expectation of its event really was; though she earnestly tried to drive away the notion of its being possible to end otherwise at last, than in the marriage of Edward and Lucy. (p. 226)

She cannot acquiesce in the total loss of Edward Ferrars, her last, best hope. Finally, her patience is gratified, her virtue rewarded. But it is *not* realism that has triumphed.

By comparison with *Sense and Sensibility, Pride and Prejudice* is much more a novel of manners. Nevertheless good behaviour *is* seen as morally significant. For Jane Austen manners are not just a matter of social appearances, as they may have been to some extent with Chesterfield – if not as much as his detractors may have wished to think. Good manners are certainly connected with upbringing. Jane Austen stresses how much Elizabeth and her sisters have been disadvantaged by being brought up by an eccentric and whimsical father who, at bottom is not much concerned with what people think, and a mother who, because of her relatively humble background is both ignorant, irresponsible and vulgar, and who has brought up Lydia and Kitty in a similar way. So Elizabeth has done well to conduct herself as well as she does. At the same time good manners are not simply a matter of social appearances. They are an indication of the sensitivity that you show to the thoughts and feelings of others. Here, many, if not all the characters in *Pride and Prejudice* offend. It is manifested at the simplest level by Mary, continuing with her recital beyond the point when anyone wishes to hear it; by Charlotte Lucas lording it over the Bennets after her engagement; even by Mr Bennet's rudeness to his wife. But it is also manifested in

more serious ways: in the boorish and bullying behaviour of
Lady Catherine de Bourgh; in the grotesque self-importance of
Mr Collins, especially as manifested in his letter after Lydia's elope-
ment; in Lydia's own shameless and unrepentant behaviour; in
Wickham's irresponsible and deceitful gossip. If Elizabeth shows
hastiness and poor judgement in accepting Wickham's account
of Darcy, this might not seem altogether unreasonable when at
their first encounter she heard him say:

> She is tolerable, but not handsome enough to tempt *me*. (p. 9)

In a sense Elizabeth shows integrity in maintaining her own self-
respect rather than believing his ten thousand-a-year. The novel
is more about *becoming* virtuous than being virtuous. Darcy is
compelled to swallow his pride. Elizabeth is forced to endure a
whole series of humiliations and mortifications because of her
readiness to jump to conclusions:

> She was humbled, she was grieved; she repented though she
> hardly knew of what. (p. 275)

The need, on both sides to retrieve their too speedily aborted
relationship, holds the possibility of being educative, of being
mutually beneficial:

> It was a union that must have been to the advantage of both;
> by her ease and liveliness, his mind might have been softened,
> his manners improved, and from his judgement, information,
> and knowledge of the world, she must have received benefit
> of greater importance. (pp. 275–6)

Nevertheless, the critical balancing of his pride and her prejudice in the novel has its dangers because the issue of pride is by
far the more crucial. *Pride and Prejudice* cannot be viewed as anything other than as a sustained attack on the selfishness and
arrogance of the aristocracy. The pride of those like Darcy and
Lady Catherine de Bourgh is corrupting, not merely to themselves but because of the way in which such attitudes percolate
down into the lower ranks of society, where clergymen, tradesmen and even servants may primp and preen themselves on their
exalted connections, imitating the pretentious behaviour of their

so-called betters. If it had not been for Darcy's arrogance the whole situation which Jane Austen describes in the novel could never have taken place. It is the fount from which all evil flows, even if he is not always personally responsible for it. Perhaps it is even not unreasonable that he should make some restitution. Darcy's confession and self-accusation is certainly a climactic moment in the novel:

> I have been a selfish being all my life, in practice, though not in principle. As a child I was taught what was *right*, but I was not taught to correct my temper. I was given good principles, but left to follow them in pride and conceit. Unfortunately an only son (and for many years an only *child*), I was spoilt by my parents, who though good themselves (my father particularly, all that was benevolent and amiable), allowed, encouraged, almost taught me to be selfish and overbearing, to care for none beyond my own family circle, to think meanly of all the rest of the world, to *wish* at least to think meanly of their sense and worth compared with my own. Such I was, from eight to eight and twenty; and such I might still have been but for you, dearest, loveliest Elizabeth! What do I not owe you! You taught me a lesson, hard indeed at first, but most advantageous. By you, I was properly humbled. (p. 328)

Darcy, like so many scions of the aristocracy, has been corrupted by a pampered and indulgent upbringing; he can only be restored to virtue from below.

However, it may be that Jane Austen regretted the more indulgent picture she painted of human nature in *Pride and Prejudice* for the depiction of virtue in the figure of the lowly born, Fanny Price, is considerably more austere. One of the most obvious signs of this is the general lack of satire in the book. Where in *Pride and Prejudice* those who were self-centred, superficial and empty-headed were generally mocked, here, with the doubtful exception of Mrs Norris, they are there to be whipped and scourged, and no prospect of redemption for the unregenerate is held out. The slant of *Mansfield Park* is distinctly Calvinist. Only Fanny, the humble, and Edmund, the clergyman, can belong to the elect group that having been mercifully saved and delivered out of the hands of the ungodly, will righteously rule over Mansfield Park. At the end of the novel the wheat have been rigorously winnowed from the chaff. All shades of grey have disappeared. Yet the sternness of this outcome is already foreshadowed at a relatively early point in the novel when Mary Crawford expresses her surprise that Edmund is to become a clergyman and enquires, very disparagingly:

> For what is to be done in the church? Men love to distinguish themselves, and in either of the other lines (i.e. professions), distinction may be gained. A clergyman is nothing. (p. 83)

In response Edmund speaks of the importance of the church's

> ... guardianship of religion and morals, and consequently of the manners which result from their influence.

He further goes on to distinguish their role in influencing manners from

> ... the arbiters of good breeding, the regulators of refinement and courtesy, the masters of the ceremonies of life. The *manners* I speak of, might rather be called *conduct*, perhaps, the result of good principles. (p. 84)

Virtue and good conduct should never be confused, even for a moment, with socially adroit behaviour.

In part it is the very fact that Fanny Price comes from such a conspicuously unpretentious background that makes it very unlikely that she should fall into any such misconception. Fanny is not only righteous and virtuous – 'the perfect model of a woman' (p. 315) – because she is young, innocent and uncorrupted but her circumstances make morally faultless behaviour well-nigh indispensable. From the time when she is miraculously translated from a poky little house in Portsmouth to the great house at Mansfield, as if seized in the beak of a giant roc, she is acutely aware of her position as a dependent. Everything, from whether she has a horse to ride or whether she is to have a fire in her room, depends not just on grace and favour but on whether anyone actually thinks about the matter at all. Any serious transgression would mean her being turned out of the house at a moment's notice. So Fanny has every reason to be virtuous as well as timid, anxious and shy. Fanny is a serious person and in a novel where virtually all the other characters are not this is in itself a powerful recommendation. Edmund notes that she is not as other girls:

> She was not to be won by all that gallantry and wit, and good nature together, could do; or at least, she would not be won by them nearly so soon, without the assistance of sentiment and feeling, and seriousness on serious subjects. (pp. 308–9)

In *Mansfield Park* Jane Austen is concerned to show that if virtue is to be rewarded then it does not come easily. There is a classic and seemingly interminable delay before it does. The novel divides into two parallel sections: the first leads up to the moral scandal of the amateur theatricals from which Fanny wisely abstains; the second – paralleling the first – to a second moment of impropriety between Henry Crawford and Maria that shakes the Bertram family and finally makes it possible for Edmund to marry Fanny. In the first part Fanny finds that her exemplary behaviour recommends her to Sir Thomas Bertram and causes her to be accepted as one of the family. But in the second part rectitude is made more difficult because Sir Thomas regards Henry Crawford, who has asked for her hand in marriage, as entirely suitable and cannot understand her objections to him, which are based not on his social position and general amiability but 'his principles'. (p. 287) Sir Thomas regards her refusal as incomprehensible and effectively banishes her to the demeaning surroundings of Portsmouth to make her come to her senses. It is *Mansfield Park* which most seriously raises the issue of a woman's autonomy and independence. There is the question originally raised in *Emmeline* as to the grounds on which a woman is justified in rejecting a suitor who possesses both rank and wealth. Jane Austen suggests that no matter how humble she might be she still has the right to refuse a man whom she neither approves of or likes. Still her situation is daunting and *Mansfield Park*, like *Northanger Abbey*, resembles a *Mysteries of Udolpho* transposed into a more humdrum key. Emily's turret at Udolpho becomes Fanny's 'little white attic' where she sits alone. (p. 135) Fanny, like her literary predecessor, possesses sensibility and can respond to the sublime, as, when contemplating the woods on an unclouded night, she exclaims:

Here's harmony! Here's repose! Here's what may leave all painting and music behind, and what poetry can only attempt to describe. Here's what may tranquillize every care, and lift the heart to rapture. (p. 102)

In such a rewriting Mrs Norris like Madame Montoni is the guardian who does not protect and Sir Thomas Bertram, despite all his kindliness, the Montoni figure, a remote patriarchal despot who wields absolute power over her existence. At Mansfield Fanny finds herself trapped. Edmund, the man she loves, is drawn into an emotional involvement with Mary Crawford, that seems to preclude a relationship, which would, in any case, involve the breaking of a tacit taboo. There seems no obvious way of escaping from the clutches of Henry Crawford. While the others have power, she alone is powerless.

However a scenario that contrasts a helpless victim with malign and oppressive forces is always in danger of collapsing into melodrama and so it proves here. Undoubtedly Jane Austen was concerned about a possible disintegration in moral standards and for her the essential precondition for it was a blurring of moral boundaries, a general disposition for people to be uncritical about standards of behaviour and to condone behaviour which was actually quite wrong. We already see this in Mrs Bennet's complacency about Lydia's wedding, but in *Mansfield Park* Jane Austen is not disposed to regard such indulgence as funny. Kotzebue's play *Lovers' Vow's* typifies this, since infidelity and illegitimacy become the justification for the most shameless attempts at seduction. Worse still, in private theatricals the play can serve as a medium through which dangerous emotions can surface. What is alarming about the Crawfords is that their very charm and personability serves to commend the fluidity of their morals, to make even the most responsible individuals lose sight of where their duty lies. They represent the new money versus the old; fashionable London versus the rather dull provinces; innovation versus tradition. Over and beyond this there is a general disposition to go along with the crowd. Even Edmund succumbs and even Fanny is put under intense pressure to do so. Only Sir Thomas's arrival, providential for her, disastrous for the others, intervenes. Nevertheless, in a fickle and changeable world, Fanny is the compass that unfailingly locks onto to a moral magnetic North when the others have lost their bearing altogether. But

the problem with taking the Crawfords as symbols of moral decadence and with contrasting, so early in the novel, their black
with Fanny's predictably spotless white, is that it precludes the
very thing that Jane Austen does best: the depiction of long delayed and complex processes of change. Had she allowed Fanny
more time to discover what the Crawfords truly were, had she
given more weight to Henry's vacillations, then the novel might
have been as masterly as it occasionally promises to be. But the
Jamesian subtlety with which she attends to nuances of social
behaviour is constantly undermined by moralism and censori-
ousness. Henry Crawford's flirtatiousness define him as a marriage-
wrecker in the making. Mary Crawford's careless letters are
evidence of criminal behaviour. Both have corrupted minds. Jane
Austen's rush to judgement strengthens neither her fiction nor
her case. That there *is* a difference between a minor fracas and
grievous bodily harm is something which *Mansfield Park*, to its
own cost, refuses to acknowledge.

But Jane Austen bears down heavily because she is determined
to convict the high and the mighty of a lack of moral integrity.
The fact that little Fanny is treated with so little regard or concern is more serious than it looks because, quite simply, it is a
particular manifestation of a more general carelessness and
indifference among the aristocracy. A faulty upbringing is to blame:
Tom, Sir Thomas Bertram's eldest son, is

. . . born only for expense and enjoyment. (p. 15)

When Edmund discusses Mary Crawford's faults with Fanny the
following interchange occurs:

She does not *think* evil, but she speaks it – speaks it in playful-
ness – and though I know it to be playfulness, it grieves me to
the soul.
　'The effect of education', said Fanny gently.
　Edmund could not but agree to it. 'Yes, that uncle and aunt!
They have injured the finest mind!' (p. 275)

He later blames the influence of London and the fashionable life
for her preoccupation with status, appearances and wealthy display.
In their own small way the theatricals, in their explosive mixture
of narcissism and frivolity epitomise all that is worst in the life

of the upper classes. But Fanny, as the outsider, is acutely conscious of

> ... the selfishness which, more or less disguised, seemed to govern them all. (p. 118)

At the end, with the Bertram family publically shamed, even Sir Thomas Bertram is forced to admit that their upbringing has been seriously at fault in its Chesterfieldian concentration on the external graces:

> He feared that principle, active principle, had been wanting, that they had never been properly taught to govern their inclinations and tempers, by that sense of duty which can alone suffice. They had been instructed theoretically in their religion, but never required to bring it into daily practice. To be distinguished for elegance and accomplishments – the authorised object of their youth – could have no useful influence that way, no moral effect on the mind. He had meant them to be good, but his cares had been directed to the understanding and manners, not the disposition; and of the necessity of self-denial and humility, he feared they had never heard from any lips that could profit them. (p. 422)

There is a moral vacuum at Mansfield Park and only the lowly Fanny can fill it.

But in *Emma* the lowly are given no special priviledges and the rich are let off very lightly indeed. Whereas Fanny is virtuous and faultless, Harriet Smith is just 'an artless, amiable girl'. (p. 431) Whereas Fanny 'judged rightly throughout' (p. 168), Harriet makes mistakes like everyone else when she misinterprets Mr Knightley's courtesy toward her as love. Emma may be rich and spoilt but this does not necessarily mean that she is on the path to damnation. There may be unfairness in this: for the lowly, like Harriet, are trampled on and the rich, like Frank Churchill emerge unscathed – but, if nothing else, this is a great deal more likely than the enthronement of Fanny. Perhaps Jane Austen herself had become too involved. Paradoxically, by writing in a lighter and more detached style, by delighting in intricacies of plot and by focusing so relentlessly on apparent trivia, she wrote in *Emma* not only her own masterpiece but one of the great novels of world literature. Part of that greatness stems from a capacity for self-criticism. Jane Austen now recognised that in life it was impossible to categorise and pigeon-hole people as if they were fixed quantities and on that basis predict what they would or would not do. In *Emma* she satirised an aspect of herself. By creating a heroine who is flawed and whose judgement of characters and events is so obviously faulty, Jane Austen denies her readers an obvious point of identification and forces them to think more critically about what they read. Despite its acute class-consciousness *Emma* is strangely democratic. It marks an astonishing step forward in the novel because it tries as far as possible to put everyone on an 'equal footing' (to quote Emma herself) (p. 362); to abolish the distinction between foreground and background; between large events and small. Quite apart from anything else *Emma* is a novel which you cannot skim. Everything contributes to the overall impression and shapes the outcome, whether it is Emma's breaking of her bootlace or her rudeness to Miss Bates, the mysterious gift of a piano to Jane Fairfax or Mr Wodehouse's fear of burglars. As in a landscape painting, delicacy and subtlety of detail and colour are not only expressive in themselves but create a sense of verisimilitude and pictorial depth. The clarity and firmness of her earlier work gives way to a delight in flux and instability of appearances, in endlessly shifting and flickering patterns of light. Yet, unlike *Mansfield Park*, the world of *Emma* could not be more stable.

Nevertheless the rich are criticised in *Emma*. The very fact that Emma is described as rich in the sixth word of the novel is Jane Austen's way of announcing to the world that she is also unmistakably flawed. Emma is stand-offish. She is patronising and condescending to those less favoured than herself. She is self-centred and thoughtless. As the result of her social position she meddles in matters that are no concern of hers, often with disastrous consequences. She is often dangerously smug. But in her defence it must be said that she bears no real malice or ill will to anyone. At worst she is the sorcerer's apprentice, whose schemes go awry. A more serious case is Frank Churchill, whose decision to go to London to have his haircut shows him to be vain and something of a fop. Mr Knightley, who admittedly has no reason to be well disposed towards him, describes him as 'proud, luxurious and selfish'. (p. 131) Emma's defence of him, that he

... can adapt his conversation to the taste of everybody, and has the power as well as the wish of being universally agreeable (p. 135)

is in Knightley's eyes no defence at all, since it simply shows that he is the Chesterfieldian hero, a social chameleon with no real integrity. He indignantly bursts out:

What! at three-and-twenty to be the king of his company – the great man – the practised politician, who is to read everybody's character, and make every body's talents conduce to the display of his own superiority; to be dispensing his flatteries around, that he may make all appear like fools compared with himself. My dear Emma, you own good sense could not endure such a puppy when it came to the point. (pp. 135–6)

The fact that Frank is also concerned to conceal his engagement with Jane Fairfax because he knows that Mrs Churchill would disapprove of it also tells against him. This is simply for his own convenience. Yet while he is relatively untroubled it creates considerable stress and anxiety in the mind of Jane Fairfax and could have seriously upset Emma had she taken his advances more seriously. As I have already suggested Jane Austen shared William Godwin's disapproval of secrecy because it created inequalities in people's relationships, distorts behaviour and offers illegitimate power over others. As Emma objects:

But I shall always think it a very abominable proceeding. What has it been but a system of hypocrisy and deceit, – espionage, and treachery? – To come among us with professions of openness and simplicity; and such a league in secret to judge us all! (p. 362)

But in the end, unlike *Sense and Sensibility*, no one is seriously harmed by this subterfuge. Frank Churchill's apologies count for more than Willoughby's. The ledger can be closed.

But Emma has a much greater capacity for redemption than Frank because even her general capacity for meddling shows that she is actually very interested and concerned about other people. It is distinctly to Emma's advantage that she is so outgoing, so sociable and so involved in the life of the community. What she lacks is the humility and respect for others – not just so as not to be rude to Miss Bates but actually to be like the Bates's, who think so much of everybody, and so little of themselves. So it becomes significant that in arranging her marriage to Mr Knightley Emma's first thought is of the welfare of her father. But if Emma becomes wiser, more thoughtful and more responsible sanctification is nevertheless a long way off. *Emma* marks a significant turning point in the development of the novel in that authenticity in the depiction of character and social milieu actually begins to preclude the idealised representation that had been so much a part of its history.

5

Provincial Virtue

On 2 March 1737 a provincial schoolmaster, Samuel Johnson, upped sticks from Lichfield with one of his pupils, David Garrick and set off for London to seek his fortune. Johnson was 28 at the time, Garrick aged 20. The two had very little money and their undertaking was both arduous and risky. But ultimately it proved to be well worthwhile since they were both to enjoy high eminence in the literary and theatrical world. Life in the metropolis could be a struggle, but eighteenth-century London was nevertheless a magnet for aspiring young men from all over the British Isles. Johnson's own closest associates were a Scotsman, Boswell and an Irishman, Oliver Goldsmith. In the theatre Garrick associated with many dramatists of Irish birth, Sheridan, Charles Macklin, Arthur Murphy, Hugh Kelly. In many ways the contrast between life in the capital and life in the provinces resembled the world of Balzac's novels and especially that of his great masterpiece, *Les Illusions Perdues*. Life in the metropolis is sophisticated but cynical and insincere, the provincials are virtuous but naive. There is an inescapable tension between the two. Johnson, though he had left it, was nevertheless proud to be a native of Lichfield and glad to return there. Yet it also carried a definite stigma. Boswell, having frequently been on the receiving end of Johnsonian witticisms about the barbarity of the Scots, was distinctly unimpressed by Johnson's claim that the local inhabitants' English was of the very purest. He noted with satisfaction:

> Johnson himself never got entirely free of those provincial accents. Garrick sometimes used to take him off, squeezing a lemon into a punch-bowl with uncouth gesticulations, looking round the company and calling out, 'Who's for *poonsh*?'

To be a provincial was a fate from which you could never really escape, yet the provincials themselves scarcely wished it, since

176

these vestiges of a world they had left behind were also a sign of their own ultimately untarnished integrity.

In the following year Johnson displayed his distrust of the city in his first significant literary work, the poem 'London'. He execrated the city as a mecca for villains, as a place where you will 'Behold rebellious quite virtue o'erthrown' and where:

All crimes are safe but hated poverty.

Johnson celebrated the virtues of the provincial existence that he had so recently left behind:

I praise the Hermit, but regret the Friend,
Who now resolves, from Vice and LONDON far,
To breathe in distant Fields a purer Air,
And, fix'd on CAMBRIA's solitary shore,
Give to St DAVID one *true Briton* more.
For who would leave, unbrib'd, Hibernia's Land,
Or change the Rocks of Scotland for the Strand?

But in later life it was to be a different story. Johnson becomes the quintessential Londoner and unimpressable metropolitan, who finds the high tide of human existence at Charing Cross and who patronisingly jests that

... the Irish are a FAIR PEOPLE; – they never speak well of one another[1]

and that

... the noblest prospect which a Scotchman ever sees is the high road that leads him to England.[2]

Johnson, a provincial himself, was to become the man who derided the claims of provincial Britain to authenticity, integrity and moral grandeur.

If I deliberately lay stress on a notion of the 'provincial' this is partly to draw attention to the diverse ways in which Scotland, America and Ireland asserted their identity against the metropolitan centre, but also because I believe that discussions of British culture in the second half of the eighteenth century are over-simplified by the tendency to focus on an opposition between country and city, between rural and urban, formulated in such very generic terms. The effect of this, on the one hand, is to speak of much poetry as pastoral without paying sufficient attention to the complex ways in which the genre was being reformulated and defined; on the other to proleptically assume that the Victorian world of industrial towns and cities is effectively already in existence because it is arguably in the process of formation. The acorn becomes the oak tree in thought rather than in time. A characteristic instance of the kind of misconstruction that can result is in Donald Davie's preface to *The Late Augustans*, where Davie, as part of a generally praiseworthy attempt to revalue the provincial, cries down the overall importance of London:

> And indeed London, though it was the commercial and political capital, was not the place to listen for the beating of the nation's heart.That was to be heard in Manchester and industrial Shropshire on the one hand (where no poet was there to listen), or else in the ravaged villages of the agrarian south, their people drifting off the land toward the cotton mills of Manchester, the foundries of Ironbridge, or Josiah Wedgwood's Staffordshire potteries. London, at neither the losing nor the receiving end, was perhaps the worst vantage-point.
>
> The move to the provinces – more often, the willingness to stay there – is related to a new liveliness and civility in many of the provincial centres. This is the period when the Assembly Rooms are built in many provincial cities; and for thirty years, off and on (1731–62), the city of York, for instance, seems to have provided the novelist Laurence Sterne with as much as he needed of civilised society and cultural amenities. What is true of English provincial cities holds still truer of Edinburgh and Dublin. This is the great age of urban culture in both these cities, as appears from their architecture.[3]

In a way this is both unexceptional and suitably corrective, yet it is also profoundly misleading in its talk of cities and centres since Davie is not comparing like with like. London was *sui generis*, a gigantic centre of shipping, commerce and manufacture, the capital of a worldwide empire stretching from India to North America and the Caribbean, whose power was as much resented by that archetypal Englishman, William Cobbett, as it was by the Americans and the Irish. Already in 1724 Daniel Defoe was presenting London as a object of wonder:

> . . . looking north, behold, to crown it all, a fair prospect of the whole city of London it self; the most glorious sight without exception, that the whole world at present can show, or perhaps ever could show since the sacking of Rome in the European, and the burning of the Temple of Jerusalem in the Asian part of the world.[4]

Defoe may not have intended to suggest that London's turn would come, but there were many later who did envisage disaster or decline on the Roman model. Commerce led to Luxury, which in turn led to Decadence, an inexorable triad. London was certainly commercial and its credentials on the luxury front were equally impressive. Exotic goods were imported from all over the world. London's tally of theatres and taverns, pleasure gardens and prostitutes, its abundant cheap alcohol was unparalleled. York may indeed have been civilised but its population prior to 1801 was 13 000, that of London 775 000. Manchester may have had 300 000 inhabitants by 1851 but before 1801 they numbered only 30 000, even Edinburgh the northern capital was one-tenth the size of London. London was a phenomenon and eighteenth-century literature reflects this.

But if the late eighteenth century was a period where great cities such as London, Paris and Rome possessed a special magnetism, it was also a time where small nations and peoples on the periphery asserted their own sense of identity against the power of the centre, whether in Scotland, Ireland or in the American colonies. It is for this reason that I find it hard to accept the arguments about British national identity put forward by Linda Colley in her book, *Britons*. It is not hard to accept that Britain was in some measure patriotically unified against France in the period of the French revolution and the Napoleonic wars, though questions of class and the suppression of dissent would still have to be addressed. But it is a rather different matter to make this figure as the culmination of a unifying *trend*, while simultaneously failing to address the very considerable body of evidence that points in a contrary direction. Moreover, her notion that

    ... Britishness was superimposed over an array of cultural differences[5]

seems inconsistent with her language elsewhere, where she speaks of British national identity being 'forged'[6] and of Protestantism being something

    ... that first allowed the English, the Welsh and the Scots to become fused together.[7]

Colley's argument is either conceptually confused or excessively plastic and its overall tendency, despite some perfunctory allusions to local and regional loyalties, is so one-sided as to involve definite distortion. At the very least it needs to be acknowledged that there are powerful counter-currents resisting such a conceptual tide.

Perhaps the exemplary instance of such a regional rebellion was in Corsica where the local people began a struggle for their independence from Genoa in 1729 which was to last off and on until 1769 – some 40 years – when the Genoese, who had been depending upon French troops to suppress these rebellions, finally sold Corsica to the French. From that moment on Corsica was a colony of France and when Napoleon, himself a Corsican, became the ruler of France in 1799 questions of Corsican independence became largely academic. But in the mid eighteenth century the cause of the Corsican people was an exemplary one. Rousseau believed that Corsica was the one country in Europe that was still sufficiently virtuous and uncorrupted to form a free and democratic state and he drew up a constitution especially for their benefit. It was Rousseau who wrote James Boswell a letter of introduction which enabled him to visit Corsica and ensured that he was hospitably received, especially by their leader General Pascal Paoli. Boswell's *Account of Corsica*, published in 1768, helped to bring the cause of the Corsican people to a wider public but, partly because of the ineffectual response of the British Government led by the Duke of Grafton, it was too late to have any effect. What was particularly significant was that Boswell, – at the time of his visit in 1765 was a young Scotsman of 25 – should have strongly identified with the Corsicans, who as a courageous and fiercely independent people from a remote and mountainous area must have strongly recalled the Scottish highlanders who had been defeated in 1745. While some might find Boswell's reported speech to the people of Bastelica slightly comical:

> I expatiated on the bravery of the Corsicans, by which they had purchased liberty, the most valuable of all possessions, and rendered themselves glorious all over Europe. Their poverty, I told them, might be remedied by a proper cultivation of their island, and by engaging a little in commerce. But I bid them remember, that they were much happier in their present state than in a state of refinement and vice, and that therefore they should beware of luxury.[8]

There can be no doubt that Boswell was sincere. He genuinely admired the Corsican people and especially their leader, Paoli. Paoli was an educated man who believed in the exemplary value of Plutarch and Livy as a school of virtue but he equally insisted that virtuous sentiments and habits were beyond the scope of philosophical reasoning and that compared with a society of professors you would find more real virtue in 'a society of good peasants'.[9] To Boswell Paoli himself seemed like a reincarnation of the spirit of antique virtue, one of the truly great men of the age, so when Dr Johnson suggested that he empty his head of Corsica, which he thought had filled it for rather too long, Boswell indignantly replied:

> Empty my head of Corsica? Empty it of honour, empty it of humanity, empty it of friendship, empty it of piety. No! while I live, Corsica and the cause of the brave islanders shall ever employ much of my attention, shall ever interest me in the sincerest manner.[10]

It was one of the few occasions when the disciple morally eclipsed the master.

There were others who felt equally strongly about Corsica. Boswell's fellow-Scot Smollett, who in 1746 had written his moving lament 'The Tears of Scotland' which he angrily concluded:

> While the warm blood bedews my veins,
> And unimpair'd remembrance reigns,
> Resentment of my country's fate
> Within my filial breast shall beat;

And, spite of her insulting foe,
My sympathising verse shall flow:
'Mourn, hapless Caledonia, mourn
Thy banish'd peace, thy laurels torn.'

In his subsequent 'Ode to Independence' Smollett saw Corsica
as an exemplary instance of the transformative power of the spirit
of Liberty:

He virtue finds, like precious ore,
Diffus'd thro' every baser mould,
Even now he stands on Calvi's rocky shore,
And turns the dross of Corsica to gold.
He, guardian genius, taught my youth
Pomp's tinsel livery to despise:
My lips by him chastis'd to truth,
Ne'er pay'd that homage which the heart denies.

Perhaps more unexpectedly the Corsican struggle is invoked at
the beginning of John Langhorne's poem 'The Country Justice'
where Langhorne, in response to his own query as to whether
the old spirit of British liberty can still prevail, continues

Were thoughts like these the Dream of ancient Time?
Peculiar only to some Age, or Clime?
And does not Nature thoughts like these impart,
Breathe in the Soul, and write upon the Heart?
Ask on their mountains yon deserted Band,
That point to Paoli with no plausive Hand;
Despising still, their freeborn Souls unbroke,
Alike the *Gallic* and *Ligurian* Yoke!

When Langhorne wrote this in 1774 the Corsicans had been
defeated by an army of 30 000 French soldiers and General Paoli
himself was in exile in England, but despite all this the remarkable example of the Corsicans as a free and virtuous people still
matters!

In the second half of the eighteenth century the contrast of
modern commercial nations such as England and those relatively
backward peoples who still wish to hang on to their own system
of values becomes particularly important. In Britain the vivid-

ness of that difference was dramatised by the second Jacobite rebellion of 1745. To the Scots themselves it was a traumatic event as it seemed to represent, as Smollett had indicated, not just the defeat of a cause or a battle lost, but the destruction of a whole culture. If the closer assimilation of Scotland into the British economy promised greater prosperity and commercial development in the long run the price paid for that might well be intolerably high. Yet England might well be thought to have equal cause to worry. The uncouth and motley army of 5000 Highlanders who marched into Derby on 4 December 1745, with London seemingly at their mercy, might have seemed only a blip in the continuing story of Hanoverian rule, but it neverthless had the effect of inculcating a powerful moral lesson. The Highlanders might be poorly armed and poorly clad but in their bravery, loyalty and determination they epitomised the military virtue and sense of collective identity that had characterised the republics of the classical world, but which England – dependent on a paid militia to save it – obviously lacked. Even if the Scots had been defeated was not Britain nevertheless on a downward path? Certainly John Brown, the author of a crude but influential diatribe against the age, *An Estimate of the Manners and Principles of the Times* (1758), certainly thought so. Modern Britain, said Brown, was vain, decadent, luxurious and effeminate and the comparative success of the rebellion proved it:

> How far the dastard spirit of Effeminacy has crept upon us, and destroyed the national Spirit of Defence, may appear from the general *Panic* the nation was thrown into, at the late *Rebellion*. When those of every Rank above a Constable, instead of arming themselves and encouraging the *People*, generally fled before the *Rebels*; while a Mob of ragged Highlanders marched unmolested to the Heart of a populous Kingdom.[11]

Writing over a decade later Brown's lurid rhetoric and sense of crisis might seem somewhat disproportionate but his general case was taken very seriously, for the issues raised were as much moral as military. Even Adam Smith, in his *The Wealth of Nations* (1776), the great advocate of commerce and free trade, in his early *Lectures on Justice, Politce, Revenue and Arms*, delivered in 1763, was prepared to concede that this invasion was proof of a decline in morale and the martial spirit that a commercial society could induce. In *The Wealth of Nations* itself Smith worried that without a citizen's army cowardice might spread:

> Even though the martial spirit of the people were of no use towards the defence of society, yet to prevent that sort of mental mutilation, deformity and wretchedness, which cowardice necessarily involves in it, from spreading themselves through the great body of the people would still deserve the most serious attention of government.[12]

Smith's earnestness on this score may well have been prompted by Adam Ferguson, who in his *An Essay on the History of Civil Society* (1767), was anxious to stress that the progress of mankind from barbarism to polished society, from hunter, herdsman and farmer to merchant and craftsman, involved significant losses as well as gains. Ferguson, himself a Highlander, drew a critical portrait of the modern commercial world, which he contrasted unfavourably with ancient Greece and Rome. The citizen of Sparta or Rome in acting as both soldier and responsible citizen was a whole man while his modern counterpart is narrow, self-centred and isolated:

> To the ancient Greek, or the Roman, the individual was nothing, the public everything. To the modern, in too many nations of Europe, the individual is every thing and the public nothing. . . . Our ancestors in rude ages, during the recess of wars from abroad, fought for their personal claims at home and by their competitions, and the balance of their powers, maintained a kind of political freedom in the state, while private parties were subject to continual wrongs and oppressions. Their posterity, in times more polished, have repressed the civil disorders in which the activity of earlier ages chiefly consisted; but they employ the calm they have gained, not in fostering a zeal for those laws, and that constitution of government, to which they owe their protection, but in practising apart, and each for himself, the several arts of personal advancement, or profit, which their political establishments may enable them to pursue with success.[13]

So the Scots in committing themselves to English ways may simply be adopting a more degraded way of life. Ferguson, of course does not say this in so many words, but not a few of his contemporaries did. Henry MacKenzie, author of *The Man of Feeling*, in an article cited by John Dwyer in his *Virtuous Discourse*, warned Scotsmen of position and rank;

> If from luxury and vain love of expense, they shall also give way to this desire for wealth; if they shall extinguish the sentiments of public virtue, and the passion for true glory, natural to that order of the state; the spring of private and national honour must have lost its force. And there will remain nothing to withstand the general corruption of manners, and the public disorder and debility which are its inseparable attendants.[14]

However, despite the fact that the prospect that loomed before the nation was menacing there remained the consoling thought Scotland had yet to go down a path that other countries had already taken. There was the opportunity to learn from the mistakes and misfortunes of others. There was still a virtue there to preserve.

The defence of small nations against the might of great powers and political empires was given a considerable boost by publication of Montesquieu's *L'Esprit des Lois* (1748), translated by Thomas Nugent as *The Spirit of the Laws* in 1750. Montesquieu divided states into three main types: republics grounded in virtue, monarchies founded on the principle of honour and despotisms based on fear. Despotism was the frightening spectre which persistently stalked through Montesquieu's voluminous and often discontinuous pages and despotism was the characteristic political system of empires. Republics tended to be comparatively small, monarchies of medium size. Europe had fortunately been saved from the pains of oriental despotism by the fact that mountainous boundaries had limited the effective size of states. But what gave Montesquieu's analysis of empire a cutting edge was his negative assessment of imperial Rome. Montesquieu did not simply point to faults and flaws in the Roman Empire, as both his predecessors had done and his successors, like Gibbon, were to do. Montesquieu suggested that the whole imperial enterprise was mistaken and self-destructive. The Roman republic not only destroyed its own values as it progressively over-extended itself; it also created a despotic empire that was doomed to collapse. Not even the wisest laws could reestablish

... what a dying republic, a general anarchy, a military government, a harsh empire, a haughty despotism, a weak monarchy, and an inane, idiotic, and superstitious court had by turns beaten down; one would have said they had conquered the world only to weaken it and deliver it defenceless to the barbarians.[15]

Montesquieu was even sceptical of Roman claims to civilisation based on refinement and manners:

The epoch of Roman politeness is the same as that of the establishment of arbitrary power. Absolute government produces idleness, and idleness gives birth to politeness.[16]

No doubt Montesquieu, though he dare not say so, was acutely conscious of parallels between the Augustan age and the court of Louis XIV. Ferguson, who always acknowledged himself to be Montesquieu's disciple was quick to pick up on these allusions and point their significance for contemporary Scotland against the imperial claims of Britain. Ferguson not only insisted that Rome should *not* be admired for her greatness and splendour which were

... ruinous to the virtue and happiness of mankind[17]

he insisted that true civilisation was more likely to be found in small nations, like Scotland, than in great and powerful states, like France and England:

Great and powerful states are able to overcome and subdue the weak; polished and commercial nations have more wealth, and practise a greater variety of arts, than the rude: but the happiness of men, in all cases alike, consists in the blessings of a candid, an active, and strenuous mind. And if we consider the state of society merely as that into which mankind are led by their propensities, as a state to be valued from its effect in preserving the species, in ripening their talents, and exciting their virtues, we need not enlarge our communities, in order to enjoy these advantages. We frequently obtain them in the most remarkable degree, where nations remain independent, and are of a small extent.[18]

This, masked as it is, is a declaration of cultural independence and a reassertion of Scottish national identity.

After Montesquieu the definitive analysis of the collapse of the Roman Empire was to be that of Edward Gibbon. Gibbon did not believe that the project of empire itself was inherently flawed. His analysis, as befitted such an extensive survey was multicausal, pointing to the character of individual emperors, the role of Christianity, the relaxation of military discipline, the introduction of barbarians into the Roman armies, the absurdity of a situation whereby emperors who were unable to protect the subjects whom they taxed so heavily were nevertheless unwilling to trust them with arms for their own defence. Indeed the enormous duration of Rome's decline and fall, continuing as it did for more than a thousand years after the accession of Commodus in 180 AD suggested that Montesquieu's notion that the empire was automatically doomed was either wrong or impossibly glib. But Gibbon nevertheless did retain some of the general terms of Montesquieu's geographical/political analysis and in the process came close to undermining his own more contingent and historical approach. At the end of Chapter 38, in his 'General Observations on the Fall of the Roman Empire in the West' he conceded that

> The decline of Rome was the natural and inevitable effect of immoderate greatness. Prosperity ripened the principle of decay; the causes of destruction multiplied with the extent of conquest; and as soon as time or accident had removed the artificial supports, the stupendous fabric yielded to the pressure of its own weight.[19]

Gibbon also accepted Montesquieu's argument that the existence of a number of small or medium-sized states in Europe had helped to preserve political freedom. Perhaps most surprisingly of all, Gibbon, the sophisticated cosmopolitan, was disposed to accept the Scottish suggestion that rude nations might actually be more civilised than those allegedly more polished. MacPherson in his introduction to *Fingal* proclaimed:

> If we have placed Fingal in his proper period, we do honour to the manners of barbarous times. He exercised every manly virtue in Caledonia, while Heliogabalus disgraced human nature at Rome . . .[20]

a suggestion that the omniverous Gibbon picked up with alac-
rity in the first volume of the *Decline and Fall* even as he conceded
the possible unreliability of the source. Gibbon was happy to
reverse the usual terms of analysis:

> ... if we could with safety, indulge the pleasing supposition,
> that Fingal lived, and that Ossian sung, the striking contrast
> of the situation and manners of the contending nations might
> amuse a philosophic mind. The parallel would be little to the
> advantage of the more civilised people, if we compare the
> unrelenting revenge of Severus with the generous clemency
> of Fingal; the timid and brutal cruelty of Caracalla, with the
> bravery, the tenderness, the elegant genius of Ossian; the
> mercenary chiefs who, from motives of fear or interest, served
> under the Imperial standard, with the freeborn warriors who
> started to arms at the voice of the king of Morven; if, in a
> word, we contemplated the untutored Caledonians, glowing
> with the warm virtues of nature, and the degenerate Romans,
> polluted with the mean vices of wealth and slavery.[21]

The contrast between nature and culture, between the tainted
metropolis and the untutored and unspoiled barbarians that Gibbon
draws is, in its romanticisation of innocence, closer to Rousseau
than to *The Spirit of the Laws*.

Since Scotland was, to all intents and purposes, a conquered
province it was perhaps to be expected that Scottish criticism of
England, though clearly stated, should nevertheless be presented
in a way that was guarded, judicious, oblique even circumspect
but this was by no means the case with the American colonists
as they protested Britain's right to impose taxation without
representation. For, although the defeat of the French in North
America during the Seven Years War and the subsequent accession
of Canada to the crown removed one threat it immediately raised
another: that the new king, George III, in extending his empire
would be correspondingly encouraged to transform monarchy into
despotism. The puritan ministers who preached against British
imperial power at the time of the American Revolution were
convinced that within this empire the American people were the
repository of the spirit of liberty and virtue, the saving remnant,
who could be replied upon to deliver themselves and ultimately
the whole world from tyranny and corruption. Moses Mather, in

his 1775 sermon justifying American rebellion 'America's Appeal to the Impartial World', referred to Montesquieu's suggestion

> ... that England could never lose its freedom, until parliament lost its virtue[22]

but went on to insist that such a moment had undoubtedly arrived when a British parliament asserted its power over the property of Americans without their consent:

> If the parliament have no such power as is claimed, their invading our rights, and in them the rights of the constitution, under pretence of authority; besieging and desolating our seaports, employing dirty tools, whose sordid souls, like vermin, delight to riot on filth; to practice every artifice to seduce, that they may the easier destroy; with money tempting, with arms terrifying the inhabitants, to induce and compel a servile submission; is treason against the kingdom, of the deepest die, and blackest complexion.[23]

In the America of the time Britain was perceived as a corrupted empire that needed to be rescued and redeemed from its own worst tendencies. The Philadelphia *Packet* of 8 August 1774 wrote:

> Those very symptoms which preceded the fall of Rome, appear but too evident in the British constitution.[24]

John Witherspoon in his sermon preached at Princeton on 17 May 1776 suggested that it had become commonplace to prophesy

> ... the downfall of the British empire, from the corruption and degeneracy of the people

and therefore rejoiced that the British restraint of commerce and trade would have the effect of denying 'articles of luxury and magnificence' to the colonists, thus compelling them to lead a life of sobriety, moderation and virtuous industry.[25] In the struggle against colonial power America would be both outwardly and inwardly cleansed.

If the Americans were so strongly convinced of their own righteousness in what they came to regard as a cosmic battle between virtue and vice, between the powers of good and evil, this was because many of their ministers viewed it as a repetition of the events that had led to the founding of the American colonies in New England in the first place. In the seventeenth century the Puritan settlers, knowing that they were not safe even in Holland, had crossed the Atlantic ocean to escape from the persecution of Archbishop Laud, chief minister of Charles I. It seemed as if the Lord had created North America as a kind of sacred and undefilable space for his anointed. So for Samuel Sherwood in his sermon 'The Church's Flight Into the Wilderness', 17 January 1776, there were important parallels between the struggle for a Protestant religion in the past and the struggle against a 'a corrupt system of tyranny and oppression' in the present.[26] It was as if, then as now, America had been established in God's dispensation as the last great place where liberty and freedom of conscience could be defended:

> This American quarter of the globe seemed to be reserved in providence, as a fixed and settled habitation for God's church, where she might have property of her own, and the right of rule and government, so as not to be controul'd and oppress'd in her civil and religious liberties, by the tyrannical and persecuting powers of the earth, represented by the red dragon.[27]

The red dragon of course was the sinister beast referred to in the verses from the book of *Revelation* that Sherwood took as the text for his sermon. In this light George III became associated with the beast and the great whore of Babylon as part of the forces of darkness. His attempt to assert despotic power over the American colonies had to be regarded as nothing less than a impious and determined attempt to flout and overturn the expressed will of God. Such a view was not confined to a handful of Calvinist divines but became part of a widespread interpretation of the world – historical significance of the American revolution.

In *Common Sense* Tom Paine made a similar connection:

> The new world hath been the place of asylum for the persecuted lovers of civil and religious liberty from every part of Europe. Hither have they fled, not from the tender embraces of the mother, but from the cruelty of the monster; and it is so

far true of England, that the same tyranny which drove the first emigrants from home, pursues their descendants still.[28]

In this way the Struggle for American independence became an apocalyptic struggle between the forces of good and evil. In his pamphlet, 'The Crisis', Tom Paine expressed his conviction that God was on the side of the colonists – indeed to believe anything else would be an impiety:

> Neither have I so much of the infidel in me as to suppose that He has relinquished the government of the world, and given us up to the care of devils; and as I do not, I cannot see on what grounds the King of Britain can look up to heaven for help against us: a common murderer, a highwayman, or a housebreaker has as good a pretense as he.[29]

Paine could not have disagreed with Abraham Ketelkas, who in his sermon of 5 October 1777, dramatically insisted that the cause of the Americans was a glorious cause:

> It is the cause of the reformation, against popery; of liberty, against arbitrary power; of benevolence, against barbarity, and of virtue against vice. It is the cause of justice and integrity, against bribery, venality, and corruption. In short, it is the cause of heaven against hell – of the kind Parent of the universe, against the Prince of darkness, and the destroyer of the human race.[30]

In the heat of the moment, the desperation of the hour, it seemed that virtuous America was locked in a cosmic struggle with corrupt Britain which they could not and would not lose.

Yet after independence was finally won a few doubts began to creep in. An important reason for this was that the language of virtue was not one that sprang readily to the lips of America's Calvinist preachers. Since they believed that man was born into sin and depravity and could only be saved, if at all, by God's grace to speak of virtue was to risk compromising the most vital tenets of their faith. It became possible only under the influence of strong patriotic emotions and fears and because it seemed to be sanctioned by Montesquieu's own insistence in the Foreword to *L'Esprit des Lois* that when he speaks of virtue he means specifically political virtue. So puritan divines could legitimately rally their congregations under the flag of colonial rebellion without necessarily compromising their belief in original sin and Moses Mather could proclaim:

> The strength and spring of every free government, is the virtue of the people.[31]

But were the American people truly virtuous? After the success of the Revolution this question became more urgent rather than less. Even in a sermon preached on the occasion of the adoption of a new constitution in the state of New Hampshire in 1784 doubts were already being raised. The dangerous analogy with Rome that had figured so prominently in the struggle with Britain now began to feature on an American political agenda. Samuel McLintock was prepared to hold up as a salutary warning to Americans the fate of the Roman people, who were corrupted by Asian luxury:

> ... it produced a entire change in the public state and manners, so that a people who had been celebrated for their virtue and courage, became effeminate and luxurious, and sold their birthright for a mess of pottage.[32]

America as a young nation was likely to be particularly vulnerable to corruption:

> ... if we do evil and fall into the vices and corruptions that have brought ruin on other nations, we may assuredly expect that we shall meet with their doom.[33]

Now it was not British power that was feared but British influence. Although Royall Tyler, one of the earliest of American dramatists, felt no shame in basing his play *The Contrast* (first performed in 1887) on Sheridan's *The School for Scandal*, the forceful and patriotic message of the play was the need to maintain the honesty and integrity of native American manners and to avoid the sophisticated but decidedly decadent behaviour that Lord Chesterfield had furnished a manual for in his *Letters to his Son*. The contrast Tyler speaks of lies between the honest and courageous Colonel Manly, who has fought for his country's independence and Billy Dimple, who, after a visit to Europe, has been transformed from a

... ruddy youth who washed his face at the cistern every morning

into an unscrupulous seducer of women,

... a flippant, palid, polite beau, who devotes his morning to his toilet, reads a few pages of Chesterfield's letters, and then minces out, to put the infamous principles in practice upon every woman he meets.

Though Colonel Manly, the patriotic hero, is deeply concerned that America may succumb to the influence of foreign manners and foreign luxury, he too is deceived by Dimple and seems likely to lose the hand of Maria Van Rough to his artful rival. But Dimple is exposed and the play concludes with Manly proclaiming:

I have learned that probity, virtue, honour, though they should not have received the polish of Europe, will secure to an Honest American the good graces of his fair countrywoman, and, I hope, the applause of THE PUBLIC.

Significantly when Dimple says 'Colonel, I presume you have been in Europe' Manly responds 'Indeed, Sir, I was never ten leagues from that continent.' Since his virtuousness is clearly bound up with the fact that he has never been exposed to alien influences. A similar morality, verging on xenophobia, is found in the novels of Charles Brockden Brown – the villainy of such figures as Carwin in *Wieland* (1798), Welbeck in *Arthur Mervyn* (1799), Clithero in *Edgar Huntly* (1799), the protagonist of *Ormond* (1799) seem inextricably linked with their transatlantic background. A comparable warning concerning the hazards of foreign travel is to be found in a letter which Thomas Jefferson wrote to Peter Carr – from Paris – in the same year, 1787, in which *The Contrast* was first performed:

There is no place where your pursuit of knowledge will be so little obstructed by foreign objects as in your own country, nor any wherein the virtues of the heart will be less exposed to be weakened.[34]

Indeed, more than half a century later Emerson – in his celebrated essay 'Self-Reliance' – was still warning of the dangers of foreign travel and the risks of imitation;

> The soul is no traveller: the wise man stays at home, and when his necessities, his duties, on any occasion call him from his house, or into foreign lands, he is at home still, and is not gadding about from himself, and shall make men sensible by the expression of his countenance, that he goes the missionary of wisdom and virtue, and visits cities and men like a sovereign, and not like an interloper or valet.[35]

The contrast between the virtuous Manly and the polished Billy Dimple is still implicitly there.

But perhaps the most striking and self-confident repudiation of the value of the Grand Tour occurs in Crèvecoeur's *Letters from an American Farmer* (1782). Crèvecoeur's first letter, which takes the form of conversations between the farmer, his wife and the local minister, which effectively justify the book, by showing why such letters would be of interest to a cultivated English reader. The farmer and the minister are puzzled by the fact that so many people are eager to visit Italy when the American scene has so many instructive lessons to offer. The minister observes:

> I am sure I cannot be called a partial American when I say that the spectacle afforded by these pleasing scenes must be more entertaining and more philosophical than that which arises from beholding the musty ruins of Rome. . . .There the half-ruined amphitheatres and putrid fevers of the Campania must fill the mind with the most melancholy reflections whilst he is seeking for the origin and the intention of those structures with which he is surrounded and for the cause of so great a decay. Here he might contemplate the very beginnings and outlines of human society, which can be traced nowhere now but in this part of the world. The rest of the earth, I am told, is in some places too full, in others half depopulated. Misguided religion, tyranny, and absurd laws everywhere depress and afflict mankind. Here we have in some measure regained the ancient dignity of our species: our laws are simple and just; we are a race of cultivators;our cultivation is unrestrained; and everything is prosperous and flourishing.[36]

Implicitly, what Rome was, America now is. Rome is the shadow, America is the substance – a young, thriving, virtuous and happy republic. Americans have nothing to learn from the corrupted old metropolitan centres of the Grand Tour; but Europeans would be well advised to study and profit from the American example.

The successful American struggle for independence had the effect of throwing into even starker relief Ireland's long standing grievances against England. For the exclusion of the possibility of political independence for Ireland was symbolised by Poyning's Law, which denied autonomy to her legislature, and was effectively manifested in the restrictions which were placed on the export of Irish manufactures. So the Irish and the American causes were directly parallel but this did not mean that Britain would concede to Ireland what she had been unable to enforce on the other side of the Atlantic ocean. Even before the American insurrection Margaret Bingham, Lady Lucan, had expressed her indignation against British rule in her 'Verses on the Present State of Ireland' (1768). She complained that the long-suffering Irish people were 'to roots confin'd', that Irish trade was unjustly restricted and that, despite British claims to religious toleration, in Ireland Protestants were unfairly privileged over Catholics. She then recounted the story of Eva and Connor, who are denied their rightful inheritance, when Murdac, the younger son, turns Protestant in order to claim the property and they are compelled to travel to the New World as 'virtuous fugitives' – among the first of many who were to embark on such a journey. After 1776 the political campaign to place Ireland on the same independent footing as America was led by the inspirational political orator, Henry Grattan. Henrietta Battier, writing under the name of Patt. Pindar, defended Grattan against Protestant libels in her poem, 'The Lemon':

> What matchless malice urged thee to profane
> Time honour'd Grattan in thy ruffian strain?
> Oh, soul of Swift, Ierne's dearest friend,
> From Heaven if possible my spirit lend
> To Grattan's offspring, and indue his breast
> With strength and rigour equal to the test;
> When patriot virtue in a chosen few
> Dares the fell fury of a sanguine crew.

Battier's reference to 'a chosen few' strikes a significant and often repeated note. For those who were actually prepared to stand up and directly challenge British rule were never quite as many as might have been expected, considering the depressed state of Ireland and the extent of the discontent that so perpetually simmered just beneath the surface. The gentry, in particular, were too narrowly self-regarding and too complacent to involve themselves in any uncertain struggle for Irish independence. At the time of the rebellion of the United Irishmen in 1798 Wolfe Tone praised his friend Sir Lawrence Parsons for resigning his command of the King's County militia because of his alarm about possible 'sanguinary measures' by the British government and commented:

> His example should be imitated by every country gentleman in Ireland; but they have neither the sense nor the virtue to see that. . . . What miserable slaves are the gentry of Ireland . . . If they had one drop of Irish blood in their veins, one grain of true courage or genuine patriotism in their hearts, they should have been the first to support this great object.[37]

But it was always easy for Britain to bribe and congenially induce Ireland's leaders away from any untoward spirit of independence. Henry Flood was in many respects an honourable man who had Ireland's best interests at heart, yet he was inveigled into accepting responsibilities under the Crown and thus into defending British government policy against Grattan's attacks. So political virtue was a very real concept in the Ireland of the time. In his speech to the Irish parliament in 1782 Grattan described Britain's claim to Ireland in Swift's terms as being nothing more than

> . . . the right of a grenadier to take the property of a naked man.

He challenged the Irish assembly to stand up to England:

> Stationed as you are, and placed as you are in relation to the community and these great objects, how do you mean to proceed? Submit and take the lead in desertion? Impossible! The strength which at your back supports your virtue, precludes your apostasy; the armed presence of the nation will not bend; the community will not be sold; nor will a nation in arms suffer the eternal blessing of freedom and renown to depend on the

experiment, whether this villain shall be a pensioner, or that pickpocket a peer.[38]

Supported by 25 000 armed volunteers, Grattan and his supporters got their way. The British government removed all existing constitutional restraints on the Irish parliament. For a moment Ireland seemed a united, independent and politically virtuous nation. As in America Roman analogies were popular. Grattan had invoked cities and counties

> . . . who have breathed a spirit that would have done honour to old Rome when Rome did honour to mankind . . .[39]

thus carefully invoking the republic rather than the empire. But the analogy was always fragile. The depressed, near starving Irish tenant scarcely enjoyed the economic and social independence of the Roman soldier/farmer. Religious divisions were damaging to political unity as had not been the case with the American colonies. The Protestant ascendancy had at best divided loyalties, at worst no interest in Irish independence whatsoever. In the event the great victory proved something of a mirage. The Lord Lieutenant continued to govern Ireland as representative of the King, with all the usual powers of patronage at his disposal. Renewed political frustration, a frustration intensified by tangible evidence of a movement in France towards democracy both before and after the French Revolution, led to the rebellion of the United Irishmen in 1798, but the sporadic outbreaks were suppressed well before the French assistance that had been promised could arrive. In what was to be one of the most familiar Irish patriotic verses, 'The Wake of William Orr' – a farmer who was sentenced to death for administering the United Irishman's oath to a soldier – William Drennan, a leading Protestant figure in the movement, wrote:

> There our murdered brother lies;
> Wake him not with woman's cries;
> Mourn the way that manhood ought –
> Sit in silent trance of thought.
>
> Write his merits on your mind;
> Morals pure and manners kind;

In his head, as on a hill
Virtue placed her citadel.

Why cut off in palmy youth?
Truth he spoke, and acted truth.
'Countrymen, UNITE', he cried,
And died for what our Saviour died . . .

Hapless Nation, rent and torn,
Thou wert early taught to mourn;
Warfare of six hundred years!
Epochs marked with blood and tears!

Hunted thro' thy native grounds,
Or flung *reward* to human hounds,
Each one pulled and tore his share,
Heedless of thy deep despair.

Significantly Drennan does not focus on William Orr as an exemplification of the struggle for independence as such; he makes him symbolic rather of a Christlike spirit of self-sacrifice, as contrasted with a wider selfishness and of the desire for national unity which is the precondition for such independence. Orr is the exemplary Irishman – the man who is the harbinger of the future 'morning light' with which the poem ends. Grattan and Orr possess the pure and disinterested patriotic virtue which is not as widespread as it should be.

In a more literary context after 1760, the distrust of the centre, the tendency to celebrate the integrity of the margins, became complexly bound up with the rejection of neo-classicism as represented by the poetry of Alexander Pope. Three works in particular provided the intellectual underpinnings for this new sensibility: Burke's *A Philosophical Enquiry into the Origin of our Ideas of the Sublime and the Beautiful* (1757), Edward Young's *Conjectures on Original Composition* (1759) and Richard Hurd's *Letters on Chivalry and Romance* (1762). Although the idea of the Sublime was by no means new, Burke revived it as a topic of interest and gave a fresh stimulus to the idea that what mattered, whether in landscape or poetry, was the capacity to overwhelm, surprise and astonish rather than simply to please. Young rejected the key assumption of neo-classicism that the goal was to imitate the best

models, insisting that Homer's greatness lay precisely in the fact
that he had no option but to be original, since there were then
no predecessors whose example must be followed. Hurd, by praising what he called 'Gothic romance', which unhesitatingly
addressed magical and fantastic subjects, and by putting forward
Spenser as the alternative to neo-classicism, encouraged poets to
shed their inhibitions. Yet, in some sense, these texts simply served
to validate verse already being written by such figures as Joseph
and Thomas Wharton and William Collins – which revelled in
mythology, used the Spenserian stanza and relished poetic diction
with an archaic flavour – such words as wight, dight, swain, fain,
courser, beldame, crew, ween, yestreen, and frith. Subsequently
with a poet like Chatterton, the use of such language became
virtually an end in itself and its exotic allure is also reflected in
Coleridge's 'Rime of the Ancient Mariner and Keats's 'The Eve
of St. Agnes'. But MacPherson, as a Scot, sought to use such antique
language as the vehicle for a heroic sensibility that could both
challenge the metropolitan centre and provide the focus for a
regional culture. This in turn became linked with the revival of
various forms of folk poetry, through such works as Evans' *Speci-
mens of the Ancient Welsh Bards (1764)*, Percy's *Reliques of English
Poetry* (1765) and Herd's *Ancient and Modern Scots Songs* (1769).
Moreover, if this ancient poetry was sublime and morally uplifting, so too was the landscape amongst which it was composed.
The beauty of the remoter and wilder parts of Britain was
celebrated in Lyttleton's *Account of a Journey Into Wales* (1774) and
a series of works by William Gilpin, his *Observations on the Wye*
(1782), *Cumberland* (1782) and the *Highlands of Scotland* (1789).
Nevertheless, although this mixture of provincialism, antiquarianism and nostalgia was powerful it did not necessarily attract
supporters or opponents from the expected quarters. David Hume,
for example was contemptuous of the superstitious ignorance of
the Druids, Celts and early Britons who in other circles were
becoming fashionable. Even those who were tempted by such
antiquarianism neverthless felt obliged to guard against succumbing
too completely to its charms. In his 'Verses on Sir Joshua Reynolds'
Painted Window' at New College, Oxford Warton begins by freely
confessing to his fascination with the Middle Ages:

> For long, enamour'd of a barbarous age,
> A faithless truant to the classic page

but ends by rejoicing in the transfiguring power of the modern:

> Reynolds, 'tis thine, from the broad window's height,
> To add new lustre to religious light:
> Not of its pomp to strip this ancient shrine,
> But bid that pomp with purer radiance shine:
> With arts unknown before, to reconcile
> The willing Graces to the Gothic pile.

The classical aesthetic still dominates. The same applies to his 'Ode Written at Vale-Royal Abbey in Cheshire', which initially conjures up a heroic past and the figure of a minstrel who celebrates it. Yet the bard who

> With fond regret surveys these ruin'd piles

is in some sense deluded and the modern sensibility, however regretfully, must take a different view:

> But much we pardon to th'ingenuous Muse;
> Her fairy shapes are tricked by Fancy's pen:
> Severer Reason forms far other views,
> And scans the scene with philosophic ken.
>
> From these deserted domes new glories rise;
> More useful institutes, adorning man,
> Manners enlarged, and new civilities,
> On fresh foundations build the social plan.

In the end the past was barbarous just as the present is progressive and civilised and it would involve bad faith to pretend anything else.

A similar ambivalence characterises Beattie's *The Minstrel* (1771). In the first part of the poem Beattie, writing as a Scottish patriot and in a manner that anticipates Wordsworth, celebrates the virtue, innocence and sensitivity of his minstrel hero, Edwin, who has been brought up in the highlands of Scotland far from the corruptions of the city. He concludes Book I by saying:

> At lucre or renown let others aim.
> I only wish to please the gentle mind,
> Whom Nature's charms inspire, and love of human kind.

But Beattie, as a representative of the Scottish Enlightenment, does not wish to be to be thought obscurantist or unappreciative of the value of progress, so in Part II Edwin is lectured by a Sage as follows:

> Lo! with dim eyes that never learn'd to smile,
> And trembling hands, the famish'd native craves
> Of Heaven his wretched fare; shivering in caves,
> Or scorch'd on rocks, he pines from day to day;
> But Science gives the word; and, lo! he braves
> The surge and tempest, lighted by her ray,
> And to a happier land wafts happily away.

Is this 'happier land' England? Beattie does not say. But if solitude, nature and virtue are good so too are the comforts of civilisation.

But if Warton and Beattie are wary of slighting science and progress this is certainly not the case with William Collins, who in a brief yet remarkable poetic career (he died aged 39 in 1759), identified strongly with many of the anti-rational tendencies which were subsequently to be associated with Romanticism. Collins felt that neo-classicism was too narrow, rigid and starchy and most of his poems are manifestoes specifically directed against it. Yet Collins's opposition itself has classical sources. His reading in the original of such classic Greek writers as Aeschylus, Sophocles, Euripides and Pindar led him to question the idea of a classical tradition centred on Virgil and Horace and such values as balance and reason. Collins embarked on a translation of Aristotle's *Poetics*, for money – a task which, like many others, he never completed – yet in many ways the project was close to his own heart since he also valued the tragic emotions of pity and fear and wrote odes addressed to them. For Collins there was sublimity in the irrational, the mysterious, the magical and the superstitious. As Dr Johnson suggested: he was

> . . . eminently delighted with those flights of imagination which pass the bounds of nature, and to which the mind is reconciled only by a passive acquiescence in popular traditions. He loved fairies, genii, giants, and monsters.[40]

As Johnson's *Journey to the Western Isles of Scotland* makes clear, Johnson himself was very far from bring prepared to acquiesce in such matters and the gulf between Collins and himself is of great significance, since for Collins the fantastic is itself poetic. Collins' fascination with folklore and legend is evident in many of his poems. He invokes 'fairy legends' and the story of Florimel's magic girdle in *The Faerie Queene*, in his 'Ode on the Poetical Character', goblins and ghosts, in his 'Ode to Fear', and in the 'Ode to Liberty' the Dutch folk superstition that they will lose their liberty if the storks disappear, and in his 'Ode on the Popular Superstitions of the Highlands of Scotland' such things as fairies, wizards, kelpies, the will-o'the wisp, pygmies and ghosts. Collins looks forward to the day when poetry will return to Nature; when 'meddling Art's officious lore' will 'Reverse the lesson taught before' –

> Alluring from a safer rule
> To dream in her enchanted school.

Although Collins could celebrate provincial virtue:

> But o! o'er all, forget not Kilda's race,
> On whose bleak rocks, which brave the wasting tides,
> Fair Nature's daughter, Virtue, yet abides!

he did not thereby identify with the Scottish point of view, also choosing in the same poem to celebrate the Duke of Cumberland, the butcher of Culloden, and, to Collins, the defender of British liberty, just four years after the event. Thomas Gray made a much greater attempt to understand the culture of the Celtic fringes. He studied the Welsh language and made a number of translations from it. He also visited Scotland in 1765 – one of the first English men of letters to do so. What is significant about 'The Bard' is that Gray, instead of writing *in propria persona* as he did in the Elegy and other poems, chose very dramatically and unexpectedly to project himself back into the past, speaking as a Welsh bard who survives the massacre ordered by Edward I on the foothills of Snowdon in 1283 but then commits suicide. Gray's poem, which touches on many of the great names in Welsh mythology is a lament for a lost culture and a plangent condemnation of the 'ruthless king' who has brought it about. What makes this all the more remarkable is that the poem, written in 1757, must have forcibly reminded contemporary readers that a similar massacre had taken place in Scotland not 600 years ago but scarcely more than a decade. In a very real sense 'The Bard' is one of the very first manifestoes that asserts the values of the periphery, that questions the whole process of domination and conquest that has led to the creation of Britain.

A particularly severe opponent of these provincial sympathies and incipiently romantic tendencies was Dr Johnson, who was quite surprisingly hostile to the poetry of both Collins and Gray. Johnson seems to have some respect for Collins's talents, despite his lack of application, and he seems to have been genuinely moved by his madness and early death. Yet this did not prevent him from concluding his brief life with a fairly comprehensive indictment of his poetry:

> To what I have formerly said of his writings may be added that his diction was often harsh, unskilfully laboured, and injudiciously selected. He affected the obsolete when it was not worthy of revival; and he put his words out of the common order, seeming to think, with some later candidates for fame, that not to write prose is certainly to write poetry. His lines commonly are of slow motion, clogged and impeded with clusters of consonants. As men are often esteemed who cannot be loved, so the poetry of Collins may sometimes extort praise when it gives little pleasure.[41]

Johnson was equally scathing in his comments on the poetry of Gray and although the life in this case concludes with some grudging praise for the Elegy much of the rest consists of a detailed demolition, as Johnson sees it, of 'The Progress of Poetry' and 'The Bard'. However, these remarks are of greater interest in that they do bring out very clearly just how opposed Johnson was to archaicising tendencies and to poetry on mythological subjects – though Johnson would certainly have been prepared to exempt classical mythology from such strictures on the grounds that the Romans would have found them true;

The fictions of Horace were to the Romans credible.[42]

In the case of Wales, however, he objects to 'the puerilities of obsolete mythology'. He complains about the harshness of 'The Bard's' poetic language, denies that it 'promotes any truth, moral or political', finds the whole narrative incredible and even purports to be indignant at its plagiarism. Johnson's objections are so factitious and contrived that, rather than take them at face value, it seems more sensible to look for his underlying motives. Certainly, Johnson genuinely believed that to try to write poetry outside the classical tradition was not to write poetry at all and that only motives of perversity could inspire any such attempt. But Johnson's mixture of violence and incomprehension displays the colonialism of the metropolitan centre. If provincialism in any way promotes or encourages cultural diversity or even suggests the possiblity of alternative identities then it needs to be ruthlessly put down. Johnson does not just *not* understand Gray and Collins, he is refusing to understand them.

In 1773, Johnson, aged 63, embarked, with Boswell, on the arduous journey to Scotland, which he recorded in his *A Journey to the Western Isles of Scotland* (1775). His motives for visiting the country, which he had heard so much about were undoubtedly very mixed. Boswell had been urging him to make the journey for some time. Moreover, Johnson as a Jacobite sympathiser was undoubtedly curious to see some of the locations associated with Bonnie Prince Charlie, as Boswell later recorded, but Johnson carefully concealed this interest in his own account. But Johnson also had a more serious intention: which was to describe as faithfully as he could the remains and vestiges of the old Scottish way of life before they finally passed away. He was never in any doubt that what he was to see and what he actually did see was the survival of a crude and barbaric way of life, which, while it might be interesting simply because it *was* different, could never be regarded as anything other than inferior. As Boswell noted in *Journal of a Tour to the Hebrides*, Johnson was

> Always for maintaining the superiority of civilized over uncivilized men.[43]

Just as Johnson – correctly – refused to believe that the poems of Ossian were authentic, so he was thoroughly determined not to be taken in by the general imposture that Scotland represented. Johnson did not believe that there was anything particularly sublime or picturesque about the Scottish landscape and he was certainly suspicious of the tendency which he detected in Boswell to gush over it. He would never have penned Boswell's description of a storm off the Isle of Skye:

I now saw what I never saw before, a prodigious sea, with immense billows coming upon a vessel so as it seemed hardly possible to escape. There was something grandly horrible in the sight.[44]

While Joseph Warton, in his poem *The Enthusiast*, said that, in preference to the fountains of Versailles, he would choose:

a pine-topped precipice
　　　　　　　　or some bleak heath,
Where straggling stands the mournful juniper.

Johnson was by no means as receptive to the wild landscape that he encountered in Scotland. Even the moment when he conceives the idea of writing the book on a bank 'such as a writer of romance might have delighted to feign' follows directly on from a passage in which he writes:

It will very readily occur, that this uniformity of barrenness can afford very little amusement to the traveller; that it is easy to sit at home and conceive rocks and heaths, and waterfalls, and that these journeys are useless labours which neither impregnate the imagination, nor enlarge the understanding.[45]

Johnson's view is not that such wild landscape is wonderful but that since wildernesses make up a large part of the earth's surface it is just as well to know about them. Johnson speaks of those

... whose curiosity pants for savage virtues and barbarous grandeur.[46]

but he himself was determined not to find any, writing

... he that goes into the Highlands with a mind naturally acquiescent and a credulity eager for wonders, may come back with a opinion very different from mine.

Johnson refused to buy the myth of bardic poetry – the bard was 'a barbarian among barbarians' and if the role was inherited then there could be no expectation that the bard would be a

poetic genius.[47] Johnson refused to believe that there could be
any virtue or any special value in such a primitive mode of existence and in any case it was almost impossible to form any accurate
picture of it since those who described it were almost certainly
inveterate liars. The whole pretence and sham of Scottish culture
seems epitomised by the moment when, after a convivial evening,
Johnson got into his bed of fine Indian cotton sheets, only to
find that his feet were in the mire and that there was a puddle
underneath. At Ostig in Skye Johnson touches on the vexed
question of the loss of virtue in a modern commercial type of
society but denies that an earlier type of society could be morally
superior:

> ... a man, who places honour only in successful violence, is a
> very troublesome and pernicious animal in time of peace; and
> that the martial character cannot prevail in a whole people,
> but by the diminution of all other virtues. . . . The strong must
> flourish by force, and the weak subsist by strategem.[48]

If all the world was once like Scotland then its disappearance
can only be for the better. There is, and indeed could not be,
anything here to trouble the metropolitan consciousness that so
remorselessly prejudges.

The celebration of provincial virtue reaches its apotheosis in the
literature of sentimentalism. The sentimental hero is typically kindly
and benevolent, spontaneous and emotional, who instinctively
follows the dictates of his heart rather than what either reason
or prudence recommend. He is not much concerned with appearances or with what kind of figure he cuts in the public world.
Sentimental literature almost inescapably has a provincial bias
since it opposes metropolitan sophistication and worldly pretence.
Precisely what defends its virtuous characters from corruption is
the fact that they are innocent and frankly naive. They are good
because that is their nature, because in their childlike simplicity
they know no better. It is directly relevant to any understanding
of sentimentalism to grasp that four of its key texts: *Tristram Shandy*,
The Vicar of Wakefield, *The Man of Feeling*, and *Humphrey Clinker*,
were written by Scottish and Irish authors. In these novels the

empire does not so much fight back as smile back, in the hope and even the expectation that the unsophisticated provinces may yet prevail.

Sterne's *Tristram Shandy* is a complex and many-sided work, but much of its complexity is actually generated by Sterne's sense of himself as a provincial figure, who has led a life set apart from the great world. His prefatory dedication describes the book as having been written in

> ... a bye corner of the kingdom, and in a retired thatched house. (p. 33)

Tristram Shandy made Sterne famous, but before that he had lived in obscurity for over 20 years as vicar of Sutton-in-the-forest in Yorkshire. This sense of a local and narrowly focused existence is strongly reflected in Sterne's great comic novel. When Tristram refers to 'the reputation in the world' of the midwife who delivers him he goes on

> ... by which word *world*, need I in this place inform your worship, that I would be understood to mean no more of it, than a small circle described upon the circle of the great world, of four *English* miles diameter, or thereabouts, of which the cottage where the good old woman lived is supposed to be the centre. (p. 42)

It is within this microcosm that everything that happens or does not happen in the novel takes place. Even the Widow Wadman, who makes such a dramatic entry into the later volumes, lives in a house directly adjacent:

> The Fates, who certainly all fore-knew of these amours of widow Wadman and my uncle Toby, had ... established such a chain of causes and effects hanging so fast to one another, that it was scarce possible for my uncle Toby to have dwelt in any other house in the world, or to have occupied any other garden in Christendom, but the very house and garden which join'd and laid parallel to Mrs. Wadman's. (p. 527)

Not only this but the fateful place by the old garden wall, when Dr Slop was thrown off his pony by the rapid onset of Obadiah's coach-horse, and thereby thrown into the mire was directly opposite the widow Wadman's house. Part of Sterne's joke is that in such a narrow little world everything that happens will necessarily be adjacent. Moreover, in such a spot on the globe as this we cannot really expect anything very dramatic to happen let alone any world-shaking events. Rather its inhabitants are content to live in their own very circumscribed sphere and to simulate the greater world as best they can. So the Duke of Marlborough's military campaigns in Flanders are reproduced by Uncle Toby and Trim in the greatly reduced form of a bowling green, one and a half rods in extent – though some encroachments into the kitchen garden may be needed.

The very idea of travelling to London was an anathema to Walter Shandy and having been incommoded by his wife's earlier insistence on travelling to the metropolis to have her baby he insisted in Tristram's case that she must stay at home. As Tristram's father saw it her obsession with London was part of a national malaise:

> He was very sensible that all political writers upon the subject had unanimously agreed and lamented, from the beginning of Queen *Elizabeth*'s reign down to his own time, that the current of men and money towards the metropolis, upon one frivolous errand or another, – set in so strong, – as to become dangerous to our civil rights; – tho', by the bye, – a *current* was not the image he took most delight in, – a distemper was here his favorite metaphor. . . . (p. 73)

It might seem that the Shandy's refusal to travel is more than a little ludicrous, but actually Sterne did have his own reasons for thinking travel over-rated. Sterne was by no means convinced that travel was as instructive or beneficial as contemporary opinion believed. Sterne himself certainly enjoyed the foreign travel that he was later able to indulge in, but at the beginning of *A Sentimental Journey Through France and Italy* he suggested the acquisition of knowledge through foreign travel was a lottery and stated:

> I am of opinion, That a man would act as wisely, if he could prevail upon himself, to live contentedly without foreign knowledge or foreign improvements, especially if he lives in a country that has no absolute want of either . . .[49]

Certainly Walter Shandy and Uncle Toby are to be numbered among those who find such knowledge superogatory but Sterne himself was certainly genuine in writing this for, in his capacity as country parson, he had earlier used the parable of the Prodigal Son to warn of the dangers of foreign travel:

> There is nothing in which we are so much deceived as in the advantages proposed from our connections and discourse with the literati, &c., in foreign parts; especially if the experiment is made before we are matured by years of study.[50]

Much of the humour of *Tristram Shandy* derives from the fact the narrative centres so determinedly on Shandy Hall and its environs that the rest of the world, seemingly so solid and impressive, takes on a rather ghostly and shadowy existence. Walter Shandy and Uncle Toby talk so relentlessly of foreign parts and exotic places that they seem to be little more than names. There is something rather unnerving about the way in which Uncle Toby can trace the topography of an idea:

> By water the sentiment might easily have come down into the *Sinus Gangeticus*, or *Bay of Bengal*, and so into the *Indian Sea*, and following the course of trade, (the way from *India* by the *Cape of Good Hope* being then unknown) might be carried with other drugs and spices up the *Red Sea* to *Joddah*, the port of *Mekka*, or else to *Tor* or *Sues*, towns at the bottom of the gulf; and from thence by karrawans to *Coptos*, but three days journey distant, so down the *Nile* directly to *Alexandria*, where the SENTIMENT would be landed at the very foot of the great staircase of the *Alexandrian* library, – and from that store-house it would be fetched, – Bless me! what a trade was driven by the learned in those days! (p. 363)

From this account it seems that not only did erudition shape the world but it is as if the world only really exists in the minds of the learned. Sterne was well aware that the idea of travel had been crucial to his fictional predecessors. Both the narrators of *Gulliver's Travels* and *Robinson Crusoe* offer the reader the wisdom of their experience. Tom Jones journeys all over the home Counties in search of Sophia. Peregrine Pickle travelled from Paris to Arras and from thence to Ghent, Antwerp and Rotterdam.

Tristram's father and Uncle Toby never go anywhere, travel in their imagination and are perfectly content.

This provincial distrust of travel is echoed in Henry Mackenzie's immensely popular and immensely influential novel, *The Man of Feeling* (1771). But here we find not simply the notion that it is best to remain within one's own locality but a positive distrust of the motives that provoke travel and of the destinations towards which it is directed. From MacKenzie onward this questioning of travel begins to be bound up with educational questions since it was increasingly felt that the best way of completing a gentleman's education, which was at the same time a way of transforming an awkward youth into a sophisticated man of the world, was to send him on a Grand Tour of Europe. But equally there was a growing tendency to question the degree of latitude and self-indulgence permitted to children in aristocratic families and also to suggest that European travel did not so much broaden the mind as corrupt the morals. Such educational ideas are particularly prominent in MacKenzie's subsequent novel in which the villainous Sir Thomas Sindall – styled in the title *The Man of the World* – is corrupt and a corrupting influence on others precisely because he has been brought up by his mother without restraint:

> In short, he did what he liked, at first, because his spirit should not be confined too early; and afterwards he did what he liked because he was past being confined at all. (p. 44)

By contrast Richard Annesly is a good parent who takes personal charge of the education of his children Billy and Harriet. They are taught reading, writing, mathematics, geography, French and Italian. Billy is taught the classics while Harriet learns the traditional female accomplishments. Above all Annesly encourages his children to perform charitable acts which he believes will lead them 'insensibly to the practice of virtue'. (p. 29) For large sections of the novel this education seems somewhat fruitless since Sindall's attempts to ruin them both make considerable headway. Nevertheless the lesson is clear: the character of children is formed early through education. In *The Man of Feeling* the emphasis is somewhat different, in that Harley, the hero, has had no particular education to speak of, but this at least means that he has not been miseducated. In the opening chapter of the book the baronet's brother suggests that young men should rub the rust of social awkwardness off by foreign travel; to which the narrator responds:

> ... that will go far; but then it will often happen, that in the velocity of a modern tour, and amidst the materials through which it is commonly made, the friction is so violent, that not only the rust, but the metal too is lost in the progress. (p. 8)

Harley later meets an eccentric gentleman in London who offers a similar critique:

> ... a raw unprincipled boy is turned loose upon the world to travel: without any ideas but those of improving his dress at Paris, or starting into taste by gazing upon some paintings in Rome. Ask him of the manners of the people, and he will tell you, That the skirt is worn much shorter in France, and that everybody eats macaroni in Italy. (p. 40)

The Grand Tour far from being genuinely instructive is simply a brusque initiation into superficiality and worldliness.

Although MacKenzie himself and his hero Harley show a great deal of sympathy with the lower orders in society and with those who have suffered adversity and misfortune, his novels place a special responsibility on the landed aristocracy to remedy the evils of an increasingly commercialised and manipulative society. At a time when the enclosure of agricultural land and the sharp raising of rents was becoming prevalent MacKenzie was concerned at the consequences that this might have for the peasants in rural society. He believed that it was incumbent on the landowner to resist this trend. The train of disaster that affect old Edwards, his son and his family follow directly on from this agricultural inflation. The local squire insists he takes responsibility for a larger farm than the family has traditionally maintained which causes him to run into trouble. He then takes on a much smaller piece of land but things take a turn for the worse when his son is press-ganged and Edwards volunteers to serve in his place and travels to India. The son and his wife die of a broken heart. By contrast in *The Man of the World* Rawlinson, who has made his fortune in India, makes a point of reducing the rents on his estates and of offering places to some of the traditional tenants who have been driven out. At the end the virtuous Harry Bolton is in charge:

> . . . their benevolence is universal; the countryside smiles around them with the effects of their goodness. This is indeed the only real superiority which wealth has to bestow. (p. 306)

Like Henry Brooke, whose interminable *The Fool of Quality* appeared between 1764 and 1770, MacKenzie believed that the idea of the gentleman was being devalued and that too much stress was being placed on clothing and externals. However, while Brooke spoke out in favour of the mercantile class MacKenzie distrusted it, and while Brooke espoused a form of Christian manliness that made Charles Kingsley see him as a precursor MacKenzie favoured a hero, who, in his sensitivity and readiness to shed tears, might almost be thought effeminate. In a very real sense Harley seems too good for the world – its seems symptomatic that not only does he die young but even his memoirs exist only in fragments, since the rest has been used by a clergyman as wadding for his gun! Harley is naive and unworldly but during his stay in London he is not taken in as often as more seasoned observers might imagine. He seems to have been duped into pawning his watch to help a prostitute, but this same girl proves to be a Miss Atkins, the daughter of an army officer who has been cruelly deceived by Sir George Winbrooke, an aristocrat. The important thing about Harley is that he is generous, open and sincere – above all, he is a good listener. Whether it is the beggar he encounters, the lady he encounters amongst the mad in Bedlam, Miss Atkins or Edwards, Harley does not snub or condescend but is prepared to give time to the sad stories of the poor or distressed and offer appropriate help. At a time when some are seeking to raise the barriers between social classes Harley is trying to lower them. Harley's seemingly grotesque judgement on the prostitute

> . . . there is virtue in these tears; let the fruit of them be virtue (p. 50)

has truth after all.

That MacKenzie as a well-born and patriotic Scotsman should have preferred Edinburgh to London is perhaps not surprising, but what is much more remarkable is that MacKenzie should have been one of the first to grasp that the dominance of London over the periphery was linked with its place as the commanding centre of a colonial empire. In *The Man of Feeling* it is abundantly clear that the military power that oppresses Edwards and his family is the very same force that tyrannises India. There are victims both near and far. Edwards, presented with the suffering of an aged Indian who is being subjected to fifty lashes daily, because the army officers are convinced that he is in possession of a vast treasure, allows him to escape. For this act of mercy Edwards is himself obliged to suffer two hundred lashes and expelled from the camp without money or guide. But the old man helps him and praises him, saying that he has an 'Indian heart'. In a British novel the phraseology is significant indeed in that MacKenzie makes no bones about suggesting that the oppressed are morally superior to the oppressors. But MacKenzie goes beyond this, questioning the very existence of empire. Harley responds to Edward's narrative by saying:

> You tell me of immense territories subject to the English: I cannot think of their possessions, without being led to enquire, by what right they possess them. (p. 102)

In the aftermath of Montesquieu the very idea of empire has become morally suspect. But it is not just a question of despotism or luxury the very idea of empire is grounded in domination, exploitation and violence. And MacKenzie cannot but have been aware that the very same system that brutally crushed Scotsmen at Culloden was now transferring its attention to crushing Americans in America and Indians in India. MacKenzie genuinely believed that those on the periphery were morally superior to those at the metropolitan and colonial centre. In *The Man of the World* Billy Annesly is capture by a tribe of native American Cherokees and compelled to undergo severe torture, but this is presented by MacKenzie, not as gratuitous sadism but as a test of character. One of the tribal elders says:

> It is thus . . . that the valiant are tried, and thus they are rewarded; for how should thou be as one of us, if thy soul were as the soul of little men? (p. 271)

These trials can be seen as morally significant since they develop in the individual a stoicism and inner strength that make him resistant to the dangerous and corrupting blandishments of civilisation. In the end Billy is grateful for the conditioning that he has received:

> When we consider the perfect freedom subsisting in this rude and simple state of society, whose rule is only acknowledged for the purpose of immediate utility to those who obey, and ceased when the process of subordination is accomplished; where greatness cannot use oppression, nor wealth excite envy; where the desires are native to the heart, and the language of satiety is unknown; where, if there is no refined sensation of delight, there is also no ideal source of calamity; we shall the less wonder at the inhabitants feeling no regret for the want of those delicate pleasures of which a more polished people is possessed. (p. 272)

MacKenzie can certainly be accused of inconsistency here. It is hard to imagine the delicate Harley undergoing such an ordeal or to reconcile the contrasting notions of virtuous conduct that they embody. But he would doubtless reply that they represent diverse, but equally valid, repudiations of a decadent metropolitan culture that erodes independence and moral autonomy.

In 1771, the same year as *The Man of Feeling*, a novel appeared, *Humphrey Clinker*, which, though it was both the most explicit and most powerful exposition of the claims of provincial virtue that had yet appeared, was by an author whose credentials were by no means impeccable. While there was strong cultural disposition for Smollett, MacKenzie's fellow Scot, to stand up for ancient virtue against the encroachments of commerce and a metropolitan civilisation, it had to be admitted that, in the past, Smollett's own orientation towards virtue had not been of the strongest. Smollett's first novel, *Roderick Random* (1748), published when he was only 27, had depicted a hero who was headstrong, violent, and always potentially capable of improper behaviour and if anything the picture became progressively worse. *Peregrine Pickle* (1751) was undoubtedly an immoralist, while *Ferdinand Count Fathom* (1753) was a wholehearted and unscrupulous villain. Smollett was generally regarded as the one early eighteenth-century novelist whose works could not possibly be regarded as morally improving. So the very fact that Smollett himself was disposed to adopt the discourse of virtue in *Humphrey Clinker* might well have proved as unexpected as the fact that in the same novel Matt Bramble's party encounters a reformed Count Fathom, now the apothecary and 'a sincere convert to virtue'. (p. 204) Part of the reason for Smollett's change of heart, if change of heart it was, can be attributed to the fact that he wrote *Roderick Random* as a comparatively young man of 27 and the other two fairly soon after, whereas *Humphrey Clinker* appeared two decades after the publication of *Peregrine Pickle*. In the interim the industrious author had published his *History of England from the Revolution of 1688* which had shown a markedly anti-Whig bias and had attributed most of Britain's ills to the combination of commerce and political corruption which they had ushered in. Representative of this interpretative emphasis are such widely separated comments as these; of Britain in 1692 he observed:

> By this time, indeed, the public virtue was become an object of ridicule, and the whole kingdom was overspread with immorality and corruption.[51]

Nearly 30 years on, with the scandal of the South Sea Bubble:

> ... luxury, vice, and profligacy increased to a shocking degree of extravagance: the adventurers ... indulged their criminal passions to the most scandalous excess; their discourse was the language of pride, insolence, and the most ridiculous ostentation; they affected to scoff at religion and morality, and even to set Heaven at defiance.[52]

Yet 60 years later, in 1752, the situation of the nation was no better and, if anything, slightly worse:

> The tide of luxury still flowed with an impetuous current, bearing down all the mounds of temperance and decorum; while fraud and profligacy struck out new channels, through which they eluded the restrictions of the law, and all the vigilance of civil policy: new arts of deception were invented, in order to ensnare and ruin the unwary; and some infamous practises, in the way of commerce, were countenanced by persons of rank and importance in the commonwealth.[53]

So, with the years, Smollett undoubtedly became considerably more censorious but he was perhaps not altogether inconsistent since in *Roderick Random* he had shown considerable indignation at the degree of corruption and indiscriminate patronage that pervaded the workings of the state – which of course was a massive disincentive to talented and ambitious Scotsmen, who invariably found others preferred to themselves. But there was a difference. In the early novels if Random and Pickle were scarcely plaster saints who could object when others were no better. A mood of harsh realism and healthy cynicism prevails. But by the time of writing *Humphrey Clinker* Smollett was not only prepared to entertain the idea of virtue but positively insisted on identifying it as a *provincial* virtue.

Neverthless, there are formidable obstacles in the way of taking *Humphrey Clinker* seriously as a novel of ideas, dedicated to the task of revealing the full extent of contemporary extravagance and cultural decadence. For even if we admit that the novel does contain many animadversions on the malign influence of contemporary commerce, this by no means commits us to the view of John Sekora that the novel is to be regarded as belonging to a polemical genre against luxury going all the way back to Plato:

> The attack upon luxury may be regarded as a relatively distinct literary mode, with its own characteristic devices and methods of persuasion. . . . It is the mode of Cato and Seneca, the *Republic* and the *City of God*, *Paradise Lost* and *Aureng-Zebe*, *Joseph Andrews* and the *Deserted Village*; of Swift and Bolingbroke, Davenant and John Brown. . . . *Humphrey Clinker* does indeed deserve to be read in the light of Western tradition, eighteenth-century controversy, and Smollett's own two decades of attack – in their light and as their epitome.[54]

The obvious problem with this is not just that it seems rather quixotic to regard *Humphrey Clinker* as the culmination of 2000 years of Western tradition, or that tradition as assembled by Sekora seems distinctly composed of bric-a-brac, but rather that anyone seeking to mount a fully fledged attack on luxury would scarcely have gone about it in such a self-consuming manner. Many contemporary readers of the novel would simply have regarded Matt Bramble's grumbles about Bath and London as fashionable half-truths and commonplaces, which they would be disposed to discount rather than take seriously. And if Bramble, like the Player Queen in *Hamlet* seems to protest rather too much, then how much more so must this be in the case of Sekora. On the other hand, there are grounds for being grateful to Sekora for retrieving a level of discourse in the novel that has too often been ignored or discounted in the readings of the new criticism. While in the twentieth century distinctions between author and persona have become inescapable, there was a much greater tendency in the eighteenth century to regard characters as mouthpieces for their authors views and to concur or object accordingly. The reviewer of *Humphrey Clinker* in the *Universal Magazine* in 1771 strongly objected to 'This most unfaithful portrait of poor Old England' and to the 'flagrant partiality towards Scotland'.[55] This reader at least did see the novel as polemic rather than as entertainment.

Nevertheless, not only is *Humphrey Clinker* a novel, it is also the most sophisticated attempt in the early history of the novel to depict reality from a variety of perspectives and points of view. Since the narrative is unfolded in a series of letters there is no authoritative narrator as in Fielding nor any privileged position as in Richardson's *Pamela*, instead we are invited to reflect on human diversity and to recognise that there can be no single way in which experienced is grasped. Matt Bramble is at his most opinionated and irascible in his early animadversions on Bath and London, but if he, in his 'crusty humours' finds Bath 'the very centre of racket and dissipation' (p. 63) we also note that Lydia Melford finds it

... a new world – All is gayety, good-humour, and diversion. (p. 68)

If Bramble finds Vauxhall Gardens in London

... a composition of baubles, overcharged with paltry ornaments, ill conceived, and poorly executed; without any unity of design, or propriety of disposition ... an unnatural assembly of objects ... contrived to dazzle the eyes and divert the imagination of the vulgar ... filled with crowds of noisy people. (p. 120)

his view is challenged by Lydia who is 'dazzled and confounded with the variety of beauties':

... a wonderful assemblage of the most picturesque and striking objects, pavilions, lodges, groves, grottoes, lawns, temples,
and cascades; porticoes, colonades, and rotundos; adorned with
pillars, statues, and painting; the whole illuminated with an
infinite number of lamps, disposed in different figures of suns,
stars, and constellations; the place crowded with the gayest
company ... (p. 124)

The very crowds and diversity that attract Lydia repel Bramble,
who is scarcely in a mood to cultivate the picturesque. In fact it
becomes almost too easy to dismiss Bramble's opinions, since not
only is he, as his name suggests both prickly and rambling, in
fact a self-confessed crotchety old man, but he is also a provincial Welshman who knows and likes little else but what he has
been accustomed to at Brambleton Hall. Moreover, his entourage
inspires little confidence. His sister, Tabitha Bramble, is distinctly
ludicrous both in the desperation of her matrimonial designs and
the eccentricity of her clothing. Her companion Win Jenkins is
an agreeable but ignorant country bumpkin, while Humphrey
Clinker, the servant Bramble acquires, is a loyal and well-meaning simpleton. Since they are all neither sophisticated nor
fashionable there is little about the party that can dispel the reader's
scepticism let alone win over the reader's respect.

But this, of course, is where Smollett is adroit. As a North Briton
he knows very well that his own exposition of provincial values
is likely to be rejected in advance, so in the early stages of the
book, when Bramble is mostly eloquent in his denunciations of
Bath and London, he gives the reader every incentive to query
them. But as the novel develops we are invited to revise our
initial impression of the principal characters and we find that
none of them is quite what they initially seemed. Here, Humphrey
Clinker himself is crucial, since as he progressively wins our
respect so too do those with whom he is associated. In particular, we are compelled to recognise that Bramble's claim to be a
misanthrope is only a pose and that in reality he is a humane,
compassionate and sensitive man. If there is anything resembling
an authoritative voice in the novel it is that of Jerry Melford,
Matt Bramble's nephew, and his increasing respect for the man
he terms 'a Don Quixote in generosity' (pp. 305–6) serves to shift
the balance of the novel. Bramble is the sentimental hero in disguise. Increasingly his assessments of the places they visit as they

travel around Great Britain, begin to look accurate, balanced, even authoritative.

Subtly and artfully, Smollett gradually pulls his critique together. But the criticism of commerce and its impact on contemporary society is only a part of this. We should perhaps remember here that Dr Johnson, like many others, not only saw no harm in luxury in itself but believed its importance over-stated because it actually affected the lives of very few people – originally a Mandevillian argument. In other words the discourse of luxury was based on exaggeration and hyperbole. So Smollett's primary intention is not to be merely negative and censorious but to redefine the idea of the good life in a way that is not automatically associated with consumer goods or the customs of the metropolis. He wants to show that the good life, which is also a virtuous life, can still be lived in the provinces, in Wales or Scotland, when this is no longer possible in London. In particular Bramble's description of the pleasures he enjoys at Brambleton Hall in his letter from London dated 8 June contrasting the purity of the air and water, the peace and tranquillity, the quality of the bread, meat, beer and cider, as contrasted with the filth and din of the city and the contamination and adulteration of its food and drink, makes both compelling and persuasive reading. By the time the party has travelled to Scotland and returned to Wales the reader has a new, provincial perspective on the over-bearing and all consuming metropolis. Such an alternative view is certainly a breath of fresh air. *Humphrey Clinker* is not a tract but its contrasted instances of Baynard who is:

> ... sucked deeper and deeper into the vortex of extravagance and dissipation. (p. 327)

and Dennison who lives prudently in the country, show that Smollett was concerned to show that there *was* an alternative lifestyle to the fashionable merry-go-round. Long before Thoreau Smollett was calling on the world to simplify.

Yet in this gallery of naive and innocent heroes it is perhaps Goldsmith's Vicar of Wakefield who is the most memorable, not because Goldsmith unequivocally celebrates him but because he is clearly so ambivalent about him, because he is so very conscious of the penalties that such unworldliness brings. The paradoxes of Goldsmith's hero are not unconnected with the circumstances under which the novel was written. As a young man Goldsmith quickly gambled away such funds as he had. Subsequently as he tried to make his way in London he got even more deeply into debt and it was only the fact that Dr Johnson was able to find a publisher for *The Vicar of Wakefield* that freed him (temporarily) from his financial difficulties. So Goldsmith himself was not a prudent person and insofar as the Vicar is not very prudent either it is clear that Goldsmith actually sympathised with what might otherwise seem to be his most serious weakness. But this equally suggests that a writer who was himself so familiar with misfortune and disaster could scarcely have envisaged the whole series of plot twists that get the Vicar out of his very serious jam without at least a tinge of irony, even if the book does conclude with the completely deadpan sentence:

> It now only remained that my gratitude in good fortune should exceed my former submission in adversity. (Vol. IV, p. 184)

On the other hand, when Goldsmith had created a character who was so admirably stoical in the face of misfortune, almost any ending might convey a trace of parody – for we might have found it even more intolerable had he really remained sanguine in the event of the death of his eldest daughter, Olivia, the seduction of the younger, Sophia, his incarceration with the rest of his family in jail. One of the real difficulties with the *Vicar of Wakefield* is that it's depiction of a world that is unpredictable and unfair is so compelling that a conclusion which cancels all this so deftly can seem almost insultingly glib.

Undoubtedly, even at this comparatively early point Goldsmith was quite consciously putting in question the morality of a commercial society, in which the display of status and possessions had come to seem more important than the practice of simple virtue, of decency and honesty. Yet the paradox of the Vicar is that while he starts off, and remains, an exponent of the simple life:

> We had no revolutions to fear, nor fatigues to undergo; for all our adventures were by the fire-side, and all our migrations from the blue bed to the brown. (p. 18)

he is sucked into a concern with social advancement by the ambitions of his wife and daughters. Symptomatically and prophetically, the Vicar wishes to name his daughter after her aunt Grissell and thus also after the patient Grissell of fairy-tale, but is twice deflected into more pretentious names – Olivia and Sophia. Virtually all the Vicar's disasters stem from the family's desire to rise in society, to wear fine clothes and to ride on horseback in the style of the gentry. The general absurdity of such ambitions is suggested by the episode in which the family is painted in the grand manner as Venus with Cupids, scholar and shepherd and Amazon, for the picture itself is so large that there is nowhere to hang it. It is by embarking on such a course that both the Vicar and his son are cheated and humiliated by Mr Jenkinson and that Olivia is seduced and that Sophia's relationship with Mr Burchill is imperilled. Contrary to his claims and beliefs the Vicar is taken in by wordly appearances and influenced by considerations other than the strictly moral. So although the Vicar is, as he says of his whole family:

> ... equally generous, credulous simple and inoffensive (p. 21)

He does become an ineffectual accomplice and partner in their upwardly mobile endeavours. But just as MacKenzie is unwilling to believe that the innocent Harley is gullible, so Goldsmith wants to believe that there is something heroic and morally admirable in the vicar's naivety; for to go through the world like Wilkinson in a spirit of perpetual cynicism is to falter and despair, while the Vicar, in all his simplicity, always perseveres and never gives up hope, no matter how black the immediate prospect may be.

Yet the irony of *The Vicar of Wakefield* lies in the fact that it preaches a virtue which has become self-evidently anachronistic. After the Vicar learns, at the outset of the novel, that he has lost his entire fortune at the hands of a dishonest merchant, he removes to a country district that epitomises provincial virtue and which seems untouched by the luxurious spirit of the age:

> The place of our retreat was in a little neighbourhood, consisting of farmers, who tilled their own grounds, and were equal strangers to opulence and poverty. As they had almost all the conveniences of life within themselves, they seldom visited towns or cities in search of superfluity. Remote from the polite, they still retained the primaeval simplicity of manners, and

frugal by habit, they scarce knew that temperance was a virtue.
(pp. 31–2)

In this rural Arcadia the vicar's family should in theory be secure
from corruption and yet it seems that even here the serpent is to
be found, in the guise of Squire Thornhill. So, although Goldsmith
is a writer who seems acutely aware of the dangers of innocence
in a sophisticated modern age, he seems equally determined to
believe that it can survive the most desperate perils. The Vicar,
despite his clerical collar, is all too reminiscent of Cervantes'
impractical hero, *Don Quixote*, yet the analogy works against him.
For while we may have a strange respect for the Knight of the
Doleful Countenance even at his most comical; it still seems wrong
that a man of the cloth should be so unable to securely guide
himself through the world when aided and instructed by the
gospels. Still, the Vicar's preposterous good fortune and his success
against all the odds, represents Goldsmith's own illogical wager
that provincial virtue, despite starting at preposterously long odds,
can nevertheless still hope to carry the day.

Yet, if Goldsmith believed this – or tried to believe this – in
The Vicar of Wakefield, by the time he came to write 'The Deserted Village' of 1770 he no longer held any such hopeful
conviction. In truth the Vicar had always been a man trying to
run down an upwardly moving escalator in a desperate attempt
to remain more or less in the same place. The very theme of
provincial virtue was generated by the sharp contrast between
London as a complex and sophisticated metropolitan centre, a
place of commerce and pleasure, and the periphery where life
seemed to continue in a simpler and morally superior way. It
was underpinned on the one hand by general worries about the
direction in which the nation was headed and on the other by
local and patriotic loyalties in a kingdom that was still very far
from being united. The persistence of virtue on the periphery
seemed so clear and so demonstrable that the case for it scarcely
called for justification – and even if the magnetic pull of London
was becoming ever stronger there would still be places where its
power could not be felt. The 'primaeval simplicity of manners'
that Goldsmith had invoked must surely continue. But Goldsmith
began to doubt this. Goldsmith had of course seen, in his native
Ireland, that there was nothing necessarily stable or tranquil about
an agricultural way of life, which could involve poverty so des-

perate as to make emigration a virtual necessity. So as a partial outsider he was more likely to discern signs of a disintegration in rural life. Auburn, in 'The Deserted Village' was based on Nuneham Courtenay, where Lord Harcourt had moved an entire village in order to create a landscaped country estate. An aestheticised 'country' devoid of people was replacing living communities. This within 50 miles or so of London was, seemingly, only the beginnings of a blight, spreading irresistibly outwards from the metropolis, that would eventually encompass the whole country. Goldsmith's own life had been beset by instability and a profound sense of insecurity. He knew that many of the landmarks that we take for granted in our everyday lives were themselves transitory and ephemeral. He begins one of his essays in *The Bee*, 'On the Instability of Worldly Grandeur', as follows:

> An alehouse keeper near Islington, who had long lived at the sign of the French King, upon the commencement of the last war pulled down his old sign, and put up that of the Queen of Hungary. Under the influence of her red face and golden sceptre, he continued to sell ale till she was no longer the favourite of his customers; he changed her, therefore, some time ago, for the King of Prussia, who may probably be changed, in turn for the next great man that shall be set up for vulgar admiration. (Vol. I, p. 470)

Perhaps the most significant feature of this description is the fact that the alehouse keeper has maintained a sign invoking the King of France for many years, yet such a familiar and long established identity can nevertheless be changed at a moments notice. We are always tempted to believe that something that has persisted will somehow go on persisting, yet even those aspects of our existence which we most take for granted can suddenly and unpredictably disappear. What is alarming about 'The Deserted Village' is not just that a whole world has gone but that it has all happened so quickly – so that the poet pursuing his vocation, presumably in the capital, finds that the place he remembered so fondly and hoped to return to has gone for good.

Although 'The Deserted Village' offers a nostalgic, even rose-tinted, view of rustic life and 'rural virtue' it is, at the same time, a powerful and urgent intervention in the controversy over the state of Britain. For, although there was on the one hand, a general disposition to believe that contemporary society was being corrupted by the dominance of commercial interests, by the spread of opulence and the erosion of traditional virtues; there was also a tendency to pooh pooh such arguments as hyperbolic and largely imaginary. Even if you genuinely believed that there were analogies between the decline of Rome and Britain, it was very hard to say what all this amounted to or what the real implications were. It all seemed highly speculative. Again, the debate over luxury quickly descended into disputes as to how luxury was to be defined. If luxuries were at once superfluous and morally damaging how could such superfluity or negative consequences be estimated. One man's luxury might be another man's necessity. It seems symptomatic that when Goldsmith and Dr Johnson argued about the matter they were reduced to discussing the possible harmful consequences of eating pickles! Dr Johnson, as usual, seems to have conquered in the encounter but Goldsmith through 'The Deserted Village' may have ultimately carried the day. What made the poem so compelling was that where there had been so much abstract discussion and so much quibbling over terms now Goldsmith pointed to Auburn, as the name for a real place within 50 miles of London and said 'Look – this has really happened – the effects of opulence and riches are real – a village has gone – a whole British way of life based on the virtue and industry of an independent peasantry is being destroyed. And while Nuneham Courtenay may not itself have been very representative, the increased poverty and insecurity of the rural labourer was very real. Goldsmith was not wrong to imply that a whole way of life was passing away even if in its twilight the contours were mellowed and softened.

It is the fact that Goldsmith chooses to write about a particular village, representative but in the end unique, that gives his poem its peculiar power. William Shenstone's 'The School-Mistress' which is often and rightly cited as offering a portrait on which Goldsmith's preacher and schoolmaster are modelled. But Shenstone's village dame is a universal type whose 'modest worth' everyone will recognise and celebrate:

> In ev-ry village mark'd with little spire
> Embower'd in trees, and hardly known to Fame,
> There dwells in lowly shed, and mean attire,
> A matron old, whom we school-mistress name . . .

She is familiar and will go on being familiar. But Goldsmith's sympathetic and benevolent parson, his strict but kindly teacher, are figures who knitted together a community and sense of community which has gone along with their presence and distinctive aura. Life in Auburn was harmonious and balanced. If there was toil there was also pleasure and relaxation, if there was indulgence there was also discipline. Virtue was instinctive when there was so little to threaten it. Broken teacups on the chimneypiece were as far as ostentation went. All this is being made irrelevant and superfluous by the 'ten thousand baneful arts' of the metropolis that promote an artificial and transitory titillation:

> And e'en while fashion's brightest arts decoy,
> The heart distrusting asks, if this be joy.

A world where things were clear and certain is being superseded by the fashionable city masquerade. What matters about 'The Deserted Village' is that it marks a very significant shift in focus – virtue may indeed have been rural and provincial but wherever it was it is now unmistakably to be located in the past. For Goldsmith, as for Scott and the Romantics, virtue is now something that has gone and will never return.

The germ of 'The Deserted Village' was a piece which Goldsmith had published in *Lloyd's Evening Post* in 1762 in which he described how he had been staying in a village of about a hundred houses, where he had learned that the villagers had 'received orders to seek for a new habitation' so that 'A Merchant of immense fortune' could 'lay out a seat of pleasure for himself'. (Vol. III, p. 196) For Goldsmith an erosion of the British way of life was an inevitable consequence of trade. He remarked:

> Let others felicitate their country on the encrease in foreign commerce and the extension of our foreign conquests; but for my part, this new introduction of wealth gives me but very little satisfaction. (p. 197)

Goldsmith linked this situation with the decline of Rome and with the invasion of Italy by the armies of Theodoric the Ostrogoth in 489 when according to his source:

The whole country was at that time one garden of pleasure; the seats of the great men of Rome covered the face of the whole kingdom; and even their villas were supplied with provisions not of their own growth, but produced in distant countries, where they were more industrious. (p. 198)

Yet is was possible to broadly accept the same terms of analysis and the possibility of a parallel between contemporary Britain and ancient Rome and nevertheless come to a very different conclusion. The poet John Dyer had been one of the very first to brood over the causes of the Roman decline in his 'The Ruins of Rome' of 1740 yet in *The Fleece*, published in 1757, only five years before Goldsmith's article, he had celebrated both the wonder of English wool and the expanding trade and Empire that were connected with it. The poem concludes with his 'exulting Muse' returning to 'her old delight'

> The shepherd's haunts, where the first springs arise
> Of Britain's happy trade, now spreading wide,
> Wide as th'Atlantic and Pacific seas,
> Or as air's vital fluid o'er the globe.

Unlike Rome, Britain could look to the future with confidence.

John Dyer, who was born in Wales, brought to his writing a very strong sense both of regional identity and provincial virtue. At the heart of this was the land he named Siluria, which invoked simultaneously the ancient Silurian people of South Wales, a particular brand of sheep, and also the border country of the Wye valley of Monmouthshire, Herefordshire and Shropshire, an area where such sheep thrive and to which Dyer had developed a strong attachment. In focusing on this part of Britain, which was famous for its sheep rearing, in *The Fleece*, Dyer effectively redefined the nation as well, by placing at the centre of her moral being and commercial prosperity a region which in other ways was very much on the periphery. The Silurian sheep's classical status is made manifest in its appearance:

>   his front is fenc'd
> With horns Ammonian, circulating twice
> Around each open ear, like those fair scrolls
> That grace the columns of th'Ionic dome.

As John Barrell has pointed out this symbolic linkage between Siluria, Greece and Britain is foregrounded by changes to the frontispiece to the second edition of the poem that quite specifically identify the sheep as belonging to this variety.[56] It is in the first book of the poem that Dyer is most successful, focusing on the day to day problems of the shepherd and offering knowledgable advice on how to tackle them in the tradition of Virgil's *Georgics*. Even when he is at his most down to earth Dyer succeeds in being poetic, as when he writes:

> Plung'd in the flood, not long the struggler sinks,
> With his white flakes, that glisten through the tide;
> The sturdy rustic, in the middle wave,
> Awaits to seize him rising; one arm bears
> His lifted head above the limpid stream,
> While the full clammy fleece the other laves
> Around, laborious, with repeated toil;
> And then resigns him to the sunny bank,
> Where, bleating loud, he shakes his dripping locks

– a description that combines accurate observation with much rhythmic dexterity. In the first book the benefits of the rural life are contrasted with the inequalities of the city and its more sordid environment;

> Far nobler prospects these
> Than gardens black with smoke in dusty towns,
> Where stenchy vapours often blot the sun.

But for much of the rest of the theme the raising of sheep is subordinated to Dyer's grander theme, the combing, spinning and dying of wool, the manufacture of garments, the export and interchange of commodities around the globe. Dyer's argument is that the benefits of trade flow naturally from the benefits of the production of wool, creating a world-wide interdependence from which all can benefit, but which both results from and creates British imperial power. But all this is far different from the idleness and luxury of imperial Rome since it is solidly founded on virtuous hard work. The work ethic becomes the thread that binds town and country here. There is to be no idleness in Arcadia or anywhere else. A characteristic admonition in *The Fleece* runs as follows:

> But chief by numbers of industrious hands
> A nation's wealth is counted: numbers raise
> Warm emulation: where that virtue dwells,
> There will be traffic's seat; there will she build
> Her rich emporium. Hence, ye happy swains!
> With hospitality inflame your breast,
> And emulation: the whole world receive,
> And with their arts, their virtues deck your isle.

Somewhere along the way wool and Siluria almost get forgotten
– indeed they are mentioned at the end of the poem almost as
an after thought. What matters is not so much wool as what
wool leads to – Book III concludes with a rhapsodic invocation
of the grandeur of London and the Thames:

> What bales, what wealth, what industry, what fleets!
> Lo, from the simple fleece how much proceeds.

In the end the sheep of the border country are just grist to the
mill of metropolitan greatness.

But Dyer's exhilarated vision of a world bound more and more
closely together by trade was very far from being universally
shared. Increasingly the metropolis was feared as an all-engulfing
force that was rapidly draining the provinces of all pretensions
to an autonomous existence. London can never simply be a physical
place or a dot on the map; London is a state of mind, a mode of
existence grounded in consumerism, luxury and mutual exploitation. The whole culture of fashionable spas, whether Bath or
Brighton, Harrogate or Scarborough, was symptomatic of the way
in which a culture of leisure and affluence was becoming more
widely diffused – to use a characteristically eighteenth-century
verb – bringing a variety of sophisticated entertainments to place
that had not known them before. The question was not simply
whether such lifestyles and such role models as Beaus Brummel
and Nash were desirable in themselves – though clearly this gave
rise to some concern – but more generally whether the sheer
power of the capital and the force with which it impacted on
the periphery was not dangerous in itself. London seemed
inherently destabilising. Town and country could no longer be
regarded as stabilised antithetical terms, as perennial opposites,
each with their own characteristic merits. Areas of Great Britain

still proud of their own history and regional identity were now subject to an invasion that was not military, as in the past, but cultural. The homogenisation of a nation seemed well under way. Perhaps just because William Cowper lived at Olney in Buckinghamshire, not a million miles from Charing Cross, his poetry expresses with particular vividness this sense of a traditional way of life under threat. Cowper is still probably best remembered for 'Yardley Oak', a poem in which he celebrated an ancient tree at the centre of the village that was reputed to be over 1000 years old. As such the oak might seem to epitomise the enduring nature of England and English culture, yet the poem is actually far more equivocal than its reputation might suggest:

> Yet is thy root sincere, sound as a rock,
> A quarry of stout spurs and knotted fangs
> Which, crook'd into a thousand whimsies, clasp
> The stubborn soil, and hold thee still erect.
> So stands a kingdom whose foundations yet
> Fail not, in virtue and in wisdom laid,
> Though all the superstructure, by the tooth
> Pulveriz'd of venality, a shell
> Stands now, and semblance only of itself.

Significantly it is only the root which still remains vital, proof of the strength and integrity of the England of a bygone age, when, as he wrote in *The Task*, she was

> plain, hospitable, kind and undebauched

and which even now is the force that sustains the tree and keeps it erect. The trunk itself is hollow, eaten away by the force of moral corruption, so that Yardley Oak as a symbol of an enduring England is more semblance than reality.

Cowper found the contemporary world of consumption and leisure distinctly threatening despite the fact that he did not necessarily see anything wrong with living a life of greater comfort and convenience. Here, Cowper might well be charged with hypocrisy since, quite apart from anything else, he can be found regularly thanking his correspondents for gifts, of oysters, salmon, fish and game, which many might think luxuries. However, it was above all the spiritual emptiness at the heart of contemporary fashionable culture that he abhorred. In true puritan fashion he genuinely dreaded the prospect of a life of vacuity, idleness and triviality – though this may perhaps not be particularly surprising given the fact that he was, in any case, subject to severe bouts of depression. His decision to begin *The Task* – at Lady Austen's suggestion – with a mock heroic celebration of the sofa seems symptomatic of his ambivalence. From a certain point of view a sofa is simply an article of furniture which makes everyday life more agreeable and which can be taken to epitomise Cowper's general intention of writing a poem which will avoid the grand themes and grand style of epic poetry and will rather cleave to the contours and subject matter of everyday experience in a rambling and discursive way – in fact much like ordinary conversation. Yet at the same time the sofa is an object that makes Cowper seem more than slightly uneasy and which he is delighted to swerve away from, since it conjures up images of lounging pashas and dangerously indolent Eastern potentates – especially when contrasted with the energies of 'arms and the man'. When in 1781 Cowper wrote a letter to his friend the Reverend William Unwin, who was staying at Brighthelmstone, he initially tried to enter sympathetically into the spirit of the thing, by agreeing with him that

... the most magnificent object under heaven is the great deep.[57]

but it was not long before he felt compelled to reveal his quite extensive reservations about the moral character of such a place:

... by your account of it it seems to be just what it was when I visited it, a scene of Idleness and Luxury, music, dancing, cards, walking, riding, bathing, eating, drinking, coffee, tea, scandal, dressing, yawning, sleeping, the rooms perhaps more magnificent because the proprietors are grown richer, but the manners and occupations of the company just the same. Though my life has long been like to that of a recluse I have not the temper of one, nor am I in the least an enemy to cheerfulness and good humour; but I cannot envy you your situation: I even find myself constrained to prefer the silence of this nook, and the snug fire-side in our diminutive parlour to all the splendour and gaiety of Brighthelmstone.[58]

For Cowper the spas were not just to be deplored because they were places of idleness and potential dissipation but because they were places in which people became superficial and distracted, where it was all too easy to 'forget' the fundamental principles that should govern human existence. The spas were places of luxury from which the corruptions of London radiated outwards into provincial areas where such entertainments had been hitherto unknown. But, of course it was London itself that was the greatest source of moral danger precisely because nothing could hope to remain unchanged and unmodified so long as London –

> opulent, enlarged, and still
> Increasing

– was developing exponentially. London, a 'noisome sew'r', was a giant vortex sucking not only the dregs of society into its polluted ambience, but also the gentlemen, the provincial knights and squires, on whom they would prey. It is the city that has created the new cynical morality which is clearly identifiable with the opinions of Bernard Mandeville. It is the 'profusion' of the city that

> Hardens, blinds
> And warps the consciences of public men,
> Till they can laugh at virtue; mock the fools
> That trust them; and in th'end, disclose a face
> That would have shock'd credulity herself
> Unmask'd, vouchsafing this their sole excuse,
> Since all alike are selfish – why not they?

Like Cobbett, Cowper saw London as a great Wen sucking the life and the goodness out of England and like Cobbett he liked to look back to the good old days when England was

> plain, hospitable, kind
> And undebauch'd. But we have bid farewell
> To all the virtues of those better days,
> And all their honest pleasures.

Cowper is torn between the fear that, in the modern world, a life of virtue may no longer be possible and the hope that there may still be rural places to which the 'stain' of the town has not spread. In his own 'blest seclusion from a jarring world' he will continue to advocate, against the grain

The cause of piety and sacred truth,
And virtue, and those scenes which God ordain'd
Should best secure them and promote them most;
Scenes that I love, and with regret perceive
Forsak'n. . . .

For a significant interval the idea of provincial virtue had held out the possibility that there would always be pockets of resistance throughout Britain where people would be able to maintain their integrity and hold out against the blandishments of the city, although Cowper was increasingly pessimistic about the prospects for such continued resistance. But with the poetry of George Crabbe – who spent much of his life at the seaside town of Aldeburgh in Suffolk, which had been his birthplace (1755) and to which he returned as a parson in 1792 – that loophole was firmly closed. The glowing or smiling landscape of Thomson is replaced by a vivid evocation of blighted trees, samphire and mud-banks, salt-ditches, 'slimy mallow' and 'clasping tares', 'Heaps of entangled weeds', the familiar sound of the dredger and the smell of boiling tar. Crabbe was acutely conscious that the bleak and forbidding environment of the Suffolk coast where he lived was very far from the rural idyll that so many poets had celebrated and he made it his mission to present it truthfully without any attempt at idealisation or even amelioration of the often harsh facts. In consequence, although Crabbe was catapaulted into prominence after the publication of *The Borough* in 1810 and his *Tales* of 1812, many contemporary readers found his work shocking because of the relentless negativity with which he seemed to view the world and refused to accept that this experience was in any way typical. The reviewer of *The Borough* in the *Monthly Mirror* observed:

There is, in Mr. Crabbe, a strange propensity to put things in their worst light; and if other poets have painted human nature better, he has certainly depicted her worse than she really is. The fact is, that Mr. Crabbe has lived a great deal in a smuggling neighbourhood, and has observed that the country there is a very different thing from what our Arcadian poets have represented it; he very naturally falls into the other extreme and sees nothing but vice in every village, and poverty in every cottage. The readers of books, who are mostly townspeople, are delighted to be told that there is quite as much vice and misery, and they know that there is more poverty, in a house that looks upon fields, than one that looks upon red bricks; and they eagerly believe in the truth of Mr. Crabbe's verse, especially since they perceive him able to discriminate and portray the characters of such men as themselves. They affect to pity the once happy cottager, and like no cottage but a *cottage ornée*. It is very true that 'the town has spoiled the country;' but there is still more simplicity more virtue, and more happiness, in a village than in a town, in a town than in a city, and in a city than in a metropolis . . . .[59]

Naturally a critic who cites Cowper is going to be unwilling to give up on Cowper's vision and when he goes on to cite 'Peter Grimes' as a prime instance of what he objects to we are bound to demur. For 'Peter Grimes' is undoubtedly Crabbe's masterpiece precisely because he is unsparingly presented as a lonely man who has ruthlessly murdered his apprentices, yet who is also the desperately alienated outcast whose crimes were generally condoned by the phrase, 'Grimes is at his exercise.' Hazlitt also objected to Crabbe's unpitying vision but more shrewdly pointed to its underlying motivation:

He does not indulge his fancy or sympathise with us, or tell us how the poor feel; but how he should feel in their situation, which we do not want to know. He does not weave the web of their lives of a mingled yarn, good and ill together, but clothes them all in the same overseer's dingy linsey-woolsey, or tinges them with a green and yellow melancholy. He blocks out all possibility of good, cancels the hope, or even the wish for it, as a weakness; checkmates Tityrus and Virgil at the game of pastoral cross-purposes, disables all his adversary's white pieces, and leaves none but black ones on the board.[60]

Crabbe's ruthless demolition of the very idea of virtue seems symptomatic. In one of his tales, Crabbe described a young man called Edward Shore, a budding writer, who seemed almost entirely admirable and who, initially at least is vastly superior to the majority of his *dramatis personae*:

With prospects bright upon the world he came,
Pure love of virtue, strong desire of fame:
Men watch'd the way his lofty mind would take,
And all foretold the progress he would make.

But Edward becomes friendly with an older man, a deist and an
atheist; becomes emotionally involved with his wife, Anna; and,
in the absence of her husband, becomes her seducer. Significantly
Shore later extenuates his actions with the argument that men
do not possess free will and that all our actions are externally
determined:

Nor good nor evil can you beings name,
Who are but rocks and castles in the game.

This is but one of many instances in Crabbe where the adoption
of advanced or radical intellectual positions is associated with
moral depravity. Shore losses his money, is tortured with guilt
and finally goes mad. Deprived of his pretensions, reduced to
the status of a harmless and contemptible simpleton, he is known
as 'Silly Shore'. It seems clear that Crabbe, though a clergyman,
has very little investment in the idea of virtue, which is simply
equated, in this story, with the pride which goeth before a fall.
This stripping away of illusions is Crabbe's forte and he therefore will not allow his readers to indulge themselves in the pleasing
fantasy that the country is any different from the town. Even in
The Village (1783), Crabbe's first significant work there can be no
misconception that this is a crime free zone. We find 'village vices'
ranging from wife-beating and 'lawless merchants' who swindle
labourers out of their money, to poaching and violence at the inn.
Slander and disguise, 'the city's vice' are present. But, of course,
The Borough, remote though it may be, is still the town, marred by
political corruption and marked by a less than idyllic environment:

Those far-extending heaps of coal and coke
Where fresh-filled lime-kilns breathe their stifling smoke.

Crabbe's often powerful realism means that there can be no ro-
manticised depiction of the lower orders and that he is scarcely
likely to depict them as virtuous. Originally, in *The Village* Crabbe's
self-confessed lack of charity:

> Yet why, you ask, these humble crimes relate,
> Why make the poor as guilty as the great

may seem to imply a refreshing candour but subsequently, in *The Borough* and the *Tales*, both published when Britain was still at war with France, it becomes clear that this severity is ideologically motivated. It has been precisely a tendency to look indulgently on the lower classes and to encourage them to become educated that has led in France to revolution and in Britain, to treasonable disaffection and a simmering discontent. The *Tales* are framed by two stories, 'The Dumb Orators' and 'The Learned Boy' that point to a contemporary political moral. In the first, Justice Bolt, a vigorous speaker and controversialist in his own community travels to a big city and attends the local debating society in the expectation of wiping the floor with his opponents in his customary manner. But he finds that the society is a forum for the most radical views and realising that he is unlikely to gain a sympathetic hearing he fails to make his opinions known. This failure makes him a good deal less overbearing. But some years later, among his own people and in a more conservative political climate, he is able to gain his revenge on the leading orator at that meeting, castigating him as follows:

> And live there those, in such all-glorious state
> Traitors protected in the land they hate?
> Rebels, still warring with the laws that give
> To them subsistence? – Yes, such wretches live.

In the second tale, Farmer Jones, a widower who remarries, has a son Stephen who is 'a whining timid lad' who, over-indulged by his stepmother, grows up to be idle and shiftless. He goes to London and eventually acquires more confidence, largely as the result of reading radical and irreligious books. When he finally returns home and discloses his new-found views to his father he is thrashed to the bone with a whip. In each case the moral is clear. Both Bolt and Jones earlier failed to insist on their own conservative views and pay the price for being too permissive. We should not foster any illusions about the depravity or the rebelliousness of the lower orders, still less assume them to be basically virtuous. They need to be put down with firmness, even brutality.

6

The Romantics and Virtue

In many ways, Wordsworth seems to be the culmination of eighteenth-century discourses about virtue. Wordsworth is the self-confident provincial who is convinced that his upbringing in the Lake District has marked him out from others as a privileged being. In *Lyrical Ballads* he celebrates the simple virtues of 'low and rustic life' and contrasts the purity of their speech with those who act under the influence of social vanity. Wordsworth distrusts London as the corrupting metropolitan centre and in 'Michael' contrast the integrity of the father who remains in Grasmere with the moral degradation of the son who leaves for the city. These concerns can be paralleled in the fiction of Sir Walter Scott, perhaps the most influential single writer of British Romanticism. Scott is proud of Scottish history and Scottish culture. Like Wordsworth, Scott is concerned to depict and dignify the lives of relatively humble people and to let them speak in their own vernacular voice. Jeanie Deans in *The Heart of Midlothian*, who walks all the way from Edinburgh to London to plead for her sister Effie's life, is a heroine who is more than able to take her place among the virtuous characters of eighteenth-century fiction. The sense of continuity is powerful and yet there are aspects of both writers that resist such assimilation to the past as can be demonstrated by a text from each, where the idea of the imagination is prominent. In Wordsworth's poem 'The Idiot Boy' Susan Gale, an old lady, has been taken seriously ill and seems close to death. Her neighbour, Betty Foy, is anxious that she should get medical attention as soon as possible and to that end sends her half-witted son Johnny into town on a pony to summon the doctor. But even at one o'clock in the morning, some five hours later Johnny has not returned and his mother is worried about what may have happened to him. She travels into town herself and bangs on the doctor's door. The doctor denys having seen the boy, is annoyed at being disturbed and goes back to bed. Betty in her worry and confusion forgets to tell him about Susan's illness. She sets out again in search of Johnny and eventually finds him on the pony in the vicinity of a waterfall. In the meantime Susan has recovered and soon all three are happily reunited. What Wordsworth celebrates here is the imagination, whether it is the intoxication of the idiot boy's involvement in a romantic landscape, or the vividness with which Betty imagines what may have happened to her son and her corresponding joy at finding him. The poem disparages everyday rational imperatives. For although Betty Foy wants to help her neighbour, in practice she acts neither well nor sensibly. It was certainly a mistake to send her idiot boy on such an important mission but she was even more at fault in first doing nothing and then failing to call out the doctor when she was actually speaking to him. Both were irresponsible – neither acted virtuously. Only Susan's miraculous recovery saved them from a lifelong burden of guilt. Whereas, for a poet of an earlier generation like Mark Akenside, author of *The Pleasures of the Imagination* virtue and the imagination were allied, Wordsworth goes out of his way to stress the lawlessness and irresponsibility of the imagination. Edward Waverley, hero of Scott's first novel *Waverley* (1814), is a dreamer and lover of literature, who enlists in the army of George II, but who on a visit to Scotland, through a romantic fascination with the Highlanders and emotional involvement with Flora Mac-Ivor, becomes implicated in the Jacobite rebellion. In a crucial scene, Waverley, in the presence of Fergus Mac-Ivor, Flora's brother and a leading figure in the rebellion removes the king's cockade from his hat and is on the point of replacing it with a Jacobite insignia but does not do so on Flora's insistence. Subsequently, Waverley is accused of desertion and high treason – crimes of which he is effectively guilty. Waverley is certainly not your unshakably virtuous man but he *is* a hero of the imagination, who through his capacity to become sympathetically involved with the predicament of others puts his very life in jeopardy. Waverley is no wimp. Scott sees real mettle in him:

> this compound of intense curiosity and exalted imagination forms a peculiar species of courage, which somewhat resembles the light usually carried by a miner.[1]

in that it can be extinguished in extreme conditions, but which is nevertheless capable of being once more rekindled with a throbbing mixture of hope, awe and anxiety.[2]

We admire Waverley more for his recklessness than his rectitude and there is something heroic about his very willingness to embrace the possibility of inconsistency and contradiction whatever the cost. Certainly the wavering hero is in total contrast to the unswerving virtuous man. Virtue and the imagination are at odds.

In the twentieth century there has often been a greater interest in the ideas which the romantics had about poetry than in the poetry itself, which has often been perceived as too subjective and self-indulgent. Coleridge's theory of the imagination was important for the new critics because it offered a way of validating the 'truths' of poetry in a world that seemed unsympathetic to them. More recently Wordsworth's desire to connect mind and nature, what Geoffrey Hartman has called

> . . . the covenant of mind and nature, the marriage of heaven and earth, center on the possibility of converting, yet not subduing, the one imagination to the other.[3]

and M.H. Abrams as

> a culminating and procreative marriage between mind and nature. . . .[4]

has served as a focus for examining the problematic claims of language to mediate between consciousness and world. For many that gap is necessarily unbridgeable. The claim that the imagination has the power to do so is one that simply cannot be sustained. Long ago Blake insisted that the Imagination and Nature were antithetical. Paul de Man, in the name of deconstruction, sees the new criticism as implicated with the Romantics in the same desire to abolish that difference:

> There is the same stress on the analogical unity of nature and consciousness, the same priority given to the symbol as the unit of language in which the subject–object synthesis can take place, the same tendency to transfer into nature attributes of consciousness and to unify it organically with respect to a center that acts, for natural objects, as the identity of the self functions for consciousness.[5]

I personally would deny that the Romantics are concerned to create such a unified consciousness precisely because in the romantic period 'virtue' is precisely the awkward and uncomfortable term that designates such a unity. It would be verging on a contradiction in terms to describe someone as 'largely virtuous'. There is a certain absolutism built into the idea of virtue: to be virtuous you have, like a stick of seaside peppermint rock, to have virtuous written all the way through. But I would also want to insist that to try to grasp Romantic poetry in such a virtual and aestheticising way is to gloss over the risks the Romantics took in elevating the imagination over everyday considerations of morals. There is a reckless, irresponsible and uncomfortable side to Romantic writing that has become invisible to us. The Romantics say: 'Yes, there is a price to be paid for this – and we are prepared to pay it!' In turning their backs on the terrain of virtue the Romantics necessarily enter territory that is both unknown and dangerous. There are no bearings. This story – of the intricate engagement of Romantic writers with the idea of virtue and of their attempts to disentangle themselves from it, the whole ethical dilemma of Romanticism – is one that remains unrecognised and untold.

In the period of the French Revolution and of Romanticism the idea of virtue, so prominent in eighteenth-century discourse as to seem well nigh inescapable, unexpectedly fades from view, like a bright sun that is suddenly overtaken by such thick banks of cloud that it can only fitfully be glimpsed behind them. The reasons for this are many and various, but on the simplest level it represents the passing of the classical paradigm: the assumption, whether in literature or ethics, that the Greek and Roman worlds offered ideals and models which later generations should follow. In the education of a gentleman in the seventeenth and eighteenth centuries a familiarity with the Latin language was deemed indispensible and this language in turn was the way in which the core values of the classical world, whether adumbrated in philosophy or exemplified in history, were transmitted. Although this education continued into the nineteenth century and beyond, the notion of virtue was so problematised and marginalised in the Romantic period that even the Victorians who might be thought to be more responsive to all that it stood for were distinctly unenthused. In the eighteenth-century virtue had seemed to represent the very pinnacle of human endeavour but now it seemed rigid, narrow and limited – something altogether insufficient to constitute the basis of a moral creed. The extent of the Victorian disengagement from virtue as an ideal can be estimated by referring to such representative figures as Tennyson, Carlyle, Matthew Arnold and John Stuart Mill. The word 'virtue' only occurs three times in the whole corpus of Tennyson's poetry and then only in very minor and marginal works. Clearly it did not constitute a significant reference point for him. In *Heroes and Hero-Worship* Carlyle might well have characterised the great men he admires, who include Luther, Mahomet, Dante and Cromwell in terms of virtue, but he prefers to praise them for their strength, their manliness, honesty, sincerity, tolerance and conviction. On the one occasion, with reference to Cromwell, where he does mention virtue he recasts it into his own idiom, deliberately differentiating it from any notion of rule governed behaviour:

> Virtue, *Vir-tus*, manhood, *hero*-hood, is not fair-spoken immaculate regularity; it is first of all, what the Germans well name it, *Tugend* .... Courage and the Faculty to do.[6]

From quite a different point of view Matthew Arnold also found the concept of virtue tarnished by connotations of limitation and complacency, perhaps particularly because he well knew how bound up it was with the idea of aristocracy. In *Culture and Anarchy* he writes of the 'lumber of phrases' about Aristotle that he had been stuffed with at Oxford in the bad old times and that

> Once when I had the advantage of listening to the Reform debates in the House of Commons, having heard a number of interesting speakers, and among them a well-known lord and a well-known baronet, I remember it struck me, applying Aristotle's machinery of the mean to my ideas about our aristocracy, that the lord was exactly the perfection, or happy mean, of virtue, of aristocracy, and the baronet the excess. And I fancied that by observing the two we might see both the inadequacy to supply the principle of authority needful for our wants, and the danger of its trying to supply it when it was not really competent for the business.[7]

In this account Aristotle's definition of virtue and the way in which it is taught emerges as badly as the class which purports to live by it. Moreover the irony of such language is very marked when Arnold's own preferred terms are 'the study of perfection', 'harmoniousness' and 'sweetness and light'. If Arnold's Hellenism is overtly offered as an alternative to the narrowness of Hebraism it is equally a corrective to the rather mechanical notion of virtue that a classical education tends to promote. By comparison, and on the face of it, John Stuart Mill seems more favourably disposed to the idea of virtue, since he acknowledges that Socrates was the most virtuous man in the Athenian society that persecuted him and regards the clash between them as decisive evidence of the need for freedom of thought and discussion in any society. But since Mill goes on to cite the example of Marcus Aurelius, who was also virtuous but who nevertheless persecuted Christianity, Mill clearly is insisting that it is toleration as a cultural goal which must take precedence. What Mill is really interested in doing is defending those who think independently and critically against the conformist majority and he does so in the name of *individuality* and *diversity* – values that are inconsistent with the monolithic logic of virtue.

Even in the eighteenth century this sense of virtue as something already *past* begins to be evident. As people become more historically aware and more intellectually sophisticated it becomes increasingly evident that a gap has opened up between ancient and modern that can never effectually be closed. The idea of emulating the classical world began to seem as impossible or irrelevant as perpetuating the ideals of chivalry in an age of windmills. Even virtue, in theory the most inescapable and universal of obligations, begins to seem problematic. The most crucial recognition is that virtue is not something that can occur at any time or in any place but a plant which flourishes under very specific conditions. Contrariwise, without these conditions it cannot be expected to thrive. The beginnings of such a sociological determinism are found in Montesquieu who specifically associated virtue with democracies and aristocracies and who argued that they could not be expected to be found in monarchies or under despotic government. But the radical implications of such a line of argument were masked by Montesquieu's insistence at the very beginning of his text that he is differentiating *political* virtue from 'moral virtue or a Christian virtue'.[8] Montesquieu's distinction is diplomatic in that it seems to offer virtue merely as a way of characterising a certain type of society which cannot be therefore read off as a critique of monarchy, the form of society which overwhelming prevailed at the time when he actually wrote. But it also averts a confrontation with Christianity since the universal possibility of virtuous behaviour is thereby preserved. However Montesquieu's successors found no reason to be either so pedantic or so circumspect. Gibbon, for example, in praising the Roman emperors who succeeded Domitian for their virtue and wisdom and for their determination to regard themselves 'as accountable ministers of the laws' suggested that they might have been able to restore the republic

> had the Romans of their days been capable of enjoying a rational freedom.'[9]

Contrariwise he suggested their predecessors had made moral behaviour virtually impossible:

> The dark unrelenting Tiberius, the furious Caligula, the feeble Claudius, the profligate and cruel Nero, the beastly Vitellius, and the timid and inhuman Domitian, are condemned to everlasting infamy. During fourscore years Rome groaned beneath an unremitting tyranny, which . . . was fatal to almost every virtue, and every talent, that arose in that unhappy period.[10]

Thus the virtue of the Roman republic is connected with a highly specific conjunction of circumstances. Under tyrants such as Tiberius and Nero virtue was so effectively proscribed that even when the emperors themselves became morally admirable the people themselves no longer possessed the virtue, independence and rationality that would have been preconditions for the effective functioning of republican government.

The increasing willingness of thinkers of the Enlightenment to examine questions of morality and virtue in the light of specific, historical conditions made it difficult to regard Plutarch's Greek and Roman heroes as the self-creating, self-determining supermen that they had for so long appeared to be. Characters such as Cato and Brutus might not have been on the winning side but it seemed that they were completely free agents in all that they did. Like the legendary Mucius Scaevola, who thrust his hand in a flame as proof of his indomitable will, the exemplary significance of the virtuous hero lay not just in his moral righteousness but in his determination to challenge overwhelming circumstances. But under the critical eye of Enlightenment history such narratives no longer seemed either very plausible or very important – in a Roman context 'virtue' might seem as much part of a Roman patriotic vocabulary as 'barbarian' had been for the Greek. Certainly Adam Ferguson, in his *An Essay on the History of Civil Society* (1767) was disinclined to take Rome at its own valuation:

> We are apt to admire the empire of the Romans, as a model of national greatness and splendour: but the greatness we admire in this case, was ruinous to the virtue and happiness of mankind.[11]

From a vantage point in Edinburgh the civilising power of empires was by no means evident. Ferguson did not simply focus on the familiar topic of Rome's own corruption and decline, he stressed the freedoms and advantages they enjoyed *before* they became Roman subjects. So, progressively we find the power of the Roman grand narrative crumbling. And as the force and clarity of what Rome represents begins to seem more doubtful so too does the greatness of the makers and perpetuators of Rome – just as the greatness of Cecil Rhodes is predicated on the fact that he extended the power of the British Empire in Africa. It seemed that to celebrate Rome was necessarily to celebrate the power of human agency; but as the historical record was more closely inspected the more tangled and enigmatic it seemed. Even Gibbon who was particularly zealous in praising and condeming the emperors of his narrative found it difficult if not impossible to regard the survival of the Empire as some kind of an achievement. Even leaving aside the awkward question as to whether the Empire continued to be the same thing he was obliged to look beyond the behaviour of individual emperors to more large scale if somewhat banal causes: immoderate prosperity, the undermining of the Empire by Christianity, the disappearance of a citizen's army, the undermining of military discipline, the incursion of barbarian hordes. Over such a huge timespan the careful weighing and evaluating of every single ruler was somewhat beside the point even if Gibbon himself never fully grasped those implications.

If the inexorable consequence of the writing of narratives on such a massive scale was to problematise the role of the individual in history, this was equally true of the events of the French

Revolution. In the history of classical Rome the great actors were always already there – it was as if Pompeii, Crassus, Julius Caesar, Antony, the Gracchi, Octavius strode out onto a stage where everyone was already expecting them. World historical events were decided by no more than a handful of key players. But the French Revolution was constituted as a series of events that involved hundreds of thousands of people. Even those who held significant power were numerous and constantly changing. In this turmoil and swirl of events the whole question of greatness, let alone virtue, becomes problematic. Although David's invocation of antique virtue in such paintings as *The Oath of the Horatii* and his *Brutus* is rightly linked with the revolution it needs equally to be stressed that such paintings initially were produced for a royalist court where they could be read off as celebrations of an aristocratic virtue. What made this art increasingly at odds with the new democratic circumstances was its frank elitism, most notably expressed in Jean-Germain Drouais's *Marius at Minturnae*, where the unknown youth who seeks to kill Marius is compelled by the sheer force of the hero's presence to cover his eyes with his robe. The two characters cannot be placed on the same symbolic or cultural level. David, in painting the death of Marat, faced a new problem, since it was by no means evident that Marat was entitled to be ranked with the illustrious icons of the past. Moreover, some might see Charlotte Corday, who killed him, as the true heroine of the narrative. So Marat is presented as a kind of martyred Christ – alone, without his assassin. But new circumstances, where chance and contingency predominate, do not lend themselves to this style of classical representation, which is constructed around the exemplary actions of an exemplary figure.

More generally, and even in its own time, the French Revolution is seen as epitomising a situation where no one has control, where everyone is at the mercy of external events. In his *Considerations on France*, published in 1797 Joseph de Maistre wrote:

> The very rascals who appear to lead the revolution are involved only as simple instruments and as soon as they aspire to dominate it they fall ignobly. Those who established the republic did it without wanting to and without knowing what they were doing. They were led to it by events; a prior design would not have succeeded.[12]

Similarly in his *The French Revolution* Carlyle writes:

> ... this Revolutionary Government is not a self-conscious but a blind fatal one. Each man, enveloped in his ambient-atmosphere of revolutionary fanatic Madness, rushes on, impelled and impelling; and has become a blind brute force.[13]

There is the vision of a world out of control before which each individual, despite his efforts, is rendered ineffectual.

In its pessimism about the possibilities for human action Weber's opera *Der Freischütz* (1821) offers fascinating evidence of the extent to which the aristocratic ethos of rationality and self-command had been undermined. Max, the hero, is an assistant forester, who is expecting to receive the hand in marriage of Agathe, daughter of Cuno, the chief forester and also to inherit the office of forester himself. But to do this he must first demonstate his prowess as a marksman in the presence of the prince. But Max has strangely lost his prowess as a marksman and in a competition on the eve of the trial he is actually defeated and humiliated by Killian, a peasant. In desperation Max is taken by Kaspar, a fellow forester to the Wolf's Glen in the forest to make a sinister compact with Samiel, the Black Huntsman, and acquires some magic bullets, which must infallibly hit their target. Max uses three of the bullets to impress the Prince on a hunting expedition and keeps back one for the trial. When he shoots at the chosen target, a white dove, Agathe his bride-to-be, falls to the ground, seemingly wounded. It is Kaspar, his initiator into evil, who is killed by the bullet. Max is forced to confess and is sentenced to banishment – but at the intercession of an old hermit is given a year to prove himself. Max's loss of skill, his resort to infernal powers, represents not only a sense that the pretensions of the aristocracy are under scrutiny – even in a country that has not had a revolution – but more pervasively a sense of a world governed by dark and mysterious forces before which the individual is powerless.

Weber's myth is particularly suggestive because it implies that the merits that supposedly define and differentiate the aristocracy from the common people are illusory and that their power and pretensions are maintained by improper means. In a similar way the very fact that virtue was linked with the aristocracy through traditions of military prowess, and through notions of honour and *noblesse oblige* meant that the political challenge to the position of the aristocracy in both France and Britain in the 1790s also involved a critique of aristocratic pretensions to virtue. In theory this leaves virtue itself intact but in practice its potential seems reminiscent of Archimedes – if only it could find a place to stand virtue would move the world, but there remains the problem of where it is to find a foothold. The radical attempt to redefine and reinvigorate virtue as an absolute moral ideal has the paradoxical effect of rendering that ideal at best hypothetical, at worst unrealisable in any conceivable temporal time frame.

In the writings of William Godwin, who was the biggest single influence on the radical intellectuals of the day, this contradiction is particularly evident. Godwin's thought represents the development of the general principles of Dissent into a political philosophy. Just as the existence of a hierarchy of bishops and an established connection between church and state serves both to corrupt and to obstruct the search for religious truth, so more generally society should be a community of individuals united in their rationality, virtue and their determination to seek happiness. Only the state and the existence of political power prevents this. People are not allowed to think for themselves but compelled to submit to a social system grounded in class distinction, which will not allow this or anything else to be questioned:

> It is supposed by many that the existence of permanent hereditary distinction is necessary to the maintenance of order, among beings so imperfect as the human species. But it is allowed by all that permanent hereditary distinction is a fiction of policy, not an ordinance of immutable truth. Wherever it exists, the human mind, so far as relates to political society, is prevented from settling upon its true foundation. There is a constant struggle between the genuine sentiments of the understanding, which tell us that all this is an imposition, and the imperious voice of Government, which bids us, Reverence and obey. In this unequal contest, alarm and apprehension will perpetually haunt the minds of those who exercise usurped power. In this artificial state of man, powerful engines must be employed to prevent him from rising to his true level. It is the business of the governors to persuade the governed that it is in their interest to be slaves. They have no other means by

which to create this fictitious interest but those which they derive from the perverted understandings, and burdened property, of the public, to be returned in titles, ribands and bribes. Hence that system of universal corruption without which monarchy could not exist.[14]

So privilege, corruption and irrationality are as indisssolubly linked together as are reason and virtue. Their role is nothing less than to prevent the coming into existence of a better world.

It follows that it is an essential part of Godwin's challenge to the *status quo* that he should be able to expose the hypocrisy and hollowness of its moral pretensions. In *Caleb Williams* Godwin made it his mission to attack the very notion of aristocratic virtue, to demonstrate that in practice no person of high social rank could ever be authentically virtuous. In the first part of the novel Falkland is the epitome of everything that the age of sentimentalism was disposed to admire. He is generous, tender-hearted, thoughtful, attentive and kind. He seeks only to help others, whether it is the weak and vulnerable Emily Melville or Hawkins, the honest hard-working tenant. It would have been very much easier for him not to get involved, since in both cases it involves crossing the violent, headstrong and tyrannical Tyrrel, who is a powerful local figure who does not take kindly to what he regards as interference. But Falkland is determined to help not just out of kindliness or pity, though he certainly feels that, but because he strongly believes in the justice of their cause. What is more, Falkland makes it clear, both in the affair of Count Malvesi and in his disputes with Tyrrel that he is anxious to resolve matters peacefully. He has no interest in conflict for its own sake – and, seemingly, no false pride. But in fact false pride is just what he does have – so that although, on the surface, he seems the total antithesis of everything that Tyrrel represents, in reality he is far closer to him than he would ever admit. His Achilles' heel is his sense of honour, which is more precious to him than anything in the world and which he will go to any lengths to protect. In *Caleb Williams* Godwin is determined to drive a wedge between true virtue, on the one hand, which is an internal, spiritual quality grounded in rationality and openness, and honour, which is ultimately hollow, since it is purely matter of how one is regarded by others, whether that reputation is justified or not. Falkland is still regarded as being a man of virtue and honour even when he is a murderer and a liar. Moreover it is precisely due to the social position that he holds that his version of events goes un-challenged – as it subsequently does in his vendetta with Caleb Williams, which ironically mirrors Tyrrel's vendetta with Hawkins. When Falkland bursts into a rage with Williams, after confessing to Tyrrel's murder, the way in which untruth preserves rank and power, and in which they in turn preserve untruth, becomes totally explicit:

> 'Do you not know, miserable wretch!' added he, suddenly alter-ing his tone, and stamping upon the ground with fury, 'that I have sworn to preserve my reputation, whatever the expense; that I love it more than the whole world and its inhabitants taken together? And do you think that you shall wound it? Begone, miscreant! reptile! and cease to contend with insur-mountable power!'[15]

Whereas virtue liberates, reputation becomes a bloodstained altar on which the most precious of human values must be sacrificed. At this moment aristocracy dramatically is exposed as the obstacle to human progress that Godwin had declared it to be in *Political Justice*:

> It is this structure of aristocracy, in all its sanctuaries and frag-ments, against which reason and morality have declared war . . . Mankind will never be, in an eminent degree, virtuous and happy, till each man shall possess that portion of distinction and no more, to which he is entitled by his personal merits. The disssolution of aristocracy is equally the interest of the oppressor and the oppressed. The one will be delivered from the listlessness of tyranny, and the other from the brutalising operation of servitude.[16]

However, the vision, in *Political Justice* of tyranny receding before the slow but relentless advance of reason and virtue was one which was barely enunciated by Godwin before it slowly began to fade as a realistic or actually realisable possibility. Admittedly there was no inclination on Godwin's part to recant and no necess-ity for him to do so. If need be aeons of time were available for its realisation, but the events of the 1790s, disquieting and intel-lectually unsettling as they were, gave Godwin considerable grounds for concern. For although he personally had disassociated himself from any attempt to realise libertarian goals through violent revolution, events in France during the reign of terror did not just discredit radicalism they were a massive setback to the very attempt to discuss all such matters rationally. Godwin's key value, that of political justice, had been so dragged through the mire and blood of political purges that it was scarcely possible any longer to invoke it as an unproblematic good. In Britain the relentless persecution of radicals seemed all too reminiscent of the irrational religious purges of the sixteenth and seventeenth centuries. Godwin himself, in his own eyes the friend and potential liberator of all humanity, found that instead of being respected and admired, he was despised, rejected and condemned. It was as if, at the very moment when Europe stood poised to take a significant step forward, she had suddenly and quite unexpectedly, turned tail and retreated in total disarray.

The extent of Godwin's pessimism at this new turn of events is manifest in *St. Leon*, a novel which was published in 1799, and which he wrote in the aftermath of the death of his much loved wife, Mary Wollstonecraft, just two years earlier. Particularly in the final section of the novel, where St. Leon, a French aristocrat of the sixteenth-century, who having been given the philosopher's stone by a mysterious stranger, travels to Hungary in order to devote his unlimited riches to some worthy purpose. The fate of the hero seems unmistakably autobiographical; St. Leon naively believes that he has been uniquely empowered to carry through a philanthropic project, to be truly benevolent and virtuous:

... spreading improvements, dispensing blessings, and causing all distress and calamity to vanish from before me.[17]

St. Leon has already learned from his earlier experiences in Italy and Spain that doing good is by no means a straightforward matter, yet, he is still cautiously optimistic that he can do much to alleviate the suffering in this war-torn country. Aware that simply pouring money into the region will be inflationary he is careful to tailor his assistance so that it will produce immediate and tangible benefits. His humanitarian goals should be uncontestable. Nevertheless his interventions meet with distrust, resentment and outright hostility. As a foreigner his intentions seem inscrutable and, since no one can believe in conduct that is at once benevolent and disinterested, there is puzzlement about his ulterior motives. But even if others could believe that he is what he says he is his activities would still be seen as a challenge to the authorities, since the ability to exert such a considerable influence on economic activity is itself a form of power, which cannot be allowed to proceed unchecked. Most paradoxical of all is the deadly enmity he provokes in Bethlem Gabor, whose estates he restores and with whom he establishes close bonds of friendship. Gabor is a particularly striking instance of Godwin's thesis that the characters of men originate in external circumstances, since the murder of his wife and children has turned him from a lover of mankind into a misanthrope. In his eyes St. Leon's desire to help anyone and everyone is not only undiscriminating but actually immoral:

> With the spirit of the slave who, the more he is beaten, becomes the more servile and submissive, you remunerated injuries with benefits. I found that there was not within you one atom of generous sentiment, one honest glow of fervent indignation. Chicken-hearted wretch! Poor soulless poltroon! to say, the best of you, to your insensate heart it was the same whether you were treated with reverence or scorn. I saw you hunted, hooted at, and pursued by the people you fed; you held on your course, and fed them still. I was compelled to witness or to hear of your senseless liberalities every day I lived.[18]

Since St. Leon, like Godwin, is a rationalist and a programmatic optimist he himself cannot fully acknowledge the power of the forces ranged against him – he must see them as temporary impediments that will in the fullness of time be brushed aside. It is left to the marchese Filosante, in an earlier episode, to articulate Godwin's own deepest fear: that there may be

> ... a principle in the human mind destined to be eternally at war with improvement and science.[19]

St. Leon problematises the idea of virtue more deeply than ever before, because Godwin has come to a kind of baffled recognition that virtue is not instantaneously recognisable as the history and mythology of Rome had predicated – that on the contrary virtue may be just as much in the eye of the beholder as beauty is. Neither Bethlem Gabor, nor Charles his own son, is prepared to acknowledge St. Leon as a virtuous man. Each in his different way sees him as a negative force rather than as a force for good. It is here that Godwin's decision to set his novel in the distant historical past – surprising in one who had so recently written of 'Things as they are' – seems particularly significant. In the face of the polarisation and partisanship surrounding the French Revolution Godwin recognised that the eighteenth-century assumption that there was such a thing as virtue, which all could identify and agree upon, was a very timebound state of affairs, which could scarcely have been comprehended when the struggle between Protestantism and Catholicism was at its height and when Hungary was threatened by Muslim invasion. So although *St. Leon* contains magical and fantastic elements it nevertheless has a strong claim to be regarded as the first historical novel, not just because Godwin researched the period before writing it but because the book displays a historical awareness, in a way that *The Mysteries of Udolpho* does not. Although Godwin's investment in the ideal of virtue is manifested in his idealised portrait of St. Leon's wife Marguerite – clearly based on Mary Wollstonecraft – it is rendered far more equivocal in Godwin's portrait of his son, Charles. We are asked to admire Charles yet Godwin shows that Charles is a fanatic and a bigot, a man totally convinced that all who oppose the armies of Charles V are infidels and scoundrels; honourable doubtless by his own soldierly and intolerant lights but scarcely an exemplary individual. Certainly, in the world of *St. Leon*, anymore than in a turn of the century Britain, living under repression and censorship, there is no place for the enlightened rationality of a William Godwin!

However, although Godwin's increasing preoccupation with the role of irrationality in human affairs must be given full weight, the fact remains that even in *Political Justice*, his most optimistic work, he had himself adduced arguments that effectively worked against all the hopes that he entertained. For if the advance of freedom and reason is blocked and thwarted by the existence of established political power, in the form of monarchy and entrenched aristocracy, then there must be some way of demonstrating, how, on a rational level, that resistance can be overcome. The obvious solution would seem to be education. If people are from birth initiated into a series of prejudices that justify the *status quo* then, by the same token, a system of education from childhood can interrogate those same prejudices and enable the individual to see them for what they are. But, perhaps surprisingly, Godwin will not allow this. Godwin's grasp of the power of ideology, particularly taking into consideration the climate of opinion in which he wrote, is impressive but his firmness on this point makes the advance of reason more problematic than he was ever prepared to admit. Godwin is remorseless:

> Should anyone talk to us of rescuing a young person from the sinister influence of a corrupt government by the power of education, it will be fair to ask who is the preceptor by whom this talk is to be effected? Is he born in the ordinary mode of generation, or does he descend among us from the skies. Has his character in no degree been modified by that very influence he undertakes to counteract? ... As long as parents and teachers in general shall fall under the established rule, it is clear that politics and modes of government will educate and infect us all. They poison our minds before we can resist, or so much suspect their malignity. Like the barbarous directors of the Eastern seraglios, they deprive us of our virility, and fit us for their despicable employment from the cradle.[20]

So Godwin presents us with a relentless dichotomy: while a virtuous and rational society would inevitably promote such qualities amongst its members, in a society based on arbitrary power these qualities will be relentlessly suppressed:

> Under a government fundamentally erronious, he will see intrepid virtue proscribed, and a servile, and corrupt spirit uniformly encouraged.[21]

So even a Darwinian timeframe actually offers no real assurance that a better world will ever come about. The self-destructing nature of Godwin's political philosophy, in conjunction with changed political circumstances, goes a long way towards explaining why virtue could no longer be a word to conjure with.

Godwin's insistence that the consequences of the wrong sort of education and upbringing are not only destructive but effectively irreversible becomes a major theme of Romantic writing, especially in the Gothic novel. It is through his monastic upbringing that Ambrosio in Lewis's *The Monk* (1796) becomes so depraved that he will not allow anything to thwart the unfettered expression of his desires. It is through the denial of any social relationship with others from the moment that his creator rejects him that the monster in *Frankenstein* (1818) is forced down a perverted path – though his initial impulses are essentially good. Virtue causes him pain because he knows that it is something he will never he able to exhibit. Watching Agatha, Felix and their old father in the cottage he laments:

> I admired virtue and good feelings, and loved the gentle manners and amiable qualities of the cottagers; but I was shut out from intercourse with them, except through means which I obtained by stealth, when I was unseen and unknown, and which rather increased than satisfied the desire I had of becoming one among my fellows. The gentle words of Agatha, and the animated smiles of the charming Arabian, were not for me. The mild exhortations of the old man, and the lively conversation of the loved Felix, were not for me. Miserable, unhappy wretch.[22]

The irony of Mary Shelley's novel is that the monster desperately struggles against the monstrosity to which he has been condemned by the universal refusal of others to accept his existence as a being with normal thoughts, feelings and desires. Yet, at bottom, he knows that there is nothing he can do about it. What Gothic fiction emphasises are the unforeseeable and uncontrollable consequences of such miseducation. In Hogg's *Private Memoirs and Confessions of a Justified Sinner* (1824) it is the fact that Robert Wringham has been indoctrinated by his natural father, of extreme Calvinist tendency, into the belief that he can do no wrong that actually leads him into evil. Most melodramatical of all in terms of its arguments about accountability is Charlotte Dacre's *Zofloya, or the Moor*, in which, despite the fact that her protagonist, Victoria, murders her husband, Beranza, Henriquez the man she obsessionally loves and Lilla, her rival for his affection, Dacre unhesitatingly blames the mother, who, through infidelity and parental neglect set the whole process in motion. It is *she* who must bear responsibility for what Victoria has done:

> From her infancy untaught, therefore unaccustomed to subdue herself, she had no conception of that *refined* species of virtue

which consists in self-denial; the proud triumph of mind over the weakness of the heart, she had ever been unconscious of; education had never corrected the evil propensities that were by nature hers: hence pride, stubbornness, the gratification of self, contempt and ignorance of the noblest propensities of the mind, with a strong tincture of the darker passions, revenge, hate, and cruelty, made up the sum of her early character. Example, a *mother's* example, had more than corroborated every tendency to evil, and the unhappy Victoria was destitute of a single actuating principle, that might, in consideration of its guilt, deter her from the pursuit of a favourite object. Her mind, alas, was an eternal night, which the broad beam of virtue never illumined.[23]

The infallible voice of conscience is no longer inescapably there – to advise, deter and admonish. The agonies of modern parenting start here.

Godwin was preoccupied with the problem of how virtue could be actualised, but William Blake was far more interested in redefining it. What gave Blake's critique of eighteenth-century notions of moral virtue such force was that he saw quite clearly how it was bound up with neo-classicism in art and how both were part and parcel of an aristocratic ideology. For Blake the Royal Academy and Reynolds's role within it typified what goes wrong when the artist's spontaneity and his own powerful sense of what is right must defer to artificial rules of taste imposed by aristocratic patrons. For Blake this was typified by William Hayley's patronising comments on his work as poet and painter, about which he complained in a letter to Thomas Butts dated 6 July 1803:

Mr. H. approves of My Designs as little as he does of my Poems, and I have been forced to insist on his leaving me in both to my own Self Will; for I am determin'd to be no longer Pester'd with his Genteel Ignorance & Polite Disapprobation.

but he was equally indignant as to the humiliations which other artists, such as Barry, were obliged to suffer, at the hands of so-called patrons of the arts who had no real understanding or responsiveness to authentic art and who exploited the artists they purported to help:

Who will Dare to Say that Polite Art is Encouraged or Either Wished or Tolerated in a Nation where The Society for the Encouragement of Art Sufferd Barry to Give them his Labour for Nothing, A Society Composed of the Flower of the English Nobility & Gentry – Suffering an Artist to Starve while he Supported Really what They, under Pretence of Encouraging, were Endeavouring to Depress. – Barry told me that while he Did that Work, he Lived on Bread & Apples. (p. 1451)

By contrast Reynolds devoted himself to the task of painting an aristocratic clientele, of formulating rules and regulations for the production of art and the conduct of artists and of legitimating art by subordinating the artist to the demands of his clients. Under Reynolds's protocols the artist was effectively denied the right to set his own agenda and to follow his own creative impulses, his task is only to be a producer for the market. Hence Blake's bitterness at the overall thrust of Reynold's *Discourses* is epitomised by his comment:

> The Enquiry in England is not whether a Man has Talents & Genius, But whether he is Passive & Polite & a Virtuous Ass & obedient to Nobleman's opinions in Art and Science. (p. 1461)

For Blake the whole discourse of virtue was a discourse of power, a dominant ideology which served to validate the superiority of the haves over the have-nots:

> . . . you cannot have Moral Virtue without the Slavery of that half of the human Race who hate what you call Moral Virtue. (p. 1025)

The very fact that virtue stemmed from the classical tradition rather than from the visionary truth of the Bible made it even more suspect. Virtue like neo-classicism was a matter of dreary and uninspiring calculation, which savoured of the cistern rather than of the fountain. In his marginalia to Berkeley's *Siris* Blake exploded:

> The Whole Bible is filled with Imagination & Visions from End to End & not with Moral Virtues; that is the baseness of Plato & the Greeks & all Warriors. (p. 1504)

In Blake's vision of things, virtue was transformed into a negative force: it was under the sign of virtue that the imagination
was thwarted and opposed. In *Milton*, with the likes of Hayley
in mind, Blake writes:

> He smiles with condescension, he talks of Benevolence &
> Virtue,
> And those who act with Benevolence & Virtue they murder
> time on time.
> These are the destroyers of Jerusalem, these are the
> murderers
> Of Jesus, who deny the Faith & mock at Eternal Life,
> Who pretend to Poetry that they may destroy
> Imagination. . . .

For Blake the discourse of virtue is hypocritical and false. It is
particularly dangerous precisely because it pretends to be idealistic and creative. It is art's false double. Yet in insisting on this
falsity Blake did not want to give up on the idea of virtue altogether. In the *Marriage of Heaven and Hell* Blake paradoxically
associates virtue with a disposition to break the rules:

> I tell you, no virtue can exist without breaking these ten
> commandments. Jesus was all virtue, and acted from impulse,
> not from rules.

This is the difference between the Old and the New Testament.
True virtue is spontaneous.

In the latter part of the eighteenth century Rousseau is generally taken to be the most influential exponent of the doctrine of
virtue and in this emphasis on spontaneity he and Blake certainly
saw eye to eye. In *Emile* (1762) Rousseau was adamant that the
dictates of the heart were always right and the influence of society
could never be other than to weaken and erode this inner and
infallible source of rectitude. However, while Blake had a clear-
sighted awareness that the qualities he advocated were not
consistent with the classical tradition, Rousseau was anxious to
convince himself that in his invocation of virtue he was simply
continuing in the tradition of Plutarch and Graeco-Roman notions
of greatness. Yet, despite the stress he placed on citizenship,
Rousseau's conception of virtue lacked the social and public

dimension that it clearly possessed in the classical world. Rousseau's virtue was always highly subjective: it represented above all his highly developed sense of personal righteousness as he measured himself against what he regarded as the all-pervasive corruptions of the modern civilised world. Rousseau had the astonishing self-confidence to believe that he alone was virtuous and that he alone could lead the world back to virtue, but the actual grounds for this conviction were astonishingly slim. In his *Confessions* Rousseau relates how, when he was about 19, he stole a ribbon and then compounded his crime by blaming it on a young servant girl called Marion. This is certainly a pivotal moment in the book, and Rousseau himself sees it as the very point of origin of *The Confessions*, but correspondingly it is easy to miss its more general significance in Rousseau's eyes. For it was the transformative influence of this episode in his life that constituted Rousseau as the virtuous man that he would henceforward always be:

> If this is a crime that can be expiated, as I venture to believe, it must have been atoned for by all the misfortunes that have crowded the end of my life, by forty years of honest and upright behaviour under difficult circumstances.[24]

Rousseau's sense of his own virtuousness was highly subjective. It was intensified by his conflict with the world, and the more that actual persecution fed the undoubted mood of paranoia that prompted the confessions, the more virtuous he believed himself to be. In Rousseau's paradoxical redefinition of it virtue was simply his sense of being right when the world was wrong – it was to be

> ... free and virtuous, superior to fortune and man's opinion, and independent of all external circumstances

It was overtly bound up with 'defying the conventions of my age'.[25] Subsequently in yet another psychological transformation, bound up with his attachment to Therese, the mother of his children, he writes:

> Until then I had been good; from that moment I became virtuous, or at least intoxicated with virtue.[26]

Rousseau took it for granted that readers of the *Confessions* would share in his intoxication with his own virtuousness, despite his confession of misdeeds, since they would recognise that the virtuous man remained intact despite the minor infractions. Nevertheless Rousseau was criticised. Burke in his *Reflections* designated him as the professor of 'the philosophy of vanity':

> He has not observed on the nature of vanity, who does not know that it is omnivorous; that it has no choice in its food; that it is fond to talk even of its own faults and vices, as what will excite surprize and draw attention, and what will pass at worst for openness and candour. It was this abuse and perversion, which vanity makes even of hypocrisy, which has driven Rousseau to reord a life not so much chequered, or spotted here and there, with virtues, or even distinguished by a single good action. It is such a life he chooses to offer to the attention of mankind. It is such a life, that with a wild defiance, he flings in the face of his Creator, whom he acknowledges only to brave. Your Assembly, knowing how much more powerful example is found than precept, has chosen this man (by his own account without a single virtue) for a model.[27]

Rousseau has not even assumed responsibility for his own children. Yet if he had actually been confronted with Burke's comprehensive indictment Rousseau would doubtless have been unabashed. He would have argued that if he claimed to be essentially virtuous this was only because his impulses, like those of every other human being, were essentially and instinctively right and that if he had been led astray this was only because of the corrupting influences of civilisation. So the debate would no longer centre on the character of Rousseau as such, but on the moral and metaphysical assumptions that underpinned two radically different conceptions of the human condition.

Nevertheless it is important to grasp that Rousseau would have found it increasingly difficult to justify himself had he lived on through the crucial years of the French Revolution. For while the complexity of these events made it difficult to assign disproportionate significance to the interventions of a single actor, their apparent openness suggested that everyone could play some part, however small, in influencing the overall direction of events, even by not actually doing anything. In the post-Revolutionary world, no one could claim to be an innocent. In some sense everyone could be regarded as having dirty hands. You did not have to be Robespierre to point an accusatory finger. Had Rousseau, from the tranquillity of some rural retreat, disassociated himself from the whole course of events that followed the storming of the Bastille, on the grounds that he had played no part in them, there would certainly have been indignant demands to know why he had remained silent and why such a eminent political philosopher had not opposed this or that tendency. That combination of naivety, complacency and self-assurance that enabled men of the eighteenth century – and perhaps especially gentlemen – to think of them-selves as benevolent and virtuous was a facility that could no longer be drawn on – rather like a highly respected bank that has unexpectedly closed its counters for good. From now on the Rousseau that came to mind was not so much the Rousseau who *was* virtuous as the Rousseau who desperately wanted to be.

Neverthless virtue had become problematic as a value precisely because it had traditionally associated with steadfastness and a certain moral rigidity, with the consistency of Shakespeare's Brutus, who was 'constant as the Northern star'. The sentimentalist con-struction of virtue, associated with benevolence, spontaneity and heart, was pulling in a different direction from the more rational, classical ideal. Yet, even before the heyday of Richardson there was the suggestion that virtue might be a more fragile and deli-cate flower – indeed if virtue was not to remain as some idol cast in marble and bronze, it needed to be infused with some sense of vulnerability in order to dramatise it. Here, a relatively pedestrian but enormously popular and internationally influen-tial work, George Lillo's *The London Merchant* (1731) represents a pivotal moment in eighteenth-century culture. On the one hand Lillo's play is unquestionably a moral tale – the more moral pre-cisely because it's setting is so humdrum – of a young apprentice who is led by erotic passion to first steal from his kindly master, Thorogood, and then to actually murder his uncle in cold blood. While it might be thought that the tragic destiny of kings was far removed from the lot of ordinary men the fate of Barnwell is far more typical and Lillo, in conclusion, firmly points a warning finger at his own audience:

With bleeding hearts and weeping eyes we show
A human gen'rous sense of others' woe,

Unless we mark what drew their ruin on,
And, by avoiding that, prevent our own.

Lillo pleased such eminent contemporaries as Pope and Richardson
– but the play was by no means as moral as it purported to be,
since by laying Barnwell's downfall at the door of the unscrupulous and manipulative courtesan, Millwood, Lillo effectively implied
that the innocent youth was more victim than criminal since he
was simply unable to cope with a wicked woman's wiles. In Lillo's
master narrative, borrowed from *Macbeth* (perhaps also *Paradise
Lost*) and repeated in *Fatal Curiosity*, it is woman who is the
instigator of crime, man the virtuous but passive subject who is
led on against his better nature and who manifests his essential
virtuousness through intense demonstrations of remorse and guilt.
But the pathos of Barnwell's predicament is based not so much
on the fact that he acts wrongly as that he seems so totally in
the power of Millwood that he loses any sense of authentic volition.
He says to Millwood

You are my fate, my heaven or my hell

and immediately after soliloquises:

What have I done! Were my resolutions founded on reason,
and sincerely made – why then has Heaven suffered me to
fall? I sought not the occasion; and if my heart deceives me
not, compassion and generosity were my motives. Is virtue
inconsistent with itself, or are vice and virtue only empty names?
Or do they depend on accidents, beyond our power to produce or prevent – wherein we have no part, and yet must be
determined by the event?

In these musings Barnwell's naivety, that leads him to trust
Millwood implicitly both in her claim to love him and in pathetic
narratives she constructs for him, becomes his strongest defence.
For if Barnwell is led astray by his own trusting nature is he not
ultimately enmeshed in vice through his very disposition to
benevolence? Of course his impressionable nature and lowly status
means that he necessarily lacks the attributes of the tragic hero,
but this is also what makes him interesting to other writers. He
is *not* in command of himself and he is readily influenced by

others – as indeed is Macbeth. But there certainly were many in the eighteenth century who regarded such vulnerability as altogether inconsistent with the idea of virtue for example, J.H. Payne in his *Brutus or the Fall of Tarquin* has Tarquin say:

> But what is honour, which a sigh can shake?
> What is his virtue, which a tear can melt?
> Truth, valour, justice, constancy of soul,
> These are the attributes of manly natures:–
> Be woman e'er so beauteous, man was made
> For nobler uses than to be her slave.

Indeed, it is interesting to consider that Macbeth was just as awkward a hero from the contemporary point of view as Barnwell. Was Macbeth manly, was Macbeth virtuous if he could be led to commit murder through the influence of women, through his wife and the prophecies of the three witches? Could Macbeth be regarded as having sufficient in the way of admirable qualities to win the reader's respect? As with *The London Merchant* the whole question of virtue was regarded as being of vital importance and yet in neither case could such a protagonist really be regarded as admirable. To Augustan eyes such characters seemed inherently paradoxical and difficult to analyse. J.P. Kemble was disposed to see Macbeth as retaining a certain virtuousness:

> Macbeth is driven into guilt by the instigation of others: his early principles of virtue are not extinct in him.[28]

but others stressed the contradictions. For Thomas Whately

> The intervention of a supernatural cause accounts for his acting so contrary to his inclinations.[29]

while William Richardson sees nothing less than a total transformation in him:

> He is exhibited to us valiant, dutiful to his Sovereign, mild, gentle, and ambitious: but ambitious without guilt. Soon after we find him false, perfidious, barbarous and vindictive. All the principles in his constitution seem to have gone a violent and total change.[30]

The same abrupt transition is found in Barnwell. It seems almost impossible to reconcile the picture of innocence drawn by his fellow apprentice Trueman:

> Never had youth a higher sense of virtue. Justly he thought, and as he thought he practised; never was life more regular than his. An understanding uncommon at his years; an open, generous manliness of temper; his manners, easy, unaffected and engaging.

with the man who violently stabs his own uncle in a wood at night while wearing a mask. So it is in *The London Merchant* that many of the difficulties surrounding the concept of virtue are clearly displayed. To be virtuous is, above all, to be unswerving in one's virtue, yet so unshakeable an individual must create difficulties in dramatic representation since he can never do anything unexpected and surprising; yet contrariwise the virtuous individual who seemingly diverges from character must appear implausible or self-contradictory. Lillo's sense of the fragility of virtue may seem more plausible and more compassionate, yet a virtue that is already being eroded by the fifth scene of the play has the air of being over before it has ever really begun. What is virtue if it cannot be tried and tested? George Barnwell's virtue only glows in the moment of its fading away. For Lillo's successors, like Prévost, the issue is not virtue but the power of love. Prévost's Manon Lescaut is no figure of evil, like Millwood, though at once naive and worldly, she seems to genuinely care for Des Grieux, the aristocrat who is so totally infatuated with her as to be prepared to risk the loss of both his fortune and his reputation. Des Grieux can only be restored to virtue when Manon Lescaux is dead. On the final page of the novel he informs his old and loyal friend, Tiberge, that

> . . . the seeds of virtue he had sown long ago in my heart were beginning to bear fruit which he would approve of.[31]

But what use is a virtue that can withstand everything but temptation?

The humble and incongruous figure of George Barnwell is thus more radical than he appears. The sober and industrious apprentice breaks away from his old identity through a traumatic initiation into sexual desire, intrigue and violence directed against the power of patriarchal oppression. The truth of Barnwell is not the youth who obeyed but the man who rebelled, and as such he becomes the humdrum prototype of the Romantic hero, a man who by creating desolation within himself, has the temerity to emulate and identify with Milton's Satan:

> Sure such was the condition of the grand apostate, when first he lost his purity. Like me, disconsolate, he wandered; and, while yet in heaven, bore all his future hell about him.

However, Barnwell crucially lacks the one thing that could make him a Romantic hero – he is not sublime. While, on the face of it, the Sublime is an aesthetic concept, Virtue a moral one, there can be little doubt that as the Sublime gained ascendancy as *the* crucial frame of reference for literary discussion so progressively the literature of Virtue goes into decline. Yet it is doubtful if this would have happened had not Milton's *Paradise Lost* been available as a compelling text on the basis of which arguments about the Sublime could be substantiated. In Longinus's original discussion the Sublime was above all a way of designating a grand poetical style, the Sublime was only obliquely and indirectly a matter of content. Moreover, though Burke's comparative analysis of the Sublime and Beautiful was extremely influential it concentrated more on the vastness and grandeur of the natural world – on oceans, great rivers and waterfalls, the sky at night – rather than on literary texts. But to call Milton's Satan sublime in some affirmative way was to generate a new set of values, since whatever it was that made Satan remarkable it certainly could not be virtue. When applied to great or heroic characters the concept of the Sublime suggested quite simply admiration as a kind of awe-inspiring force, rather akin to a phenomenon of nature, in which moral judgement always verges on being suspended. Thus Coleridge could subsequently write of Shakespeare and *King Lear*:

> But in this tragedy the story or fable constrained Shakespeare to introduce wickedness in an outrageous form in the persons of Regan and Goneril. He had read nature too heedfully not to know, that courage, intellect, and strength of character are the most impressive forms of power, and that to power in itself, without reference to any moral end, an inevitable admiration

and complacency appertains, whether it be displayed in the conquests of a Buonoparte or Tamerlane, or in the foam and thunder of a cataract.[32]

In saying this Coleridge is not necessarily refusing condemnation of these characters, but is rather recognising that – in imaginative literature especially – we may well be impressed by that which we do not necessarily approve of. Similarly, James Beattie, in his *Dissertations Moral and Critical* (1783), distinguishes between our moral and aesthetic response and makes it clear that we have other motives in our response to literary texts other than a desire to embrace virtue:

> For the test of moral sublimity is not moral approbation, but that pleasurable astonishment wherewith certain things strike the beholder.... Achilles, though in many respects not virtuous, is yet a most sublime character... Julius Caesar was never considered a man of strict virtue. But, in reading his *Memoirs*, it is impossible not to be struck with the sublimity of his character.... Nay even in Satan, as Milton has represented him in *Paradise Lost*, though there are no qualities that can be called good in a moral view... there is boldness, which no power, but what is Almighty, can intimidate. These qualities are astonishing: and though we always detest his malignity, we are often compelled to admire that very greatness by which we are confounded and terrified.[33]

Under the aegis of the Sublime and of *Paradise Lost*, its exemplary text, there was no longer the same pressure to see virtue rewarded and to insist on the strict operation of poetic justice. A particularly clear instance of a play that the eighteenth century found uncomfortable because of it failure to end in a morally acceptable way was *King Lear*. Although Dr Johnson conceded that

> A play in which the wicked prosper, and the virtuous miscarry, may doubtless be good, because it is a just representation of human life

but he nevertheless felt that it was morally preferable to see

> ... the final triumph of persecuted virtue.[34]

This demand had long been met by the version of Nahum Tate, where Cordelia and Edgar marry at the end and the play concludes with Edgar saying to Cordelia:

> Thy bright example shall convince the world
> (Whatever Storms of Fortune are decreed)
> That Truth and Virtue shall at last succeed.

But by the time of the Romantics it had become possible to view Lear in terms of the Sublime. In Hazlitt's reading of the play Lear's character is a towering instance of it:

> ... sustained, reared to a majestic height out of the yawning abyss, by the force of the affections, the imagination, and the cords of the human heart – it stands a proud monument, in the gap of nature, over barbarous cruelty and filial ingratitude.[35]

Similarly for De Quincey Lear's greatness is spiritual: Lear is the Kantian sublime, he communicates:

> a feeling of the infinity of the world within.[36]

The same stress on spirituality underpins Lamb's famous argument that *Lear* cannot be represented on the stage:

> The greatness of Lear is not in corporal dimension, but in intellectual. ... On the stage we see nothing but corporal infirmities and weakness, the impotence of rage; while we read it, we see not Lear, but we are Lear, – we are in his mind, we are sustained by a grandeur which baffles the malice of daughters and storms.[37]

What is particularly interesting about Lamb's analysis of Shakespearean tragedy in this essay is that he constantly uses Lillo and his hero George Barnwell as a foil. What differentiates Shakespeare from Lillo is not so much the nature of the story as it is dramatically represented as Shakespeare's intellectual power and the sublimity of his conception:

> The truth is, the characters of Shakespeare are so much the objects of meditation rather than of interest or curiosity as to

their actions that while we are reading any of his great criminal characters, – Macbeth, Richard, even Iago, – we think not so much of the crimes which they commit, as of the ambition, the aspiring spirit, the intellectual activity, which prompts them to overleap those moral fences. Barnwell is a wretched murderer; there is a certain fitness between his neck and the rope; he is the legitimate heir to the gallows; nobody who thinks at all can think of any alleviating circumstances in his case to make him a fit object of mercy.[38]

Lamb goes on to say that with Shakespeare's heroes 'the crime is comparatively nothing'.[39]

Here we find not just the characteristic romantic disposition – as in *Hamlet* – to privilege thought over action, but even, under the sign of the intellect, virtually to dismiss action altogether. Complexity, above all, is what is valued and the case of George Barnwell, revolving as it does around rather antiquated notions of virtue, now seems so simple as to be positively laughable!

A play that epitomises the new cult of the sublime hero is Charles Maturin's *Bertram or the Castle of St Aldobrand*, first performed to tremendous acclaim in 1816. In the first place the scenic dimension of the play is certainly calculated to induce fear and terror. The entire action takes place at night and in darkness – Maturin specifies thunder, lightning, rain and wind; there are dark woods, caverns, rocks and precipices. But it is Bertram himself who epitomises the superhuman, morally ambiguous hero. In the early scenes of the play Bertram, incognito, is cast ashore on the coast of Sicily near the castle of St Aldobrand as the result of a shipwreck. We subsequently learn that Bertram, like Milton's Satan, was an over-reacher, who in

> his mad ambition
> Strove with the crown itself for sovereignty.

He was forced by Aldobrand into a protracted exile leaving behind Imogine, the mother of his child, who was then compelled to marry Aldobrand. An important part of Bertram's sublimity is the air of mystery and general obscurity that hangs around him. Before she discovers who he is Imogine says:

> There is a mystery of woe about him
> That strongly moves my fancy.

In a time-honoured Romantic tradition, initiated by Schiller's *The Robbers* Bertram is revealed to be the leader of a robber band, which in turn must be regarded as indisputable evidence of his wickedness, but Maturin nevertheless contrives to suggest that Bertram has been more sinned against than sinning. In particular, given that the context is medieval Sicily, where legitimacy was always based on superior force, the question as to who should be regarded as a brigand must always have been a perplexing one. Moreover, the deference that the Prior, in particular pays to him, makes him seem a grand rather than a disreputable figure, who compels respect even from those who disapprove of him

> High-hearted man, sublime even in thy guilt,
> Whose passions are thy crimes, whose angel-sin
> Is pride that rivals the star-bright apostate's. –
> Wild admiration thrills me to behold
> An evil strength, so above earthly pitch –
> Descending angels only could reclaim me.

What is paradoxical about Bertram is that he seems to be condemned almost before he has done anything and equally that his revenge on Aldobrand at the end of the play seems almost like an afterthought. Here, with redoubled force, we feel the pertinence of Lamb's suggestion that the crime itself may be comparatively nothing. What seems more significant is Bertram's guilt at his desertion of Imogine, his moral isolation, misanthropy and despair that lead him, at the end of the play, to stab himself with the words:

> Bertram hath but one fatal foe on earth –
> And *he is here.*

Since Bertram identified himself on his first appearance as 'a man of woe' it is as if nothing that has actually happened in the play had materially altered the situation. Maturin deliberately makes it difficult for us to arrive at a confident assessment of Bertram and he anyway insists, prefiguring Byron's *Manfred*, that the moral verdict of others must be both superficial and beside the point; from being indispensible and incontestable morality has become something of an irrelevance.

Nevertheless, it remains something of a mystery, why the Romantic hero (or heroine) should so rarely be an individual with a clear and unclouded conscience. If Robert Bage's character Hermsprong could argue that 'Servile compliance is a crime',[40] then surely we might expect the Romantic rebel, who challenges the *status quo* in the name of freedom and justice, would be firmly convinced of his own virtuousness and sense of right. This would be all the more to be expected since the state was increasingly being viewed as a purely secular institution, as an instrument of coercion without any genuine moral basis. As the leader of the gang of thieves in Godwin's *Caleb Williams* philosophically observes:

> Since, by the partial adminstration of our laws innocence, when power was armed against it, had nothing better to hope for than guilt, what man of true courage would fail to set these laws at defiance, and, if he must suffer by injustice, at least take care that he had first shown his contempt of their yoke.[41]

The severity of the laws protecting property and the ruthlessness with which land enclosure was being pushed forward made the narrow class basis of the state all too clear. While the American revolution had not merely challenged the authority of the British monarch and parliament, it had exposed with blinding clarity the commercial nature of the whole enterprise in which Ireland and the colonies were viewed as simply being there to be exploited by the imperial centre. It was no longer self-evident that the individual had no right to contest the legitimacy of the state or other established form of power. The clearest evidence of this shifting climate of opinion is Hegel's celebrated analysis of *Antigone*:

> Creon, the king, had issued, as head of the state, the strict command that the son of Oedipus, who had risen against Thebes as an enemy of his country, was to be refused the honour of burial. This command contains an essential justification, provision for the welfare of the entire city. But Antigone is animated by an equally ethical power, her holy love for her brother, whom she cannot leave unburied, a prey to the birds. Not to fulfill the duty of burial would be against family piety, and therefore she transgresses Creon's command.[42]

Against the power of the Theban state Antigone not only has a clear right and responsibility to demand her brother's burial but can be regarded as being virtuous for doing so. Of course, *Antigone* ends tragically but it still remains highly perplexing that Romantic literature that focuses so intensively on individual transgressions against the social order seems to concede so readily that such actions are illegitimate. One possible approach to this would be to argue that the validation offered by Hegel was not one that would have seemed plausible much earlier. In particular, social contract theory from Hobbes and Locke to Rousseau made it difficult to think in terms of rights *against* the state when it seemed that it was the state itself which guaranteed such rights or benefits as the individual enjoyed. So to speak as Hegel does of a conflict between the claims of Antigone and the claims of the Theban state might appear as a contradiction in terms. Again, it could be argued that the acts of self-assertion by an Antigone, a Socrates, or a Cato predicate a highly structured and disciplined social context in which only elite individuals can challenge the social order, since few would either have the courage to do so or be regarded as significant enough to present such a challenge. Just as only an aristocrat can challenge an aristocrat to a duel so, by the same token only a person of considerable social standing, indeed a person who already possesses authority, could offer an alternative focus for authority. Arguably, in the modern world, the situation is very different. Any challenge to authority challenges authority itself and in a less hierarchical, if not wholly democratic world, any gesture of political disobedience invites a process of multiplication and imitation where chaos must necessarily ensue. To strike a match is in itself comparatively harmless, but to strike it in an atmosphere filled with petrol fumes is dangerous in the extreme. Otway had already suggested this in *Venice Preserved*, a play that was popular throughout the eighteenth century, but which acquired even greater pertinence after the French Revolution, that the consequences of revolutionary violence might be incalculable, however exalted the cause. Venice is unquestionably decadent and corrupt and Pierre, in dreaming of overthrowing it, says that they will

> Openly act a deed, the world shall gaze
> With wonder at, and envy when it's done.

But at a very early date it is clear that the insurrection has no hope of being authentically realised. The other conspirators, rightly suspecting Jaffier, are prepared to kill him without evidence. The conspiracy is indeed betrayed by Jaffier, but if it actually had gone ahead it is clear that its idealistic goals and affectation of discipline would have been compromised by indiscriminate violence on the part of Renault and others. Burke, against, Rousseau and other radical thinkers who insisted that the state must ultimately rest on the will of individuals, denied this right and insisted on the anarchy that must ensue if such a claim were to be taken seriously. He concedes that society is a contract but denies that consent to it can be withdrawn:

> Each contract of each particular state is but a clause in the great primaeval contract of eternal society, linking the lower with the higher natures, connecting the visible and invisible world, according to a fixed compact sanctioned by the inviolable oath which holds all physical and all moral natures, each in their appointed place. This law is not subject to the will of those, who by an obligation above them, and infinitely superior, are bound to submit their will to that law . . . if that which is only submission to necessity should be made the object of choice, the law is broken, nature is disobeyed, and the rebellious are outlawed, cast forth, and exiled, from this world of reason, and order, and peace, and virtue, and fruitful penitence, into the antagonistic world of madness, discord, vice, confusion, and unavailing sorrow.[43]

Burke's vision of a universe linked together in a great chain of being was undoubtedly anachronistic, yet the idea that it could be challenged even by a single act of wilful self-assertion had a deep fascination for the Romantic generation, left or right. For if even one single transgressive gesture can send powerful reverberations through the cosmos that this serves to dramatise and exalt the individual who presents that challenge. Indeed, in an age of compliance and subservience to the law, it seems that the very idea of the individual can only be actualised as disobedience and defiance, through behaviour that will almost inevitably be regarded as criminal. In Schiller's *The Robbers* Karl Moor, who becomes leader of a robber band after being rejected by his old father, deplores the fact that the modern world has no place for heroism:

No, I'll not think of it. I am supposed to lace my body in a corset, and strait-jacket my will with laws. The law has cramped the flight of eagles to a snail's pace.

So if the Romantic hero is wrong in being at odds with the world he is also perversely right, since this is the only way in which he can assert himself. Coleridge, in *The Statesman's Manual*, deplored such prideful assertions of individual will in a manner very reminiscent of Burke:

> But in its utmost abstraction and consequent state of reproba-
> tion, the Will becomes satanic pride and rebellious self-idolatry
> in the relations of the spirit to itself, and remorseless despot-
> ism relatively to others; the more hopeless as the more obdurate
> by its subjugation of sensual impulses, by its superiority to toil,
> pain and pleasure; in short, by the fearful resolve to find in
> itself alone the one absolute motive of action, under which all
> other motives from within and without must be either subor-
> dinated or crushed.
> This is the character which Milton has so philosophically as
> well as sublimely embodied in the Satan of his *Paradise Lost*.[44]

Such an instinctive and unreflective assertion of the will occurs in *The Rime of the Ancient Mariner* when the Mariner shoots the Albatross with his crossbow. In so doing the Mariner does not merely behave arbitrarily, he also acts unjustly and in a way which goes against the grain of the entire universe. Such behaviour cannot be permitted. As Moser says to Franz, Karl's unscrupulous brother, who turns their father against him:

> And now do you suppose that God will allow one man to dwell
> in His creation like a raging demon, and turn His works to
> nothing.

For violating the entire order of the cosmos and for setting him-
self above it, the Mariner is compelled to endure the most intense isolation and terror; to feel himself completely alone. It is only by recognising the depth of his transgression that he can be saved. Yet through his sin the Mariner has acquired a wisdom not available to ordinary men. His disobedience leads to grasp the significance of harmony in the universe in a way that the majority never

can. The individual who transgresses opens himself up to a dialectical progression quite beyond the narrow and rigid path of virtue.

Clearly an important reason why few of the Romantic writers
were able to offer a wholly unequivocal endorsement of the righteous and self-willed hero stems from the rapidity with which
the outbreak of the French Revolution in 1789 was followed by
the Reign of Terror of 1793. The terrifying consequences of the
demands of Robespierre and others for revolutionary justice on
those who opposed them and otherwise stood in their way could
scarcely be ignored. So it is certainly of interest that the two texts
that do endorse the auto-authorising hero or heroine were both
completed in 1793 – Southey's *Wat Tyler* and *Joan of Arc*. For many
it might seem that there was a significant difference between Tyler,
the leader of an insurrectionary mob, and Joan, a woman inspired
by God whose struggle against the English is endorsed by the
French king, but Southey, without explicitly linking the two works,
undoubtedly viewed their protagonists in a similar light. Sincerity
and spontaneity are undoubtedly important. Tyler kills a tax-
gatherer when several of them seize his daughter because he is
unable to pay their unjust demand for a tax of three groats on
her head. John Ball subsequently criticises Tyler's action-

His mangled feeling prompted the bad act

but there is nevertheless a sense that such a revolt against intolerable oppression has a powerful justification. In the case of *Joan
of Arc* Southey is at pains to diminish any possible religious justification for her actions – precisely what interests him in the
story is that here is a strong and self-willed heroine who is
prompted by mysterious impulses from within:

The aid of angels and devils is not necessary to raise her above
mankind; she has no gods to lackey her, and inspire her with
courage, and heal her wounds: the Maid of Orleans acts wholly
from the workings of her own mind, from the deep feeling of
inspiration. The palpable agency of superior powers would
destroy the obscurity of her character, and sink her to the mere
heroine of a fairy tale.

We must see not see Joan's sense of mission as being in some
way prompted – it is wholly personal and based on her own

mysterious conviction that she is in the right. But after Robespierre such an unfathomable sense of righteousness could scarcely be given an unequival endorsement. Now, it seemed doubly dangerous for an individual to take the law into his own hands no matter how clear and self-evident the cause. In *The Borderers* – a work which may well have been written in response to Southey – Wordsworth not only unequivocally rejected the auto-authorising hero but also suggested that intellectuals might be peculiarly prone to the kind of deluded moralism that was involved. Rivers, who, in his days as a sailor, has himself been misled into abandoning an innocent man on a deserted island, endeavours to make Mortimer repeat his crime by persuading him to punish a very old man called Herbert. According to Rivers, Herbert has deceived Matilda into believing that she is his daughter and is now plans to make her the harlot of Clifford, a corrupt and lascivious aristocrat. Mortimer is the more ready to perform ruthless actions because he believes that they are dictated by the noblest of motives. He stifles the promptings of his heart that tell him that Herbert is innocent. Because Mortimer is leader of a band of outlaws, operating in territory where no established authority prevails, he can do as he pleases. He repeats the mistake of Schiller's robber chief, Karl Moor, who finally confesses:

> Oh, fool that I was, to suppose that I could make the world a fairer place through terror, and uphold the cause of justice through lawlessness.

The point is not just that he was mistaken about the old man, but that the very project of subjectively motivated 'justice' is self-contradictory. Rivers, the tempter figure, says:

> You have obeyed the only law that wisdom
> Can ever recognise: the immediate law
> Flashed from the light of circumstances
> Upon an independent intellect.

But this word 'independent' is fraught with sinister overtones. The individual who places himself above any public morality is guilty of the most dangerous kind of pride and one, potentially linked to an atheistic sensibility, as Wordsworth suggests of Rivers:

When the name of God is spoken of
A most strange blankness overspreads his face.

Yet Mortimer has been egged on to impiety and crime by the
language of virtue – by Rivers' insinuation that Herbert fears
Mortimer's presence because he knows that only a virtuous person will find him out:

He dreads the presence of a virtuous man
Like you, he knows your eye would search his heart,
Your justice stamp upon his evil deeds
The punishments they merit.

The Romantics find such possibilities disturbing, and yet they
find such moral confusions more fascinating than situations where
the moral imperatives are incontrovertable and binding.

Nevertheless, the most fundamental reason why the idea of
virtue had come to seem almost unimaginably remote for the
Romantics was that virtue predicated a wholeness in the poet,
an unwaveringness in his makeup which they knew they simply
did not, and perhaps could not, possess. The characteristic figures
of Romantic writing are exiled, haunted, maimed and blighted.
De Quincey, in citing Euripides' characterisation of sleep as a
balm for that characteristic Romantic malady, a 'wounded heart
and a haunted brain' significantly added that this, because of his
incessant dreams, was not available to him.[45] The Romantic writer
took this condition almost as a given and saw it as his task to
offer a psychological exploration of this predicament rather than
purport to overcome it. Above all, the virtuous individual, by
definition, was insulated from the world. Whatever others might
or might not do such a person would always act with instinctive
rectitude, confident that such an act was self-validating. Implicitly, virtue would always be acknowledged and remembered. Virtue
always seemed to carry with it the inevitability of its own triumphal
restoration, even when seemingly in mortal danger. So virtue was
not just a set of values but a purposive, confident attitude of mind.
This, the Romantics, for many reasons lacked. In theory, perhaps,
there need be no contradiction between the poet's sense of his
own vulnerability and a belief in virtue. After all, Cowper was
one of the first to confess to be a 'stricken deer' and yet *The Task*
was nevertheless a call to moral order written by a poet who felt

empowered to make it. But between Cowper and his Romantic successors the shadow of the French Revolution intervened. Increasingly the poet became entangled in the intricate webs of a constantly changing political world, more and more prone to doubt his own judgement and to question whether there could be any such authority as the idea of virtue predicated – whether uttered by Robespierre or anybody else. Indeed, as Wordsworth certainly felt, it was no longer the task of the poet to offer familiar or conventional answers – although in the nature of things he might eventually be forced to fall back on such justifications, but rather to offer a frank disclosure of his own perplexity and puzzlement. To share a problem would be salutary in itself. In relation both to the argument I am pursuing – the swerve of the Romantics away from virtue – and to the overall trajectory of Romanticism, *The Excursion* is a crucial text because of the prominence it assigns to the despondency and disillusionment of The Solitary, who like Wordsworth and so many of the radical intellectuals of his generation, found themselves looking into a black hole of despair when the French Revolution failed. For how could anything so indisputably and morally right have gone so terribly wrong. The failure of the world to take the right path became inextricably bound up with the fact that every individual who had supported the whole undertaking had gone similarly astray –

> a troubled mind,
> That, in a struggling and distempered world
> Saw a seductive image of herself.

Images of illness become inescapable. As Mortimer says in *The Borderers* :

> The deeper malady is better hid –
> The world is poisoned at the heart.

Such a thought, of course, is not a Christian one, but it is one that is likely to surface in the consciousness of a disillusioned radical. For in the horrors of the Reign of Terror all optimistic hopes for the future seemed to die simultaneously. The idea of Justice so central in the radical lexicon seemed to have been emptied of all conceivable meaning. And what prospects could there be for democracy if the people had actually descended –

as Conservatives had melodramatically warned – into a raging, implacable mob. Worst of all it seemed as if the very thought of rectifying the manifest evils of the world must be given up. Hope itself must be given up. No wonder the Romantics identified with Milton's Satan. Wordsworth's solitary is a sick man and his malaise is primarily spiritual. Wordsworth's resumé of Book III speaks of

> His languor and depression of mind, from want of faith in the great truths of Religion, and want of confidence in the virtue of Mankind.

There it is – the word 'Virtue' centrally installed in a Romantic text and Wordsworth's formulation suggests that virtue is alive and well. But the Solitary no longer believes in it or mankind and that is the problem. Wordsworth purports to correct such errors in the following book and notably fails to do so. For Wordsworth himself knows all to well that a spiritual malaise will not respond to textbook answers and that hope destroyed cannot readily be rekindled.

Perhaps because they are so unequal in quality there has been little tendency to read *The Excursion* in the light of *The Prelude* and *The Prelude* in the light of *The Excursion*. Yet to do can often be illuminating, since what is veiled or obscure in one text is often dealt with more openly in the other. From *The Prelude* and especially from the account of Wordsworth's friend, the aristocrat and friend of the people, Michel Beaupuy, we can gain a much fuller picture of not just how Wordsworth himself became disillusioned with the idea of virtue in a political context, but of how fervently he had believed in it in the first place. From Wordsworth's account it would seem that Beaupuy had a stronger faith in the people than Wordsworth had and that Wordsworth was the more inclined to advocate a political system with checks and balances and to prefer a model in which the virtuous few would be able to exercise leadership over the ignorant multitude. But as their discussions progressed the tone became yet more optimistic – 'the honourable deeds of ancient story' that is, the virtuous deeds of the heroes of the Roman and Greek republics must be portents and presages of the higher morality that would prevail in a polity freed from domination and injustice, while their faith in the common people received an overwhelmingly endorsement in the pattern of contemporary events:

                and, finally, beheld
A living confirmation of the whole
Before us in a people risen up
Fresh as the morning star. Elate we looked
Upon their virtue, saw in rudest men
Self-sacrifice the firmest, generous love
And continence of mind, and sense of right
Uppermost in the midst of fiercest strife.

Yet, sadly, all such hopes for a virtuous republic were shattered
in Beaupuy's own short-lived career as a distinguished military
leader. Wordsworth is anxious to place Beaupuy alongside the
virtuous heroes of old:

                So Beaupuy – let the name
Stand near the worthiest of antiquity –
Fashioned his life, and many a long discourse
With like persuasion honored we maintained,
He on his part accoutred for the worst.
He perished fighting, in supreme command,
Upon the borders of the unhappy Loire,
For liberty, against deluded men,
His fellow countrymen; yet most blessed
In this, that he the fate of later times
Lived not to see, nor what we now behold
Who have as ardent hearts as he had then.

The passage is rich in ironies. Beaupuy despite it all remained
virtuous, yet in some sense he could only still be virtuous then,
while the cause still could be seen as both clear and right. Yet
even at the moment of Beaupuy's death the issues have become
desperately confused, the waters muddied, for Beaupuy is fighting against his own people and they, 'deluded' are opposing the
liberty which they should regard as their birthright. Really,
Wordsworth himself has ceased to believe in virtue because this
in itself predicates and depends on a controllable and rational
field of political action. Virtue itself is ephemeral – as the Solitary acknowledged:

And the more faithful were compelled to exclaim,
As Brutus did to Virtue, 'Liberty,

I worshipped thee, and did but find a shade!'
Such recantation had for me no charm . . .

An understatement certainly, when it causes such a colossal moral
vacuum to open up. Effectively, Nature supplanted man as the
only stable and enduring element in human existence.
It was as a result of his experiences during the French Revolution that Wordsworth was brought to a spiritual crisis, a veritable
sickness unto death, in which he not only doubted humanity
but the very meaning of existence. It was this morbid condition
that led to the writing of *The Prelude* and to the whole convoluted process by which Wordsworth endeavoured to trace a path

Through Nature to the love of humankind.

Yet, having done so Wordsworth was reluctant to fully acknowledge the crisis of values that he had experienced – which must
have involved doubting God himself – for in so doing he would
have undermined the very sense of confidence, in himself and
others, that he was endeavouring to create. Certainly when
Wordsworth wrote the original version of the poem in 1805 he
must have felt intensely isolated. For one who had been as deeply
involved in the French Revolution as he had been there must
have been little hope that anyone could even begin to understand what he had been through, at a time when England was
at war with France and Napoleon was readying his troops for an
invasion. His position emotionally would have been akin to that
of someone during the Blitz, who had travelled to Germany as a
Nazi sympathiser in the 1930s. Still, there was always Coleridge
to whom he could – at least partially confess – and so for Coleridge
he wrote the poem, predicating absolution in advance. But as
Paul de Man perceptively wrote of Rousseau's *Confessions* – a
perceptiveness which, we can now see, was sharpened by his
own concealment of past pro-Nazi sympathies:

to confess is to overcome guilt and shame in the name of truth . . .

yet paradoxically:

Excuses generate the very guilt they exonerate, though always
in excess or by default. At the end of the Reverie there is always a lot more guilt around than we had at the start.[46]

Wordsworth had become so deeply entangled in the world of revolutionary France that he also had feelings of guilt and shame to overcome – both over his desertion of Annette Vallon but also because he almost certainly wished, not that he had become caught up in the Revolution but that, in so doing, he had not played a more active part than he had. In his role as bystander and voyeur he had all the sense of complicity without any clear sense of having done all he could according to his lights. Autobiography endeavours to place the writer in a position of power in relation to his (or her) life: through truth-telling it seeks to be authoritative and through that very authoritativeness more deeply underpins its own credibility; but in reality the project turns out to be ever more elusive. For confession throws up gaps, omissions and quirks of emphasis that would otherwise never come to our attention. So that instead of offering conclusive answers it raises yet more questions – rather like the Warren Report! Wordsworth obliquely acknowledged his involvement with Annette Vallon in the Julia and Vaudracour section of 1805, yet by 1850 was anxious to eliminate it altogether. The intense self-accusation of the 1805:

> Through months, through years, long after the last beat
> Of those atrocities (I speak bare truth,
> As if to thee alone in private talk)
> I scarce had one night of quiet sleep,
> Such ghastly visions had I of despair,
> And tyranny, and implements of death,
> And long orations which in dreams I pleaded
> Before unjust tribunals, with a voice
> Labouring, a brain confounded, and a sense
> Of treachery and desertion in the place
> The holiest that I knew of – my own soul

with its insistent repetition of I's and ands and frank and potentially sacriligeous exaltation of his own conscience is deliberately lost in the expanded version of 1850, which seeks to insinuate that such self-recrimination was indeed nightmarish and unjust rather than serious and substantive. Again, in Book 12 Wordsworth's admission:

> Long time in search of knowledge desperate,
> I was benighted heart and mind

became the blander

> Long time in search of knowledge did I range
> The field of human life

precisely because such a desperate seeker could scarcely hope to
acquire credibility as the wise and philosophic visionary that
Wordsworth now sought acceptance as. Wordsworth had not
always been stoical and tranquil and if his poetry had a consoling power then that must necessarily appeal to readers who were
as intellectually disturbed as he had been. The poet who offered
plenitude could not afford to dwell longer in the company of a
man so afflicted by a sense of lack.

Wordsworth certainly felt that a deep sense of communion with
Nature was the remedy – indeed the only remedy – to the malaise of the age and in some sense he certainly thought that a life
spent in solitude in natural surroundings as a virtuous one, but
it was in practice awkward to assert this because so many of the
connotations of virtue were connected with society and social
existence. The virtuous Roman hero was concerned with the fate
of the republic. For Shaftesbury virtue is expressed through benevolent feelings towards others and to be 'well affected towards
the public interest'. Anyone who is 'wholly destitute of the com-
municative or social Principle' will feel 'slender Joy in Life'.[47] Many
eighteenth-century thinkers such as William Godwin thought that
solitude was morally and pyschologically harmful. Most eighteenth-
century poets took their cue from Milton's antithetical but
complimentary poems, 'L'Allegro' and 'Il Penseroso' – solitude is
good but 'the busy hum of men' is good too. If the poet, as a
reflective and contemplative had a instinctive inclination to solitude and melancholy, this did not necessarily preclude him playing
a more active part in society. Morever there was an acute awareness of the dangers of solitude and an attendent disposition to
melancholy, since it was well recognise that they could lead to
madness, misanthropy and suicide. Wordsworth tacitly acknowledges this in 'Resolution and Independence' where he imagines
the old leechgatherer – a figure whom few eighteenth-century
readers could have felt very enthusiastic about – wandering

> About the weary moors continually

and becomes concerned that the old man's sanity may be threatened – so he is reassured to find

> In that decrepid man so firm a mind.

Wordsworth's precursors took such possibilities very seriously and hence could hardly have endorsed a solitary existence as fervently as he did. Although Thomas Warton notably celebrated 'the Pleasures of Melancholy' he could also suggest in his 'Ode to Solitude' that such isolation was not necessarily congenial and in 'The Suicide' he warned of its dangers:

> Full oft, unknowing and unknown,
> He wore his endless noons alone,
> Amid th'autumnal wood:
> Oft was he wont, in hasty fit,
> Abrupt the social board to quit,
> And gaze with eager glance upon the trembling flood.
> Beckoning the wretch to torments new,
> Despair, for ever in his view,
> A spectre pale, appear'd.

A similar figure, though not a suicide, is the anonymous figure, whose epitaph concludes Gray's 'Elegy in a Country Churchyard' who would wander

> Now drooping, woeful wan, like one forlorn,
> Or crazed with care, or cross'd in hopeless love.

Yet interestingly Gray, nevertheless, shows a Wordsworthian inclination to celebrate the solitary – such a man is as entitled to be remembered quite as much as the virtuous great of 'storied urn or animated bust'!

For Wordsworth Nature was the virtue behind virtue: the tutelary presence to turn to when virtue itself had failed. In Book 2 of *The Prelude* he writes

> if in this time
> Of dereliction and dismay, I yet
> Despair not of our nature, but retain
> A more than Roman confidence, a faith

That fails not, in all sorrow my support,
The blessing of my life, the gifts is yours
Ye mountains, thine, O Nature.

The rocklike security and dependability once attributed to Roman
virtue has now been transferred to Nature. Yet given Wordsworth's
powerful sense of himself as a being uniquely privileged and set
apart by the good fortune of having grown up in the natural
surroundings of the Lake District, it then becomes hard to see
how Wordsworth could have subsequently lost his way – surely
he of all people should never have doubted humanity, should
never have been brought, as he undoubtedly was, to the very
brink of despair. It is here that we can begin to see why the
model of human behaviour predicated by the classical ideal of
virtue will not meet the new circumstances of Romanticism. The
contemporary hero is no unshakeable monolith, but a divided
character pulled between different alternatives, who is often led
to doubt his true path and to be perplexed as to whom he owes
his allegiance. There is a significant parallel between Scott's
Waverley, who is torn between a romantic sympathy for the Jacobite
cause and a rational support for the Hanoverian *status quo* and a
symmetrical conflict in Wordsworth's mind between the need for
solitude and the desire for political action. We can also see very
clearly how a recognition of the way in which human beings are
determined by their environment produces such splits. In particular Wordsworth sees the modern world of the city as morally
corrupting and psychologically confusing. In the countryside,
surrounded by natural objects, people retain their dignity, their
sense of morality, their autonomy. It is only in urban surroundings, as in London's Batholemew fair that we find mobs and riots,
a 'parliament of monsters'. Moreover even intellectuals can be
affected by all this:

O, blank confusion, and a type not false
Of what the mighty city is itself
To all, except a straggler here and there –
To the whole swarm of its inhabitants
An undistinguished world to men,
The slaves unrespited of low pursuits,
Living amid the same perpetual flow
Of trivial objects, melted and reduced

To one identity by differences
That have no law, no meaning and no end –
Oppression under which even the highest minds
Must labour, whence the strongest are not free.

Part of the significance of 'Michael' is that it imaginatively con-trasts these alternatives – splits Wordsworth's own personality in two – part of him is Michael the old shepherd, who never left Green-head Ghyll, the other is Luke who left home and succumbed to the temptations and urgencies of the city. Yet the problem remains as to how these contradictions can be resolved or worked through. For if the city cancels the world of Nature, the world of Nature *would* if only it had the opportunity to do so. The power of Nature is that it can repair its own loss: virtue is reformulated not as an unchanging state but as a medicinal power to heal the sick and restore the patient to health. The experiences of Nature are spots of time whose 'renovative virtue' can overcome malig-nant invaders of the system, like white corpuscles in the bloodstream. Wholeness is not an abstract and remote ideal but a realisable possibility.

Of all the Romantic poets the one who was most deeply com-mitted to the idea of virtue was undoubtedly Shelley. It would seem that Shelley's early commitment to virtue was both the product of a classical education and intimately bound up with his development of an atheist point of view – since a recurrent theme of his letters is the impossibility of being virtuous if one is a Christian. From the time when Shelley was 18 until his comple-tion of *Queen Mab* in February 1813, when he was 20, Shelley was positively obsessed with the idea of virtue and with an attempt to define it. There are upwards of 100 references to 'virtue' and 'virtuous' in his letters over this period. He was clear that virtue was opposed to selfishness but would not identify it either with prudence, or follow Godwin in linking it with expediency. Shelley's own preferred definition was in terms of disinterestedness. How-ever, it is also clear that Shelley did come under Godwin's influence at this period. Early in 1812 Shelley entered into a correspondence with Godwin praising him as

. . . the personal exciter and strengthener of my virtuous habits . . .

and spoke of his own ambition to improve his powers and to

... diffuse true and virtuous principles.[48]

At this point his adulation of Godwin was such that he wrote to the revered master:

> It appears to me that on the publication of 'Political Justice', you looked to a more rapid improvement than has taken place; it is my opinion that if your book had been as general as the Bible human affairs would now have exhi(bi)ted a very different aspect.[49]

Although Shelley was later to disassociate himself from the idea of writing in a directly didactic manner, at this point he was very insistent that poetry must serve to promote virtue:

> I therefore write, and I publish because I will publish nothing that shall not conduce to virtue, and therefore my publications so far as they do influence shall influence to good. – My views of society, and my hopes of it meet with congenial ones in few breasts. – But virtue and truth are congenial to many.[50]

The preoccupation with virtue is particularly evident in Shelley's two major productions of 1812, *Queen Mab* and his *An Address to the Irish People*, which together yield 80 references to virtue – infinitely more than in the rest of his published works put together. The Godwinian cast of all this is particularly evident in the *Address to the Irish People* where virtue is characteristically linked either with wisdom or justice. *Queen Mab*, the definitive exposition of the young Shelley's radical views, is a text which combines a Godwinian critique of kingship and the power of the state with a condemnation of religion based on Volney's *The Ruins of Empires* and a wide-ranging indictment of the influence of commerce on human society, which is very much in the spirit of eighteenth-century protests against 'luxury'. We cannot fail to be aware in reading Shelley of his hostility to economics in its widest sense. He read and was disturbed – but also impressed – by Malthus's claim that population must always outstrip the food supply. He was hostile to Adam Smith's suggestion that the commercial stage of civilisation was the highest, since he believed that economic development could be destructive of other values. More surprisingly, since the reputation of Mandeville was certainly fading, he remained as disturbed as any eighteenth-century writer by Mandeville's apparent espousal of selfishness and self-interest, contrasting, on the one hand

> Commerce! beneath whose poison-breathing shade
> No solitary virtue dares to spring

with a genuine virtue based on human contact and communication:

> This commerce of sincerest virtue needs
> No meditative signs of selfishness.

In Shelley's view there is no truth in the reactionary and repressive ideology that asserts essentialist arguments about 'Man's evil nature'. If there is evil in the world it is primarily the product of human culture. The crucial question for Shelley is to establish how man had become alienated from the harmony and tranquillity of nature. His answer is that this had come about through the distinctively human institutions of government and religion. Shelley rejects the pantheistic connection of God and Nature that is so prominent in the poetry of Wordsworth and Coleridge. On the contrary it is religion that has made man tortured and unhappy, that has exiled him from the happiness that is rightfully his. But there is a progressive account of human history, unveiled by the fairy Mab, in which man will develop in the direction of virtuousness and this virtue will in turn overcome the obstacles that bar humanity from felicity, truth and justice. The virtuous individual has a particularly important role to play in bringing this better world about. Shelley celebrates

> The virtuous man,
> Who, great in his humility, as kings
> Are little in their grandeur; he who leads
> Invincibly a life of resolute good,
> And stands amid the silent dungeon-depths
> More free and fearless than the trembling judge,
> Who, clothed in venal power, vainly strives
> To bind the impassive spirit.

Such virtuous individuals are crucial – for it is only because they persist uncorrupted that there is hope for humanity. Gradually

the sphere of virtue will expand and in the face of an unflinching and unswerving virtue the forces of darkness will be overcome.
In the 'ebb and flow of human things' virtue is a fixed beacon
which shows

> Somewhat stable, somewhat certain still,
> A lighthouse o'er the wild of dreary waves,

virtue that will guide mankind along

> The gradual paths of an aspiring change.

Queen Mab was, of course, written before the defeat of Napoleon and while radicals like Shelley could not approve of all that
Napoleon had done, his continuing dominance of European politics
nevertheless seemed an assurance both of the eclipse of the old
political order and of the possibility of an opening to a more
genuinely radical politics. However, his defeat in 1815 and the
comprehensive restoration of reactionary regimes made the new
political situation seem bleak indeed. Shelley began his sonnet
'On the Fall of Bonaparte' with the words;

> I hated thee, fallen tyrant!

but more significantly acknowledged that the supporters of
democracy now faced yet more intransigent obstacles:

> I know
> Too late, since thou and France are in the dust,
> That virtue owns a more eternal foe
> Than force or fraud: old Custom, legal Crime,
> And bloody Faith the foulest birth of time.

This is the context for Shelley's next significant political intervention, *Laon and Cythna* (1817). In writing it Shelley was
undoubtedly influenced by the more fatalistic and pessimistic
climate of opinion that followed Waterloo. He found this tendency
disturbing:

> Thus many of the most ardent and tender-hearted of the wor-
> shippers of public good, have been morally ruined by what a

partial glimpse of the events they deplored, appeared to shew as the melancholy desolation of all their cherished hopes Hence gloom and misanthropy have become the characteristic of the age in which we live, the solace of a disappointment that unconsciously finds relief only in the wilful exaggeration of its own despair.

Given the characteristic disparaging allusions to Shelley's weakness initiated by Arnold it is important to stress just how false this is. It was in Byron rather than Shelley that this mood found its characteristic expression. Shelley refused to concede defeat. He wanted to show that the failure of the French Revolution did not necessarily mean that a better world could not be envisaged or that men must necessarily come to terms with tyranny and injustice as an inescapable state of affairs. *Laon and Cythna* (subsequently *The Revolt of Islam* with the intimation of incestuous love between the protagonists removed) is an imaginative representation of a revolt against the power of religion and despotism in the Middle East in which women are given particular prominence:

Can man be free if woman be a slave.

In so doing Shelley both insisted that women must be part of any democratic transformation but also suggested that they might help to ensure that any radical political change could be brought about with the minimum of violence. Shelley identifies himself with those in the poem who

sternly struggle to relume
The lamp of Hope o'er man's bewildered lot

but, despite this, the overall perspective is significantly more pessimistic than *Queen Mab*. Since Shelley's defeated revolt in the Middle East allegorises the contemporary situation in Europe it is as if he is suggesting that any follow up to the French Revolution, however idealistically motivated and however pure in its eschewal of violence, would also be inexorably defeated by the forces of political reaction. Of course, as a disciple of Godwin, Shelley is prepared to take the long view and to envisage the final triumph of democracy and virtue as something that must be projected very far into the distant future. From this stand-point it is crucial that a radical politics should not betray its own best principles in the short term if it is to have any hope of pre-vailing in the long term. In *Laon and Cythna* Shelley presents exemplary figures who can give substance to the paradox that any political revolt must necessarily be committed to modera-tion. Shelley urged the same thing in his *Address to the Irish People*. However, although Shelley wanted his poem to help the reader to see 'the beauty of true virtue' he is now considerably less con-fident that the cause of virtue would automatically identify itself. His concluding reference to the possibility that individuals might suffer from

> . . . the bigoted contempt and rage of the multitude

is proof of that. It was becoming increasingly evident to Shelley that great and good causes are not necessarily regarded as such and that one of the most baffling circumstances that any idealist can encounter is to find himself reviled, like Socrates, as a cor-ruptor rather than an enlightener of humanity. It is at the conclusion of *Laon and Cythna*, where hero and heroine are trans-lated to a higher world, that Shelley finally cashes the ephemeral connotations of the Spenserian stanza:

> And ever as we sailed, our minds were full
> Of love and wisdom, which would overflow
> In converse wild, and sweet, and wonderful;
> And in quick smiles whose light would come and go,
> Like music o'er wide waves, and in the flow
> Of sudden tears, and in the mute caress –
> For a deep shade was cleft, and we did know,
> That virtue, tho' obscured on Earth, not less
> Survives all mortal changes in lasting loveliness.

But the concession is significant. The beauty and permanence of virtue is by no means evident in the material world where we only ever see through a glass darkly. The very notion of an eventual triumph of virtue is itself to be indefinitely dissolved and deferred. In practice Shelley sees little real prospect of attaining anything through political action even though he continues to engage in it and believe in it.

After *Laon and Cythna* the mood of Shelley's poetry – indeed the mood of much of his greatest and most memorable poetry – becomes much darker and more pessimistic. Yet in some respects this is puzzling, since his transformed attitude is nevertheless filtered through an overall perspective that always contains some element of hope, even optimism. Shelley always viewed the immediate social and political situation as unpromising and always believed that any hope of a better world would have to be realised in the much longer term – certainly not within his own lifetime. From *Queen Mab* to such later works as his *Ode to the West Wind*, *Prometheus Unbound* and his *Defence of Poetry*, Shelley is always engaged in some colossal wager on the Future. Indeed his sense of himself as poet and prophet is grounded in his conviction that

Poets are the hierophants of an unapprehended inspiration; the mirrors of the gigantic shadows which futurity casts on the present. (p. 297)

In a very real sense it is the poet's duty to make vivid to mankind the ideal of a future freed from oppression and domination that may otherwise seem abstract and remote. However, perhaps the very fact that Shelley was ready to assume this task made the burden of it seem all the more intolerable. In the ensuing years there were many reasons for him to feel discouraged. In Britain the determination of the ruling classes to resist any democratic advance was epitomised by the decision of the local militia to fire on a peaceful crowd in St Peter's Fields, Manchester. Shelley must also have been disappointed by the lack of any positive response to either *Queen Mab* or *The Revolt of Islam* – a sense of disappointment that must have been sharpened by his friendship in exile with Byron, the most famous and successful poet in Europe. This was compounded by a whole series of tragic circumstances in Shelley's own personal life, especially the suicide of Harriet, his first wife, and his estrangement from Mary Shelley as the result of many obscure events, which certainly included the death of their daughter Clara and may well have involved Mary's awareness of infidelities on Shelley's part. Again, it is evident from *Julian and Maddalo* that Shelley, for so long a rather programmatic optimist, found the constant exposure to Byron's cynicism and worldweariness rather hard to take. Shelley felt alienated from what he increasingly perceived as a hostile and unfeeling world and he was unable to respond to this with such a lofty Byronic shrug as

I have not loved the world, nor the world me.

Shelley felt hurt, demoralised and confused. His refers in his *Letter to Maria Gisborne* to

The jarring and inexplicable frame
Of this wrong world,

and to a 'cold world' in *Julian and Maddalo*. In 'The Sensitive Plant' the beautiful garden is overtaken by

mandrakes, and toadstools, and docks, and darnels.

In 'Lines Written Among the Euganean Hills' he refers to 'The deep wide sea of misery', in 'Epipsychidion' to 'The dreary cone of our life's shade' and in 'Adonais' he speaks of finding shelter 'in the shadow of the tomb', 'From the world's bitter wind'. Even the idea of virtue as something rocklike and enduring is a casualty in all this. In 'Mutability' he writes

Virtue how frail it is!
Friendship how rare!
Love, how it sells poor bliss
For proud despair!

Everything is transitory and even the most lauded of human qualities lack real substantive existence when the chips are down.

Of all the poems that Shelley wrote at this time it is perhaps *Julian and Maddalo* (1818) that offers the most subtle and faithful portrait of his state of mind. The poem introduces us to Julian, 'an Englishman of good family' who is convinced of the 'immense improvements' to which 'human society may yet be susceptible' (clearly Shelley) and Count Maddalo, whose pride – and consequent contempt for others – leads him to 'an intense apprehension of the nothingness of human life' (undoubtedly Byron), and who must be regarded as something of a tempter figure. The two men are depicted riding in a landscape that can express symbolically their contrasting attitudes, since on the one hand it is desolate and barren, yet on the other it is sublime, it is a place

> where we taste
> The pleasure of believing what we see
> Is boundless, as we wish our souls to be.

But as they are subsequently rowed by the Count's men in a gondola and experience the beauty of a Venetian sunset

> Like the fabrics of enchantment piled to Heaven

the Count attempts to enforce the validity of his own perspective by drawing attention to the sombre tolling of a 'deep and heavy bell', which comes from a solitary building on an island

> A windowless, deformed and dreary pile,

from the belfry of a madhouse, which is calling the maniacs to vespers. The following day Count Maddalo is there and introduces him to an individual, whom he claims once cherished optimistic views of humanity, who, like Julian tirelessly sought to discover 'soul of goodness' in the things essentially ill. The maniac has lost his reason because he has been unhappy in love. He has been rejected and reviled, deceived and disappointed by a woman. The plight of the maniac is moving – the more so because Maddalo has done all he can to ease and relieve his condition. The maniac's unhappiness and his manifest inability to cope with the betrayal he has experienced seems to offer decisive corroboration of the Count's pessimism but Shelley, though undoubtedly despondent himself, has not conceded quite as much to Byron as it might appear. For one thing the maniac's systematic despair is itself Byronic when he says

> So let Oblivion hide this grief

He strikes a note that constantly recurs in Byron's later poetry. So it is possible to turn the argument around and suggest that it is such a negative view of life, rather than life itself, that is so damaging. But what is equally significant is that the story is *not* closed. The lady returned. They parted again. There is much that is never disclosed, which the 'cold world' will never know. Shelley implies that in appropriating the experience of another human being simply to illustrate an argument Maddalo, sensitive as he is, has nevertheless gone too far. The maniac is frozen as a moral exemplum like one of the characters in Dante's *Inferno*. Here, as so often, albeit in a much more muted vein, we find Shelley's characteristic appeal to the future. Life *can* unexpectedly change, new possibilities may always emerge. A determination to face the worst may well be misguided – the bitter 'truth' that seemingly lies behind pleasing illusions may itself be a half-truth at best. Still, all this is very far from being optimism. What cannot be evaded is that Shelley is no longer writing about strong and virtuous characters who struggle against injustice but about sensitive souls who find the pain of the world very hard to bear. Here we encounter a series of doubles for Shelley himself – the sensitive plant, the maniac (based on the Italian poet Torquato Tasso), in Keats's 'Adonais'. There is the repeated suggestion that death would be a release. Moreover, Shelley's strong sense that the nature of reality is itself shaped and determined by human consciousness:

> Where is the love, beauty, and truth we seek
> But in our minds

is itself at odds with traditional accounts of virtue – since virtue must be self-evident and must begin to dissolve in the face of the suggestion that it must be subject to interpretation.

In a way, evidence of such a dissolution of the idea of virtue is to be found in Shelley's drama, *The Cenci*, even though from another point of view it can be seen as evidence of Shelley's determination to keep faith with the idea of virtue even in the most unpromising of circumstances. Some might want argue that the very idea of exhibiting moral deformity to such an extent as here must nullify any such intention. Certainly there is something both paradoxical and disturbing about *The Cenci*, which on its first appearance in 1820 elicited comments ranging from a reference to Shelley's 'strange perversity of taste'[51] to the exclamation:

> Of all the abominations which intellectual perversion, and poetical atheism, have produced in our times, this tragedy appears to be the most abominable.[52]

Yet in his introduction Shelley is careful to distance himself from any unqualified endorsement of Beatrice's complicity in her father's murder, despite the fact that she has strong justification – besides the fact that he is a murderer many times over – not only in the fact that he has raped her, but that he is committed to going on doing so. Shelley writes:

> Revenge, retaliation, atonement, are pernicious mistakes. If Beatrice had thought in this manner she would have been wiser and better; but she would never have been a tragic character.

Shelley's moral disavowal of Beatrice's actions is convincing, yet it also seems disingenuous since there can be no point in writing about her if not to validate – as Shelley does – her courage in standing up to her father, whose continued existence can only represent the indefinite perpetuation of a reign of infamy, so in this respect at least Beatrice is sister to Laon and Cythna. In Shelley's development the significance of *The Cenci* is that it represents his concession – one that he would never have made at the time of *Queen Mab* – that there is or can be such a thing as absolute evil, that is not explicable in social and political terms. Count Cenci is unquestionably evil, although he can only survive and even prosper because of the Pope's determination to maintain patriarchal authority no matter how exercised. Count Cenci is evil not just because of what he does but because of his determination to actively destroy goodness and virtue as manifested in Beatrice, whose existence provokes him, as it does Iago:

> this my bane and my disease,
> Whose sight infects and poisons me; this devil
> Which sprung from me as from a hell, was meant
> To aught good use; if her bright loveliness
> Was kindled to illumine this dark world;
> If nursed by thy selectest dew of love
> Such virtues blossom in her as should make
> The peace of life, I pray thee for my sake,
> As thou the common God and Father art
> Of her, and me, and all; reverse that doom!

Of course, Shelley, as an atheist must have relished the idea of such an impious and immoral prayer! Yet the Italian Renaissance world that he depicts is one that offers few grounds for levity or optimism, so deeply corrupted is it. As in Greek tragedy we have the sense that evil is not something localised and containable but appears as an irresistably spreading and deepening stain of pollution. In this context Beatrice can only remain gentle, pure and virtuous if she does nothing and barely even then since she cannot but be aware of what is going on around her. While Shelley may be on morally high ground to suggest that

> ... the fit return to make to the most enormous injuries is kindness and forebearance.

we must nevertheless wonder whether Shelley anymore than Milton could really reverence a fugitive and cloistered virtue, a virtue that must always remain passive, never active. Personally I cannot believe this. I feel sure that he felt that Beatrice remained virtuous even in her actions – as Beatrice herself refers to

> the faith that I,
> Tho' wrapt in a strange cloud of crime and shame,
> Live ever holy and unstained.

For Shelley the real worry is the possibility that Beatrice is damned if she does and damned if she doesn't; that in the moral miasma created by Count Cenci it is well nigh impossible to escape corruption. Virtue, it seems, is only hanging on to its existence by the slenderest of threads.

As a poet Shelley is haunted by repetition. He sees human history as the endless recurrence of tyranny and domination sanctioned and reinforced by religion. He sees endless analogies between past and present and predicts further repetitions of things that have already occurred. He sees Tasso's fate, Keats's fate, as potentially his own. Yet, ironically, Shelley is mesmerised by his own need to repeat: to go on saying what he has said already, to reaffirm that despite the ongoing and seemingly inescapable nightmare of political oppression there will nevertheless be deliverance some magical day. But what is the status of Shelley's assurance that this is so – is it a confident prediction of an inevitable state of affairs; a profound hope and expectation that that will indeed be the case but which needs completion in a human desire and will to achieve it; or is it, rather more pessimistically, simply a taunting and tantalising dream that human life could actually be other than it is? Shelley's mind oscillates insatiably between these and other variations on the 'same' overall scenario and in many respects blurs the differences between them, despite the fact that your mood will be significantly different according to the version you decide to follow. But Shelley understood better than anyone that that choice is itself shaped by your state of mind when you make it; so that everything becomes circular and self-validating.

Shelley, completing *Prometheus Unbound* in 1819 was, on the face of it, simply rearticulating the narrative of despair to hope, of the ultimate triumph of freedom and democracy, that he had already written in *Queen Mab* just seven years earlier, but in the sheer anxiety of thinking and rethinking it, it came out as something rather different and considerably more complex and poetic. Not least of these differences was the fact that Shelley had hoped for a popular success with *Queen Mab* – which he was to achieve posthumously with the Chartists – but *Prometheus Unbound* was a difficult work, which, like *Paradise Lost*, was aimed at a fit audience though few (Shelley estimated perhaps 20 readers):

> . . . to familiarise the highly refined imagination of the more select classes of poetical readers with beautiful idealisms of moral excellence; aware that until the mind can love and admire, and trust, and hope, and endure, reasoned principles of moral conduct are seeds cast upon the highway of life which the unconscious passenger tramples to dust.

We should note the crucial implication of what Shelley is saying here: it is only through an affirmative attitude to life that morality can be called into existence. Virtue only becomes a possibility where love and hope have already taken root. So there is something Nietzschean in all this. Morality is not just something out there – it has to be created and indeed made beautiful and attractive! A further significant difference is that both here and in *A Defence of Poetry* Shelley disowns his earlier desire to subordinate poetry to moral and political science. In *A Defence* he praises Milton for his 'bold neglect of a direct moral purpose' (p. 290) and in the Preface to *Prometheus* he writes

> Didactic poetry is my abhorrence.

Shelley's work now takes a distinctly aesthetic turn. He recognises more clearly than ever before that the role of poetry is not just to advocate a better world but to offer the reader beautiful and compelling images of what it would be like. For the real problem that humanity faces is that with evil and suffering seemingly dominant it is all too easy to imagine that the struggle can never be won; so the poet must be able to generate a radiant vision that can keep hope itself alive. When in *A Defence of Poetry* Shelley wrote:

> A poet is a nightingale who sits in darkness and sings to cheer its own solitude with sweet sounds (p. 282)

and described poetry as

> . . . the light of life, the source of whatever beautiful or generous or true can have place in an evil time (p. 286)

of no work was this more true than *Prometheus Unbound*. What Shelley now recognised was that virtue itself was not enough. In *Queen Mab* he had written:

> O human Spirit ! spur thee to the goal
> Where virtue fixes universal peace

– in the belief that what mankind needed was to be spurred on ever more urgently towards liberation. Now, writing in an evil time he recognised that what poetry had to offer was a consoling power, the ability to reassure man that in the very long run all would nevertheless be well. Here the mood of *Prometheus* approaches that of *Paradise Lost*, a work also written under the most discouraging circumstances. While Prometheus is the very embodiment of a virtue that will never capitulate or yield, in some sense Prometheus's defiance is simply negative – a refusal to accept that tyranny or domination will prevail – only the artistry of the poet can actually depict the free and beautiful world that that struggle is actually for. Moreover, Shelley was one of the first British writers to consciously privilege Greece over Rome, so the whole discussion of morality and virtue is radically aestheticised. Athens is characterised by 'energy, beauty and virtue'

(p. 283) and even with Rome its 'true poetry' lived in its institutions. (p. 287) Most radically of all Shelley claimed that 'the greatest poets have been men of the most spotless virtue.' (p. 295) On a literal level this is rather hard to take seriously, but the real thrust of Shelley's discussion is to insist on the importance of the aesthetic dimension. For men to follow the path of virtue it must be made both beautiful and appealing – and only the poet can do this. Only poetry can offer mankind a way out of the impasse that it finds itself in. Only poetry can make the future real!

Perhaps, of all the romantic poets, it is Keats who illustrates most dramatically the extent of their disposition to move away from virtue and all the intellectual baggage associated with it. For one thing Keats does not use the word 'virtue' anywhere in his poetical works but in addition to this demonstrable fact there is quite a lot of evidence to show that Keats was hostile to moralistic discourse in general. As the son of an oastler he associated it with the readiness of the upper classes to speak critically and condescending about their inferiors, but if it was not this, it was either employed to repress freedom and spontaneity, or else it was the vehicle for a clichéd and trivial response to life in general. To put it no higher, moral judgements of any kind got Keats's back up, as we see repeatedly in his letters. When Benjamin Bailey failed to get the curacy he had hoped for in Lincoln Keats could not contain his indignation, speaking of 'barefaced oppression and impertinence' and of 'a self-willed yawning impudence in the shape of conscience'. What made the Bishop of Lincoln's behaviour so very objectionable was precisely his 'sacred Profession' and his pretension to have acted honourably. (Vol. I, p. 178) Keats had little time for the Church in general – in Scotland he saw the damage done to young people especially by the proscription of pleasure and enjoyment: 'These kirkmen have done Scotland harm.' (Vol. I, p. 319) But Keats could also see how even a popular play, like Sheil's *Evadne*, which the Scottish church would certainly have disapproved of, became vapid and unrealistic through its instinctive employment of cardboard cut-out moral categories:

> . . . the whole was made up of a virtuous young woman, an indignant brother, a suspecting lover, a libertine prince, a gratuitous villain, a street in Naples, a Cypress grove, lillies &

roses, virtue and vice, a bloody sword, a spangled jacket. (Vol. II, p. 68)

Keats's general reluctance to be judgemental created quite a few problems for him in his attempt to carve out a career for himself as a poet. For, in practice, achieving greatness as a poet meant writing an epic poem and this in turn meant adopting a hero whom the world had deemed great or valiant or virtuous. But Keats, again because of his own lowly background, regarded the whole notion of greatness as some kind of agreed but nevertheless implausible imposture. In a letter of 21 February 1818 Keats reports reading both Voltaire and Gibbon, the great eighteenth-century historians, no doubt in search of a worthy poetic subject but Keats developed a dislike of historical writing and quite deliberately chose mythological subjects instead. His reluctance to take on board the whole cult of greatness is manifest in *Endymion* – a *romance* not an epic – where he protests at those

>   who lord it o'er their fellow-men
>   With most prevailing tinsel'
> who
>   With unladen breasts,
>   Save of blown self-applause, they proudly mount
>   To their spirit's perch, their being's high account,
>   Their tiptop nothings, their dull skies, their thrones –
>   Amid the fierce intoxicating tones
>   Of trumpets, shouting, and belabour'd drums,
>   And sudden cannon.

What Keats is really saying here is that it is impossible for him to write an epic poem, despite the pressure on any ambitious poet to do so, because he simply can have no respect for the values, attitudes and individuals that the epic has characteristically held up for admiration. Repudiating the dubious impositions of Gibbon and history :

> Hence, pageant history! hence, gilded cheat!

Keats insists that lovers are of greater interest and more worthy of celebration than heroes:

What care, though striding Alexander past
The Indus with his Macedonian numbers?
Though old Ulysses tortured from his slumbers
The glutted Cyclops, what care? – Juliet leaning
Amid her window-flowers, – sighing, – weaning
Tenderly her fancy from its maiden snow,
Doth more avail than these: the silver flow
Of Hero's tears, the swoon of Imogen,
Fair Pastorella in the bandit's den,
Are things to brood on with more ardency
Than the death-day of empires.

Given Keats's own temperament and predicament as a man
dying of consumption it was certain that he would have more
sympathy for the vulnerable passionate than for those apparently
impregnable figures whose effigies were cast in bronze, but we
must also add that, after Waterloo, the very idea of the hero
required quotation marks. Few apart from Hazlitt could see
Napoleon as the hero pure and simple, not least because he seemed
to be at the mercy of events. Discussing his plans for *Hyperion*
and contrasting them with the already completed *Endymion* Keats
observed:

> . . . the Hero of the written tale being mortal, led like Buonaparte,
> by circumstance; whereas the Apollo in Hyperion being a fore-
> seeing God will shape his actions like one. (Vol. I, p. 207)

However, as *Hyperion* was never completed we can reasonably
assume that Keats found omniscience no more appealing.

There were more personal reasons why Keats found the ideas
of virtue difficult. His decision to give up medicine for poetry –
though it was one that he never for one moment regretted –
nevertheless had the effect of making him feel psychologically
uncomfortable. Whereas becoming a poet presented few obstacles
or financial difficulties for Byron, Shelley or Wordsworth, Keats
undoubtedly felt uneasy about both his prospects as a poet and
the degree to which he was obliged to depend on loans and assistance from his relatives and friends. In becoming a poet Keats
felt that he had chosen beauty, pleasure and indolence over hard
work and self-sufficiency. Keats criticised Wordsworth for his
egotism and pride, but from another point he recognised that it

was necessary for the ambitious poet to have this intense self-belief and to be totally self-centred if he were to achieve anything of any importance. In one of his very last letters he wrote that the artist must have

> ... self-concentration selfishness perhaps. (Vol. II, pp. 322–3)

In his letters Keats repeatedly, and self-deprecatingly referred to his sins, his vices, his selfish nature – no doubt to be taken with a pinch of salt, but it does show that Keats thought of himself as having taken an amoral path in devoting himself to writing. For him the poet's very occupation implied rebellion and thus made him akin to Milton's rebel angel. The poet defied conventional wisdom and morality by putting beauty before all else:

> ... with a great poet the sense of Beauty overcomes every other consideration. (Vol. I, p. 194)

Like Nietzsche, that other celebrated invalid, Keats valued health, vitality and dynamism over morality, custom and inertia, or as he also put it

> I must choose between despair and Energy. (Vol. II, p. 113)

So that these, rather than virtue and vice, became Keats's crucial polarities. For Keats as for Pater, beauty and intensity were the only things that either did matter or could possibly matter. Everything else was irrelevant.

'The power to dream deliciously', invoked in *Endymion*, was a gift neither especially common nor reputable yet it was one that was crucial to Keats's sense of what poetry involved. Moreover, if the artist is devoted to his own pleasure and with communicating that pleasure to others, it is likely that he will be thought of as both immoral and irresponsible. When, in one of his exceedly few references to virtue, Keats writes:

> What shocks the virtuous philosop(h)er, delights the chameleon poet (Vol. I, p. 387)

He not only implies that the poet may feel free to tackle subjects that the philosopher or moralist might disapprove of, but also that he is free to change his attitude or perspective – he is not duty bound to be consistent. Although Keats in this passage was distinguishing his own position from 'the Wordsworthian or egotistical sublime' we do need to ponder whether Keats was hijacked by the new critics, who found it all too easy to identify Keats' 'negative capability' with T.S. Eliot's emphasis on impersonality, for what Keats is really insisting on is the right of the artist to suspend moral categories and to present human actions without necessarily being obliged to be judgemental about them or to use them to display models of virtuous conduct. Ultimately what is at the back of this is the widespread discontent with allegory amongst Romantic writers, typified by Goethe's definition:

The allegorical differs from the symbolic in that what the latter designates indirectly, the former designates directly.[53]

For Keats there had been a definite advance in human awareness since Milton's time, a 'general and gregarious march of intellect', and therefore Milton's deployment of simple and all too legible moral oppositions, though understandable in historical context, could no longer satisfy the modern reader:

... who could gainsay his ideas on virtue, vice, and Chastity in Comus, just at the time of the dismissal of Cod-pieces and a hundred other disgraces? who would not rest satisfied with his hintings at good and evil on the Paradise Lost, when just free from the inquisition and burning in Smithfield? (Vol. I, pp. 281–2)

What makes for art is not such clear-cut moral judgements but precisely the representation of situations where such judgements are very difficult if not impossible to make:

... the excellence of every Art is its Intensity, capable of making all disagreeables evaporate, from their being in close relationship with Beauty & Truth – Examine King Lear & you will find this exemplified throughout. ... I had not a dispute but a disquisition with Dilke, on various subjects; several things dovetailed in my mind, & at once it struck me, what quality went to form a Man of Achievement especially in Literature & which Shakespeare possessed so enormously – I mean *Negative*

Capability, that is when a man is capable of being in uncertainties, Mysteries, doubts, without any irritable reaching out after fact and reason. . . . (Vol. I, pp. 192–3)

True art does not offer the security afforded by allegory or any clear-cut moral perspective. Its representative power and emotional impact will be diminished by any didactic intention. So from Keats's point of view if Beauty equals Truth it must also be seen as antithetical to Virtue. This, almost certainly is what Keats is getting at in the 'Ode on a Grecian Urn' when he suggests that the aesthetic impact of the urn is to 'tease us out of thought' – we are left contemplating the enigma both of life and the art that contrives to represent it, to accept and be glad of beauty without a moral. Undoubtedly the Greek emphasis on beauty was extremely important to Keats – but Keats was drawn not just to Greece rather than to Rome but to Greek mythology rather to the virtuous classical heroes celebrated by Plutarch. In so many Greek myths it is personal beauty that is the supreme value, whether in the story of Cupid and Psyche, that of *Hyperion* in which the Titans are superseded by the Olympian gods according to the eternal law

That first in beauty should be first in might . . .

or even mythic, quasi-historical narrative of the Trojan war – provoked not by a desire for territorial conquest but to reclaim the transcendent beauty of Helen. Yet, for Keats, to choose beauty is not the easy option because beauty is fleeting and ephemeral. Keats's phrase 'slippery blisses' is often seen, perhaps justifiably, as one of his most ridiculous expressions, yet it does convey a pyschological truth. The recognition of the desire for beauty in another manifests itself as a lack. It makes the individual painfully conscious of his dispossession whereas the virtuous individual is unwavering, self-contained and necessarily complete. To desire is to open oneself to the possibility of torment: in the words of *Endymion*:

> 'Tis the pest
> Of love, that fairest joys give most unrest;
> That things of delicate and tenderest worth
> Are swallow's all, and made a seared dearth,

By one consuming flame: it doth immerse
And suffocate true blessings in a curse.
Half-happy, by comparison of bliss,
Is miserable.

Lovers, through their very vulnerability, their desperate entangle-
ment in indeterminacy, are heroic in a way that the conventional
hero can never be or even glimpse. Indeed, Aeneas, the prototype of the virtuous hero in classical epic poetry notoriously
refuses to dally any longer with Dido and set forth for Rome,
thus making the *Aenead* a tale of arms and men rather than love.
The desperate dilemma of all those who desire but who can never
possess is epitomised by Isabella who loses her lover, reclaims
him from death and places his head in the pot of basil, only to
lose even that. It is reflected more mercifully, by the lover in
the 'Ode on a Grecian Urn' who, though unable to attain the
consummation of love, can nevertheless be consoled by the
thought that that teasing denial of fulfilment has itself been
immortalised:

She cannot fade, though thou hast not thy bliss,
For ever wilt thou love, and she be fair!

Certainty, security are always lacking.

Keats, with Blake, was the most determined opponent of all
that the idea of virtue represented among the Romantic poets
and yet the general decline in respect for the idea of virtue is
more conspicuously flagged in the poetry of Byron. In its eighteenth-century heyday virtue was always taken extremely seriously.
Even Fielding, despite the insouciance with which he satirised
human behaviour and pretensions, could be almost as po-faced
about virtue as Samuel Richardson. In the 1720s Mandeville, in
showing such disrespect towards virtue shocked a great many
people and was widely viewed as a self-conscious promoter of
depravity and wickedness and as a danger to society and yet
when Byron also mocked virtue one hundred years later he was
viewed rather as an irresponsible jester and a tease – if Byron
was 'wicked' it was always in inverted commas, like a habitual
stage villain who can't resist hamming it up even when off-duty.
Byron typically ridicules virtue and its pretensions:

They accuse me – *Me* – the present writer of
The present poem – of – I know not what –
A tendency to underrate and scoff
At human power and virtue, and all that.

Byron's posture, rather like Mandeville's is that he will believe it when he sees it. For Byron the whole idea of virtue is bound up with hypocrisy; an agreed social pretence that people are better or nobler than they actually are. Byron delights in confounding the reader's expectations. In only the second stanza of *Childe Harold's Pilgrimage* Byron announces that his hero 'ne in virtue's ways did take delight' and that he was 'a shameless wight,/ sore given to revel and ungodly glee'. In *Don Juan* he lays particular emphasis on the fact that Juan's mother, Donna Inez, was a pious hypocrite and that she took great pains to give him a virtuous education. Byron stresses the disconcerting aspect of classical education that was already of concern to many educationists: that although the classics are supposed to promote virtue, in practice they may promote much that is licentious and lewd:

His classic studies made a little puzzle,
Because of filthy loves of gods and goddesses,
Who in the earlier ages raised a bustle,
But never put on pantaloons or bodices
His reverend tutors had at times a tussle,
And for their Aeneads, Iliads, and Odysseys,
Were forced to make an odd sort of apology,
For Donna Inez dreaded the mythology.

Which was of course precisely the thing that appealed to Keats. But Byron's doubts about virtue and the cultural tradition that underwrites it go quite a lot deeper, since Byron is also sceptical of the credentials of history and finds it hard to believe that the great men of the past were really quite as admirable as they are supposed to be. In *Don Juan* he notes:

And glory long ago made the sages smile;
'Tis something, nothing, words, illusion, wind –

while in *Lara* his flawed protagonist gazing at the portraits on his walls:

There were the painted forms of other times,
'Twas all they left of virtues or of crimes,
Save vague tradition; and the gloomy vaults
That hid their dust, their foibles, and their faults;
And half a column of the pompous page,
That speds the specious tale from age to age;
Where's history's pen its praise or blame supplies,
And lies like truth, and still most truly lies.

Here Byron stresses an important truth – that it is precisely the moralising intention of the historian that is most likely to produce misrepresentation and distortion. The very discourse that aims to produce virtue is most likely to misrepresent and deceive.

Byron believes that all individuals are a mixture of good and evil, worthy and unworthy characteristics and this obviously leads him to reject representations of human behaviour in terms of one-sided stereotypes. Yet Byron does not interpret this conflict in terms of the traditional Christian model whereby each individual struggles to develop his or her good side and conquer their less admirable impulses. On the contrary what Byron emphasises is the fact that people are determined by their experiences and can have little control over what they become. He sees in human nature a jarring and irresolvable incongruity: we are, says Manfred:

Half dust, half deity, alike unfit
To sink or soar, with our mix'd essence make
A conflict of its elements, and breathe
The breath of degradation and of pride,
Contending with low wants and lofty will
Till our mortality predominates,
And men are – what they name not to themselves,
And trust not to each other.

So the Byronic hero is necessarily an enigma. He is shaped by a mysterious past which he simultaneously defies, glories in and regrets. Every revelation, however oblique only serves to opens up yet further empty Chinese boxes so that disclosure is ultimately denied. The Giaour is a man whose life has been incomprehensibly blighted through his love for and loss of

Leila, so that he feels himself to be more a spectre than a human being:

> And she was lost – and yet I breathed,
> But not the breath of human life:
> A serpent round my heart was wreathed,
> And stung my every thought to strife.

The Corsair freely acknowledges himself to be a villain and yet we learn that he is not quite the reckless, if gallant, desperado that he seems:

> His heart was form'd for softness – warp'd to wrong;
> Betray'd too early, and beguiled too long

So that behind the Byronic parade of cynicism verging on nihilism we also glimpse a Rousseauistic vision of tender young innocents who have been irretrievably damaged by their early experiences of society, which have educated them in bitterness not hope. Similarly Count Lara is an ambiguous character, who either soars above or sinks beneath the common norm. His very idealism is the cause of his subsequent moral confusion when he finds his hopes betrayed by experience:

> With more capacity for love than earth
> Bestows on most of mortal mould and birth
> His early dreams of good outstripp'd the truth,
> And troubled manhood follow'd baffle youth;
> With thoughts of years in phantom chase misspent,
> And wasted powers for better purpose lent;
> And fiery passions that had pour'd their wrath
> In hurried desolation o'er his path,
> And left the better feelings all at strife
> In wild reflection o'er his stormy life.

For Byron the ideology of virtue is actually corrupting because it creates expectations that cannot be fulfilled and necessarily leads towards a disillusionment from which there can be no exit. The real point about Byron's critique of virtue is not so much that he refuses to believe in it but that at one time he quite genuinely did!

It is with such mixed and contradictory feelings about virtue and the very possibility of heroism that underlie Byron's great poem *Childe Harold's Pilgrimage*. Here, Byron powerfully expresses his own sense of belatedness and a pervasive sense of desolation and exhaustion in the Europe after Waterloo. Indeed, Byron is the first genuinely European poet in the sense that his words and feelings elicited an almost universal sense of recognition; he spoke more for the weakened and despirited nations of the Continent than for a triumphant England. The sense of melancholy for a vanished past that, Gibbon experienced in Rome as he heard friars chanting in the ruins of the Capitol, is intensified in *Childe Harold* into a Byronic despair at the ultimate emptiness of human history, where, seemingly, so many noble deeds and idealistic beginings have petered out and run into the ground. After Waterloo disillusionment was doubled, since not only had the course of the French Revolution destroyed the great hopes that had been invested in it; but then Napoleonic justice proved to be nothing more than a hollow idol. In the end Napoleon, the man of destiny, was himself the victim of circumstance. By no means a hero unqualified, he epitomised in his very contradictions the perverse dualities that Byron perceived in human nature:

Oh, more or less than man – in high or low,
Battling with nations, flying from the field;
Now making monarch's necks thy footstool, now
More than thy meanest soldier taught to yield;
And empire thou couldst crush, command, rebuild,
But govern not thy pettiest passion, not,
However deeply in men's spirits skill'd,
Look through thine own, nor curb the lust of war,
Nor learn that tempted Fate will leave the loftiest star.

But in searching and sifting through the pages of history for a genuine greatness that remains truly worthy of respect Byron finds little that does not crumble to the touch. Certainly the struggles for Greek and Swiss independence at Marathon and Morat are more worthy to be commemorated than the destruction of empires at Cannae and Waterloo. Venice in its early days under Dandolo has its appeal. Indeed, in general Byron subscribes to the cyclical theories of history so prevalent in the eighteenth century, whereby virtuous beginnings irresistably lead to luxurious and corrupt endings, which may be why, in his own time he was impressed by the American spirit, as exemplified in Washington, Franklin and Daniel Boone. But in general he can find little to commemorate and whatever may have been achieved in the past it is indisputable that Greece, Rome and Venice are all sad relics of what they once were. Time destroys everything:

> A thousand years scarce serve to form a state;
> An hour may lay it in the dust: and when
> Can man its shatter'd splendour renovate,
> Recall its virtues back, and vanquish Time and Fate?

If history for Plutarch was an inexhaustable storehouse of human virtue and greatness; for Byron, much as he would like to believe otherwise, it is little better than a box of broken toys.

In his historical dramas, *Sardanapalus*, *Marino Faliero* and *The Two Foscari*, Byron significantly chose to focus on the losers of history, on those who had been condemned, derided or forgotten, rather than those who had been immortalised and celebrated. The decadent Sardanapalus, King of ancient Ninevah and Assyria, was a particularly suggestive choice since it gave Byron the opportunity to call into question the values that have traditionally driven the writing of history. Sardanapalus spends virtually all his time enjoying himself and the conventional wisdom is that he is neglecting his kingly duties and needs to be prodded and stimulated into performing noble actions – that is, waging war. Salemenes, the King's brother-in-law, is the principal spokesman for this point of view and it is he who opens the play with a lengthy indictment of the King's failings, which strongly recalls the introduction to *Antony and Cleopatra* in which Philo laments the fact that 'the triple pillar of the world' has been transformed into 'a strumpet's fool'. According to Salamenes virtue to Sardanapalus is an 'unknown word' and the strong implication is that until Sardanapalus takes it on board he has no hope of being a world–historical character. But Sardanapalus takes the reader offguard by putting forward a very plausible defence of his inaction. He has no interest in glory, war or military conquest. His failure to be heroic is not only sensible but is in the very best interests of his subjects: Decrying epic inscriptions and monuments Sardanapalus observes;

> I leave such things to conquerors; enough
> For me, if I can make my subjects feel

The weight of human misery less, and glide
Ungroaning to the tomb; I take no licence
Which I deny to them.

Sardanapalus, like Antony is fettered:

I am the very slave of circumstance
And impulse – borne away with every breath!
Misplaced upon the throne – misplaced in life.
I know not what I could have been, but feel
I am not what I should be – let it end.

Trapped in a position he has not sought, saddled with moral
obligations he cannot acknowledge and presented with challenges
whose purpose is doubtful Sardanapalus can only be perplexed
and tortured by a sense of incongruity. He is a Hamlet who must
be Fortinbras. The later scenes of the play shows Sardanapalus,
spurred on by his concubine Myrrah, trying, rather belatedly and
ineffectually, to be heroic in a way which seems to muddy what
had been relatively clear waters. For Sardanapalus, as for Byron,
virtue and courage have a certain glamour even if they don't
necessarily have much point!

Byron's two dramas of Venetian politics, *Marino Faliero* and *The
Two Foscari*, are much more pessimistic because the very possibility of heroism is excluded and in practice his protagonists are
only offered a choice between different forms of powerlessness
and ignominy. Marino Faliero, despite the fact that he is both
Doge and a faithful servant of the city who acquitted himself
with honour at the battle of Zara, finds that he is unable to obtain
redress when he and his wife are publicly insulted. Indignant,
he joins a conspiracy directed against the aristocratic group of
Ten and is condemned to be executed when the plot is discovered. Frances Foscari is condemned to stand by helpless and his
son Jacopo, who, having already been exiled, is tortured, condemned once more, and finally dies in prison just as he is due
to leave for a further period of exile. Speaking of his office Marino
Faliero says:

I sought it not, the flattering fetters me
Returning from my Roman embassy

and the imagery recurs when one of the conspirators, Philip
Calendaro, complains about the delay in taking action:

>   day on day
> Crawl'd on, and added but another link
> To our long fetters.

It is as if all those caught up in the history and reputation of
Venice are accomplices in their own downfall, inevitably doomed
and defeated from the very start. What makes the plays seem so
very depressing is that the characters are so transparently the
victims of circumstance and even of trivial accident. Marino
Faliero's destiny is determined by an insult written on a wall
and by Bertram's suggestion to Lioni that he should not go out
the next day. Jacopo dies in prison just as he is about to leave it.
His father, the Doge, is not allowed to give up the office that has
become so burdensome to him because of an oath that he has
previously sworn. According to Francis Foscari everything is
determined by fate and fortune – the individual can do nothing:

>   So, we are slaves,
> The greatest as the meanest – nothing rests
> Upon our will; the will itself no less
> Depends upon a straw than on a storm;
> And when we think we lead, we are most led.

So although both Marino Faliero and the Foscaris try to act both
virtuously and nobly their behaviour is emptied of morality and
significance because they are on the losing side. So there is at
once pathos and irony in the speech that Marino Faliero makes
at the end of Act I, after he has decided to become part of the
conspiracy:

> For I should rest in honour with the honour'd.
> Alas! I must not think of them, but those
> Who have made me thus unworthy of a name
> Noble and brave as aught of consular
> On Roman marbles; but I will redeem it
> Back to its antique lustre in our annals,
> By sweet revenge on all that's base in Venice,
> And freedom to the rest, or leave it black

To all the glowing calumnies of time,
Which never spare the fame of him who fails,
But try the Caesar, or the Catiline,
By the true touchstone of desert – success.

But, inevitably, the Doge's wager is not vindicated. All that is base in Venice continues as usual and those who have the power to convey honour are precisely Faliero's ignominious and ruthless adversaries. So there is no portrait of him in the ducal palace – only a painted black veil on which is written the words:

HIC EST LOCUS MARINI FALIERI DECAPITI PRO CRIMINIBUS.
Not only has he been condemned – he cannot even be represented!

In the aftermath of the French Revolution and Romanticism virtue was no longer what it once had been. Virtue as an ideal was clear, definite, uncompromising, as sharply chiselled in stone as an heroic statue. Virtue could not be qualified or blurred. Yet now virtue seemed all too reminiscent of the friezes from the Parthenon which Lord Elgin had so recently brought back from war-torn Greece and which were placed in the British Museum in 1816 – noble and beautiful undoubtedly, but nevertheless shattered, dislocated, defaced, verging on the indecipherable.

Notes

1 Introduction

1. John Locke, *Some Thoughts Concerning Education*, eds J.W. and J.S. Yolton (Oxford, 1989), p. 195.
2. Jeffrey Hart (ed.), *Political Writers of Eighteenth Century England* (New York, 1964), p. 176.
3. Viscount Bolingbroke, *Letters on the Study and Use of History etc.* (London, 1870), pp. 242–3.
4. Ibid., p. 170.
5. Edmund Burke, *Pre-Revolutionary Writings*, ed. I. Harris (Cambridge, 1993), pp. 30–1.
6. Ibid., p. 187.
7. Edmund Burke, *Reflections on the Revolution in France*, ed. L.G. Mitchell (Oxford, 1993), p. 95.
8. Ibid., p. 35.
9. Ibid., p. 96.
10. Edward Gibbon, *The History of the Decline and Fall of the Roman Empire*, 3 vols., ed. D. Womersley (London, 1994), Vol. III, p. 353.
11. Ibid., Vol. II, p. 121.
12. Ibid., Vol. I, p. 56.
13. Bernard Mandeville, *The Fable of the Bees*, ed. P. Harth (London, 1970), pp. 336–7.
14. Ibid., p. 87.
15. Ibid., p. 88.
16. Frances Hutcheson, *Collected Works*, 7 vols, (Hildesheim, Germany, 1971), p. 129.
17. Ibid., p. 164.
18. Ibid., p. 114.
19. Joseph Butler, *Works* 2 vols (Oxford, 1836), Vol. II, p. 41.
20. Adam Smith, *The Theory of Moral Sentiments*, ed. D.D. Raphael and A.L. MacFie (Oxford, 1989), p. 166.
21. Ibid., p. 152.
22. Adam Ferguson, *An Essay on the History of Civil Society 1767*, ed. D. Forbes (Edinburgh, 1966), pp. 57–8.
23. Smith, *Moral Sentiments*, p. 316.
24. Adam Smith, *An Inquiry into the Nature and Causes of the Wealth of Nations* ed. R.H. Campbell, A.S. Skinner and W.B. Todd, 2 vols (Oxford, 1976) Vol. I, pp. 26–7.
25. Smith, *Moral Sentiments*, p. 185.
26. Smith, *Wealth of Nations*, Vol. I, pp. 23–4.
27. Locke, *Some Thoughts*, p. 132.
28. Ibid., p. 107.
29. Ibid., p. 234.

30. Ibid., p. 230.
31. Bolingbroke, *Letters etc.*, p. 6.
32. Ibid., p. 39.
33. Lord Chesterfield, *Letters to his Son* Introduction R.K. Root (London, 1969), p. 4.
34. Quoted in David Allen, *Virtue, Learning and the Scottish Enlightenment* (Edinburgh, 1993), p. 174.
35. James Beattie, *Essays Moral and Critical* (London, 1776), p. 747.
36. William Robertson, *History of Ancient Greece* (Edinburgh, 1790), pp. v–vi.
37. Thomas Tomkins (ed.), *Poems on Various Subjects selected to enforce the Practice of Virtue* (London, 1780), p. vii.
38. Jean-Jacques Rousseau, *Emile*, trans. B. Foxley (London, 1974), p. 5.
39. Ibid., p. 57.
40. Ibid., p. 56.
41. Ibid., p. 215.
42. Ibid., p. 182.
43. Thomas Carlyle, *Sartor Resartus and On Heroes, Hero-Worship and the Heroic in History* (London, 1927), pp. 461–2.

2 Virtue's Vicissitudes

1. George Savile, Marquis of Halifax, *Works* 3 vols, ed. M.N. Brown (Oxford, 1989), Vol. I, p. 192.
2. John Dryden, *Of Dramatic Poesy etc.*, 2 vols, ed. G. Watson (London, 1962), Vol. I, p. 165.
3. Thomas Hobbes, *Leviathan*, Introduction K.R. Minoghue (London, 1973), p. 49.

3 Virtue Excluded

References to works by Swift included in the text are to *A Tale of a Tub and Other Works*, ed. A. Ross and D. Woolley (Oxford, 1986) and to *Gulliver's Travels*, ed. P. Turner (London, 1986). All others references are to H.J. Davis *et al.*, *The Prose Works of Jonathan Swift*, 14 vols (Oxford, 1939–68). References to Defoe are to *Moll Flanders*, ed. P. Rogers (London, 1993) and to *Roxana*, ed. J. Jack (Oxford, 1981).

1. Sir William Temple, *Five Miscellaneous Essays*, ed. S.H. Monk (Ann Arbor, 1963), p. 68.
2. Ibid., p. 115.
3. Ibid., p. 71.
4. Ibid.
5. Ibid., pp. 186–7.
6. Ibid., p. 201.
7. *v.* Ian Higgins, *Swift's Politics: a Study in Disaffection* (Cambridge, 1994), p. 43.
8. *v.* Ibid., p. 107.
9. Thomas Hobbes, *Leviathan* Introduction K.R. Minoghue (London, 1973), p. 40.

10. Ibid., p. 22.
11. Ibid., p. 217.
12. Ibid., p. 380.
13. Quoted in J.A. Downie, *Jonathan Swift : Political Writer* (London, 1984), p. 147.
14. Lord Macaulay, *Critical and Historical Essays* (London, 1877), p. 756.
15. Edward Young, *The Complete Works*, 2 vols, ed. J. Nichols (Hildesheim, 1968), Vol. II, p. 583.
16. Macaulay, *Essays*, p. 775.
17. Joseph Addison, *Miscellaneous Works*, 2 vols, ed. A.C. Guthkelch (London, 1914), Vol. II, pp. 271–2.
18. Geoffrey Holmes, *The Making of a Great Power* (London, 1993), pp. 334–5.
19. J.G.A. Pocock, *The Machiavellian Moment: Florentine Political Thought and the Atlantic Republican Tradition* (Princeton, 1975), p. 486.
20. John Trenchard and Thomas Gordon, *Cato's Letters*, 2 vols, ed. R. Hamory (Indianapolis, 1995), Vol. I, p. 13.
21. Ibid., Vol. I, p. 23.
22. Ibid., Vol. I, p. 41.
23. Ibid., Vol. I, p. 211.
24. Ibid., Vol. II, pp. 868–9.
25. Ibid., Vol. I, p. 56.
26. Ibid., Vol. I, p. 251.
27. Ibid., Vol. I, p. 57.
28. Ibid., Vol. I, p. 278.
29. Ibid., Vol. I, p. 146.
30. Ibid., Vol. I, p. 259.
31. Ibid., Vol. I, p. 282.
32. Pocock, *The Machiavellian Moment*, p. 472.
33. Daniel Defoe, *The Complete English Tradesman* (Gloucester, 1987), pp. 140–1.
34. Daniel Defoe, *A Tour through the Whole Island of Great Britain*, ed. and abridged P. Rogers (London, 1971), p. 307.
35. Bernard Mandeville, *The Fable of the Bees*, ed. P. Harth (London, 1970), p. 81.
36. Ibid., p. 214.
37. Ibid., p. 88.
38. Ibid., p. 241.
39. Ibid., p. 57.
40. Ibid., pp. 134–5.
41. J. Martin Stafford (ed.), *Private Vices, Public Benefits: The Contemporary Reception of Bernard Mandeville* (Solihull, 1997), p. 77.
42. Ibid., p. 149.
43. Ibid., p. 176.
44. Ibid., p. 275.
45. Ibid., p. 544.
46. Ibid.
47. John Locke, *An Essay concerning Human Understanding*, 2 vols, ed. J.W. Yolton (London, 1965), Vol. II, p. 287.

48. Hobbes, *Leviathan*, p. 23.
49. G.W. Leibnitz, *New Essays on Human Understanding* trans. P. Remnant and J. Bennett (Cambridge, 1982), p. 473.
50. Locke, *Essay*, Vol. I, p. 126.
51. Mandeville, *Fable*, p. 81.
52. G.W. Leibnitz, *Philosophical Essays* ed. and trans. R. Ariew and D. Garber (Indianapolis and Cambridge, 1989), p. 39.
53. G.W. Leibnitz, *Theodicy*, ed. and abridged D. Allen (Don Mills, Ontario, 1966), p. 95.
54. Leibnitz, *New Essays*, p. 306.
55. Ibid., p. 307.
56. Hobbes, *Leviathan*, p. 44.
57. Quoted in Arthur O. Lovejoy, *The Great Chain of Being* (Cambridge, Mass. and London, 1978), p. 196.
58. Joseph Butler, *Works*, 2 vols, (Oxford, 1836), Vol. I, pp. xii–xiii.
59. David Hume, *Enquiries*, ed. L.A. Selby-Bigge, 2nd edn (Oxford, 1962), pp. 138–9.
60. Alexander Pope, *Correspondence*, ed. G. Sherburn Vol. IV (1736–44) (Oxford, 1956), pp. 138–9.
61. J. Barnard, ed., *Pope: The Critical Heritage* (London, 1973), p. 345.
62. Colley Cibber, *An Apology for the Life of Colley Cibber*, ed. B.R.S. Fone (Ann Arbor, 1968), p. 21.
63. Mandeville, *Fable*, p. 269.
64. Stafford (ed.), *Private Vices, Public Benefits*, p. 548.

4 Virtue from Below

References in the text to works by Richardson are to: *Pamela* (2 vols), Introduction by M. Kinkead-Weekes (London, 1976), *Clarissa*, ed. A. Ross (London, 1985), *Sir Charles Grandison* ed. J. Harris (Oxford, 1986).

References to Fielding are to the Wesleyan Edition of the Works of Henry Fielding: *Joseph Andrews*, ed. M.C. Battestin (Oxford, 1967), *The History of Tom Jones, A Foundling* ed. F. Bowers 2 vols (Oxford, 1975), *Amelia*, ed. M.C. Battestin (Oxford, 1983).

Other references are to: Fanny Burney, *Evelina*, eds E.A. and L.D. Bloom (Oxford and New York, 1982), Thomas Day, *The History of Sandford and Merton*, repr. 3 vols, Preface I. Kramnick (New York and London, 1977), Charlotte Smith, *Emmeline*, ed. A.H. Ehrenpreis (London, 1971).

References to novels by Jane Austen are to the World's Classics editions edited by J. Kinsley (Oxford and New York, 1990) (*Northanger Abbey*, ed. J. Davie).

1. Daniel Defoe, *The Compleat English Gentleman*, ed. K.D. Bulbring (London, 1890), p. 24.
2. Daniel Defoe, *The Complete English Tradesman* (Gloucester, 1987), pp. 76–7.
3. John Locke, *Some Thoughts Concerning Education* eds J.W. and J.S. Yolton (Oxford, 1989), p. 127.
4. Ibid., p. 128.

5. Mark Kinkead-Weekes, *Samuel Richardson, Dramatic Novelist* (Ithaca, NY, 1973) p. 150.
6. Bernard Mandeville, *The Fable of the Bees*, ed. P. Harth (London, 1970), p. 174.
7. *v.* Martin Battestin, *The Moral Basis of Fielding's Art* (Middletown, Conn., 1959), pp. 14–25 and pp. 70–84.
8. John Tillotson, *Works*, 10 vols, (London, 1820), Vol. IX, pp. 2–3.
9. Ibid., Vol. IX, p. 114.
10. Isaac Barrow, *Theological Works* 8 vols (Oxford, 1830), Vol. III, pp. 382–3.
11. R. Paulson and T. Lockwood (eds), *Fielding: the Critical Heritage* (London and New York, 1969), p. 446.
12. Mandeville, *Fable*, p. 233.
13. Locke, *Some Thoughts*, p. 122.
14. Paulson and Lockwood (eds), *Fielding: the Critical Heritage*, pp. 174–5.
15. Quoted in J. Sekora, *Luxury* (Baltimore and London, 1977), p. 193.
16. Lord Chesterfield, *Letters to his Son*, Introduction R.K. Root (London, 1969), p. 53.
17. Ibid., p. 122.
18. James Boswell, *The Life of Samuel Johnson*, Introduction John Wain (London, 1976), Vol. I, p. 159.
19. Chesterfield, *Letters*, p. 145.
20. Ibid., p. 272.
21. James Keir, *Account of the Life and Writings of Thomas Day*, repr. (New York, 1970), p. 82.

5 Provincial Virtue

References in the text are to: Lawrence Sterne, *The Life and Opinions of Tristram Shandy*, ed. G. Petrie (London, 1967), Henry MacKenzie *The Man of Feeling*, ed. B. Vickers (London, 1970), Henry MacKenzie, *Miscellaneous Works*, 3 vols (Edinburgh, 1819) Vol. II, *The Man of the World*, Tobias Smollett, *Humphrey Clinker*, ed. A. Ross (London, 1967), Oliver Goldsmith, *Collected Works* 5 vols, ed. A. Friedman (Oxford, 1966).

1. James Boswell, *The Life of Samuel Johnson*, 2 vols, Introduction John Wain (London, 1976), Vol. I, p. 522.
2. Ibid., Vol. 1, p. 264.
3. Donald Davie (ed.), *The Late Augustans* (London, 1958), pp. xii–xiii.
4. Daniel Defoe, *A Tour through the Whole Island of Great Britain*, abridged and edited by P. Rogers (London, 1971), pp. 176–7.
5. Linda Colley, *Britons: Forging the Nation 1707–1837* (New Haven and London, 1992), p. 6.
6. Ibid., p. 1.
7. Ibid., pp. 367–8.
8. James Boswell, *An Account of Corsica*, 3rd edn (London, 1769), p. 291.
9. Ibid., p. 329.
10. Boswell, *The Life of Samuel Johnson*, Vol. I, pp. 349–50.

11. John Brown, *An Estimate of the Manners and Principles of the Times*, (London, 1758), Vol I., p. 91.
12. Adam Smith, *An Inquiry into the Nature and Causes of the Wealth of Nations*, 2 vols, eds R.H. Campbell, H.S. Skinner and W.B. Todd (Oxford, 1976), Vol. II, pp. 787–8.
13. Adam Ferguson, *An Essay on the History of Civil Society 1767*, ed. D. Forbes (Edinburgh, 1966), p. 56.
14. Quoted in John Dwyer, *Virtuous Discourse* (Edinburgh, 1987), p. 44.
15. Montesquieu, *The Spirit of the Laws* trans. and eds A.M. Cohler, B.C. Miller and H.S. Stone (Cambridge, 1989), p. 451.
16. Ibid., p. 331.
17. Ferguson, *Essay*, p. 59.
18. Ibid.
19. Edward Gibbon, *The History of the Decline and Fall of the Roman Empire*, 3 vols, ed. D. Womersley (London, 1994), Vol. II, p. 509.
20. *The Poems of Ossian*, trans. James MacPherson (Leipzig, 1847), p. 16.
21. Gibbon, *Decline and Fall*, Vol. I, p. 152.
22. Ellis Sandoz (ed.), *Political Sermons of the American Founding Era 1730–1805* (Indianapolis, 1990), p. 446.
23. Ibid., p. 475.
24. Quoted in Gordon S. Wood, *Creation of the American Republic 1776–1787* (Chapel Hill, 1969), p. 35.
25. Sandoz (ed.), *Political Sermons*, pp. 556–7.
26. Ibid., p. 502.
27. Ibid., p. 508.
28. Tom Paine, *Rights of Man, Common Sense and other Political Writings* ed., M. Philp (Oxford and New York, 1995), p. 22.
29. Ibid., p. 64.
30. Sandoz (ed.), *Political Sermons*, p. 603.
31. Ibid., p. 487.
32. Ibid., pp. 804–5.
33. Ibid., pp. 810–11.
34. Thomas Jefferson, *Complete Papers*, Vol. 12, ed. J.P. Boyd (Princeton, 1955), p. 17.
35. Ralph Waldo Emerson, *Collected Works* Vol. II (Harvard and London, 1979), p. 46.
36. J. Hector St John de Crevecoeur, *Letters from an American Farmer* (New York, 1963), p. 37.
37. Wolfe Tone, *The Autobiography 1763–1798*, 2 vols (Dublin, 1893), Vol II, pp. 166–7.
38. Henry Grattan, *Speeches*, 4 vols, edited by his son (London, 1822), Vol. I, pp. 166–7.
39. Ibid., Vol. I, p. 43.
40. Samuel Johnson, *Lives of the English Poets*, 2 vols (London, 1946), Vol. II, p. 314.
41. Ibid., Vol. II, p. 316.
42. Ibid., Vol. II, pp. 390–1.
43. Samuel Johnson and James Boswell, *A Journey to the Western Isles and the Journal of a Tour to the Hebrides*, ed. P. Levi (London, 1984), p. 226.

44. Ibid., p. 331.
45. Ibid., pp. 60–1.
46. Ibid., p. 74.
47. Ibid., p. 117.
48. Ibid., p. 99.
49. Lawrence Sterne, *A Sentimental Journey through France and Italy* (Oxford, 1929), p. 12.
50. Lawrence Sterne, *The Sermons of Yorick*, 2 vols (Oxford, 1927), Vol. I, p. 237.
51. Tobias Smollett, *History of England from the Revolution of 1688* 4 vols (Paris, 1836), Vol. I, p. 109.
52. Ibid., Vol. II, p. 206.
53. Ibid., Vol. III, p. 98.
54. John Sekora, *Luxury*, (Baltimore and London, 1977), pp. 216–17.
55. L. Kelly (ed.), *Tobias Smollett: the Critical Heritage* (London and New York, 1987), p. 217.
56. *v.* John Barrell, *English Literature in History: an Equal, Wide Survey 1730–80* (London, 1983), p. 95.
57. William Cowper, *Letter and Prose Writings*, 2 vols, eds J. King and C. Ryskamp (Oxford, 1979), Vol. I, p. 523.
58. Ibid., Vol. I, p. 527.
59. A. Pollard (ed.), *Crabbe: the Critical Heritage*, (London, 1972), p. 114.
60. Ibid., p. 303.

6 The Romantics and Virtue

References in the text are to G.E. Bentley (ed.), *William Blake's Writings*, Vol. II (Oxford, 1978), John Keats, *The Letters of John Keats, 1814–1821* 2 vols, ed. H.E. Rollins (Cambridge, Mass., 1958), D.L. Clark (ed.), *Shelley's Prose* (London, 1988).

1. Walter Scott, *Waverley*, ed. C. Lamont (Oxford, 1981), p. 181.
2. Ibid.
3. Geoffrey Hartman, *Wordsworth's Poetry 1787–1814* (Cambridge and London, 1987), p. 267.
4. M.H. Abrams, *Natural Supernaturalism* (New York, 1971), p. 27.
5. Paul de Man, *Blindness and Insight*, 2nd edn. (London, 1983), pp. 199–200.
6. Thomas Carlyle, *Sartor Resartus and On Heroes, Hero-Worship and the Heroic in History* (London, 1927), p. 471.
7. Matthew Arnold, *Complete Prose Works*, Vol. 5, *Culture and Anarchy*, ed. R.H. Super (Ann Arbor, 1965), p. 127.
8. Montesquieu, *The Spirit of the Laws*, trans and eds A. Cohler, B. Miller and H. Stone (Cambridge, 1989), p. xli.
9. Edward Gibbon, *The History of the Decline and Fall of the Roman Empire*, 3 vols, ed. D. Womersley (London, 1994), Vol. I, p. 103.
10. Ibid., Vol. I, p. 104.
11. Adam Ferguson, *An Essay on the History of Civil Society 1767*, ed. D. Forbes (Edinburgh, 1966), p. 59.

12. Joseph de Maistre, *Considerations on France*, ed. R.A. Lebrun (Cambridge, 1994), p. 5.
13. Thomas Carlyle, *The French Revolution*, 2 vols (London, 1933), Vol. II, pp. 329–30.
14. William Godwin, *Enquiry concerning Political Justice*, ed. I. Kramnick (London, 1976) pp. 436–7.
15. William Godwin, *Caleb Williams*, ed. M. Hindle (London, 1988), p. 160.
16. Godwin, *Political Justice*, p. 475.
17. William Godwin, *St. Leon*, ed. P. Clemit (Oxford, 1994), p. 167.
18. Ibid., p. 426.
19. Ibid., pp. 289–90.
20. Godwin, *Political Justice*, pp. 113–14.
21. Ibid., p. 114.
22. Mary Shelley, *Frankenstein*, ed. M.K. Joseph (Oxford and New York, 1980), pp. 120–1.
23. Charlotte Dacre, *Zofloya, or the Moor*, ed. K.I. Michasiw (Oxford and New York, 1997), pp. 132–3.
24. Jean-Jacques Rousseau, *The Confessions*, trans. J.M. Cohen (London, 1953), p. 89.
25. Ibid., p. 332.
26. Ibid., p. 388.
27. Edmund Burke, *Reflections on the Revolution in France*, ed. L.G. Mitchell (Oxford, 1993), pp. 270–1.
28. J.P. Kemble, *Macbeth and King Richard the Third*, repr. (London, 1970), p. 170.
29. B. Vickers (ed.), *Shakespeare: the Critical Heritage*, Vol. VI (1774–1801) (London, 1981), p. 411.
30. Ibid., p. 119
31. Prévost, *Manon Lescaut*, trans. L.W. Tancock (London, 1949), p. 140.
32. Jonathan Bate (ed.), *The Romantics on Shakespeare* (London, 1992), pp. 387–8.
33. Andrew Ashfield and Peter de Bolla (eds), *The Sublime* (Cambridge, 1996), p. 183.
34. Samuel Johnson, *Works* Vol. VIII, *Johnson on Shakespeare*, ed. A. Sherbo (New Haven and London, 1968), p. 704.
35. Bate, (ed.) *The Romantics on Shakespeare*, p. 401.
36. Thomas de Quincey, *Literary Criticism*, ed. H. Darbishire (London, 1909) p. 153.
37. Bate, (ed.) *The Romantics on Shakespeare*, p. 123.
38. Ibid., p. 122.
39. Ibid.
40. Robert Bage, *Hermsprong*, ed. P. Faulkner (Oxford, 1985), p. 237.
41. Godwin, *Caleb Williams*, p. 229.
42. G.W. Hegel, *On Tragedy*, eds A. and H. Paolucci (New York, 1962), p. 133.
43. Burke, *Reflections*, p. 97.
44. Samuel Taylor Coleridge, *The Collected Works*, Vol. VI, ed. R.J. White (London and Princeton, 1972), p. 65.

45. Thomas de Quincey, *Confessions of an English Opium Eater*, ed. A. Hayter (London, 1971), p. 68.
46. Paul de Man, *Allegories of Reading* (New Haven and London, 1979), p. 299.
47. Shaftesbury, *Characteristics of Men, Manners, Opinions, Times*, 2 vols, ed. J.M. Robertson (Indianapolis, 1964), Vol. I, pp. 282–3.
48. Frederick L. Jones (ed.), *The Letters of Percy Bysshe Shelley*, 2 vols (Oxford, 1964), Vol. I, pp. 229–31.
49. Ibid., Vol. I, p. 277.
50. Ibid., Vol. I., p. 259.
51. James E. Barcus (ed.), *Shelley: The Critical Heritage* (London and Boston, 1975), p. 181.
52. Ibid., p. 164.
53. Quoted in Tzvetan Todorov, *Theories of the Symbol*, trans. C. Porter (Oxford, 1982) p. 199.

Select Bibliography

History and Politics

Black, J. *Britain in the Age of Walpole* (London, 1984)
—— *Robert Walpole and the Nature of Politics in Early Eighteenth Century Britain* (London, 1990)
Blum, C. *Rousseau and the Republic of Virtue: The Language of Politics in the French Revolution* (Ithaca and London, 1986)
Brewer, J. *The Sinews of Power: War, Money and the English State 1688–1783* (London, 1989)
Christie, I.R. *Wars and Revolutions: Britain 1760–1815* (London, 1982)
Clark, J.C.D. *English Society 1688–1832* (Cambridge, 1985)
—— *The Language of Liberty 1660–1832* (Cambridge, 1994)
Colley, L. *In Defiance of Oligarchy: the Tory Party 1714–60* (Cambridge, 1982)
Dickinson, H.T. *Liberty and Property: Political Ideology in Eighteenth Century Britain* (London, 1977)
Goldsmith, M.M. *Private Vices, Public Benefits: Bernard Mandeville's Social and Political Thought* (Cambridge, 1985)
Harris, T. *Politics under the Later Stuarts: Party Conflict in a Divided Society 1660–1715* (London, 1993)
Henshall, N. *The Myth of Absolutism: Change and Continuity in Early Modern European Monarchy* (London, 1992)
Holmes, G. *British Politics in the Age of Anne* (London, 1967)
—— *Politics, Religion and Society in England, 1679–1742* (London, 1986)
—— *The Making of a Great Power: Late Stuart and Early Georgian Britain 1660–1722* (London and New York, 1993)
Kenyon, J.P. *Revolution Principles: the Politics of Party 1689–1720* (Cambridge, 1977)
Kramnick, I. *Bolingbroke and His Circle: the Politics of Nostalgia in the Age of Walpole* (Ithaca and London, 1992)
MacDowell, R.B. *Ireland in the Age of Imperialism and Revolution, 1760–1801* (Oxford, 1979)
Matthews (ed.), *Virtue, Corruption and Self-Interest: Political Values in the Eighteenth Century* (Bethlehem, Pa., 1994)
Monod, P.K. *Jacobitism and the English People, 1688–1788* (Cambridge, 1989)
Pares, R. *King George III and the Politicians* (Oxford, 1953)
Plumb, J.H. *The Growth of Political Stability in England 1675–1725* (London, 1967)
Pocock, J.G.A. *The Machiavellian Moment: Florentine Political Thought and the Atlantic Republican Tradition* (Princeton, 1975)
—— *Virtue, Commerce and History* (Cambridge, 1985)
Robbins, C. *The Eighteenth Century Commonwealth Man* (Cambridge, Mass., 1961)

Rogers, N. *Whigs and Cities: Popular Politics in the Age of Walpole and Pitt* (Oxford, 1989)

Speck, W.A. *Stability and Strife: England 1714–1760* (London, 1977)

Thomas, P.D.G. *John Wilkes: a Friend to Liberty* (Oxford, 1996)

Thomson, E.P. *Whigs and Hunters* (London, 1977)

Worrall, D. *Radical Culture: Discourse, Resistance and Surveillance 1790–1820* (London, 1992)

The Social and Cultural Context

Allen, D. *Virtue, Learning and the Scottish Enlightenment* (Edinburgh, 1993)

Ayres, P. *Classical Culture and the Idea of Rome in Eighteenth-Century England* (Cambridge, 1997)

Barker-Benfield, G.J. *The Culture of Sensibility, Sex and Society in Eighteenth Century Britain* (Chicago and London, 1991)

Brewer, J. *The Pleasures of the Imagination: English Culture in the Eighteenth Century* (London, 1997)

Browne, A. *The Eighteenth Century Feminist Mind* (Brighton, 1987)

Colley, L. *Britons: Forging the Nation 1707–1837* (New Haven and London, 1992)

Downie, J.A. *To Settle the Succession of the State: Literature and Politics 1678–1750* (London, 1994)

Dwyer, J. *Virtuous Discourse: Sensibility and Community in Late Eighteenth-Century Scotland* (Edinburgh, 1987)

Fairchild, H.N. *The Noble Savage: a Study in Romantic Naturalism* (New York, 1961)

Goldgar, B.A. *Walpole and the Wits: the Relation of Politics to Literature, 1722–1742* (Lincoln, Nebraska, 1977)

Klein, L. *Shaftesbury and the Culture of Politeness* (Cambridge, 1994)

Kramnick, I. *Bolingbroke and his Circle: the Politics of Nostalgia in the Age of Walpole* (Ithaca and London, 1968)

Levine, J.M. *The Battle of the Books: History and Literature in the Augustan Age* (Ithaca and London, 1991)

Linebaugh, P. *The London Hanged* (London, 1991)

Meek, R.L. *Social Science and the Ignoble Savage* (Cambridge, 1976)

Motooke, W. *The Age of Reasons: Quixotism, Sentimentalism and Political Economy in Eighteenth-Century Britain* (London, 1998)

Newman, G. *The Rise of English Nationalism: a Cultural History, 1740–1830* (New York, 1987)

Porter, R. *Gibbon: Making History* (London, 1988)

Rivers, I. *Books and their Readers in Eighteenth-Century England* (Leicester, 1982)

Sambrook, J. *The Eighteenth Century: the Intellectual and Cultural Context of English Literature 1700–1789* (London, 1986)

Sekora, J. *Luxury* (Baltimore and London, 1977)

Stephen, L. *History of English Thought in the Eighteenth Century* (2 vols) (London, 1962)

Thomson, E.P. *Customs in Common* (London, 1991)

Wasserman, E.R. (ed.) *Aspects of the Eighteenth Century* (Baltimore and London, 1965)

Wilson, K. *The Sense of the People: Politics, Culture and Imperialism in England 1715–1785* (Cambridge, 1995)

Weinbrot, H.D. *Augustus Caesar in 'Augustan' England: the Decline of a Classical Norm* (Princeton, 1978)

Whitney, L. *Primitivism and the Idea of Progress* (New York, 1973)

Williams, R. *The Country and the City* (London, 1985)

Wroth, W. and A.E. *The London Pleasure Gardens of the Eighteenth Century* (London, 1979)

Philosophy and Religion

Abrams, M.H. *Natural Supernaturalism* (New York, 1971)

Berlin, I. (ed.) H. Hardy *The Sense of Reality: Studies in Ideas and Their History* (London, 1996)

Bradley, J.E. *Religion, Revolution and English Radicalism: Non-conformity in Eighteenth-Century Politics and Society* (Cambridge, 1990)

Brown, V. *Adam Smith's Discourse: Canonicity, Commerce and Conscience* (London and New York, 1994)

Bryson, G. *Man and Society: the Scottish Inquiry of the Eighteenth Century* (Princeton, 1945)

Carpenter, S.C. *Eighteenth Century Church and People* (London, 1950)

Cassirer, E. *The Philosophy of the Enlightenment* trans. F.C. Koelln and J.P. Pettegrove (Princeton, 1953)

Cragg, G.R. *Reason and Authority in the Eighteenth Century* (Cambridge, 1964)

Fitzgibbons, A. *Adam Smith's System of Liberty, Wealth and Virtue: the Moral and Political Foundations of the Wealth of Nations* (Oxford, 1995)

Forbes, D. *Hume's Philosophical Politics* (Cambridge, 1975)

Foucault, M. *The Order of Things* (London, 1970)

Fussell, P. *The Rhetorical World of Augustan Humanism: Ethics and Imagery from Swift to Burke* (Oxford, 1965)

Harris, R.W. *Reason and Nature in the Eighteenth Century 1714–1780* (London, 1968)

Hazard, P. *The European Mind, 1680–1715* (London, 1953)

Herrick, J.A. *The Radical Rhetoric of the English Deists: the Discourse of Skepticism 1680–1750* (Columbia, South Carolina, 1997)

Horne, T.A. *The Social Thought of Bernard Mandeville: Virtue and Commerce in early Eighteenth-Century England* (London, 1978)

Jeffner, A. *Butler and Hume on Religion: a Comparative Analysis* (Stockholm, 1966)

Jones, P. (ed.) *The 'Science of Man' in the Scottish Enlightenment: Hume, Reid and their Contemporaries* (Edinburgh, 1989)

Lovejoy, A.O. *Essays in the History of Ideas* (Baltimore, 1948)

—— *The Great Chain of Being* (Cambridge, Mass., 1964)

Lyles, A.M. *Methodism Mocked: the Satiric Reaction to Methodism in the Eighteenth Century* (London, 1960)

Mandelbaum, M. *Philosophy, Science and Sense Perception: Historical and Critical Studies* (Baltimore, 1964)

MacIntyre, A. *After Virtues: A Study in Moral Theory* (London, 1985)

MacPherson, C.B. *The Political Theory of Possessive Individualism, Hobbes to Locke* (London, 1962)

Manuel, F.E. *The Eighteenth Century Confronts the Gods* (Cambridge, Mass., 1959)

Miller, D. *Philosophy and Ideology in Hume's Political Thought* (Oxford, 1981)

Miller, P.N. *Defining the Common Good: Empire, Religion and Philosophy in Eighteenth-Century Britain* (Cambridge, 1994)

Philp, M. *Godwin's Political Justice* (Cambridge, 1986)

Roberts, T.A. *The Concept of Benevolence: Aspects of Eighteenth Century Moral Philosophy* (London, 1973)

Rupp, G. *Religion in England 1688–1791* (Oxford, 1986)

Spadafora, P. *The Idea of Progress in Eighteenth-Century Britain* (New Haven and London, 1990)

Vereker, C. *Eighteenth Century Optimism* (Liverpool, 1967)

Walker, W. *Locke, Literary Criticism and Philosophy* (Cambridge, 1994)

Watts, M.R. *The Dissenters*, Vol. I: *From the Reformation to the French Revolution*

Willey, B. *The Eighteenth Century Background* (London, 1940)

Yolton, J. *Thinking Matter: Materialism in Eighteenth-Century Britain* (Oxford, 1983)

Literature

Alter, R. *Fielding and the Nature of the Novel* (Cambridge, Mass., 1968)

Armstrong, N. *Desire and Domestic Fiction: a Political History of the Novel* (New York, 1987)

Backman, S. *This Singular Tale: a Study of 'The Vicar of Wakefield' and Its Literary Background* (Lund, Sweden, 1971)

Barbeau, A.T. *The Intellectual Design of John Dryden's Heroic Plays* (New Haven and London, 1970)

Barrell, J. *English Literature in History: an Equal, Wide Survey* (London, 1983)

Battestin, M.C. *The Moral Basis of Fielding's Art: a Study of Joseph Andrews* (Middletown, 1959)

Brissenden, R.F. *Virtue in Distress* (New York, 1974)

Brown, M. *Preromanticism* (Stanford, 1991)

Butler, M. *Romantics, Rebels and Reactionaries* (Oxford, 1981)

Bygrave, S. *Coleridge and the Self: Romantic Egotism* (London, 1996)

Castle, T. *Masquerade and Civilisation* (Stanford, 1986)

Clark, J.C.D. *Samuel Johnson: Literature, Religion and English Cultural Politics from the Restoration to Romanticism* (Cambridge, 1994)

Clifford, J.L. (ed.) *Eighteenth Century Literature: Modern Essays in Criticism* (London, 1959)

Cohen, R. *The Art of Discrimination: Thomson's 'The Seasons' and the Language of Criticism* (Berkeley, 1964)

Dawson, P.M.S. *The Unacknowledged Legislator: Shelley and Politics* (Oxford, 1980)

Donoghue, J.W. *Dramatic Character in the English Romantic Age* (Princeton, 1970)

Downie, J.A. *Jonathan Swift: Political Writer* (London, 1984)

Eagleton, T. *The Rape of Clarissa* (Oxford, 1982)

Ellis, M. *The Politics of Sensibility: Race, Gender and Commerce in the Sentimental Novel* (Cambridge, 1996)

Erskine-Hill, H. *The Augustan Ideal in English Literature* (London, 1983)

Evans, B. *Gothic Drama from Walpole to Shelley* (Berkeley and Los Angeles, 1947)

Foot, P. *Red Shelley* (London, 1980)

Fox, C. *Locke and the Scriblerians: Identity and Consciousness in Early Eighteenth-Century Britain* (Berkeley, 1988)

Gerrard, C. *The Patriot Opposition to Walpole: Politics, Poetry and National Myth 1725–42* (Oxford, 1994)

Goldstein, L. *Ruins and Empire* (Pittsburgh, 1977)

Hartman, G. *The Unremarkable Wordsworth* (London, 1987)

Higgins, I. *Swift's Politics: a Study in Disaffection* (Cambridge, 1994)

Hume, R.D. *The Development of English Drama in the Late Seventeenth Century* (Oxford, 1976)

Johnston, K.R. *The Hidden Wordsworth: Poet, Lover, Rebel, Spy* (New York and London, 1998)

Jones, C. *Radical Sensibility: Literature and Ideas in the 1790s* (London, 1993)

José, N. *Ideas of the Restoration in English Literature 1660–71* (Cambridge, Mass., 1984)

Kelsall, M. *Byron's Politics* (Brighton, 1987)

Knapp, S. *Personification and the Sublime* (Cambridge, Mass., 1985)

Landsdown, R. *Byron's Historical Dramas* (Oxford, 1992)

Levinson, M. *Wordsworth's Great Period Poems* (Cambridge, 1986)

Liu, A. *Wordsworth: the Sense of History* (Stanford, 1989)

Loftis, J. *The Politics of Drama in Augustan England* (Oxford, 1963)

McFarland, *Romanticism and the Forms of Ruin* (Princeton, 1981)

Meehan, M. *Liberty and Poetics in Eighteenth Century England* (London, 1986)

Mullan, J. *Sentiment and Sociability: the Language of Feeling in the Eighteenth Century* (Oxford, 1988)

Nussbaum, F. and L. Brown (eds) *The New 18th Century* (New York and London, 1987)

Nuttall, A.D. *A Common Sky: Philosophy and the Literary Imagination* (London, 1974)

Paulson, R. *Satire and the Novel in Eighteenth-Century England* (New Haven, 1967)

—— *Representations of Revolution* (New Haven, 1983)

Price, M. *To the Palace of Wisdom: Studies in Order and Energy from Dryden to Blake* (Garden City, N.Y., 1964)

Roe, N. *Wordsworth and Coleridge: the Radical Years* (Oxford, 1988)

—— (ed.) *Keats and History* (Cambridge, 1995)

Rogers, P. *Grub Street: Studies in a Subculture* (London, 1972)

—— *Eighteenth Century Encounters: Studies in Literature and Society in the Age of Walpole* (Brighton, 1985)

Sheriff, J.K. *The Good-Natured Man: The Evolution of a Moral Ideal, 1660–1800* (Alabama, 1982)

Shroff, H.J. *The Eighteenth Century Novel: the Idea of a Gentleman* (London, 1979)

Spacks, P.M. *The Poetry of Vision* (Cambridge, Mass., 1967)
Summerfield, G. *Fantasy and Reason: Children's Literature in the Eighteenth Century* (London, 1984)
Thomson, E.P. *Witness against the Beast: William Blake and the Moral Law* (Cambridge, 1993)
Todd, J.M. *Sensibility: an Introduction* (London, 1986)
Van Sant, A.J. *Eighteenth-Century Sensibility and the Novel: the Senses in Social Context* (Cambridge, 1993)
Watt, I. *The Rise of the Novel* (London, 1957)
Weinbrot, H.D. *Britannia's Issue: the Rise of British Literature from Dryden to Ossian* (Cambridge, 1993)
Wendorf, R. *William Collins and Eighteenth Century Poetry* (Minneapolis, 1981)

Art and Aesthetics

Ashfield, A. and P. De Bolla *The Sublime: a Reader in British Eighteen-Century Aesthetic Theory* (Cambridge, 1996)
Barrell, J. *The Political Theory of Painting from Reynolds to Hazlitt* (New Haven and London, 1986)
—— (ed.) *Painting and the Politics of Culture: New Essays in British Art 1700–1850* (Oxford and New York, 1992)
Bindman, D. *Hogarth* (London, 1981)
Bryson, N. *Word and Image: French Painting of the Ancien Regime* (Cambridge, 1981)
Cohen, R. *Studies in British Art and Aesthetics* (Berkeley, 1985)
Copley, S. and P. Garside (eds) *The Politics of the Picturesque: Literature, Landscape and Aesthetics since 1770* (Cambridge, 1994)
Craske, M. *Art in Europe 1700–1830* (Oxford and New York, 1997)
Crow, T.E. *Painters and Public Life in Eighteenth Century Paris* (New Haven and London, 1985)
—— *Emulation: Making Artists for Revolutionary France* (New Haven and London, 1995)
Dabydeen, D. *Hogarth, Walpole and Commercial Britain* (London, 1987)
Donald, D. *The Age of Caricature: Satirical Prints in the Reign of George III* (New Haven and London, 1996)
Fried, M. *Absorption and Theatricality: Painting and Beholder in the Age of Diderot* (Berkeley, 1980)
Irwin, D. *English Neoclassical Art* (London, 1966)
Lipking, L. *The Ordering of the Arts in Eighteenth Century England* (Princeton, 1970)
Mattick, P. *Eighteenth Century Aesthetics and the Reconstruction of Art* (Cambridge, 1993)
Monk, S.H. *The Sublime* (London, 1935)
Solkin, D. *Painting for Money: the Visual Arts and the Public Sphere in Eighteenth Century England* (New Haven and London, 1993)
Todorov, T. *Theories of the Symbol* trans. C. Porter (Oxford, 1982)
Zammato, J.H. *The Genesis of Kant's Critique of Judgement* (Chicago and London, 1992)

Index